During the twentieth century, American attitudes about drugs and governmental drug control policies have vascillated between prohibition and laissez faire. The current debate is polarized between two extremes: those favoring stronger drug enforcement laws and those favoring legalization or decriminalization. *Dealing with Drugs* divides the monolith typically called the drug problem into more analytical categories and expands the debate beyond simplistic solutions. The authors—leading psychiatrists, criminologists, pharmacologists, and economists—provide solid research about every major aspect of drug policy, including the sources of addiction; long-term effects of controlled use; the economic nature of the illegal drug market and the costs of current enforcement policies; drug-related crime; and the toxicity and medicinal use of illicit drugs.

The authors find a disturbing pattern of failure. Vast and enormously expensive enforcement policies drain economic resources, distort American foreign policy, and trample civil liberties. These policies have not made a serious dent in drug traffic or abuse, but they have led to sharp increases in street crime, the corruption of numerous public officials, and a weakening of the social fabric.

From this devastating critique, *Dealing with Drugs* points the way toward new policy options, based on informed decision-making, enforceable and consistent laws, and reliance on social controls. Such policies, argue some of the authors, can involve the prudent use of police power, but more often than not the role of the police is shown to be counterproductive. The authors urge that greater emphasis be given to the development of alternative private solutions for social control of drug use and abuse. This, perhaps, is the most important contribution provided by the authors: the understanding that government policies are no substitute for the more complex knowledge embedded in custom and social arrangements that arise independent of deliberate planning.

DEALING WITH DRUGS

Consequences of Government Control

Pacific Studies in Public Policy

PACIFIC RESEARCH INSTITUTE FOR PUBLIC POLICY
San Francisco, California

Edited by

Ronald Hamowy

Foreword by

Dr. Alfred Freedman

Lexington Books

D.C. Heath and Company/
Lexington, Massachusetts/Toronto

Hardback ISBN 0-669-15678-7
Paperback ISBN 0-936488-07-7 (available only from the Pacific
Research Institute for Public Policy)

Library of Congress Catalog Card Number 86-46340

Printed in the United States of America

Pacific Research Institute for Public Policy
177 Post Street
San Francisco, California 94108
(415) 989-0833

Library of Congress Cataloging-in-Publication Data

Dealing with drugs.

    (Pacific studies in public policy)
    Includes bibliographies and index.
    1. Narcotic laws—United States. 2. Drug
abuse—United States. I. Hamowy, Ronald,
1937-   . II. Series.
HF3890.D4 1987   344.73'0545   86-46340
ISBN 0-669-15678-7 (hbk. alk. paper) 347.304545
ISBN 0-936488-07-7 (pbk. alk. paper)

CONTENTS

iii

PART III   POLICY REFORM: EVIDENCE AND ETHICS

LIST OF TABLES

FOREWORD

Dealing with Drugs: Consequences of Government Control is the sort of book that commands attention. Both the professional and nonprofessional reader will be rewarded for their efforts. The book offers a vigorous and at times provocative presentation, but it is a scholarly, well-documented volume, with scientific data and numerous quotations and references.

Many of the chapters stress the failure of existing laws in regard to the control of illegal drugs and recommend the necessity of modifying present policies. The work is of inestimable value in understanding our current drug problem which, as the volume's contributors emphasize, has not disappeared in spite of draconian legislation and repeated declarations of "war" on drugs.

Dealing with Drugs will challenge the reader to scrutinize today's troubled situation concerning drug use and encourage the formulation of new, more rational approaches to our seemingly intractable dilemma. The book compels attention, not only to the increasing problems of the present time, but to the importance of studying the foreseeable consequences of legislation. Too often, legislation has been based on rigid, linear thinking that results in simple-minded proposals—for example, tough sentences, including even the death penalty, for very sensitive and complex situations. It is evident as one reads these chapters that there are no gimmicks or easy solutions. Some of the authors do not agree with those who advocate the decriminalization of various illicit substances—but throughout the book there are strong arguments for a major reconsideration of current laws. In making their arguments, the authors provide a range of options for reform.

The book is well written and the layperson will find it very readable. But its high standards of academic presentation will also be gratifying to the expert. Each and every chapter has something to offer. It is strongly recommended for all who are concerned about the future welfare of our nation and particularly the younger segments of our population.

Dr. Alfred Freedman
New York Medical College
Former president, American
Psychiatric Association

ACKNOWLEDGMENTS

I should like to thank Mr. Leonard Szabo of the University of Alberta for his help in researching the material contained in the editor's introductory essay. Professor John Kaplan of the Stanford Law School was kind enough to read the papers that comprise this volume and to offer a number of helpful recommendations. Finally, the largest debt is owed Professor Ralph Raico of the State University College at Buffalo, who commented on the entire manuscript and whose painstaking reading of each of the essays led to a wealth of invaluable suggestions. Much of the credit usually accorded the editor of a collection such as this properly belongs to him.

Ronald Hamowy

INTRODUCTION
Illicit Drugs and Government Control

Ronald Hamowy

In terms of expenditures, the federal government's attempt to enforce the laws against illicit drugs constitutes the most expensive intrusion into the private lives of Americans ever undertaken in the nation's history. Even compared to the costs of enforcing Prohibition, the expenses incurred by the various federal agencies in their seemingly endless war against illicit drugs are massive. Consider the following: During the first ten years of Prohibition, between 1920 and 1929, the Congress authorized expenditures of $88.1 million for the purpose of enforcing the National Prohibition Act.[1] This amount

1. Charles Merz, *The Dry Decade,* originally published in 1930 (Seattle: University of Washington Press, 1969), p. 329. The figures for each year (exclusive of those amounts allocated for enforcement of the Harrison Narcotic Act), with their 1983 values as adjusted by the Consumer Price Index, are as follows:

Year	Amount Appropriated	1983 Dollars
1920	$ 2,200,000	$ 10,941,300
1921	6,350,000	35,351,500
1922	6,750,000	40,123,500

(continued)

1

translates into 506.2 million 1983 dollars. In fiscal year 1983, on the other hand, the federal government budgeted no less than $836.3 million for drug law enforcement.[2] Nor does this figure include the large sums spent on prevention, treatment, and research programs, nor the costs of state and local police measures aimed at controlling the traffic in drugs. Indeed, in June 1982 President Reagan announced a new major campaign against the illegal use of drugs, which led to an escalation in the resources devoted to drug enforcement at the federal level to a minimum of $1.2 billion in 1985. One newspaper has estimated that the total amount devoted by all levels of government to the battle against the illegal consumption and distribution of drugs, together with all prevention and rehabilitation projects, is in the area of $5 billion annually.[3]

Yet despite these staggering costs, the availability and use of the major illicit drugs do not appear to have decreased. Although government estimates of the number of drug users are seldom the most reliable, since they are, by their very nature, subject to manipulation for political purposes,[4] recent figures released by the President's

Continued from previous page

Year	Amount Appropriated	1983 Dollars
1923	8,500,000	49,636,000
1924	8,250,000	48,082,000
1925	10,012,330	56,908,200
1926	9,670,560	54,447,100
1927	11,993,005	68,821,400
1928	11,990,965	69,748,600
1929	12,401,620	72,137,300
Totals	$88,118,480	$506,196,900

2. The amount originally allocated for fiscal 1983 was $702.8 million. See *Federal Strategy for Prevention of Drug Abuse and Drug Trafficking, 1982* (Washington, D.C.: Drug Abuse Policy Office, 1982), p. 74. Following President Reagan's "declaration of war" on drugs, the Congress increased its funding for drug enforcement by $127.5 million, plus an additional $6 million to cover the costs of the newly established South Florida Task Force. See Steven Wisotsky, "Exposing the War on Cocaine: The Futility and Destructiveness of Prohibition," *Wisconsin Law Review* (1983): 1307, n. 10.

3. "Society Pays Price for Drug Haunting America," *Washington Times,* 25 September 1984. The drug legislation passed in 1986 has, of couse, added a minimum of a half-billion dollars to that sum.

4. For a particularly dramatic instance of political exploitation of the available data on drug users, see Edward Jay Epstein, *Agency of Fear: Opiates and Political Power in America* (New York: Putnam, 1977), pp. 173–77, and Charles E. Silberman, *Criminal Violence, Criminal Justice* (New York: Random House, 1978), pp. 174–76.

Commission on Organized Crime appear consonant with other data currently available.

The commission, employing figures supplied by the Drug Enforcement Administration, has estimated the number of heroin users in 1981 at 490,000, about the same as was the case two years earlier.[5] However, although there is no evidence to support the conclusion that this number has increased significantly in recent years, domestic heroin consumption is estimated to have increased from 3.85 metric tons in 1981 to 6.04 metric tons in 1983 and 5.97 metric tons in 1984.[6] While heroin use seems to be limited to a small group, ingestion of cocaine is far more prevalent and the drug appears to have gained steadily in popularity over the past decade. The Drug Enforcement Administration calculates the number of users estimated to have employed the drug at least once per month as follows:

Year	Number of Regular Users
1976	1,200,000
1977	1,542,330
1978	1,950,000
1979	4,400,000
1980	N/A
1981	N/A
1982	4,200,000
1983	N/A
1984	5 to 6 million

SOURCE: President's Commission on Organized Crime, *America's Habit: Drug Abuse, Drug Trafficking and Organized Crime* (Washington, D.C.: 3 March 1986, Mimeographed), figure 1.

Although there is no clear explanation of why the number of regular users should have more than doubled between 1978 and 1979, there appears to be general agreement that approximately 5 million people currently routinely use cocaine.[7]

5. President's Commission on Organized Crime, *America's Habit: Drug Abuse, Drug Trafficking and Organized Crime* (Washington, D.C.: 3 March 1986, Mimeographed), figure 5. There is an inexplicable drop in the estimates supplied by the Drug Enforcement Administration, from 740,000 in 1977 to 467,000 in 1979 and 465,000 in 1980.

6. Ibid., figure 6.

7. The rise in popularity of cocaine in the late 1960s appears to have been accompanied by a shift in the method by which the drug has been most commonly ingested. While intravenous injection had been the customary mode of ingesting cocaine before its reappearance some twenty years ago, snorting is currently the preferred means. This method prevents large amounts of the drug from being taken in quickly. See James Lieber, "Coping with Cocaine," *The Atlantic Monthly* 257 (January 1986): 42.

The National Narcotics Intelligence Consumers Committee (NNICC), a government interagency group, has estimated that in 1978 between 19 and 25 metric tons of cocaine were smuggled into the country and that this amount increased to between 40 and 48 metric tons in 1980, between 54 and 71 metric tons in 1983, and between 71 and 137 metric tons in 1984.[8] Thus, based on the lowest NNICC estimates, the amount of illicit cocaine entering the United States has increased by 274 percent between 1978 and 1984.[9]

Unlike cocaine use, the consumption of marijuana appears to have decreased somewhat over the past few years, although there is no evidence whatever that this decline can be credited to more vigilant law enforcement. Estimates supplied by the Drug Enforcement Administration indicate that about 20 million people used the drug at least once per month in 1982, down from 25.5 million in 1980 and 22.7 million in 1979, but up from 16.2 million in 1977 and 14.2 million in 1976.[10] Total marijuana consumption in the United States since 1982, however, seems to have remained relatively constant. The NNICC estimates consumption in 1982 at between 8,200 and 10,200 metric tons, dropping slightly to between 8,000 and 9,600 metric tons in 1983 and between 7,800 and 9,200 metric tons in 1984.[11]

If we assume that these figures respecting heroin, cocaine, and marijuana use are accurate, at least with respect to their variation from year to year, then it is evident that the huge sums expended by the federal government in the past few years to interdict the supply of these drugs has proved a total waste of funds, even if one were sympathetic to the ends toward which they were used. Indeed, it has been shown that even if the government were to substantially improve its current levels of interdiction, the street price of these drugs would not be seriously affected. Thus, in the case of marijuana, doubling the amount of the drug seized would generate a retail price increase of no more than 12 percent,[12] and the consequent drop in

8. President's Commission on Organized Crime, *America's Habit,* figure 4.

9. If one were to use the higher estimates supplied by the NNICC, the amount of cocaine smuggled into the country in 1984 would have reached 548 percent of its 1978 levels.

10. President's Commission on Organized Crime, *America's Habit,* figure 10. In 1982 approximately 11.5 percent of teenagers 12 to 17 years old and 27 percent of young adults 18 to 25 years old used marijuana at least once per month (ibid., p. 34).

11. Ibid., figure 11.

12. J. Michael Polich et al., *Strategies for Controlling Adolescent Drug Use,* R-3076-CHF (Santa Monica, Calif.: Rand Corporation, 1984), p. x.

supply would almost certainly prove temporary inasmuch as the marijuana plant is so easily cultivated domestically. With respect to cocaine, the effects of interdiction are even less effective. Doubling the seizure rate from its currently estimated 20 percent would raise the retail price by less than 4 percent, since the importer's selling price (approximately $50 per gram of pure cocaine "on the beach") constitutes such a small portion of the ultimate retail price (about $625 per gram).[13]

Having failed dramatically in its attempt to limit the available supply of illicit drugs, the Reagan administration has proposed to use the massive power of the federal government to control demand. On March 3, 1986, the President's Commission on Organized Crime, under the chairmanship of Judge Irving R. Kaufman of the U.S. Court of Appeals for the Second Circuit, recommended that a nationwide program of drug testing be instituted, to apply to all federal employees, together with all employees working for private firms awarded government contracts. In addition, the commission urged that all private employers not otherwise covered initiate similar "appropriate" programs.[14]

Neither the questionable constitutionality of so intrusive a program nor its immense cost seems to have deterred its defenders on the commission. When Rodney Smith, the commission's deputy executive director and the author of the report, was confronted with its civil libertarian implications, one newspaper reported him as having "urged those 'who say it is too intrusive' to consider that Federal drug-enforcement officers are 'putting their lives on the line' because of the drug users' 'weekend activities.' "[15]

This same perverse reasoning is reflected in the supplementary comments of a group of four commission members, including Jesse A. Brewer, deputy chief of police of Los Angeles, and Eugene Methvin, a senior editor of *Readers Digest*. "Federal employees," they noted,

13. Ibid. The actual street price of a gram of cocaine is usually considerably less than $625, since the drug sold at the retail level is commonly heavily adulterated.
14. President's Commission on Organized Crime, *America's Habit,* recommendations 3 and 8 in section entitled "Reducing the Demand for Drugs."
15. "U.S. Panel Urges Testing Workers for Use of Drugs," *New York Times,* 4 March 1986, p. 14. The general argument, of course, is that the government may institute any measure, no matter how oppressive, if its aim is the enforcement of a law that has proved dangerous to law-enforcement officers. The same rationale could be used to support more stringent apartheid legislation or any measure calling for preventive detention.

should shun the use of illegal drugs and set an example of intolerance of those who do use or traffic in them. Brave federal officers risk their lives daily trying to stop the criminals and terrorists who run this trade. *The user is a part of the trafficking.*[16]

Included in the category "criminals and terrorists" are no less than 25 million regular users of cocaine and marijuana, in addition to the millions more who occasionally employ these drugs. Indeed, the federal government has recently estimated that Americans are spending approximately $110 billion annually on illicit drugs and that this amount is increasing at the rate of about 10 percent per year.[17]

In the fall of 1986, the Congress adopted many of the recommendations of the President's Commission and passed a $1.7 billion bill that provides for increased efforts to educate people about the harmful effects of illicit substances and to more effectively enforce the laws against their use.[18] It is unlikely, however, that anything short of establishing a police state would prove to have significant long-term consequences either on the amount of drugs smuggled into the country or the quantity consumed.[19] This, at least, has been the traditional pattern of legislation and dealer response. Thus, Governor Nelson Rockefeller orchestrated passage of a stringent new drug law in New York in 1973, one of the more drastic provisions of which called for mandatory prison sentences of fifteen years, with a maximum sentence of life imprisonment, for all those convicted of possessing more than two ounces of heroin or who sold more than one

16. President's Commission on Organized Crime, "Supplemental Views of Commissioners Brewer, Manuel, Methvin, and Rowan," *The Impact: Organized Crime Today* (Washington, D.C.: April 1986, Mimeographed), p. 179 (italics in the original).

17. "Meese's Ambitious War Against U.S. Drug Abuse Is Faltering as Cocaine Use Continues to Spread," *Wall Street Journal,* 9 January 1986, p. 44.

18. *The New York Times* reported that the commission recommended that the "Defense Department, now involved in helping civilian drug-enforcement agencies in a limited way, should recognize that drug-traffickers constitute a 'hostile threat' to the United States and the military should expand its role in drug law-enforcement" (4 May 1986, p. 14). With respect to the legislation passed in the fall of 1986, however, a proposal to employ military forces alongside civilian drug agencies for purposes of domestic enforcement was dropped from the final bill. There is some question that the use of the military for this purpose violates the provisions of the Posse Comitatus Act [18 U.S.C.§ 1385 (1982)], which forbids employing the armed forces to enforce civil law.

19. With respect to heroin, one authority has concluded that changes in law enforcement do contribute to determining which potential customers have access to the drug and which do not. See John Kaplan, *The Hardest Drug: Heroin and Public Policy* (Chicago: University of Chicago Press, 1983), p. 78.

ounce. Yet heroin use appears to have been as widespread in 1976 as before passage of the new act.[20] What occurred was that dealers began employing juveniles, who were not subject to the penalties stipulated in the Rockefeller law, to engage in the riskier aspects of distribution. As a result, the juvenile division of the criminal justice system could not cope with the sheer volume of arrests for violations of the narcotics laws, with the consequence that the New York police ceased arresting juveniles for these offenses altogether.[21]

Yet, notwithstanding the rigidity and severity of our current drug laws and despite their having proved ineffective, serious legal reform in this area seems unlikely. As Randy Barnett has observed (Chapter 2: "Curing the Drug-Law Addiction: The Harmful Side-Effects of Legal Prohibition"), there are large numbers of people, principally employees of law enforcement agencies, who have a vested interest in seeing to it that ever increasing amounts are expended to stamp out the distribution and sale of illicit drugs. These groups are economically dependent on the existence of restrictive drug legislation; and even though the evidence might point to relaxing or repealing our current laws, their own economic benefit will be best served by supporting comprehensive legislation and a massive campaign of drug enforcement. Those whose primary concern is the enforcement of the nation's narcotics laws, together with all those who staff the institutions responsible for the treatment and rehabilitation of drug users—from administrators and physicians on down—all stand to lose if these laws were substantially liberalized; so too would the people assigned the task of instructing us concerning the evils of narcotics, and the researchers who, operating under government grants, investigate the dangerous effects of opiates, cocaine, and marijuana and who replicate experiments that have already suggested that these drugs invariably produce harmful effects on our minds and bodies.

In addition, the American government's attempts to curtail the cultivation of opium, coca, and marijuana outside the country have

20. In addition, the 1976 study of the effects of the Rockefeller law, commissioned by the Association of the Bar of the City of New York, found "no evidence of a sustained reduction in heroin use after 1973" and noted that "the pattern of stable heroin use in New York City between 1973 and mid-1976 was not appreciably different from the average pattern in other East Coast cities." See Joint Committee on New York Drug Law Evaluation, *The Nation's Toughest Drug Law: Evaluating the New York Experience* (New York: Association of the Bar of the City of New York; Drug Abuse Council, 1977). p. 3.

21. See Kaplan, *The Hardest Drug*, p. 79.

served far more elaborate purposes in the area of foreign policy, purposes that the government is unlikely to easily abandon. Jonathan Marshall (Chapter 4: "Drugs and United States Foreign Policy") notes that the involvement of the government in the drug war has become an extension of U.S. policy intimately linked to counterinsurgency operations and covert actions in the Third World. Profits from the international drug traffic can be truly enormous,[22] and have proved a potent weapon in international politics. By tolerating the complicity of high foreign officials in the international drug traffic, American administrators engaged in foreign operations believe that the United States is contributing to the security of these regimes and providing some stability to particularly unstable regions of the world. At the same time, this policy furnishes foreign governments friendly to the United States with vast sums with which to engage in counterinsurgency operations.[23]

Any serious reform of the nation's drug laws is bound to meet powerful resistance from these groups within the American bureaucracy—certain officials operating in the area of foreign policy, drug

22. The most widely quoted estimate of the income accruing to organized crime from narcotics is that of James Cook, who in 1980 estimated this amount at $63 billion annually. See Sima Fishman, Kathleen Rodenrys, and George Schink, "The Income of Organized Crime" prepared for the President's Commission on Organized Crime (Philadelphia: Warton Econometric Forecasting Associates, 6 March 1986, Mimeographed), p. 25. Those involved in drug trade outside the country are reputed to have amassed various fortunes. According to one report, Gonzalo Rodríguez, one of Colombia's top drug traffickers, collects about $20 million per month from drug operations, while Roberto Suárez Gómez is estimated to earn $33 million per month from the production of coca leaves in Bolivia. See Laurence Gonzales, "Why Drug Enforcement Doesn't Work," *Playboy* 32 (December 1985): 104.

23. In April 1985, Mark Kleiman, writing in the *Wall Street Journal,* observed: "Governments, their agencies, their employees and their foreign surrogates are rather frequently involved in drug dealing because it is a way to make quick, substantial and untraceable money; they often need or want money they don't have to account for; they have powers, resources, immunities and organizational capabilities that give them advantages in some aspects of drug dealing, and these make them more competitive in moving narcotics than they are in making steel or automobiles." (See "We Can't Stop Friend or Foe in the Drug Trade," *Wall Street Journal,* 9 April 1985).

On May 29, 1986, two American journalists filed a federal lawsuit in Miami, Florida, which accused "a group of Americans and Nicaraguan guerrillas [Contras] of smuggling cocaine to finance military operations against the Nicaraguan government." The suit charged that several of the thirty defendants, resident in Florida, employed seafood importing firms as fronts for the purpose of smuggling cocaine into the United States to finance Contra operations. It need hardly be added that the State Department immediately denied all charges. See Reuter's dispatch, "Cocaine dealing finances contras, two reporters say," *Globe and Mail* (Toronto), 30 May 1986, p. A5.

enforcement officers, administrators of drug prevention and rehabilitation facilities, and so on—who have capitalized on our current
policy and who have a great deal to gain from its maintenance. And
the longer this policy remains unchanged, the more entrenched those
forces working for its preservation will become. Of course, American attitudes and laws relating to the use of drugs have not always
had the shape they do now. David F. Musto has provided an overview of the history of legislative constraints over the sale and
consumption of the major illicit drugs (Chapter 1: "The History of
Legislative Control Over Opium, Cocaine, and Their Derivatives");
however, it remains worthwhile to touch briefly on several aspects
of the history of social control over drugs, if for no other reason
than to compare the situation as it existed a century ago with that
obtaining today.

Throughout the nineteenth century there existed no laws regulating the sale of cocaine and opium and its derivatives in any of the
states and territories of the Union. There were a few exceptions to
this generalization in the last few years of the century—the Territory
of Montana, for example, enacted legislation in 1889 that limited the
sale or disposition of cocaine, opium, morphine, or any of their compounds to prescription of a physician only—but enforcement of these
early statutes was sporadic, and the penalties imposed for violation
were usually limited to a small fine. (Table I-1 provides a summary
of the earliest state laws, to 1930, that required a physician's prescription before certain drugs could be dispensed.)

As Table I-1 indicates, there were no effective legal impediments
to purchasing either cocaine or opiates throughout the country before the twentieth century. These drugs were sold over the counter
by pharmacies and were also available from general stores, groceries,
and through mail-order houses. A survey of Iowa during the period
1883-1885, which then had a population of less than 2 million, un-
covered the fact that, besides physicians who dispensed opiates
directly, no less than 3,000 stores in the state sold opiates.[24] In addition, patent medicine manufacturers regularly used opiates or
cocaine in their remedies. Indeed, given the limitations of the nineteenth-century physician's armamentarium, it is no wonder that so
many consumers took advantage of the analgesic qualities of certain

24. Edward M. Brecher, *Licit and Illicit Drugs* (Boston: Little, Brown, 1972), p. 3.

Table I-1. Dates of First Enactment of State Laws Prohibiting the Sale of Certain Drugs Except by Prescription.

	Cocaine	Opium	Morphine	Heroin	Marijuana	Peyote
Alabama (1887)	1907	1909	1907	1909		
Arizona (1903)	1899	1899	[1899]	[1899]	1923	1923*
Arkansas (1891)	1899	1923	1923	1923	1915	
California (1897)	1907	1907	1907	1907	1917	1917*
Colorado (1897)	1897	1915	[1915]	[1915]		
Connecticut (1881)	1905	1913	1913	1913		
Delaware (1883)	1913	1913	1913	[1913]		
Dist. of Columbia (1878)	1906	1906	1906	[1906]		
Florida (1889)	1909	1909	1909	[1915]		
Georgia (1881)	1902	1907	1907	[1907]		
Idaho (1887)	1909	1909	1909	1909	1927	
Illinois (1881)	1897	1915	[1915]	[1915]		
Indiana (1899)	1907	1907	1907	1913	1913	
Iowa (1880)	1902	1923	1923	1923	1921	1925
Kansas (1885)	1901	1921	1901	[1921]	1927*	1920*
Kentucky (1874)	1902	1912	[1912]	[1912]		
Louisiana (1888)	1898	1918	1918	1918	1924*	
Maine (1877)	1899	1913	1913	1913	1913	
Maryland (1908)	1904	1912	1904	1912		
Massachusetts (1885)	1906	1910	1910	1910	1914	
Michigan (1885)	1905	1915	1909	[1909]	1929	
Minnesota (1885)	1905	1915	1915	1915		
Mississippi (1892)	1900	1924	1924	[1924]		
Missouri (1881)	1905	1915	1915	1915		
Montana (1895)	1889	1889	1889	[1889]	1927	1923*
Nebraska (1887)	1905	1915	1915	[1915]	1927	
Nevada (1901)	1911	1877	1911	[1911]	1917	1917

New Hampshire (1875)	1909		1915	1915		
New Jersey (1877)	1904		1908	1915		
New Mexico (1889)	[1909]		[1909]	[1909]	1923	
New York (1900)	1907		[1914]	[1914]	1927	
North Carolina (1881)	1905		1905	1907		
North Dakota (1890)	1905	1885	1917	1915	1927	1923*
Ohio (1884)	1902		1902	[1902]		
Oklahoma (1890)	1910		1910	1910		
Oregon (1891)	1913		1913	1913	1923	
Pennsylvania (1887)	1903		[1917]	[1917]		
Rhode Island (1870)	1906		1906	1906	1918	
South Carolina (1876)	1907					
South Dakota (1890)	[1915]	1885	[1915]	[1915]		1923*
Tennessee (1893)	1901		[1913]	[1913]	1919	
Texas (1889)	1903		1911	[1903]	1915	
Utah (1892)	1907		1911	1911	1915	1917
Vermont (1894)	1915		1915	1915		
Virginia (1886)	1908		1904	1908		
Washington (1891)	1909		1909	[1909]	1923	
West Virginia (1881)	1907		1907	1907		
Wisconsin (1882)	1907		1907	1907		
Wyoming (1886)	1903		[1903]	[1903]	1913	1929*

Notes: Statutes to 1930 only.

Dates in parentheses following the name of each state or territory are those of passage of the first statewide pharmacy act, mandating the licensing of all pharmacists. Such laws were often enacted under intense pressure from the various state pharmaceutical societies, under the general direction of the American Pharmaceutical Association.

Dates enclosed in brackets indicate that the drug is not explicitly mentioned in the statute referred to but is covered by virtue of such language as "any salt or compound" or "any alkaloid or derivative" of opium, coca leaves, etc.

*Unavailable even by prescription of a physician.

SOURCE: The statutes of the various states and territories.

proprietary medicines that in fact contained opium or morphine. Equally effective—as tonics and for their stimulating properties— were the syrups and "wines" containing cocaine, including the most famous of these, Coca-Cola.

The movement to limit access to opium and its derivatives appears to have been precipitated not by a concern for the addictive properties of the drug, which physicians were aware of, but by anti-Chinese sentiment. Thousands of Chinese laborers had been imported into the United States between 1850 and 1880, primarily to help build the nation's transcontinental railroad system. Census figures show that between 1860 and 1880, the Chinese male population increased from 33,000 to over 100,000.[25] Many of these workers eventually took up residence in the larger population centers of the west, while others migrated to the major eastern cities. These immigrants brought with them the custom of smoking opium in opium dens, a practice that appears to have become fashionable among certain segments of the white population as well.[26] Concerned that opium smoking would spread to larger numbers of whites, the city of San Francisco enacted an ordinance in 1875 making it illegal, under penalty of a substantial fine, imprisonment, or both, to keep or frequent an opium den.[27] San Francisco's ordinance was only the first of many such laws, most passed at the state level, aimed at stamping out the increasing popularity of opium houses. As Table I–2 shows, twenty-two states and territories enacted legislation respecting opium dens between 1877 and 1896.

That the impetus for passage of legislation prohibiting opium dens was racist in origin there can be little doubt. The intent of physicians, legislators, and other social reformers who lobbied for these laws was to protect whites from what was commonly regarded as a

25. Bureau of the Census, *Historical Statistics of the United States: Colonial Times to 1970,* 2 vols. (Washington, D.C.: Government Printing Office, 1975), Vol. 2, p. 14 (Series A 91–104). During the same period, the Chinese female population grew from 1,800 to 4,800!

26. One contemporary account notes that "men and women, young girls—virtuous or just commencing a downward career—hardened prostitutes, representatives of the 'hoodlum' element, young clerks and errand-boys who could ill afford the waste of time and money, and young men who had no work to do, were to be found smoking together in the back rooms of laundries in the low, pestilential dens of Chinatown, reeking with filth and overrun with vermin, in the cellars of drinking saloons, and in houses of prostitution." See H. H. Kane, *Opium-Smoking in America and China* (New York: Putnam, 1882; facsimile edition: New York: Arno Press, 1976), p. 2.

27. Ibid., p. 1. A similar law was passed in Virginia City, Nevada, in 1876 (ibid., p. 3).

Table I-2. Dates of Enactment of Statutes Prohibiting the Keeping of an Opium Den.

	Date		*Date*
Nevada	1877	Ohio	1885
Dakota Territory	1879	Oregon	1885
Utah	1880	Pennsylvania	1885
California	1881	Maryland	1886
Montana	1881	Idaho	1887
Washington	1881	Missouri	1887
New York	1882	New Mexico	1887
Wyoming	1882	Minnesota	1889
Arizona	1883	Wisconsin	1891
Connecticut	1883	Georgia	1895
Massachusetts	1885	Iowa	1896

Note: Most laws were similar in language to that of California's 1881 statute, which provided that "every person who opens or maintains, to be resorted to by others persons, any place where opium, or any of its preparations, is sold or given away to be smoked at such place; and any person who, at such place, sells or gives away any opium or its said preparations to be there smoked or otherwise used; and every person who visits or resorts to any such place for the purpose of smoking opium or its said preparations, is guilty of a misdemeanor." (1881 *Cal. Stat.*, c. 40, p. 34.)

SOURCE: The statutes of the various states and territories.

loathsome Oriental vice. What Orientals themselves did was of minor concern. Indeed, Idaho's original statute of 1887, making it unlawful to maintain or frequent a house where opium was smoked, explicitly referred solely to "any white person."[28] It was not until 1893 that the law was amended to apply to "any person."[29] In an interesting parallel, a strong element of bigotry contributed to the criminalization of marijuana several decades later.

The statutes making opium dens unlawful, like the various later enactments by the states prohibiting the sale of cocaine, opium, or their derivatives without a physician's prescription, proved ineffective. While the larger, well-publicized smoking-houses were forced to close, smaller dens appear to have multiplied and flourished.[30] Similarly, efforts to enforce the states' antinarcotics laws passed in the period before the First World War were easily nullified by a thriving interstate traffic from jurisdictions that either had not yet enacted legislation in the area or had passed comparatively weak

28. 10 February 1887; *Rev. Stat.* 1887,§6830.
29. 1893 *Idaho Sess. Laws* 22.
30. Kane, *Opium-Smoking in America and China*, p. 2.

statutes. It was partly to rectify this situation and partly to fulfill the obligations that the United States had undertaken to control the production and distribution of, among others, cocaine, opium, morphine, and heroin at the International Conference on Opium held at The Hague in 1912,[31] that the Harrison Narcotic Act was passed by Congress in 1914.[32]

One of the chief proponents of the Harrison narcotic bill was Secretary of State William Jennings Bryan, aptly described as "a man of deep prohibitionist and missionary convictions and sympathies," who regarded its passage as a moral duty owed the international community in light of America's diplomatic leadership in convening the Hague Conference.[33] In addition, the bill had the strong support of Dr. William C. Woodward, director of the American Medical Association's Committee on Medical Legislation, and of the American Pharmaceutical Association.[34] The bill, as finally enacted in December 1914, did not appear to be a prohibition statute. However, it was quickly interpreted by law enforcement officers, who were sustained by the courts, as prohibiting physicians from prescribing narcotics to any addict.[35] Thus what at first seemed to be a simple record-

31. The full text of the International Opium Convention, which was signed at The Hague on 23 January 1912, appears as Appendix I to Charles E. Terry and Mildred Pellens, *The Opium Problem* (New York: American Social Health Association, 1928; facsimile edition: Montclair, N.J.: Patterson Smith, 1970), pp. 929ff.

32. Public Law No. 233, 63rd Congress, 17 December 1914 [38 Stat. 785 (1914)]. Earlier the same year, Congress enacted a statute imposing a prohibitively high tax ($300 per pound) on opium prepared for smoking within the United States. See Public Law No. 47, 63rd Congress, 17 January 1914 [38 Stat. 277 (1914)]. Since the Congress had earlier banned the importation of all smoking opium [Public Law No. 221, 60th Congress, 9 February 1909 [35 Stat. 614 (1909)], the effect of this additional legislation was to close off all supplies of smoking opium within the country.

33. Brecher, *Licit and Illicit Drugs,* pp. 48–49.

34. David F. Musto, *The American Disease: Origins of Narcotic Control* (New Haven: Yale University Press, 1973), pp. 55–56.

35. Dr. Hamilton Wright, who was later given the title "the father of American narcotic laws" and who served as the United States representative at the Shanghai Opium Convention of 1909 and the International Conference on Opium held at The Hague in 1912, had hoped that the Harrison Act would be interpreted precisely in this manner. Wright believed that "since the statute was the outcome of an international agreement, . . . it could employ police powers within a state in addition to the traditional powers associated with a federal revenue measure. This would give great importance to the words 'prescribed in good faith,' enabling the federal government to argue, as it did, that this phrase prevented addiction maintenance. Without some legal sanction for federal police powers in the states, the Act would be limited to record keeping. Wright based his optimistic expectation on the principle that a treaty to which the United States had become a signatory and which had been ratified by the Senate,

keeping law was turned into a prohibition statute, with predictable consequences: the formation of a widespread black market in opiates and the establishment of a well-coordinated national organization devoted to smuggling and distributing drugs outside the law.[36] These effects were exacerbated in 1924, when Congress made it illegal to manufacture heroin altogether, even for medicinal purposes,[37] despite the fact that morphine and heroin do not differ in any significant pharmacological respect.[38] Indeed, the harm this seemingly innocuous act has done is singularly extensive, given the fact that the Harrison Act, with its numerous amendments and supplements, has served as the basic law governing narcotics in the United States for almost fifty-six years.[39]

One of the more striking aspects of the language of the act, and those which followed it, was the inclusion of cocaine and other derivatives of the coca leaf as narcotics. These drugs cannot be regarded as "addictive" in the same sense as are the opiates, with which they were classed and from which they were seldom distinguished. Robert Byck (Chapter 6: "Cocaine, Marijuana, and the Meanings of Addiction") has observed that cocaine, like marijuana, does not

---

would take precedence over state law" (ibid., p. 62). In the event, the Supreme Court did not regard this broad interpretation of the Harrison Act as requiring the existence of a prior treaty.

A summary of the major court decisions sustaining the constitutionality of the Harrison Act and the government's argument that "mere addiction" did not constitute a disease that warranted treatment "in good faith" appears in Terry and Pellens, *The Opium Problem,* pp. 758–61, and in Arnold S. Trebach, *The Heroin Solution* (New Haven: Yale University Press, 1982), pp. 125–31. See especially the excellent study by Alfred R. Lindesmith, *The Addict and the Law* (Bloomington: Indiana University Press, 1965). Among the more important cases are *United States* v. *Doremus* 249 U.S. 86 (1919) (upholding the constitutionality of the Harrison Act); *Webb* v. *United States* 249 U.S. 96 (1919) (holding that it was a violation of the act to prescribe to addicts); *Jin Fuey Moy* v. *United States* 254 U.S. 189 (1920) (addictive maintenance a contravention of the statute); and, *United States* v. *Behrman* 258 U.S. 280 (1922) (the amount of narcotic prescribed may itself determine "prescribing in bad faith").

36. Brecher, *Licit and Illicit Drugs,* p. 51.

37. Public Law No. 274, 68th Congress, 7 June 1924 [43 Stat. 657 (1924)].

38. President's Committee on Law Enforcement and Administration of Justice, *Task Force Report: Narcotics and Drug Abuse* (Washington, D.C.: Government Printing Office, 1967), p. 3. Dr. Lawrence Kolb noted as early as 1925 that "if there is any difference in the deteriorating effects of morphine and heroin on addicts, it is too slight to be determined clinically." See "Pleasure and Deterioration from Narcotic Addiction," *Mental Hygiene* 9 (1925): 724; quoted in Brecher, *Licit and Illicit Drugs,* p. 51).

39. In 1970 the federal government consolidated the pertinent provisions of its various previous statutes dealing with narcotics into the Comprehensive Drug Abuse Prevention and Control Act (Public Law No. 513, 91st Congress, 27 October 1970 [84 Stat. 1236]).

have a pharmacologically significant withdrawal syndrome that would "enforce" continued ingestion of the drug. Indeed, the purely physiological withdrawal effects of cocaine are minor. Additionally, since users of cocaine do not seem to develop tolerance to the drug, they do not need ever larger doses to produce similar effects. This, of course, does not imply that cocaine is "harmless," but neither are alcohol and cigarettes, drugs that are currently legal. Why use of these drugs is permitted to remain within our individual purview, while use of cocaine or marijuana is not, is by no means obvious. Certainly there are no scientific reasons to support this position. *Addiction,* Dr. Byck has noted, is open to a variety of definitions, some of which can be made scientifically operational, but many of which cannot, while *drug abuse* is a purely relative term, subject to a host of social presuppositions that are almost never made explicit. The resulting confusion in terminology serves certain ends, specifically those of that group of people whose self-interest depends in part on the continued criminalization of these substances. These people are greatly benefited by the confusion generated when a statement about the value of certain political ends appears under the guise of a scientific observation.

There is perhaps no clearer example of this distortion than in the original campaign by the federal government to criminalize the possession and sale of marijuana without a medical prescription. Marijuana's popularity as a recreational drug in the United States emerged largely as a result of passage of the Eighteenth Amendment, which raised the price of alcohol to prohibitively high levels for many poorer drinkers, leading them to substitute use of this far less expensive weed.[40] Apparently sufficient marijuana to achieve a "high" could be had for less than twenty-five cents and the drug was easily available in almost all of the larger cities, where marijuana "tea pads," similar to opium dens, were quickly established.[41] Before Prohibition, marijuana use had been almost completely confined to immigrants from the West Indies and Mexico. Mexican immigration had increased substantially during the first twenty years of the cen-

40. Brecher, *Licit and Illicit Drugs,* p. 410.
41. Mayor's Committee on Marihuana (1944) (LaGuardia Report), "The Marihuana Problem in the City of New York," in David Solomon, ed., *The Marihuana Papers* (New York: Bobbs-Merrill, 1966), p. 246.

tury, and the number of American residents born in Mexico had reached almost half a million by 1920. By 1930, it had approached 650,000.[42] Despite the growing popularity of marijuana among non-Hispanics, however, the drug remained associated with Mexicans; much of the propaganda respecting its dangers centered on its association with what was commonly viewed as an inferior ethnic group embracing alien habits, with which decent people could have little sympathy.[43]

During the 1920s and 1930s, marijuana was commonly linked with the worst excesses of lawless behavior. Users were reported to be oblivious to human life, shooting down even casual passers-by while engaged in spectacular holdups and other crimes.[44] This preposterous description of the effects of marijuana use was perpetuated by none other than the Surgeon General of the United States, who issued a report in 1929 in which he observed that "those who are habitually accustomed to the use of the drug are said to develop a delirious rage after its administration during which they are temporarily, at least, irresponsible and liable to commit violent crimes." In support of this view, its author invoked, among others, "the murderous frenzy of the Malay," drunk on hashish, and the brutality of the "hashshashin," who killed without remorse on the order of their Mohammedan leaders.[45] The report further concluded that marijuana was a narcotic and suggested that it was addictive and ultimately caused the habitual user to lapse into insanity.[46]

Although by 1930 a number of states had enacted laws prohibiting

42. Bureau of the Census, *Historical Statistics,* vol. 1, p. 117 (Series C 228-295). In 1900, the Mexican-born population was less than 104,000.

43. See Jerome L. Himmelstein, *The Strange Career of Marihuana: Politics and Ideology of Drug Control in America* (Westport, Conn.: Greenwood Press, 1983), pp. 50–54.

44. Brecher, *Licit and Illicit Drugs,* p. 411. Even a periodical as respected as *Scientific American* referred to marijuana as "more dangerous than cocaine or heroin" ("Marihuana More Dangerous than Heroin or Cocaine," *Scientific American,* May 1938, p. 293. A good summary of the hysteria surrounding the use of marijuana that prevailed before passage of the federal Marihuana Tax Act of 1937 appears in Richard J. Bonnie and Charles H. Whitebread II, *The Marihuana Conviction: A History of Marihuana Prohibition in the United States* (Charlottesville: University Press of Virginia, 1974), pp. 92–153.

45. Hugo S. Cummings, Surgeon General, *Preliminary Report on Indian Hemp and Peyote* (Washington, D.C.: Government Printing Office, 1929), quoted in Bonnie and Whitebread, *The Marihuana Conviction,* p. 128.

46. Ibid., p. 60.

the use of marijuana without a prescription,[47] there was strong pressure from a variety of sources, including local law enforcement officials and a number of congressmen, for passage of a federal statute banning the drug. This was eventually accomplished in great measure through the efforts of Harry J. Anslinger, who directed the Federal Bureau of Narcotics from its creation in 1930. With the repeal of Prohibition, Congress had transferred the antinarcotics activities of the Bureau of Prohibition to a new division of the Treasury Department, the Federal Bureau of Narcotics (FBN), and had confirmed Anslinger as its first commissioner, a position he was to hold for thirty-two years. Anslinger had been an ardent supporter of government control over the distribution and sale of alcohol, and in 1928, as chief of the Foreign Control Section of the Prohibition Unit of the Treasury Department, he had drawn up an extensive program aimed at revitalizing enforcement of the provisions of the Volstead Act.[48] Doubtless it was in part due to this crusading spirit that he was chosen to head the new narcotics bureau.

Anslinger's zeal to expand the operations of his new bureau, coupled with his indifference to the facts respecting the actual effects of marijuana on the behavior of its users, made the drug a natural choice with which to extend and publicize the FBN's role as the principal agency responsible for drug control in the United States. Anslinger apparently decided first to move at the state level in publicizing the menace of marijuana and in agitating for a prohibitory law. As early as 1924 a growing concern respecting the relation between the ingestion of drugs and criminal behavior had led the National Conference of Commissioners on Uniform State Laws to appoint a committee to draft a uniform state narcotics act. Although several attempts had been made to draft a bill, no acceptable version emerged from the committee until 1932, some time after Commissioner Anslinger had become a participant in the drafting process. Anslinger placed the full weight and authority of the FBN behind total prohibition of the cultivation, sale, and possession of marijuana, even for medicinal purposes.[49] This position was to bring the

47. See table I-1 and map 1 in ibid., p. 52. Of the twenty-four jurisdictions passing prohibitory statutes before 1930, there is a discrepancy in the dates of enactment of four states, which appear to have passed legislation limiting the sale of marijuana before the dates indicated by Bonnie and Whitebread.

48. Musto, *The American Disease,* p. 211

49. Bonnie and Whitebread, *The Marihuana Conviction,* p. 83.

bureau into conflict with elements of the medical profession and of the pharmaceutical industry, who either opposed any reference at all to the drug in the draft law or who supported availability of the drug by prescription. The result was that the clause respecting marijuana in the final draft of the Uniform Narcotic Drug Act, as submitted to the states in 1932, was made optional and provided only that cannabis be added to the list of narcotic drugs otherwise included in the act.[50] The ultimate effect of this change was to define marijuana as a narcotic, subject to all of the penalties attached to the possession and sale of narcotics, in each of the states.

In order to encourage quick passage of the act by the various states, including its provisions respecting marijuana, the FBN and Commissioner Anslinger launched a comprehensive propaganda campaign to warn the public of the horrors incident to marijuana use. At the same time, the bureau spent substantial sums of money lobbying state legislators to enact that section of the draft law dealing with marijuana. In the FBN's report for 1935, Anslinger noted: "In the absence of Federal legislation on the subject, the States and cities should rightfully assume the responsibility for providing vigorous measures for the extinction of this lethal weed, and it is therefore hoped that all public-spirited citizens will earnestly enlist in the movement urged by the Treasury Department to adjure intensified enforcement of marihuana laws."[51] More typical because less restrained were Anslinger's comments on the drug made in 1937: "If the hideous monster Frankenstein came face to face with the monster Marihuana, he would drop dead of fright."[52]

---

50. Ibid., pp. 84–91.

51. Bureau of Narcotics, U.S. Treasury Department, *Traffic in Opium and Other Dangerous Drugs for the Year Ended December 31, 1935* (Washington, D.C.: Government Printing Office, 1936), p. 30. See also Anslinger's comments made in a radio broadcast in early 1936: "Another urgent reason for the early enactment of the Uniform State Narcotic Act is to be found in the fact that it is THE ONLY UNIFORM LEGISLATION yet devised to deal effectively with MARIHUANA. . . .

"There is no Federal law against the production and use of Marihuana in this country. The legal fight against its abuse is largely a problem of state and municipal legislation and law enforcement.

"All public spirited citizens should enlist in the campaign to demand and to get adequate state laws and efficient state enforcement on Marihuana." ("The Need for Narcotic Education," speech over NBC, 24 February 1936; quoted in Bonnie and Whitebread, *The Marihuana Conviction,* p. 98.)

52. *Washington Herald,* 12 April 1937; quoted in Bonnie and Whitebread, *The Marihuana Conviction,* p. 117.

The FBN cooperated with several organizations that shared their views on marijuana, most notably the Women's Christian Temperance Union, and with a large number of newspapers, including the Hearst chain, in inciting the public against marijuana through a series of horror stories purporting to show that the consumption of even one marijuana cigarette could lead to the most gruesome criminal acts. The following examples are typical of the approach to marijuana taken by the public press between 1932 and 1938, under the aegis of the FBN. On November 5, 1933, the *Los Angeles Examiner* carried the following headline above one of its feature articles: "Murder Weed Found Up and Down Coast—Deadly Marihuana Dope Plant Ready For Harvest That Means Enslavement of California Children"; and two days later, the *San Francisco Examiner* observed, "Dope Officials Helpless To Curb Marihuana Use."[53] In early 1936, Kenneth Clark, writing for the Universal News Service, syndicated a story on the dangers of marijuana that reflected the FBN's propaganda. Under the headline "Murders Due to 'Killer Drug' Marihuana Sweeping United States," Clark wrote:

> Shocking crimes of violence are increasing. Murders, slaughterings, cruel mutilations, maimings, done in cold blood, as if some hideous monster was amok in the land.
> Alarmed Federal and State authorities attribute much of this violence to the "killer drug."
> That's what experts call marihuana. It is another name for hashish. It's a derivative of Indian hemp, a roadside weed in almost every State in the Union. . . .
> Those addicted to marihuana, after an early feeling of exhilaration, soon lose all restraints, all inhibitions. They become bestial demoniacs, filled with the mad lust to kill. . . . [54]

The relation between marijuana use and criminal activity had been "officially" adopted by the FBN in the mid-1930s, when Commissioner Anslinger submitted a memorandum on "The Abuse of Cannabis in the United States" to the Cannabis Subcommittee of the League of Nations Advisory Committee on Traffic in Opium

53. Quoted in Larry Sloman, *Reefer Madness: The History of Marijuana in America* (Indianapolis: Bobbs-Merrill, 1979), p. 44.
54. Quoted in ibid., p. 48. See also Himmelstein, *The Strange Career of Marihuana*, pp. 54–68, which contains a synopsis of the popular literature of the period on the subject.

and Other Dangerous Drugs in November 1934. Anslinger there observed:

> Reports from narcotic officers who have consulted the police in various cities of those States in which the abuse of cannabis is most widespread, are to the effect that marihuana addicts are becoming one of the major police problems. While it is admitted by these officers that marihuana offenses do not show up directly in many cases, they state their estimate to be that fifty percent of the violent crimes committed in districts occupied by Mexicans, Turks, Filipinos, Greeks, Spaniards, Latin-Americans and Negroes, may be traced to the abuse of marihuana.
>
> A prosecuting attorney in Louisiana states that the underworld has been quick to realize the possibility of using this drug to subjugate the will of human derelicts. It can be used to sweep away all restraint and many present day crimes have been attributed to its influence.
>
> Police officials in the South have found that, immediately before undertaking a crime, the criminal will indulge in a few marihuana cigarettes in order to remove any natural sense of restraint which might deter him from committing the contemplated acts and in order to give him the false courage necessary to his purpose.[55]

There is good evidence that Anslinger himself did not believe such arrant nonsense concerning the effects of marijuana. Several scientific studies, all of them familiar to the FBN, indicated, in the words of the Indian Hemp Drug Commission Report of 1893-94, that "the moderate use of hemp drugs is practically attended by no evil results at all." The commission also concluded that "moderate use . . . produces no injurious effects on the mind" and results in "no moral injury whatever."[56] Similar findings were reached by the Panama Canal Zone Study of 1925, which was charged with investigating marijuana use among American troops stationed on the Isthmus. Despite the concern of the military authorities that increasing use of the drug could well pose a threat to discipline, the members of the committee, including its military advisers, found that "there is no

55. League of Nations, Advisory Committee on Traffic in Opium and Other Dangerous Drugs, *The Abuse of Cannabis in the United States (Addendum)* [O.C. 1542 (L)], 10 November 1934, (Memorandum forwarded by the representative of the United States of America); quoted in Bonnie and Whitebread, *The Marihuana Conviction,* pp. 146–147.

56. *Marijuana: Report of the Indian Hemp Drugs Commission, 1893-1894* (Silver Spring, Md.: Thomas Jefferson Co., 1969), p. 263; quoted in ibid., pp. 130–31. The commission was convened to investigate the effects of cannabis use on the native population of India.

evidence that marihuana . . . is a 'habit-forming' drug in the sense in which the term is applied to alcohol, opium, cocaine, etc., or that it has any appreciably deleterious influence on the individuals using it," and recommended that "no steps be taken by the Canal Zone authorities to prevent the sale or use of marihuana."[57]

There seems little doubt that Anslinger chose to neglect what scientific evidence existed concerning the consequences of marijuana use for purely political purposes. In the event, he proved successful in his campaign to gain passage of the Uniform Narcotic Drug Act by the various states. Between 1933 and 1937, forty states had enacted the statute and in twenty-nine of these the state legislatures had included the optional provision respecting marijuana, which the FBN had so strongly supported. By 1937, Tennessee and South Carolina remained as the only two jurisdictions in the United States without laws against marijuana.

Having succeeded in the first stage of his crusade, Anslinger next turned his attention to agitating for enactment of a federal law governing the drug.[58] The publicity mounted by the FBN against marijuana during the previous several years now served to advance support for federal controls. Indeed, Anslinger's accounts of the connection between marijuana and violent crime became even more intemperate when, in 1937, the Treasury Department submitted to Congress the draft of a bill that was to become the Marihuana Tax Act of 1937. Perhaps the most famous of Anslinger's numerous horror stories concerned a young man named Victor Licata, who was reputed to have gone berserk and hacked his family to pieces while under the influence of a marijuana cigarette. In an article published

57. "Canal Zone Report," 18 December 1925 (Colonel W. P. Chamberlain, chairman), pp. 2–3; quoted in Bonnie and Whitebread, *The Marihuana Conviction,* p. 134. A second committee was established in 1932, under the chairmanship of Dr. J. F. Siler, Dr. Chamberlain's successor as chief health officer of the Canal Zone, to reinvestigate the question of whether marijuana was in fact a habit-forming drug. In October, the committee reported that based on a sample of thirty-four users, only 15 percent missed the drug when deprived of it while 71 percent expressed a preference for tobacco (J. S. Siler et al., "Marihuana Smoking in Panama," *Military Surgeon* 73 [1933]: 269–80; quoted in ibid., p. 138).

58. As one historian of the subject has noted, the FBN's reports from the early 1930s "clearly show that it sensed the pressure for a national law, and Commissioner Anslinger personally regarded marihuana use as a vice requiring federal attention. From his first year as head of the FBN, his correspondence advocated eventual national control." (Himmelstein, *The Strange Career of Marihuana,* p. 56.)

in collaboration with Courtney Ryley Cooper in 1937, Anslinger recounted the particulars of the case:

> An entire family was murdered by a youthful addict in Florida. When officers arrived at the home, they found the youth staggering about in a human slaughterhouse. With an ax he had killed his father, mother, two brothers, and a sister. He seemed to be in a daze. . . . He had no recollection of having committed the multiple crime. The officers knew him ordinarily as a sane, rather quiet young man; now he was pitifully crazed. They sought the reason. The boy said he had been in the habit of smoking something which youthful friends called "muggles," a childish name for marihuana.[59]

Anslinger's testimony before the House Ways and Means Committee and a subcommittee of the Senate Finance Committee was filled with such spectacular reports of users driven mad by even the most casual contact with the drug. Thus, during the one day of Senate hearings on the bill, Anslinger, whose knowledge of pharmacology was about as extensive as his mastery of early Byzantine architecture, offered the following analysis of the effects of marijuana in reply to a question regarding what dosage was thought to be dangerous.

> I believe in some cases one cigarette might develop a homicidal mania, probably to kill his brother. It depends on the physical characteristics of the individual. Every individual reacts differently to the drug. It stimulates some and others it depresses. It is impossible to say just what the action of the drug will be on a given individual, or the amount. Probably some people could smoke five before it would take effect, but all the experts agree that the continued use leads to insanity. There are many cases of insanity.[60]

---

59. Harry J. Anslinger, with Courtney Ryley Cooper, "Marihuana: Assassin of Youth," *American Magazine* 124 (July 1937): 19, 150.

60. U.S. Congress, Senate, Finance Committee Subcommittee, *Hearings on H.R. 6906,* 75th Cong., 1st sess., 1937, pp. 11–14; quoted in Bonnie and Whitebread, *The Marihuana Conviction,* p. 157. At the outset of hearings in the House, the FBN submitted a brief written statement regarding the relationship between marijuana use and psychosis: "Despite the fact that medical men and scientists have disagreed upon the properties of marihuana, and some are inclined to minimize the harmfulness of this drug, the records offer ample evidence that it has a disastrous effect upon many of its users. Recently we have received many reports showing crimes of violence committed by persons while under the influence of marihuana. . . .

"The deleterious, even vicious, qualities of the drug render it highly dangerous to the mind and body upon which it operates to destroy the will, cause one to lose the power of connected thought, producing imaginary delectable situations and gradually weakening the physical pow-

Despite the perfunctory nature of these hearings, the bill passed both the House and the Senate with practically no debate and was signed into law on August 2, 1937. The Marihuana Tax Act[61] was nominally a revenue-producing act that imposed a tax on, among others, physicians who prescribed, and pharmacists who dispensed, the drug. Only the nonmedical possession and sale of marijuana was made criminal by the statute, while all persons engaged in the legal chain of cultivation and sale for medicinal purposes—growers, manufacturers, druggists, doctors, etc.—had to comply with the extensive record-keeping provisions of the act and to pay an annual license fee. The law, however, effectively called a halt to continued use of the drug as a medicinal agent.

Not content with the dampening effects the Marihuana Tax Act alone was to have on the medical uses of the drug, Anslinger immediately began to mobilize support within the medical profession itself to eliminate marijuana from the physician's armamentarium. In 1941, Anslinger was successful in convincing Dr. Ernest Fullerton Cook, chairman of the Commission on Revision of the *United States Pharmacopeia,* to remove cannabis from the *USP.* The results of this action followed quickly; marijuana was no longer prescribed as a medicinal agent, and research on possible medical uses of the drug came to an abrupt halt. It is impossible to assess the damage caused by marijuana's removal from the *USP.* It is also difficult to understand why Anslinger should have displayed such mean-spiritedness in attempting to stamp out the drug even when employed for medical purposes. We do know that the legacy of his campaign to criminalize a drug as comparatively harmless as marijuana at both the state and federal levels[62] was the humiliation and suffering of hundreds of

---

ers. Its use frequently leads to insanity." There followed an outline of cases purporting to show the intimate connection between cannabis use and "revolting crimes." (U.S. Congress, House, Committee on Ways and Means, *Hearings on H.R. 6385,* 75th Cong., 1st sess., 1937, p. 30; quoted in ibid., p. 155.)

61. Public Law No. 238 (75th Congress), 2 August 1937 [50 stat. 551 (1937)].

62. Anslinger's public posture on the relation between marijuana and insanity appears to have remained unchanged, at least into the 1950s, despite the mounting evidence that his position was scientifically totally untenable. Indeed, the FBN was still distributing Anslinger's essay on "Criminal and Psychiatric Aspects of Marihuana" as the leading publication in the field as late as March 1950 (Bonnie and Whitebread, *The Marihuana Conviction,* p. 194). An extensive treatment of the attitude of the FBN and of Anslinger's personal pronouncements respecting marijuana also appears in Rufus King, *The Drug Hang-Up: America's Fifty-Year Folly* (New York: Norton, 1972), pp. 69–107.

thousands of people who were to endure the indignity of arrest and, in many cases, imprisonment. Equally important, the medical advances that might have been made through more extensive research into the possible beneficial effects of cannabis have been denied us for almost half a century.

As Drs. Lester Grinspoon and James Bakalar observe (Chapter 5: "Medical Uses of Illicit Drugs"), the official representative of the American Medical Association at the congressional hearings on marijuana in 1937 had taken strong exception to the language of the bill on the ground that cannabis might prove to have substantial medical benefits.[63] Indeed, that legal difficulties prevented further research on the drug is just one more regrettable aspect of its criminalization. Among the recent studies to which Grinspoon and Bakalar call our attention are those that suggest that marijuana is useful in the treatment of alcohol dependence and that, under certain conditions, it can act as an efficacious analgesic and as an anticonvulsant. In addition, the authors report that cannabis appears to be of value in treating glaucoma and as an antiemetic. They point to the significant fact that the legal problems connected with research on the effects of marijuana, as with narcotics and other controlled substances, cannot but discourage such studies; further, official attitudes toward the recreational use of illicit drugs commonly spill over into a biased perception of the medical potential of these substances.

There is a further problem, which we would do well to underscore, respecting research on the effects of controlled substances. More and more scientific research is funded through agencies either directly or indirectly answerable to various levels of government, particularly the federal government.[64] Before a scientific hypothesis becomes scientific fact, it must first have undergone empirical investigation and

63. Dr. William C. Woodward of the American Medical Association's Committee on Medical Legislation had not been consulted in the drafting of the bill and took strong exception to its provisions, which he felt unnecessarily inhibited the prerogatives of physicians. Much of his testimony before Congress on the Marihuana Tax Act appears verbatim in Bonnie and Whitebread, *The Marihuana Conviction*, pp. 164–72.

64. In 1970, $1,969 million was spent on medical research in the United States, of which $1,754 million, or 89 percent, was funded through public expenditures. By 1984, the total expended had risen to $6,798 million, of which $6,426 million, or about 95 percent, were government funds. See Bureau of the Census, *Statistical Abstract of the United States, 1986* (Washington, D.C.: Government Printing Office, 1985), p. 97 (Series 147).

rigid testing, and in the ordinary course of research, this testing must have been replicated with similar results. Now, it is clearly going to prove more difficult to receive a grant to replicate an experiment the conclusions of which defy the prevailing orthodoxy than to procure funds for projects that conform to current scientific doctrine. It follows that the increasing concentration of research funds in the hands of government or quasi-government agencies will serve to reinforce the official prejudice that controlled substances are dangerous even when ingested in moderate amounts and, for the most part, are of limited medical value.

There is something especially distressing in fact that scientific research should be colored by the legal treatment accorded certain drugs, particularly when we recall the history of the various prohibitory laws to which the opiates, cocaine, and marijuana are now subject. It is surely more than a curiosity that the original motive impelling state legislatures to control the use of opium was to be found in anti-Chinese sentiment and that the early history of agitation for legislation prohibiting the use of marijuana was associated with anti-Mexican attitudes. Similarly, laws governing the sale and possession of cocaine can, in part, be explained by the notion popular at the beginning of the century that the use of the drug was intimately connected with the bestial rage of blacks involved in crimes of violence.[65] From their origins in an ignorant racism, the various statutes governing opiates, cocaine, and marijuana have become an unquestioned part of American law. That this approach to the use of these substances might be not only ineffective but actually destructive is seldom considered. Yet, the smugness long shown by the drug enforcement bureaucracy has begun to fade as the figures indicate that our drug laws, despite the huge amounts expended in enforcing them, have done nothing to decrease drug use. Indeed, as Arnold Trebach has reported (Chapter 3: "The Need for Reform of International

65. See Musto, *The American Disease,* pp. 7–8. Immediately before passage of the Harrison Narcotic Act of 1914 the claim was made that most attacks made by blacks on white women in the South were directly attributable to a "coke-crazed negro brain," and that blacks were made temporarily immune to the "knockdown effects of fatal wounds" made by .32 caliber bullets while under the effects of the drug. As a consequence, a large number of Southern police departments replaced their firearms with .38 caliber revolvers. See Wisotsky, "Exposing the War on Cocaine," pp. 1414–15.

Narcotics Laws"), the evidence points to the fact that the United States is not alone in this regard but is in the vanguard of a worldwide escalation in illicit drug use.

Trebach has mustered a substantial amount of impressionistic data showing that opiate use has increased substantially in both Europe and the Orient in the past twenty-five years,[66] to the point where even the most draconian penalties have not been able to deter an increase in illicit consumption.[67] One of the more worrisome features of this situation, Trebach notes, is the response of many foreign governments, which have followed the United States in attempting to deal with drug use through the enactment of prohibitory laws with harsh punishments. Such laws, besides being inhumane, have proved incapable of deterring drug use while encouraging the creation of a complex illegal system of supply. In light of this, some reform in the structure of drug legislation is essential. Although Trebach stops short of recommending the total decriminalization of illicit drugs, he does support a program along the lines that prevailed in Great Britain prior to 1968, whereby regular opiate users were able to maintain their habit through the mediation of a physician.[68] Whether or not one is sympathetic to this specific program, there is little question that reform of our current drug laws is imperative if billions of dollars more are not to be wasted and if more lives are not to be ruined by such legislation.

It we were in fact to remove all prohibitory laws respecting illicit drugs, is there some way of determining the most likely number of users? Robert Michaels (Chapter 8: "The Market for Heroin Before

66. See especially the issue-length study of the extent of drug abuse in twenty-five countries that appeared in the journal *Addictive Diseases: An International Journal* 3 (1977): 1–134. Unfortunately, the enormous difficulty in obtaining reliable figures and the fact that the statistics on drug use are consistently manipulated for political ends make these data at best suggestive.

67. The severity of sentences for heroin possession in certain Third World countries was brought home in dramatic fashion recently when two Australians were hanged at Pudu jail in Kuala Lumpur, Malaysia, for possession of more than 15 grams of heroin. See Reuter's dispatch, "Two Australians Hanged in Malaysia," *Globe and Mail* (Toronto), 17 July 1986, p. A8. It is difficult to imagine how the imposition of such sentences could occasion any feeling other than revulsion among civilized people or what the purpose of such barbaric penalties are.

68. This system of narcotics control is dealt with in some detail in Alfred R. Lindesmith, *The Addict and the Law* (Bloomington: Indiana University Press, 1965), pp. 164–79.

and After Legalization'') has undertaken to answer this question with respect to heroin. As Michaels points out, any reasonable attempt to predict how many users there would be if heroin were decriminalized is predicated on the existence of more or less reliable data on the current user population. These data, however, simply are not available. The government, which provides such statistics, has consistently manipulated the figures it publishes for one political purpose or another, fully aware of the fact that such data on the number and characteristics of users are essential if researchers are to realistically extrapolate to conditions in which heroin is legal. As Michaels observes, there exist organized interests outside of government that are concerned with accurate demographic statistics in other areas, and these interests will pressure the government to collect and provide reliable figures if this is not being done. However, no such pressure group exists for unambiguous and precise data respecting heroin users.

Even the term *addict* is subject to immense variation, depending on when the term is used, the purpose for which it is being used, and the agency using it. When a new ''war on drugs'' is declared, or when the government agencies charged with enforcement of the drug laws are seeking larger appropriations, the number of addicts tends to rise sharply. Not all heroin users, of course, are ''addicts,'' in the sense that they exhibit the classic symptoms of physical withdrawal. Indeed, the overwhelming majority are only occasional users, known as ''chippers.'' Nor is addiction inevitable after prolonged use. (The Drug Enforcement Administration's claim that anyone having used heroin more than six times becomes addicted to the drug[69] is contravened by all the scientific evidence.) In addition, large numbers of heroin addicts apparently go through voluntary withdrawal and many, after having been briefly addicted, give up heroin permanently.[70] All these factors contribute to imprecision in the use of the term, an imprecision reflected in the fact that the number of current ''addicts'' in the United States has been variously es-

69. U.S. Congress, House, Committee on Appropriations, Oversight Hearings before a Subcommittee of the Committee on Appropriations, 90th Cong., 2d sess., 1968, Testimony of Henry L. Giordano, Commissioner of Narcotics, Bureau of Narcotics, p. 623; quoted in Kaplan, *The Hardest Drug,* p. 32.

70. Ibid., pp. 15–38.

timated as 69,000 (Bureau of Narcotics and Dangerous Drugs, 1969) to 740,000 (Drug Enforcement Administration, 1977).

Attempts to determine the number of addicts immediately after passage of the Harrison Narcotic Act in 1914 seem to have varied almost as widely as do current estimates. In 1917, it was claimed that there were 300,000 addicts in New York City alone,[71] and in 1924 one physician calculated that more than 1,000,000 people throughout the country were addicted to opiates.[72] Perhaps the most reliable figures, however, were those offered by Dr. Lawrence Kolb of the U.S. Public Health Service, who carefully analyzed all available data pertinent to the subject in 1924 and who concluded that the addict population at that time was between 110,000 and 150,000, and had never been higher than 264,000 when, after 1900, the number of addicts steadily decreased.[73]

In the absence of any more reliable data, it does not appear likely that, under decriminalization, the number of heroin addicts—as opposed to occasional users, whose normal living patterns would remain essentially unchanged—would exceed the current "best estimate" of 500,000. More important, there is evidence to suggest that a clear positive correlation exists between heroin use and certain crimes, particularly robberies, burglaries, and thefts. Indeed, a recent study has concluded that daily heroin users commit twice as many robberies and burglaries as those sentenced to California prisons for such crimes.[74] The authors conclude that "on an annual basis, the average heroin abuser probably committed about twenty-five crimes (robbery, burglary, and larceny) against individual victims who would complain to police. But he also committed an additional seventy-five nondrug crimes without clear victims (mainly shoplifting

71. "The Problem of the Drug Addict," *American Medicine* 23 (December 1917): 794; quoted in H. Wayne Morgan, "Introduction," in H. Wayne Morgan, ed., *Yesterday's Addicts: American Society and Drug Abuse, 1865–1920* (Norman: University of Oklahoma Press, 1974), p. 9.

72. S. Adolphus Knopf, "One Million Drug Addicts in the United States," *Medical Journal and Record,* 119 (6 February 1924): 135–39.

73. Lawrence Kolb and A. G. Du Mez, "The Prevalence and Trend of Drug Addiction in the United States and Factors Influencing It," *Public Health Reports* 39 (23 May 1924): 1179–1204. (*Public Health Reports* was issued weekly by the United States Public Health Service of the Treasury Department.)

74. Bruce D. Johnson et al., *Taking Care of Business: The Economics of Crime by Heroin Abusers* (Lexington, Mass.: Lexington, 1985), pp. 73–80.

for resale, burglaries of abandoned buildings, and larcenies considered as losses by victims).''[75] These conclusions are consistent with earlier studies, including an analysis of the effects of the price of heroin on crime-rates in Detroit.[76] Researchers there found that a 10 percent increase in the street price of heroin consistently led to a rise of 2.9 percent in reports of revenue-raising crimes, particularly those crimes associated with heroin use, armed and unarmed robberies and burglaries of residences.[77] Whether a substantial portion of the crimes engaged in by heroin-users is committed for the purpose of raising revenue in order to buy the drug, or whether users would commit these crimes regardless of their drug-use, can never be proved conclusively, but the data strongly suggest the former. If such a correlation does indeed exist, as is commonly assumed, then one immediate effect of the legalization of the opiates would be a reduction in certain crimes that most people find particularly oppressive since, as Michaels reports, twenty 10-milligram tablets of legally produced heroin cost approximately $1.00, while the average heroin habit is limited to about 50 milligrams per day.

Estimates of the number of addicts and the crime-rates that would follow decriminalization are not the only issues that deserve serious consideration in any discussion of the legalization of illicit drugs. Dr. Norman E. Zinberg (Chapter 7: "The Use and Misuse of Intoxicants: Factors in the Development of Controlled Use") makes the important point that the use of illicit drugs, like all substance gratification, is a function of a variety of factors beyond the simple desire to enjoy the substance. More particularly, how, when, where, and how much of the substance we use is in part determined by the social sanctions and rituals that surround the substance's use. An especially unfortunate aspect of our current drug laws, which have now been in place for half a century or more, is that our culture has been deprived of the natural means by which we would ordinarily accommodate and adapt ourselves to drug use, in the way most of

75. Ibid., p. 184.

76. Drug Abuse Council, *Heroin Supply and Urban Crime* (Washington, D.C.: Drug Abuse Council, Inc., 1976). The data contained in this pamphlet are extracted from a study undertaken by the Public Research Institute of the Center for Naval Analyses and commissioned by the Drug Abuse Council in 1975. See Lester Silverman, Nancy Spruill, and Daniel Levine, *Urban Crime and Heroin Availability,* PRI 75-1 (Arlington, Va.: Public Research Institute, 1975).

77. Ibid., [5].

us have accommodated and adapted ourselves to the socially acceptable use of alcohol. Zinberg rightly characterizes our current policy toward drug use as naive, since it assumes that all use is misuse, that is, uncontrolled use. Thus, any policy that apparently reduces the total amount of current use is advertised as a victory in the war on drugs. What is lacking in this simplistic analysis is an awareness that only a percentage, possibly a fairly modest percentage, of use is uncontrolled and therefore warrants legal sanctions in the eyes of many. There is a certain fanciful quality to the rationale of most government action (and in far too many discussions) concerning illicit drugs, that only two possibilities exist, either total abstinence enforced by the police power of the state or uncontrolled use leading to addiction. Drug enforcement agencies have done everything in their power to promote this notion and the media, taking their cue from the government, have bombarded us with this view of drug use. In fact, as Zinberg makes clear, the great bulk of such use falls somewhere between these two extremes and is governed by a series of informal controls that have arisen despite the presence of prohibitory laws.

Implicit in Zinberg's analysis is the view that social arrangements of more than passing value are, at their inception, fragile and require time to take on the status of convention. The laws respecting drugs under which we operate, however, have acted as serious obstacles to the development of more systematic rules of behavior respecting drug use which arise independent of government command. These laws are predicated on the theory that complex social structures are, of necessity, the product of conscious design (that is, can only come about through the action of the legislature). It has become increasingly apparent over the past century, however, that the actions of government are no substitute for the more complex knowledge embedded in the customs and social arrangements that arise independent of deliberate planning. It is absurd to suppose that men obey rules only when the punishment for breaking them involves legal sanctions. The overwhelming majority of us accommodate our behavior to a host of social conventions without the need for police enforcement, and there is every reason to believe that we would adjust our actions to conform to acceptable social practice with respect to drug use, were we permitted to.

In light of the total failure of our current policy toward illicit drugs, it seems clear that earnest consideration must be given to complete abandonment of all prohibitory laws. Both prudential reasons and principle dictate that the decriminalization of marijuana, cocaine, and the opiates would halt the current massive drain of public funds and the substantial suffering brought about through attempts to enforce these unenforceable laws. Evidence indicates that legalization would do much to reduce the current crime-rate and thus contribute to restoring the safety of our city streets. It would reduce the amount of government corruption, which is partly a function of the immense fortunes that are constantly made in the drug trade, and it would play a large part in decreasing the profits that flow to organized crime. All these arguments have recently been offered by a host of writers calling for repeal of our drug laws.[78] Of far greater importance, however, is the fact that any statute aimed at preventing behavior that does harm to no one but the actor—that is, legislation that creates victimless crimes—raises significant ethical questions in a society the most important of whose founding principles is individual freedom.[79] The argument that the ingestion of drugs is in reality a crime with many victims since it harms the family and community of the drug-user, who are denied his productive capabilities and his forgone earnings, as well as the drug-user himself, who is deprived of his rationality and his health, has no more merit than similar arguments applied to wastrels, layabouts, and chronic overeaters.[80] Drug use is a victimless crime and defenders of criminali-

78. See, for example, the editorial supporting the decriminalization of marijuana and possibly of cocaine that appeared in *The New Republic*, 15 April 1985, pp. 7–8; the statement of the federal public defender for eastern California, as reported in the *San Francisco Chronicle*, 2 December 1985; and, especially, the syndicated column by William F. Buckley, Jr., calling for the legalization of all illicit drugs (Universal Press Syndicate, 28 March 1985).

79. One of the few commentators on our drug laws who has supported the legalization of narcotics and other drugs for purely principled reasons is the economist and Nobel laureate Milton Friedman. See "Prohibition and Drugs," *Newsweek*, 1 May 1972, p. 104.

80. John Stuart Mill, in his classic discussion of the nature of liberty, argued that a free society is one based on the principle that, in a civilized community power cannot rightfully be exercised over an individual against his will except to prevent harm to others and that the physical or moral good of the individual did not constitute a sufficient excuse to exercise such power. See *On Liberty*, David Spitz, ed. (New York: Norton, 1975), pp. 10–11. John Kaplan has taken issue with this view, concluding that, even on Mill's own terms, it would be possible to support statutes that criminalized the distribution of narcotics. Kaplan argues that since Mill exempted children from his principle and inasmuch as it would be impossible to prevent children from having access to these drugs unless their sale were universally halted, the protection of children could well constitute sufficient grounds within the structure of Mill's argument, to prohibit all sales of opiates (*The Hardest Drug*, pp. 104–5). I find no merit whatever in this contention. It seems obvious that Mill would have rejected Kaplan's argument on the

zation cannot avoid the problem of how to reconcile these laws with a society based on personal liberty and individual responsibility.[81]

The importance of the moral dimension of our drug laws makes it particularly fitting that the last essay in this volume deals with the ethical aspects of drug control in a free society. Dr. Thomas Szasz (Chapter 9: "The Morality of Drug Controls") has written passionately in defense of the notion that the freedom to eat and drink what we choose can be no less a basic right in a society dedicated to individual liberty than the freedom to speak and to worship as our consciences dictate. It is an unfortunate commentary on how far this nation has strayed from its political foundations that some writers have regarded the most appropriate way of describing the relation between the individual and government as comparable to the relation of a public ward to a benign magistrate.[82] If we were to accept this metaphor as an accurate description of the essential nature of political life then, of course, we can offer no principled objections to laws prohibiting drug use. It is uncertain, however, how many people would embrace this view of the nature of American society if they were fully aware of all its implications. This country was not founded on the principle that our governors are our parents, to whom we have entrusted the power to prevent us from harming ourselves. Nor is our legal system predicated on the notion that we are not responsible for our own actions. To accept this view is to accept that the ideal state is a beneficent totalitarianism, staffed by an endless number of well-meaning, albeit intrusive, bureaucrats.

The genius of American society since its founding has consisted in its openness and its diversity. We have embraced a multiplicity of

---

simple grounds that it could serve to prevent the sale of any good or service whatever, the effect of which would be to subject adults to a marketplace structured by laws created solely for children.

Kaplan's second argument, that Mill did not extend his notion of individual liberty to include selling oneself into slavery and that opiate addiction constitutes a species of slavery to which the user is at least at risk, is equally weak (ibid., pp. 105–6). The slavery of which Mill is writing has reference solely to our subjugation to another person's will and not to anything else, whether it be the laws of God or the forces of nature, to which we are all, depending on our beliefs and our circumstances, more or less subject.

81. Kaplan has managed to circumvent this difficulty by the simple expedient of abandoning the principles commonly associated with a free society. See ibid., pp. 106–9.

82. See ibid., p. 107, and Robert Bartels, "Better Living through Legislation: The Control of Mind-Altering Drugs," *Kansas Law Review* 21 (1973): 439–92.

values and customs, and have grown stronger for it. Drug laws, of which Prohibition was simply the most spectacular example, strike at the very root of our pluralistic society and constitute a surrender of our traditional toleration for disparate values. The analogy with religion that Szasz invokes is a particularly apt one. For centuries it had been thought that a common religion comprised the cement that held society together and that its absence would lead to social and political chaos. Yet religious toleration has in fact strengthened society, not weakened it. There is every reason to believe that the effect would prove no different were we to tolerate those groups who wish to ingest drugs other than those we currently find socially acceptable.

A truly liberal society, without violating the principles under which it operates, cannot concern itself with preventing some people from using certain drugs because a segment of the community condemns such pleasures any more than it can prohibit some of us from reading certain books because some portion of the population finds these works offensive. We may choose to eliminate what we consider to be vice and depravity through exhortation and discussion, or we may opt to root out sin by using the police power of the state. It is only the first method, however, that is compatible with a society of free people who have the courage to take responsibility for their own actions.

PART I

THE EFFECTS
OF PROHIBITION

1

THE HISTORY
OF LEGISLATIVE CONTROL
OVER OPIUM, COCAINE,
AND THEIR DERIVATIVES

D. F. Musto

Legislative control over dangerous drugs may be dated from attempts in the nineteenth century to prevent acute poisoning by certain substances that might be purchased in ignorance of their lethal potential or might be too easily available to would-be suicides. Opium was being sold in a crude form containing about 10 percent morphine, as well as in concoctions derived from crude opium: paregoric, laudanum, and a solution in acetic acid known as "black drop." Morphine had been isolated from opium in 1805 by the German pharmacist, F. W. Sertürner, but production of the powerful active ingredient of opium on a large scale was delayed until the 1830s.[1] From that time onward, in factories in Germany, Great Britain, and the United States, morphine was produced in great quantities. Thus when in 1868, Great Britain came to enact pharmacy laws to control dangerous substances, "opium and all preparations of opium or of

---

1. Rudolf Schmitz, "Friedrich Wilhelm Sertürner and the Discovery of Morphine," *Pharmacy in History* 27 (1985): 61–74.

poppies" was listed alongside such substances as oxalic acid as commodities that could not be sold without being labeled "poison."[2]

The Pharmacy Act of 1868 is an important symbol of legislative control in a Western country. The act was not the most strict among nations; perhaps the Prussian regulations were stricter and more comprehensive, but establishment by the British of some limitation on the availability of dangerous drugs—drugs that would eventually become more serious a problem for society as addictive agents than as tools for suicide—was a policy also followed by other European nations. It had an apparently discouraging effect on the per capita consumption of opium, opiates, and cocaine in the late nineteenth century and contributed to the low level of British consumption (at least compared to the American) right up to the 1960s.[3]

The experience of the United States stands in contrast to Britain's. The Pharmacy Act of 1868 was regulated in large part by the organized association of pharmacists, the Pharmaceutical Society (established 1841). In order to retail, dispense, or compound "poisons," or to assume the title of chemist, druggist, pharmacist, or dispensing druggist or chemist, the individual had to be registered by the Pharmaceutical Society. As well as being the testing and registering body, the Society was also given the initial responsibility for adding new drugs to the poison list. Thus the law, which ultimately would be enforced in British courts, was monitored by local members of the Pharmaceutical Society as a tool in competition with unregistered druggists, grocers, and anyone else who might attempt to purvey these drugs to the public.

While the act presumably aided the public health by having dangerous drugs sold or dispensed by individuals knowledgeable about their qualities, it was also a convenient aid to the trade of registered pharmacists. Although the drugs could be obtained with no specific restraint on the amount or frequency of sale, the bottles had to be labeled "poison." A stricter category of substances also required that the purchaser be an acquaintance of the pharmacist or someone the pharmacist knew. This list included arsenic and "strychnine and all poisonous alkaloids and their salts." The impact of this modest ob-

2. 31 and 32 Vict. ch. 121, 1868: Act to Regulate the Sale of Poisons and Alter and Amend the Pharmacy Act 1852 (1868 Pharmacy Act).

3. Virginia Berridge and Griffith Edwards, *Opium and the People: Opiate Use in Nineteenth-Century England* (New York: St. Martin's, 1981), pp. 147–49, 227, 254.

stacle to the acquirement of dangerous drugs should not be under-estimated. Further, the self-interest that would motivate registered pharmacists to monitor breaches of the law provided an unpaid, but interested, drug enforcement cadre scattered throughout Great Britain. "Patent medicines" were excepted from these controls, and this led to a campaign against them later in the century, but the pure forms of the drugs, e.g., morphine suitable for injection, were restricted in availability from the time of the Pharmacy Act onward.[4]

In the United States, throughout the nineteenth century, both medicine and pharmacy remained essentially unorganized, although there were some physicians and pharmacists attempting to organize their professions. The American Medical Association, which was founded in 1847 and which we now might think of as the dominant medical organization, was a small and nationally unrepresentative group until about World War I.[5] The American Pharmaceutical Association, founded four years later, grew slowly and, like the AMA, lacked the authority to license practitioners. The pharmacy establishment was divided sharply among drug manufacturers, wholesalers, and retailers, whose divergent interests the APhA tried to coordinate, but each segment of the profession came to work through its own organization: the National Wholesale Druggists' Association (1882), the National Association of Retail Druggists (1898), and many other groups.[6] There was no national group for the health professions to which government could turn for regulation, even if the American constitutional system had permitted such an arrangement.

Licensing of pharmacists and physicians, which was the central government's responsibility in European nations, was, in the United States, a power reserved to each individual state. In the era of Andrew Jackson, any form of licensing that appeared to give a monopoly to the educated was attacked as a contradiction of American democratic ideals. State after state repealed the medical licensing laws adopted in earlier days. Practical concerns also supported repeal: Legislators preferred to leave it to the patients to decide which of

4. Ibid., pp. 113–31.

5. James G. Burrow, *AMA: Voice of American Medicine* (Baltimore: Johns Hopkins Press, 1963), pp. 51–52, 62ff.

6. Glenn Sonnedecker, *Kremers and Urdang's History of Pharmacy,* 4th ed. (Philadelphia: Lippincott, 1976), pp. 198–212.

the many competing theories of medicine was the best. Instead of moving toward a national system of licensing for health professionals, therefore, individual states were deregulating the professions. American medical schools were similarly unregulated, and many flourished—some no better than diploma mills. The states did not begin reestablishment of medical licensing until the 1880s, and even then the movement was spotty, with a wide range of standards.[7] Pharmacists, also seeking to raise standards and limit competition, likewise fought at the state level for licensing, since the U.S. Constitution placed in the hands of states the regulation of the health professions. Although some requirements for labeling of over-the-counter medicines would come with the Pure Food and Drug Act of 1906 as an exercise of the federal right to regulate interstate commerce, in general, the nineteenth and early twentieth century interpretation of the Constitution favored a strict division between state and federal powers.

The status of legislative control of dangerous drugs during the nineteenth century may be summed up as follows: The United States had no practical control over the health professions, no representative national health organizations to aid the government in drafting regulations, and no controls on the labeling, composition, or advertising of compounds that might contain opiates or cocaine. The United States not only proclaimed a free marketplace, it practiced this philosophy with regard to narcotics in a manner unrestrained at every level of preparation and consumption.

Through a slower pace of professional development, the United States also lagged behind Britain and other European countries in establishing broadly based organizations representing the nation's physicians or pharmacists to which the central government could turn for regulation. Second, the form of government adopted in the United States, a federation of partly independent states, was a conscious attempt to prevent establishment of an all-powerful central government characteristic of Europe. In the nineteenth century, this remarkably successful form of government entailed each state making its own regulation if it wished to; the result was an array of controls that varied from one state to another. In fact, states made little

7. R. H. Shryock, *Medical Licensing in America, 1650–1965* (Baltimore: Johns Hopkins Press, 1967), p. 32ff.

attempt to control addictive drugs until quite late in the last century, and those efforts did not prove very effective.

During the first part of the nineteenth century, the amount of opiates used in the United States may have been comparable to that used in Britain, where some areas, notably the fen counties, had a fairly large per capita consumption. Inhabitants there often took a dose of laudanum or some form of opium daily to keep away the fevers associated with the marshlands.[8] More generally, parents reputedly purchased one or another form of opium to rub on the gums of teething infants or to spoon-feed a child to induce sleep so that the mother without provision for child care could work in the local factory. These accounts are anecdotal, but recent historical studies do suggest that the taking of some form of opium for pain, sleep, or to ward off illness was not uncommon. The occasional death of an infant from an overdose of opium or the suicide of an adult by means of opium prompted parliamentary interest in the distribution and labeling of the drug. In large measure, the 1868 Pharmacy Act was the result. One should note however, that through the provisions of the act and the designation of the Pharmaceutical Society as the most responsible body, the pharmacists also achieved some control over the profession and a lead on the other health professions. A somewhat similar victory for U.S. pharmacy would be found in the details of the Harrison Narcotic Act in 1914.[9]

In nineteenth-century America, the unimpeded importation of opium and the free economy in opiates do give an advantage to the historian, for estimates of per capita consumption are more reliable when there are few restrictions on the importation, sale, and consumption of a product. Because the growth of poppies within the country and preparation of opium from them seem to have been a minor contributor to American use, the import statistics, begun in 1840 and continued to the present day, are reliable as a guide to domestic consumption until the Harrison Act of 1914. Certainly the minimum level and the trend can be observed. After the Harrison Act, these statistics grew less reliable, for smuggling becomes a more uncertain variable, but we can say that at least during the nineteenth

8. Virginia Berridge, "Fenland Opium Eating in the Nineteenth Century," *British Journal of Addiction* 72 (1977): 275-84.

9. David F. Musto, *The American Disease: Origins of Narcotic Control* (New Haven: Yale University Press, 1973), p. 54ff.

century the annual per capita consumption rose steadily from about 12 grains in 1840 (an average single dose being one grain) until the mid-1890s, when it reached 52 grains annually per capita. Then statistics show that average individual consumption gradually subsided up to 1914, by which time the per capita rate had fallen back to the level of about 1880.[10] In Great Britain, the per capita consumption declined during the latter half of the nineteenth century.[11] During that same period, opium use in the United States rose dramatically. The peak of opiate addiction in the United States occurred about the turn of the century, when the number probably was close to 250,000 in a population of 76 million, a rate so far never equaled or exceeded.[12] Heroin had been introduced into the pharmacy in 1898 and had contrasting impacts in Britain and the United States. In New York City, the addiction capital of the United States, heroin became the drug of choice for recreational addicts, and the number of addicts was measured in the tens of thousands by 1920. In Britain, the addiction rate for heroin addicts by 1920 was minuscule.[13] Of course, the use of drugs is determined by many factors, but I would like to suggest that the contrast in easy availability of narcotics in America and Britain—created by political and social factors removed from considerations of addiction—underlay the strikingly different rates of addiction each country experienced well into this century. The rise in addiction with which we are more familiar, that of the 1950s and more recently, appears to be associated with additional factors that will be discussed later.

Americans have something to learn from their earlier and extensive consumption of opiates, including heroin, and also massive consumption of cocaine, which occurred before World War I. This era

10. Ibid., p. 3
11. Berridge and Edwards, *Opium and the People*, p. 145ff.
12. Musto, *American Disease*, p. 5; David T. Courtwright, *Dark Paradise: Opiate Addiction in America before 1940* (Cambridge: Harvard University Press, 1982), chap. 1, "The Extent of Opiate Addiction," pp. 9–34. Opiate addiction is the regular use of opiates to prevent painful and uncomfortable bodily and psychic symptoms that would occur if the drug's use were abruptly stopped. Estimates of the number of addicts in the United States have often been susceptible to ideological and political influences. After carefully considering contemporary surveys, importation statistics, and other estimates, and subjecting his findings to modern statistical analysis, Professor Courtwright concluded that the highest rate of addiction in the United States occurred in the 1890s at the maximum rate of 4.59 per 1,000. Today that rate would result in 1.1 million addicts, about twice the current official estimate.
13. Musto, *American Disease*, p. 236.

is forgotten. We commonly act as if the heroin "epidemic" of the 1960s or the current cocaine "epidemic" is a new phenomenon in the United States, that the widespread use of a drug implies that legalization or "decriminalization" is the only reasonable response. The history of attempts at legislative control in the United States suggests that other courses may be effective and that these alternatives to legalization appear to have reduced enormous opiate and cocaine consumption in the United States earlier in this century. Therefore, it is worthwhile to consider these early efforts at narcotic limitation if we are to approach contemporary policy issues with an appreciation of the range of policy options that reduce or encourage ingestion of these substances. For in spite of the great difference in addiction rates between the United States and Great Britain in 1920, the United States did reduce its addiction rate to a relatively small number. On the other hand, the low heroin addiction rate in Great Britain prior to the 1950s did not prove a protection against drug problems in that nation, although the level of use in Britain has not reached the proportions to which we are accustomed in the United States. Clearly the social and legal factors affecting drug use are complex, and there is no single influence that determines a particular level of drug use and abuse.

AMERICAN LEGISLATIVE CONTROL OVER OPIUM AND OPIATES TO 1914

The role of opium and its derivatives in the United States can be traced independently from cocaine until 1914, when these substances were linked together as "narcotics" through the Harrison Act. Technically, only the opiates are narcotics, that is, sleep-inducing, and they all have different effects. Nevertheless, most dangerous drugs, including cannabis, were grouped under the rubric "narcotics" from at least the 1920s until the 1960s.

As mentioned above, opium was available in many forms derived from crude opium long before the nineteenth century. In America, the two developments that spurred both consumption and concern about opium were (1) the isolation of morphine and its injection into the body with hypodermic syringes and (2) the introduction of smoking opium, which had been brought to the United States mainly by a feared minority, Chinese laborers imported to help build western railroads. The much greater ease of addiction through use of morphine compared to the more dilute forms employed previously focused attention on the drug, medical practitioners, and modern technology in the form of the hypodermic syringe.

Consumption of opium in the United States rose steadily before and after the Civil War. There had been complaints before the war about "opium drunkards" by such prominent and progressive physicians as Oliver Wendell Holmes, but in the second half of the century, physicians, as well as the general public, widely deplored opium and morphine addiction. To be addicted to morphine was to harbor a shameful secret to be hidden from others at whatever cost, a point illustrated in Eugene O'Neill's moving play about his own family, *Long Day's Journey into Night*. Written in his later years, it was based on his mother's addiction by a thoughtless physician, and the pain of this memory had remained so great that O'Neill would not permit the play's production during his lifetime. The leading American surgeon and the first professor of surgery at The Johns Hopkins Hospital, William Stewart Halsted, was a morphine addict for the last several decades of his life. His secret was kept hidden carefully until the publication of Sir William Osler's private diary in 1969.[14] Osler had been Halsted's physician while Osler was on the Hopkins faculty. Halsted's addiction did not appear to interfere with his work.

Americans received opium and morphine not only from their physicians for pain; they could receive what they wanted, for whatever reason they chose, over the counter or from mail order catalogues. The American free enterprise system, coupled with the federal system of government, meant that a bottle heavily laced with morphine could be sold across state lines as an "addiction cure" and affirmed on the label to contain no morphine whatsoever, quite within the law. States could pass laws restricting such advertising, but they were not inclined to do so. Patent medicine companies were the leading advertisers in American newspapers. They developed an ingenious protection from prying investigations or public pressure to reveal secret formulas, or from any state requirement to make only valid claims for effectiveness: The proprietary manufacturers included in their lucrative contracts with newspapers a proviso that the advertising agreement would be void if the state in which the newspaper was

14. Wilder Penfield, "Halsted of Johns Hopkins: The Man and His Problem as Described in the Secret Records of William Osler," *Journal of the American Medical Association* 210 (1969): 2214–18.

published enacted any laws affecting the sale or manufacture of the nostrums.[15]

In the nation's capital, the manufacturers also fought off requirements that their nostrums be labeled as to contents. Bills to enact such a law under the interstate commerce clause of the Constitution were defeated repeatedly, but in the 1890s a new reforming spirit was evident in the nation. These reforms were extensive, ranging from control over the use of forest land, to government inspection of meat and other comestibles and laws relating to adulterants in foods, and to drugs considered unsafe. Attention to the danger of narcotics—using the term broadly—accompanied the peak of per capita consumption in the United States. It is clear that what were regarded as the most negative aspects of drug use led to the passage of the new legislation. The simplest reform, correct labeling, was part of the Pure Food and Drug Act of 1906. Any over-the-counter medicine—commonly these would be "patent medicines"—had to be labeled correctly as to inclusion of any of the following drugs: morphine, cocaine, cannabis, or chloral hydrate. A long-desired reform, it simply informed the purchaser whether any of these drugs were present; it did not prevent purchase or restrict the amount of the drug.[16] Nevertheless, reports at the time indicate that the amount of these substances dropped from a third to a half as a response to public concern.[17] Although the newspapers remained quiet, widely read magazines such as *Collier's* and *Ladies Home Journal* railed against patent medicines, especially against morphine and cocaine. Even after passage of the truth-in-labeling laws, the magazines continued their exposés unabated until the next major step, which was restriction on the availability of the drugs themselves.[18]

Tracing the movement to restriction, as opposed to labeling accuracy, requires a step back to the mid-nineteenth century. Patent medicines are thought to have created some addiction, but the number of addicts is difficult to estimate. That physicians addicted or

15. James Harvey Young, *The Toadstool Millionaires: A Social History of Patent Medicines before Federal Regulation,* (Princeton, N.J.: Princeton University Press, 1961), p. 211ff.
16. Public Law No. 384, 59th Congress, Session I, 30 June 1906. Section 8 names the drugs that need to be listed on the label.
17. J. P. Street, "The Patent Medicine Situation," *American Journal of Public Health* 7 (1917): 1037–42.
18. Young, *Toadstool Millionaires,* p. 213ff.

assisted in the addiction of patients is more certain. The problem of iatroaddiction initially was approached by limiting renewal of prescriptions for opiates. These legal controls were mostly in the form of additions to the health statutes and depended for their efficacy on the judgments of physicians and pharmacists. These controls would not, of course, affect interstate commerce in narcotics or the familiar patent medicines, which still could be bought over the counter. No consistent police efforts to enforce these laws appear to have been undertaken.[19]

As the public and leaders of the health professions became more aware of the growing number of those addicted to opiates, chiefly morphine, state laws were amended to be more stringent, and the police occasionally staged crackdowns. As will be recalled, however, the professions were pretty much unorganized and struggling to achieve mandatory licensing; a threat to take away a license could not hold much fear until a license was required to begin with. Legislators also felt, or at least claimed, a helplessness when neighboring states did not enact strict laws—a circumstance more familiar to us with variations in the legal drinking age between states—with the result that enforcement was weak. This circumstance, combined with a poorly trained medical profession, a lack of professional organization, and an absence of laws controlling either patent medicine or interstate commerce in drugs, left local controls more symbolic than effective.

The nineteenth century's last decade brought the rise of what would come to be called the Progressive Movement, a set of reforms usually taking the form of federal laws affecting the entire nation with the ostensible purpose of improving the nation's morals or resisting the selfish actions of the rich and powerful. Alongside it grew a temperance, soon a prohibition, movement that would eventuate in the Eighteenth Amendment mandating prohibition of alcohol distribution for nonmedical purposes in the United States. In many ways, of course, the antialcohol movement was part of the Progressive Era; its startling success and later dramatic repeal have given the alcohol issue a somewhat separate development in our minds,

19. Martin I. Wilbert and Murray Galt Motter, *Digest of Laws and Regulations in Force in the United States Relating to the Possession, Use, Sale and Manufacture of Poisons and Habit-Forming Drugs,* Public Health Bulletin no. 56, Nov. 1912 (Washington, D.C.: Government Printing Office, 1912).

but the interrelation between the battles against alcohol and against narcotics is an important one. The antialcohol crusade helped establish the attitude that there could be no compromise with the forces of evil, that "moderation" was a false concept when applied to alcohol: Prohibition was the only logical or moral policy when dealing with this great national problem. By the nineteenth century a new wave of state prohibition laws was enacted. These were tempered by the contemporary constitutional understanding that a state prohibition law did not prevent purchase of liquor from a "wet" state, for that would be a form of interstate commerce and not subject to the states' powers. This assumption helped placate some doubters about prohibition, but the staunch fighters against alcohol also sought to remove that loophole. This they did through the Webb-Kenyon Act of 1913. Without going into the details of the broad and involved movement that led to national prohibition, we should note that the significance for the control of narcotics is that another dangerous substance, over which there was even more dispute as to the means of control, progressed inexorably toward a policy of "no maintenance" and no compromise. The moral question of how to deal with a dangerous substance was being fought out over alcohol, but the case would be stronger even with narcotics when that issue was brought to national deliberation.

The means by which the narcotics issue arose at the federal level was accidental. Certainly it would have come to the attention of Congress and the president eventually as a corollary to the alcohol prohibition movement or as a way of controlling addiction, which was becoming a target of journalist reformers and physicians. It was acquisition of the Philippines through the Spanish-American War that occasioned action by the federal government.

Again, in order to understand how the Philippines forced the central government to take action on opium, it is necessary to appreciate the divisions between federal and state powers that were so marked until the last half-century. The Philippines, unlike a state, came directly and wholly under the control of the federal government. At last, Congress could not avoid making decisions on such matters as the local availability of opium. Opium had been provided to Chinese on the Philippine Islands through a Spanish government monopoly. Civil Governor William Howard Taft considered whether the monopoly should be reinstituted. It was his judgment that this would be reasonable and that the profits from the opium monopoly could be used to help educate Filipinos, a task the United States eagerly accepted as it sought to provide a model government for its first colony.[20]

It was at the point in 1903, when this reinstitution was passing through the Philippine government under the eye of Civil Governor Taft, that the moral question of compromising with "evil" affected the future of opium's legal availability in that land. Missionaries in Manila and in the United States had learned that "tainted money" from opium sales was to be employed for education, and they besought President Theodore Roosevelt to prevent this moral wrong. He ordered Taft to stop the bill, and that was the end of it. The mood of moral leaders in the United States was sufficient during the first few years of this century to prevent any such "maintenance" program, even if it was restricted, as promised, to the Chinese in the Philippines. This immediate reaction to allowing opium to be used for purely "recreational" purposes, coming even before the Food and Drug Act, gave a signal as to how the federal government would respond to later questions regarding the legal supply of opium to individuals, not for medical reasons but for enjoyment or to satisfy their addiction.

In response to the veto from Washington, Governor Taft appointed an Opium Investigation Committee to consider how other Asian territories handled the opium problem. This committee introduces us to Bishop Charles Henry Brent, the Protestant Episcopal bishop of the Philippines, who had come out with Taft to help in Americanization of this new possession. Bishop Brent later would become world famous for his pioneer efforts to launch the ecumenical movement among Christian churches, but his second claim to fame was as a world leader against nonmedicinal uses of narcotics. He was appointed to the committee, which traveled to Japan, Formosa, Shanghai, Saigon, and Singapore examining how other nations dealt with the opium user. He and the other members of the committee found the Japanese policy in Formosa, a Japanese possession since its seizure from China in 1895, to be the most effective and enlightened. Japan opposed smoking opium but did not try to stop confirmed addicts abruptly from indulging in their habit. Japan hoped to "mature out" the opium smokers and leave an opium-free

20. Musto, *American Disease*, p. 25ff.

colony. In Japan, itself, opium use was controlled stringently by the government, rare even among Chinese aliens, and strongly deprecated by Japanese society.

The Philippine Opium Investigation Committee recommended that (1) male opium smokers over 21 should be registered in order to receive opium from a reinstituted government monopoly and (2) after a three-year period, the amount provided the smokers be reduced gradually until the smokers had been completely weaned from the drug.[21] But Congress reacted more sternly. Congress decreed immediate opium prohibition, except for medicinal purposes, for all native Filipinos; non-Filipinos—mostly Chinese—were allowed a three-year period of use. Over 12,000 non-Filipino opium users were registered, and their usual dosage was maintained for two-and-one-half years. During the final six months of the three-year leniency period ending March 1908, the opium provided was gradually reduced to zero. For official purposes, opium smoking had stopped in the Philippine Islands.[22] One additional point: The opium dispensing stations established under these laws were the first American narcotic clinics, although their goal was not long-term maintenance but rather registration and detoxification.

The Philippine situation forced the federal government to take a stand on opium use for nonmedicinal purposes, and the decision was to prohibit. To Congress, once the question was posed, compromise with narcotics was not a politically practical alternative. The Philippines also gave the United States leadership of the international control of narcotics, a role it still holds. It was apparent to the Opium Investigating Committee that the solution to the Philippine opium problem lay in the control of international trafficking in opium, as well as in the curtailment of opium production in the original producing states, such as India, China, Burma, Persia, and Turkey, to name some of the most prominent sites for the cultivation of the opium poppy.

At the time that the Philippines were perceived to be a victim of external sources of opium, the United States was having increasing problems with the Chinese Empire. Owing to maltreatment of

---

21. *Report of the Committee Appointed by the Philippine Commission to Investigate the Use of Opium and the Traffic Therein . . .* , Bureau of Insular Affairs, War Department, 1905.

22. Musto, *American Disease,* pp. 261–62.

Chinese in the United States, merchants in China planned a voluntary embargo on American goods. This worried American industrialists, wholesalers, exporters, and the federal government. China had also embarked on a vigorous effort to rid itself of opium use and, employing draconian methods, was having some success. As a means to indicate good will to China, to aid the Philippine opium problem, and to take an international leadership position on a moral issue of the times, the United States proposed, following Bishop Brent's suggestion to President Roosevelt, to convene an international meeting at Shanghai to consider the opium traffic among nations and to suggest ways in which China's antiopium campaign might be aided.

Thus, the Shanghai Opium Commission came into being. It would meet during February 1909, with Bishop Brent as its elected president. The group was designated a "commission" because the United States was unable to gain approval for a more powerful convocation, a "conference," which under international law could draft a treaty that would, if ratified, bind the signatory states. A "commission," on the other hand, could make findings of only fact or opinion. In addition to the United States and China, those who accepted invitations to Shanghai were Great Britain, France, the Netherlands, Persia, Japan, Italy, Austria-Hungary, Germany, Portugal, Siam, and Russia. Turkey accepted but did not send a representative. Persia was represented by a local merchant.

The resolutions adopted by the commission were merely recommendations and, even as such, had a comfortable vagueness that allowed a latitude of interpretations. For example, Resolution Three, taking cognizance of the near unanimous agreement that opium for nonmedicinal uses should be prohibited or "carefully regulated," called upon nations to "reexamine" their laws. This could hardly be considered a clarion call for prohibition of nonmedical uses, but it was Brent's goal to achieve a series of resolutions that at least pointed in the direction of action to control traffic in narcotics, with the hope that a future conference would enact a treaty initiating such control.[23]

The road from the Shanghai Opium Commission to the Hague Opium Conference, which convened in December 1911 and resulted in the Opium Convention of 1912, was a tortuous one, but after the Shanghai meeting, the United States continued to press for a second and more significant gathering. Eventually, the nations gathered in

23. Arnold H. Taylor, *American Diplomacy and the Narcotics Traffic, 1900–1939* (Durham, N.C.: Duke University Press, 1969), pp. 47–81.

The Hague, and once again Bishop Brent was elected the presiding officer.

The Hague Opium Convention (which concerned cocaine as well as opium) placed the burden of narcotic control on the domestic legislation of each nation. Chapter Three of the convention called for control of each phase of the preparation and distribution of medicinal opium, morphine, heroin, cocaine, and any new derivative that could be shown to have similar properties.[24]

The convention was not put into force by the dozen nations who attended the First Opium Conference, for it was agreed that the requirements would be held in abeyance until all forty-six world powers had signed and ratified the convention. Eventually three conferences were held, the second in 1913 and the third in 1914, only weeks before the outbreak of World War I. A compromise was reached regarding the implementation of the treaty: Any ratifying nation was permitted to put the treaty into effect in 1915, even if ratification had not been unanimous. But only seven nations did this by the end of the World War and the beginning of the Versailles treaty negotiations in 1919. The United States supported incorporating the Hague Convention into the Versailles treaty, so that ratification of the treaty ending World War I would at the same time bring the nation under the requirements of the Hague Convention, which required national and domestic legislation to control the preparation and distribution of opiates and cocaine. Of course, the United States never did ratify the Versailles treaty, but it had already ratified the Hague Convention in 1913 and had put it into effect in 1915. One significant result of the inclusion of the Hague Convention in the Versailles treaty was the passage in Britain of the Dangerous Drugs Act of 1920, an action taken not because of any serious problem with addiction but because, by ratifying the Versailles treaty, Britain had committed itself to comprehensive domestic legislation.[25]

DOMESTIC NARCOTIC LEGISLATION IN THE UNITED STATES

During the year or so prior to the Shanghai Opium Commission, the United States suggested topics to be discussed in 1909, and one of the topics was a report on domestic antinarcotic legislation. Amer-

24. Ibid., p. 82ff.
25. Berridge and Edwards, *Opium and the People*, p. 268.

icans understood that strong and enforced domestic legislation in other nations would result in diminishing the flow of drugs into the United States, but would other nations understand why the United States had no national antinarcotic legislation whatsoever? Americans knew that federal-state separation of powers made a national antinarcotic law rather difficult, but the State Department decided that something should be on the books when the U.S. delegation arrived in Shanghai.

The simplest law that could be framed and stand a chance of passage by the U.S. Congress before the commission opened was one that excluded from the United States opium not intended for legitimate medical uses or, in other words, opium prepared for smoking. Here there was an ironic combination of political factors. The United States hoped one of the major effects of the Shanghai Commission would be to placate China with regard to the poor treatment given Chinese nationals in the United States. Such treatment was in violation of our treaty obligations with China. The impetus for banning smoking opium from the United States, however, had developed from the fear and loathing of the Chinese, who were associated intimately with this particular manner of ingesting opium. Thus, the negative American attitude toward Chinese aliens gave the push that passed a "face saving" law designed to show China the good will of the United States.

After the law was enacted on February 9, 1909, it was announced dramatically in Shanghai to the other nations as proof of American sincerity.[26] And yet no one in the American delegation or within the State Department had any illusions that this law would control domestic narcotic use. Additional legislation was seen as imperative both to curtail the American narcotics problem and to display an American example to other nations where the implementation of narcotics control programs was essential to the solution of the American domestic problem.

Dr. Hamilton Wright, a physician with political interests who had been appointed opium commissioner by the State Department in 1908, oversaw the State Department's preparation for the Shanghai meeting, which included culling information from police departments, physicians, pharmaceutical houses, etc., regarding the nar-

26. United States 60th Congress, Public Law No. 221. An Act to prohibit the importation and use of opium for other than medicinal purposes. Approved 9 February 1909.

cotic problem and consumption in the United States. Bishop Brent was the chairman of the delegation, but after his elevation to the commission's presidency, Wright became the acting head. Back in Washington after the commission meeting, Wright took up the battle for an international meeting that could frame a treaty and played a leading role in the preparation of domestic antinarcotic legislation. He had opposition within the State Department on both questions, but he finally won the assent of Philander C. Knox, the secretary of state, and moved ahead.

Wright, who combined an aggressive personal style with self-right-eousness and a thirst for political preferment, was less effective than he otherwise might have been. He never got the prize plum for which he yearned, the ministry to China, and his chief claim for notability, the Anti-Narcotic Act of 1914, known even then as the "Harrison" Act, left him at the moment of achievement with almost no further role in the antinarcotic movement. Eventually, he volunteered to help the wounded on the western front during World War I, was injured there in an automobile accident, and died in 1917 in Washington.[27] His indomitable wife, Elizabeth Washburn Wright, carried on his battle for world control of narcotics until her death in 1952.[28]

In late 1909 Dr. Wright proposed a domestic law that would be based on the federal government's power of taxation. The alternative federal power was that over interstate commerce, but Wright believed that taxation would result in a detailed accounting of narcotics from their introduction into the United States to their distribution to manufacturers, wholesalers, and retailers, including pharmacists and physicians. Heavy fines would be levied on anyone not keeping records accurately or selling and transferring these products without proper reporting and payment of taxes.

Wright tried to solve the federal/state dichotomy in this manner: The information obtained by this proposed law would be made available to state boards of pharmacy and medicine, which would then take appropriate action to ensure that "the proper relations . . . should exist between the physician, the dispensing druggist, [and] those who have some real need of the drugs."[29] So it is evident that at this early stage, two years before the Hague Convention, Wright

27. Musto, *American Disease,* pp. 31–37, 40–45, 61–62.
28. Ibid., pp. 31, 198, 202.
29. Ibid., p. 41.

and the State Department did not envision a federal role in policing the relationships between, say, an addict and his or her supplying pharmacist or physician. The sanctity of the state's police powers would be maintained; the federal government would supply only information. Reformers believed that the information, however, could lead a responsible state agency to take only one action, that is, to curb the supply of narcotics to those who did not have a medical need for it—and "mere" addicts did not fall into that category.

The Foster Anti-Narcotic Bill (1910–1911)

Republican Congressman David Foster of Vermont introduced Wright's bill in April 1910. In addition to opium and cocaine, as in the eventual Harrison Act, the bill was aimed at cannabis (marijuana) and chloral hydrate, the same substances the Food and Drug Act of 1906 required to be revealed on labels. It did not allow small amounts of the drugs in mild remedies such as cough syrup to be exempt from the stringent reporting requirements and their severe penalties. Druggists feared the multitude of stamps and labels at each stage; the fines, which would range from $500 to $5,000; and the one-to-five-year jail sentences. The word "knowingly" did not qualify the prohibited actions, making it likely that simple errors without any intention to deceive would result in horrendous punishments. Although support for the bill could be found, the individuals in the drug trade would not endorse the detailed and hazardous provisions of the Foster Bill. It never came to a vote in the Sixty-first Congress, which ended in March 1911.[30]

The next Congress was marked by a significant change: For the first time in almost two decades, the Democrats gained control of the House of Representatives. The South now had achieved new importance, in that committee chairmanships changed hands. In the Sixty-second Congress the Foster Bill became the Harrison Bill, named after Francis Burton Harrison, a New York City Democrat who served on the Foreign Relations Committee. Dr. Wright continued his difficult task of trying to obtain the most stringent bill consistent with winning essential political support from the medical and pharmaceutical interests and now from the Democratic Party. In order to mitigate the severity of the original Foster Bill, the drug trades

30. Ibid., pp. 40–48.

established the National Drug Trade Conference, which would represent the major trade associations and try to reach a compromise position on the complex antinarcotic bill. The NDTC, which first met in Washington, D.C., in January 1913, provided the most powerful influence on the writing of what would become known as the Harrison Act.[31]

The attitude of the newly influential southern Democrats toward any potential invasion of states' rights now had to be taken more seriously. These politicians feared an interference with the South's local laws, which enforced racial segregation and Negro disenfranchisement. They remembered the era of "reconstruction," when the North ruled the South following 1865, and wanted to maintain the authority the white citizenry had subsequently won with the withdrawal of troops and "carpetbaggers." The narcotic control proposals threatened to intrude federal authority into the states, affecting local pharmacists and physicians and threatening to reach right into a neighborhood and send an individual to federal prison. Furthermore, this example of using the federal tax power primarily to achieve a moral end—for the taxes were not intended to bring in a significant revenue but rather to force disclosure and compliance with rules of narcotics distribution—could be a precedent for other concerns brewing in the United States, such as protecting Negro voting rights in the South.

Dr. Wright, therefore, faced a new set of attitudes in the Democratic-controlled House. He reacted by stressing the impact of narcotics, especially cocaine, on Negroes. He attributed attacks on whites to the crazed Negro cocaine fiend. He also argued that many poor Negroes would not have the energy or knowledge to send away for the cocaine, so the conclusion must be that northern businessmen who did not care about the South's concerns were shipping—via interstate commerce—cocaine to Negroes. Further, unscrupulous or ignorant employers were said to be supplying cocaine to their Negro workers.[32]

One further concern about the precedent the antinarcotic law would provide related to the flourishing prohibition movement. As

31. Ibid., pp. 54–68.

32. Hamilton Wright, "Report on the International Opium Question as Seen within the United States and Its Possessions," in *Opium Problem: Message from the President of the United States,* Senate Document no. 377, 61st Congress, 3rd Session, 21 February 1910, p. 49.

prohibition was achieved in state after state, the loophole for at least the upper and middle classes was that alcohol could be ordered across state lines and shipped into a dry state, for interstate commerce was regulated by the federal government, which so far was not teetotal. The Webb-Kenyon Act of 1913, however, was passed to close this loophole, survived President Taft's veto, and, much to the surprise of many, was declared constitutional by the Supreme Court. This occurrence removed one of the stumbling blocks to the Harrison Bill, for now a national antinarcotic law could not serve as a precedent for curtailing interstate commerce in a dangerous substance.

In the course of all this maneuvering, no one rallied to the defense of any of the drugs named for control except that occasionally cannabis was described by someone as not habit-forming or not as serious as opium or cocaine. Perhaps because the cannabis problem was not seen to be serious or because the drug did not seem so dangerous, it was dropped from the proposed law. Chloral hydrate, a sleeping medicine, was also dropped. The attitude toward opium and cocaine, however, was almost totally condemnatory. The only question was how to control their distribution most efficiently, since they had medicinal value but were also considered dangerously addicting. This was in sharp contrast with alcohol; its use divided the nation, and huge legitimate industries depended upon its continued consumption.

The government and the trades eventually reached agreement on the proposed law by moderating the record-keeping provisions, reducing penalties, and allowing the sale of patent medicines with small amounts of narcotics in them. Repesentative Harrison introduced it in June 1913, and it was passed quickly by the House. In the Senate some amendments were offered, a few with an apparent goal of destroying the bill's chances of passage. In August of 1914, though, the Senate passed the bill, albeit with a few modifications that were compromised in Conference Committee. Finally, on December 17, 1914, President Wilson signed it into law, to become effective March 1, 1915. At last the United States had redeemed its pledge to other nations that it would enact a stringent law, as it had urged every other nation to do.

The significance of the Harrison Act to strategists like Dr. Wright, though, was more than just the satisfaction of redeeming pledges made to questioning representatives of other nations. For him, the Harrison Act was the implementation of the Hague Convention of

1912, which called upon signatories to enact domestic legislation controlling narcotics supplies and distribution. The Understood as the fulfillment of treaty obligations, the Harrison Act would have the authority to usurp the states' police powers, for the Constitution in Article Six gives treaties concluded by the United States supremacy over the laws of states. This would resolve the problem of states' rights interfering with the ability of a national law to require a uniform compliance with strict narcotics control.[33]

Unfortunately, the Supreme Court at first did not give a very strict interpretation to the Harrison Act. In the first *Jin Fuey Moy* case (1916), the Court declared by a six-to-two majority that the Harrison Act could not be understood as having been required by the Hague Convention and that physicians could prescribe as they saw fit, even to simple addicts.[34] This decision was a stunning blow to federal enforcement, which, from the first day of the act's implementation, was directed at pharmacists and physicians who sold prescriptions or treated addicts without any intent to cure them.

World War I, arriving at almost the same time as the Harrison Act, profoundly affected American attitudes, creating an intense desire to purify the nation as it girded itself to fight for democracy against the barbarism of the Kaiser. The fall of Russia and the spread of Bolshevism intensified fears of contagion and the desire to be sure that the United States remained pure and strong. Prohibition took giant strides during World War I. The Prohibition Amendment in an early form nearly passed the House in December 1914, a week after the passage of the Harrison Act. In 1916 it did pass, and by January 1919 Prohibition had become part of the Constitution as the Eighteenth Amendment. Earlier, Congress had passed wartime prohibition, which was intended to save grain for the war effort as well as to promote efficiency in war production plants. Similarly, a battle was being fought to overturn the *Jin Fuey Moy* decision, which had weakened the government's intention for the Harrison Act. A Treasury Department committee reported that the number of addicts in the nation was over a million.[35] These exaggerated figures, as well

33. Hamilton Wright to Charles Evans Hughes, 28 June 1916, in Papers of Dr. Hamilton Wright, U.S. National Archives, Record Group 43, entry 36.

34. *U.S.* v. *Jin Fuey Moy,* 241 U.S. 394 (1916).

35. *Special Committee of Investigation, Appointed March 25, 1918, by the Secretary of the Treasury: Traffic in Narcotic Drugs* (Washington, D.C.: Government Printing Office, 1919).

as a fear about returning veterans having become addicted on the battlefield and the specter of alcohol prohibition, which might drive alcoholics to morphine and cocaine, led to a new attempt to put teeth into the Harrison Act. This time the government was successful.

In March 1919, two months after the ratification of the Eighteenth Amendment (which would go into effect a year later), the Supreme Court ingeniously decided, five to four, that to call a prescription for narcotics intended to supply a "mere" addict with maintenance doses was an error, for such a script could not be considered a true prescription given in the proper conduct of medical practice. Since it was not a prescription, the issuing physician had conveyed narcotics without the required tax; he had therefore violated the Harrison Act and could be arrested. The four dissenting justices were the conservatives, who argued that this was an invasion of states' police powers, while the majority, including Holmes and Brandeis, felt that more power had to be given the government if it was to carry out its duty to protect the public from such an insidious evil.[36]

At last, the intent of the reformers had been achieved: Simple maintenance was outlawed, and the federal government could take action nationwide to arrest and convict health professionals who practiced it. Narcotics now had a no-maintenance policy, which a few months later would also be the policy for alcohol. Enforcement of both prohibitions would be the responsibility of a unit in the Bureau of Internal Revenue, reflecting the similarity of the two conceptions.

Enforcement During the 1920s

Several additional laws completed the early legislative structure of American control of opium and cocaine. Some were minor, such as a stipulation that no finished products such as heroin or morphine could be imported into the United States.[37] The law stated that only coca leaves and crude opium could be imported and that the finished products, cocaine, morphine, heroin, codeine, etc., were to be manufactured in American pharmaceutical factories, which were given a monopoly to produce these substances. This may have made up for

36. *Webb et al.* v. *U.S.,* 249 U.S. 96 (1919); *U.S.* v. *Doremus,* 249 U.S. 86 (1919).
37. 67th Congress, Public Law No. 227. To amend the act of February 9, 1909, as amended, to prohibit the importation and use of opium for other than medicinal purposes. Approved 26 May 1922.

revenues lost, as the amounts sold legally in the United States fell after the Harrison Act. Other laws dealt with transshipment of drugs across the United States for foreign markets.[38]

Heroin

Perhaps the most important addition to the Harrison Act's control of opiates and cocaine came in 1924, when the United States banned the importation of opium to be used for the manufacture of heroin.[39] The observance of federal-state boundaries is evident in this law, for it does not ban the manufacture of heroin altogether but only the importation of crude opium for that purpose. Just that much seemed to be within the power of the federal government. Also, this did not require the seizure of heroin legally available in the United States for cough medicines (the original claim for heroin's value) or for certain other purposes, chiefly pain control or "twilight sleep" during child birth.

Heroin had been made available commercially by the Bayer Company of Germany in 1898 as a superior cough suppressant.[40] The Bayer Company believed that the addition of acetyl groups to the basic molecule would make morphine more palatable, and this product, diacetylmorphine, the company named Heroin, a trademark that was protected until Germany lost such protections as a result of losing the First World War. Similarly, by adding an acetyl group to salicylic acid to make it less irritating to the stomach when taken for joint pains, the Bayer Company launched another successful venture. In 1899 the company named sodium acetyl salicylic acid Aspirin, which similarly was protected by trademark until World War I. Few pharmaceutical firms can take credit for naming and distributing two drugs that remain among the most popular in Western society even after nearly a hundred years.

Heroin essentially had been unrestricted in the United States prior to the Harrison Act, and by 1912 in New York City it had replaced morphine as the drug of recreational choice among youthful males, according to the records of Bellevue Hospital. The addictive nature

38. 68th Congress, Public Law No. 274. Prohibiting the importation of crude opium for the purposes of manufacturing heroin. Approved 7 June 1924, Section 2.

39. Ibid., Section 1.

40. David F. Musto, "Early History of Heroin in the United States," in P. G. Bourne, ed., *Addiction* (New York: Academic Press, 1974), pp. 175–85.

of heroin had been recognized rather quickly, for the AMA issued a warning in 1902. Heroin was popular because it could be inhaled by sniffing, like cocaine, as well as injected by needle. When injected into the bloodstream, heroin crossed the blood-brain barrier more quickly than morphine and therefore gave a more intense, but briefer, "high." During the years of intense concern over social control, which began with the First World War, heroin became linked with male gang violence and the commission of crimes. Some believed that heroin stimulated the user to commit crimes or at least provided the courage to pull off a bank robbery or mugging. In the early 1920s most of the crime in New York City was blamed on drug use, chiefly the opiates, including heroin.[41]

The preference for heroin over morphine by recreational users, and the belief that other opiates could fulfill heroin's role as a pain-killer and cough suppressant, led to a move to ban heroin for medical purposes. The heroin problem also contributed to American fear of foreign nations after World War I, for the drug was being manufactured in other countries and then smuggled into the United States. The Swiss drug industries, for example, produced large amounts of heroin, which found its way into this country. Heroin's image as a foreign product popular with feared domestic groups helped support an isolationist stance, illustrated by the American refusal to join or even recognize the League of Nations. Influential congressmen, such as Stephen G. Porter, Republican chairman of the House Committee on Foreign Relations, urged that all heroin production in the United States be stopped. As an example he would try to get other nations to follow at the Geneva Opium Conferences of 1924 and 1925.[42]

The United States did enact the legislation sought by Congressman Porter, but it failed to achieve its goals at the meetings in Geneva. In fact, in disgust at the refusal of other nations to agree to curb production of poppies and coca bushes, the ultimate source of heroin and cocaine, the United States walked out of the conference.[43] The United States, which had founded the world antinarcotic movement

41. Gerhard Kuhne, "Statement of Gerhard Kuhne, Head of the Identification Bureau, New York City Department of Correction," in *Conference on Narcotic Education: Hearings before the Committee on Education of the House of Representatives, December 16, 1925* (Washington, D.C.: Government Printing Office, 1926), p. 175.

42. *Prohibiting the Importation of Opium for the Manufacture of Heroin: Hearings on HR 7079,* House of Representatives, Committee on Ways and Means, 68th Congress, 1st Session, 3 April 1924 (Washington, D.C.: Government Printing Office, 1924), p. 41ff.

43. Taylor, *American Diplomacy and Narcotics Traffic,* p. 200ff.

in Shanghai and The Hague, now saw it taken over by the League of Nations (as the Versailles treaty had mandated) and controlled by the very nations the United States sought to shame or force into a narcotics policy that the United States viewed as responsible. American participation in the worldwide effort then fell to a low point until the 1930s, when participation was resumed in international meetings. By the outbreak of World War II, the United States was again achieving significant participation in international antidrug activities.

AMERICAN DOMESTIC CONTROL TO THE MARIJUANA TAX ACT OF 1937

The use of cocaine, which had been in "soft" drinks like Coca-Cola until 1903 and was available easily to sniff as a treatment for sinusitis or hay fever, fell precipitously after reaching a peak somewhere around 1905. By the 1930s cocaine use had receded, and during the 1950s physicians and narcotics agents alike described cocaine use as a problem that once was serious in the United States but now was practically absent. Several reasons for its reduced use can be suggested. The drug had been introduced as a wonder substance—Freud had called it the first medicine that worked as an antidepressant. The Parke-Davis Company manufactured it after 1885 in many forms for drinking, smoking, inhaling, or rubbing on the skin. Within about a decade, warnings surfaced. Consumption peaked about twenty years after its initial distribution, and around the same time the accounts of its effect on the lives of its users and its popularly believed—although questionable—special link with southern blacks created in the public's mind an image so fearful that cocaine's effects became the extreme against which other drugs would be compared. Cocaine's association with violence, paranoia, and collapsed careers made laws against it by 1910 a popular matter. The first strict antinarcotic law in New York State was passed in 1913 and was directed at cocaine. Al Smith, later to be an anti-Prohibition candidate for president and critic of Prohibition in his state while he was governor, drew the strict anticocaine measure in his early years as a state assemblyman.[44] The combination of strict laws and intense public support of control measures brought on a reduction in consumption,

44. Musto, *American Disease,* pp. 6–8; *Laws of New York,* 1913, ch. 470, pp. 9984–91, approved 9 May 1913.

which, at the peak of its popularity, must have seemed most unlikely if not impossible.

The effect of the Harrison Act, its court interpretations, and supplementary legislation also appear to have reduced greatly the number of opiate addicts. The medical and pharmacy professions were denied an easy way of providing drugs. Although it is clear that only a fraction of either profession was liberal in their provision, this nevertheless had been enough to maintain a large number of users. It had been argued recently that the recreational users began to stand out more prominently, as the medically addicted and more sedate group declined in numbers, and that the relatively small number of addicts in the United States, about 50,000 in 1940, would have had an "underworld" or unsavory character even without the Harrison Act's criminalization of drug use.[45] This point of view contrasts sharply with the argument that the Harrison Act changed citizens who were normal except for their addiction into criminals who had to violate the law to obtain their daily supply of opiates.[46] Whatever the reason, the number of those addicted fell from about a quarter-million around 1900 to much less than half that number by World War II. The war effectively reduced supplies of narcotics to the United States, and in 1945 the United States probably had its lowest number of opiate addicts since the mid-nineteenth century. The rise of addiction after World War II may have built on the core of addicts left in the nation, but the dynamics of the addiction epidemic that began in the 1960s appear in certain respects to have had a different character.

NARCOTIC CLINICS, 1913-1925

In order to close the story of the decline in addiction after 1900, it is necessary to consider the legendary narcotic clinics that, like the Philippine opium dispensaries, were intended to deal with addicts who no longer could receive opiate or cocaine supplies from local physicians.[47] The first in the United States was opened in 1912 by Charles Terry, the public health officer of Jacksonville, Florida, where he provided both opiates and cocaine to men and women,

45. Courtwright, *Dark Paradise,* pp. 146-47.
46. Alfred R. Lindesmith, *The Addict and the Law* (New York: Vintage Books, 1965), pp. 3-34.
47. Musto, *American Disease,* pp. 151-81.

blacks and whites. Dr. Terry went on to become a student of the opium problem in the United States and compiled a classic book of reports, excerpts from articles, and statistical information in *The Opium Problem,* published in 1928 and co-authored by Mildred Pellens.

Other clinics followed, particularly after the Treasury Department, in enforcement of the Harrison Act, prosecuted or threatened with prosecution health professionals who supplied addicts indefinitely. A series of clinics in New England were established at the suggestion of officials of the Internal Revenue Bureau. In New York State, the crackdown on druggists and physicians emanated from state law, and clinics were established in upper New York State through state planning and authorization. Registration of addicts was permitted so that physicians would restrict maintenance to those already addicted.

In New York City, the Health Department did not wish to provide opiates, morphine, and heroin on an indefinite basis but did open a clinic at the city Health Department headquarters. This clinic provided heroin, but only as an inducement to registration and eventual detoxification and rehabilitation. About 7,500 addicts registered, received their drug of choice in dosages gradually decreased until uncomfortably small, usually three to eight grains of morphine daily, and were offered curative treatment. Most declined to be cured. Those who did receive treatment, at North Brother Island, seemed both unappreciative and very liable—the estimate was 95 percent—to return to narcotics available on the street or from a physician or druggist.

The Treasury Department, armed with fresh Supreme Court decisions of March 1919, started to close down the clinics, along with prosecuting the dispensing physicians and druggists. One argument was that the availability of easy maintenance inhibited cures and also that giving legal permission for maintenance clinics undercut the Treasury Department's position when it brought action against a professional for reckless provision of drugs. From a legal point of view, the "reckless" provider was obeying the tax laws, as was the clinic, unless the federal government wanted to get into the question of medical competence, which was a state, not a federal, concern.

Gradually the clinics were closed, the last one in 1925 in Knoxville, Tennessee. Some had been operated poorly, others quite responsibly with community support. Yet, because of the intricacies of the tax powers under which the federal law operated, all were closed, even if unfair harassment was necessary to discourage the operation. The number of registrants was not large, about 3,000 if we exclude the New York City clinic, which was not intended for maintenance but for bait to get addicts into detoxification. The number of addicts registered under the New York State law, which provided for maintenance not only in clinics but also from private physicians and pharmacists, eventually totaled about 13,000 in 1920. It can be assumed, therefore, that the clinics were not a major element in the maintenance of addiction in the United States. One side note: The 13,000 addicted registrants in New York State in 1920 add up to the largest number of legally supplied addicts recorded in any Western country this century, a number not approached yet by Britain under the so-called "British System." Although the "American System" preceded and surpassed in size any scheme attempted then or subsequently in Britain, it was in fact the large number of addicts in America that made maintenance so unwieldy and unpopular.

The demise of the clinics left drug peddlers and individual members of the health professions as the major targets of the federal government. Generally, the physicians did not wish to treat addicts, nor did they have any sympathy with addicts. Those physicians who, for whatever reason, did continue to treat addicts with maintenance doses were threatened and arrested, unless the maintenance had been approved by the local narcotic agent. Some maintenance was permitted, but only on a case-by-case evaluation. From reports prepared by agents upon investigating narcotic clinics, it appears that an acceptable life-style was a requirement for permission to be maintained.[48]

A theory had been advocated, mostly among maintaining physicians in New York City, that longstanding addiction changed the body's physiology in such a way that opiates were necessary for the patient to remain normal.[49] Too little opiate and the patient would experience withdrawal, too much and the patient would be "high," but just the right amount would allow normal feelings and behavior.

48. Ibid., p. 167ff.
49. Ernest Bishop, *The Narcotic Drug Problem* (New York: Macmillan, 1920); see also, David F. Musto, "Social and Political Influences on Addiction Research," in Seymour Fisher and Alfred M. Freedman, eds., *Opiate Addiction: Origins and Treatment* (Washington, D.C.: Winston, 1973), pp. 93–98.

This, of course, is close to the argument made in the 1950s by Drs. Dole and Nyswander to justify methadone maintenance. After a series of scientific studies shortly after World War I, the government concluded otherwise.[50] Those physicians who insisted on maintaining patients without approval from a narcotics agent ran a serious risk of arrest and, if convicted, loss of a medical license and time in a federal penitentiary. In spite of the danger, of course, some physicians supplied narcotics without restraint or with very poor judgment, but evidence shows that other, responsible physicians were entrapped without good reason in order to boost the number of an agent's arrests and thereby bolster his chances for promotion.[51] An aura of fear, therefore, accompanied a physician's decision to give an opiate to a patient, especially a new patient. On the other hand, the casualness with which physicians once handed out morphine or some other opiate was reduced considerably.

Along with the rejection of maintenance, physicians unfortunately had no effective medical cure available for addiction. Several had been promoted in many forms in the nineteenth and early twentieth century, but each had been found to have no scientific merit.[52] The problem devolved into a decision of whether to stop opiates abruptly and thereby cause the patient to go directly into full withdrawal— the so-called "cold turkey" approach—or gradually to reduce the opiate over a few days or a few weeks. Because the addicted person frequently has a threshold of average daily consumption below which the user becomes acutely uncomfortable, and because a yearning for heroin or morphine often persists for months or years after the beginning of withdrawal, the decision to detoxify abruptly or gradually usually was a difficult path for the patient. Nevertheless, detoxification was the preferred route for legal reasons. Two ancient warnings about detoxification, that the patient would die in withdrawal, or that a supply cutoff would precipitate a rash of suicides, did not materialize.

During the 1920s and 1930s the number of addicts diminished in

50. David F. Musto, "The American Antinarcotic Movement: Clinical Research and Public Policy," *Clinical Research* 19 (1970): 601–5.

51. H. T. Nugent, Field Supervisor of the FBN, Fourth Annual Conference of Pharmaceutical Law Enforcement Officials, Toronto, Canada, 25 August 1932, Stenographic typescript of Proceedings, Archives of the American Pharmaceutical Association, Washington, D.C., box 31, pp. 86–87.

52. Musto, *American Disease,* pp. 69–90.

the United States. Grossly exaggerated estimates came from antidrug entrepreneurs like Captain Richmond Pearson Hobson, who had been a Prohibition advocate before unleashing his energies against heroin and later marijuana as the head of several national and international voluntary groups.[53] Captain Hobson attacked heroin in a most melodramatic manner, claiming there were 4 million addicts in the United States and comparing them all to lepers. In spite of Hobson, the concern over opiate addicts and cocaine users declined during the two decades after World War I.

MARIJUANA TAX ACT OF 1937

With the battle against opiate addiction apparently at a more stable, less alarming level in the 1930s and the use of cocaine having declined dramatically, a new dangerous drug appeared on the American horizon: marijuana. Marijuana smoking arrived in the United States with Mexican farm workers who had crossed the border, mostly to labor in agricultural fields in the Southwest and in sugar beet fields as far north as Montana and Michigan. During the prosperous 1920s, about half-a-million farm workers came to the United States, but as the Depression's widespread unemployment laid an increasingly heavy burden on the country's citizens, the Mexicans became an unwelcome group, encouraged in all ways to return to Mexico. Entwined with the troubles they were said to cause local citizens was the Mexicans' custom of growing marijuana for their own use. Hence, marijuana was linked to violence, dissolute living, and Mexican aliens.[54]

The greatest fear of marijuana in the United States lay in the West and Southwest. The government was importuned to take action, but the recent experience with alcohol prohibition (which had ended in 1933) made the Federal Bureau of Narcotics (FBN) and its head, Harry J. Anslinger, formerly of the Prohibition Bureau, hesitant to get involved in a drug that grew domestically and prolifically. Cocaine and heroin were both foreign imports and therefore, at least theoretically, could be regulated more easily, but marijuana appeared to be almost impossible to curb, let alone eradicate. The FBN tried

53. Ibid., pp. 190–94.
54. David F. Musto, "Marijuana Tax Act of 1937," *Archives of General Psychiatry* 26 (1972): 101–8.

to address this drug by including it in a recommended uniform state narcotic law that would leave to localities the question of prosecution and allocation of enforcement resources. Then a curious law intended to reduce the number of machine guns provided the federal government with a mechanism to attack marijuana nationally and at the federal level.

The Firearms Act of 1934 decreed that a machine gun could not be transferred in any way without the payment of a transfer tax (from which law enforcement personnel were exempted). As odd as this mechanism may sound, the law was upheld by the Supreme Court in 1937 as a legitimate use of the power of taxation for a moral objective. Within weeks of this decision, the Treasury Department, which housed the FBN, appeared before Congress asking for a transfer tax for marijuana. Without a stamp permit and the proper tax stamps, marijuana could not be sold, bartered, or given away. Congress quickly approved the bill, and President Franklin Roosevelt signed it into law later in 1937. Unfortunately for the enforcement of this law, the FBN did not receive any more money or agents. Therefore, the FBN relied on obnoxious descriptions of marijuana to do the job. The substance was described to the public as a danger at least equal to cocaine or morphine, and the penalties for its illegal use or possession were severe. Because use of marijuana does not seem to have been great in the 1930s, the law's extraordinary severity did not concern the general public until the 1960s, when thousands of users were arrested as marijuana's popularity burgeoned. Furthermore, the contrast between the effects of marijuana observed in the 1960s and the longstanding claims of the FBN regarding marijuana led to a problem concerning the credibility of official statements, which still affects popular perceptions.

WORLD WAR II TO THE PRESENT

The Second World War ended with relatively few opiate addicts and very little use of cocaine or marijuana in the United States. The only closely controlled drug rising in use was alcohol, consumption of which had increased in per capita rates since the repeal of Prohibition. During all this period, sleeping pills and other barbiturates were prescribed widely but did not appear to be a similar problem. The same holds true for the amphetamines, which had been made available in the 1930s and continued to be manufactured and prescribed without restriction.

Treatment of hard-core addicts did take place at the two federal narcotics hospitals in Lexington, Kentucky, and Fort Worth, Texas. Each was, in fact, a prison in which addicts were treated and forced to detoxify, but the patients/prisoners frequently resumed their drug habits when they returned to their previous environments. Around 1950 a younger age group began to be admitted for heroin addiction, an abuse that reached a very high level in 1970 and remains high today. This threat elicited two responses. First, the federal government enacted more severe laws that levied mandatory sentences for conviction of dealing in narcotics. The laws, enacted in 1951 and 1956, are the peak of legal penalties against narcotics, including marijuana, in the United States.[55]

The second response reflected the domestic and international tensions of the time. The heroin menace—and it should be reemphasized that cocaine and marijuana were not seen as anything but potentially major problems in the 1950s—was ascribed to the infiltration of the drug trade by Chinese Communists who had taken over the China mainland in 1949. The Red Chinese purportedly sent heroin to the United States to undermine our democracy and at the same time obtain specie, for which they had a desperate need.[56] By the 1970s, however, the United States was defending the People's Republic of China against the same charge, now levied by Soviet newspapers.[57] Such are the vagaries of international relations and the domestic drug problem.

Heroin addicts in the 1950s mainly were young males concentrated in black and Hispanic urban ghettos. These addicts concerned the federal government, as well as reform-minded lawyers, academics, and physicians. The latter groups found the harsh penalties and the loathing attitude toward the addicts to be inhumane. Leaders of this countermovement included sociologist Professor Alfred Lindesmith and the attorney Rufus King. They believed a more relaxed approach

---

55. 82nd Congress, Public Law No. 255, approved 2 November 1951; 84th Congress, Public Law No. 728, approved 18 July 1956.

56. H. J. Anslinger and W. F. Tomkins, *Traffic in Narcotics* (New York: Funk and Wagnalls, 1953), pp. 69–116.

57. For example, "Poisoners: How the Maoists Smuggle Opium," *Literaturnaya gazeta,* 19 March 1969, translated and reprinted in *Current Digest of Soviet Press* (Ann Arbor, Mich.: Joint Committee on Slavic Studies, 1969), vol. 21, p. 7.

would be much more successful, as well as more kind. Rather than depriving addicts of heroin, heroin should be provided them. Rather than jailing addicts, they should be hospitalized, if necessary, or just left alone.[58]

This alternative view competed with the more hard-line style of law enforcement exemplified by Commissioner Anslinger. After forty or more years, treating addicts medically, which had been popular before World War I and had then been found inadequate to the task of reducing addiction, became part of public policy in the 1960s. Methadone, a synthetic opiate developed in Germany in World War II, was used by Dole and Nyswander to provide maintenance under theories similar to those which had justified maintenance prior to the restrictive Supreme Court decisions in 1919. This marked a major break in American narcotic control policies; maintenance again was legal, although not with heroin or morphine.

Along with the possibility of maintenance, other milder forms of control were invoked by the federal government. Civil commitment to a narcotic treatment center, thought more humane than prison sentences, became possible legally in 1966, although in subsequent years this did not prove a practical method either to reduce addiction or to cure addicts in any marked number.[59]

Also in the 1960s, an enthusiasm for drug consumption of all kinds, polydrug abuse, replaced the habitual use of one or two drugs, which had been more common in the past. Marijuana became very popular with young people, and then gradually its popularity expanded in both directions to even younger and to older ages. Psychedelic drugs, such as LSD, appeared on the scene, along with injectable methedrine or "speed." Drugs came to symbolize opposition to the government and older mores. The turmoil and dissension caused by the Vietnam War added to the sense of alienation many young people already felt from the older generation, which frowned on drug use other than alcohol and tobacco. In addition to cultural alienation and the rapid increase in multidrug use, the drug problem in the 1960s was intensified by the extraordinarily large number of young people in the ages most likely to experiment with

58. Lindesmith, *Addict and the Law;* Rufus King, *The Drug Hang-up: America's Fifty Year Folly* (New York: Norton, 1972).

59. Narcotic Addict Rehabilitation Act of 1966, Public Law 89-273, 89th Congress, approved 8 November 1966.

drugs; the post–World War II "baby boom" generation had reached the teenage years.

By 1970, marijuana was used commonly, and research was showing that it did not have the awful effects ascribed to it from the 1930s onward. Various groups and individuals initiated movements to legalize the substance, perhaps along the lines of tobacco. The drug situation was perceived by the public and the federal government to be so bad and yet so difficult to control that this seemed a good time to reevaluate the nation's entire policy. A National Commission on Marijuana and Drug Abuse was established in 1971.

In general, the members of the commission reflected traditional views on the subject of drug control, and therefore it was with even greater impact that the commission recommended in its first report, "Marijuana: A Signal of Misunderstanding," that the substance be "decriminalized." By decriminalization was not meant legalization but a step short of that position: Marijuana possession for individual use no longer would be a crime, but its sale and distribution would be against the law. The purpose of control at this stage would be to relieve law enforcement agencies of the nuisance of arresting individual users and thereby allow more resources to be concentrated on investigating large-scale crime and more dangerous drugs.[60] The notion of "decriminalization" proved difficult for all to understand. Some foreign nations considered it to mean legalization. President Nixon refused to receive the report in public or to comment on it except to affirm that marijuana was not going to be legalized if he had anything to say about it.

The second and final report, published in 1973, dealt with drugs more broadly.[61] It attempted to draw attention to the actual, measurable damage done by drugs, reflected in hospital admissions and drug-related deaths, as opposed to the myths that had evolved around many of them. Heroin, for example, was misperceived as causing more deaths annually than barbiturates. This approach intended to make more rational the discussion over drug policy, but it also laid the groundwork for the inclusion of cigarettes and alcohol in the

60. *Marijuana: A Signal of Misunderstanding: First Report of the National Commission on Marijuana and Drug Abuse* (Washington, D.C.: Government Printing Office, 1972), p. 150ff.

61. *Drug Use in America: Problem in Perspective, Second Report of the National Commission on Marijuana and Drug Abuse* (Washington, D.C.: Government Printing Office, 1973).

antidrug crusade. It de-emphasized, however, the effects a drug such as cocaine has on judgment and efficiency, the less quantifiable but still real aspects of drug use.

The enforcement of laws against individual possession or use of marijuana has fallen in the United States to a very low level. Moreover, dealers in relatively small amounts are reportedly not prosecuted either, because the largest dealers and smugglers, who are involved with tons, not ounces or pounds of marijuana, require all the time of officials. There has been a de facto decriminalization throughout large parts of the country, even if laws against individual use remain on the books. Possession of marijuana in some states is a small-scale misdemeanor, and the penalty is a ticket, like a parking violation. Yet, the frequency of marijuana use by high school seniors has been dropping since 1978, and this reduction, coupled with a more conservative national mood, has slowed further moves toward formal federal decriminalization or more liberality in the drug laws.

The rise in cocaine's availability and popularity, for the second time this century, has further complicated the control of drugs in the United States. The fact that first millions should use marijuana, then millions more take cocaine raises questions about the ability of local and national governments to control narcotics. The corruption that follows the drug traffic and the restraints on resources that may be allocated to drug control combine to leave a sense of frustration with enforcement policy. What will be the result of these trends? It all remains uncertain. We appear to be in an era of widespread drug use that would seem to make reasonable the revocation of antidrug statutes. We should recall, however, that a similar condition prevailed around 1900, shortly before an onslaught against drug use led to a substantial reduction in the use of opiates, heroin, cocaine, and alcohol. That such a national response could occur must make us pause before offering predictions for the future.

2

CURING THE DRUG-LAW ADDICTION
The Harmful Side Effects of Legal Prohibition

Randy E. Barnett

INTRODUCTION

Some drugs make people feel good. That is why some people use them. Some of these drugs are alleged to have side effects so destructive that many advise against their use. The same may be said about statutes that attempt to prohibit the manufacture, sale, and use of drugs. Using statutes in this way makes some people feel good because they think they are "doing something" about what they believe to be a serious social problem. Others who support these laws are not so altruistically motivated. Employees of law enforcement bureaus and academics who receive government grants to study drug use, for example, may gain financially from drug prohibition. But as with using drugs, using drug laws can have moral and practical side-effects so destructive that they argue against ever using legal institutions in this manner.

One might even say—and not altogether metaphorically—that

some people become psychologically or economically *addicted*[1] to drug laws. That is, some people continue to support these statutes despite the massive and unavoidable ill-effects that result. The psychologically addicted ignore these harms so that they can attain the "good"—their "high"—they perceive that drug laws produce. Other drug-law users ignore the costs of prohibition because of their "economic dependence" on drug laws; these people profit financially from drug laws and are unwilling to undergo the economic "withdrawal" that would be caused by their repeal.

Both kinds of drug-law addicts may "deny" their addiction by asserting that the side effects are not really so terrible or that they can be kept "under control." The economically dependent drug-law users may also deny their addiction by asserting that (1) noble motivations, rather than economic gain, lead them to support these statutes; (2) they are not unwilling to withstand the painful financial readjustment that ending prohibition would force them to undergo; and (3) they can "quit" their support any time they want to (provided, of course, that they are rationally convinced of its wrongness).

Their denials notwithstanding, both kinds of addicts are detectable by their adamant resistance to rational persuasion. While they eagerly await and devour any new evidence of the destructiveness of drug use, they are almost completely uninterested in any practical or theoretical knowledge of the ill effects of illegalizing such conduct.

Yet in a free society governed by democratic principles, these addicts cannot be compelled to give up their desire to control the con-

---

1. For those who would object to my use of the word *addiction* here because drug laws cause no physiological dependence, it should be pointed out that, for example, the Illinois statute specifying the criteria to be used to pass upon the legality of a drug nowhere requires that a drug be physiologically addictive. The tendency to induce physiological dependence is just one factor to be used to assess the legality of a drug. Drugs with an accepted medical use may be controlled if they have a potential for abuse, and abuse will lead to "psychological *or* physiological dependence" *Illinois Revised Statutes,* ch. 56½, § 1205 (emphasis added). See also, id. § § 1207, 1209, 1211. Thus, applying the same standard to drug-law users as they apply to drug users permits us to characterize them as addicts if they are psychologically "dependent" on such laws.

Personally, I would favor limiting the use of the term *addiction* to physiological dependence. As John Kaplan puts the matter: "While the concept of addiction is relatively specific and subject to careful definition, the concept of psychological dependence, or habituation, often merely reflects the common-sense observation that people who like a drug will continue to use it if they can—so long as they continue to like its effects." John Kaplan, *Marijuana— The New Prohibition* (New York: World, 1970), p. 160. The same might be said about those who like drug laws.

sumption patterns of others. Nor can they be forced to support legalization in spite of their desires. In a democratic system, they may voice and vote their opinions about such matters no matter how destructive the consequences of their desires are to themselves, or—more importantly—to others. Only rational persuasion may be employed to wean them from this habit. As part of this process of persuasion, drug-law addicts must be exposed to the destruction their addiction wreaks on drug users, law enforcement, and on the general public. They must be made to understand the inherent limits of using law to accomplish social objectives.

In this chapter, I will not attempt to identify and "weigh" the costs of drug use against the costs of drug laws. Instead, I will focus exclusively on identifying the harmful side-effects of drug law enforcement and showing why these effects are unavoidable. Such a "one-sided" treatment is justified for three reasons. First, a cost-benefit or cost-cost analysis may simply be impossible.[2] Second, discussions by persons who support illegalizing drugs usually emphasize only the harmful effects of drug use while largely ignoring the serious costs of such policies. By exclusively relating the other side of the story, this chapter is intended to inject some balance into the normal debate. Third, the effects of drug use will be discussed by other contributors to this volume.

The harmful side-effects of drug laws have been noted by a number of commentators,[3] although among the general public the facts are not as well known as they should be. More important, even people who agree about the facts fail to grasp that it is the nature of the means—coercion—chosen to pursue certain ends—the suppression of voluntary consumptive activity—that makes these effects una-

2. I discuss some of the problems with efforts at cost-benefit calculation in Randy E. Barnett, "Public Decisions and Private Rights (Review Essay)," *Criminal Justice Ethics* 4 (Summer/Fall 1984): 50.

3. While there certainly is no consensus on the conclusions that ought to be drawn from the facts of this tragic story, the facts themselves are not unknown in law enforcement or in academia. See, for example, John Kaplan, *The Hardest Drug: Heroin and Public Policy* (Chicago: University of Chicago Press, 1983), and Arthur D. Hellman, *Laws Against Marijuana: The Price We Pay* (Champaign: University of Illinois Press, 1975). Nor have they escaped the attention of the popular press. See, for example, the series on "The Drug Trade" in the *Wall Street Journal,* 27, 29 November and 3 December 1984, p. 1; and the series on "Heroin: The Unwinnable War" in the *Washington Times,* 24–28 September 1984, p. 1A. See also, "Research Suggests That Crime Caused by Drugs Is Less Than Public Believes," *Wall Street Journal,* 29 November 1984, p. 20.

voidable. This vital and overlooked connection is the main subject of this chapter.

Clarifying Our Terms

Before we can discuss the destructive effects of drug laws, it is necessary to clarify the nature of (1) the legal approach to social problem-solving and (2) the conduct that is the subject of these particular laws.

The Nature of the Legal Approach.   There are two senses in which we regularly use the word *law*. The term *law* may refer simply to a command that has been enacted according to procedures recognized by a community to be legitimate.[4] In contrast, the same term may also be used to describe a rule or principle that is both duly enacted and sufficiently "right" that it merits at least a prima facie moral duty of obedience.[5] Using the term *law* in the second sense, it may be said that a duly enacted statute or "law" that is unjust is not really a law at all.[6]

This difficulty arises, at least in part, from our using the same word in two ways, where other societies employ two different words.[7] In this discussion, when I use the phrase "drug laws," I am only speaking descriptively about duly enacted statutes regulating drug use. When, however, I speak of the institution of law generally, I mean those rules that are not only duly enacted, but are also in ac-

4. The original statement of this view was John Austin's. See John Austin, "The Province of Jurisprudence Determined," in *Lectures in Jurisprudence, or the Philosophy of Positive Law* (1832), vol. 1, ed. Robert Cambell (New York: James Cockcroft, 1875), pp. 3–209. The most famous modern statement of this position, which attempts to correct weaknesses in Austin's approach, is H. L. A. Hart, *The Concept of Law* (Oxford: Oxford University Press, 1961).

5. See, for example, Lon L. Fuller, "Positivism and Fidelity to Law—A Reply to Professor Hart," *Harvard Law Review* 71 (1958): 630–72; George Fletcher, "Two Modes of Legal Thought," *Yale Law Journal* 90 (1981): 970–1003.

6. See, for example, Thomas Aquinas, *Summa Theologica,* as it appears in J. Arthur and W. Shaw, eds., *The Philosophy of Law* (Englewood Cliffs, N.J.: Prentice-Hall, 1984), p. 10: "The force of a law depends upon the extent of its justice. . . . If at any time it departs from the law of nature, it is no longer a law but a perversion of law."

7. See Fletcher, "Two Modes of Legal Thought," pp. 980–84. "Because we have no clear concept of *Right* in English, the single word 'law' does double duty. Until the time of Blackstone and after, the 'common law' clearly had the connotation of law in the sense of Right. At least since the seventeenth century, however, positivist philosophers have sought to equate the word 'law' with enacted law (*Gesetze*)" (p. 982).

cord with principles of right or justice. I expect that the context will also help clarify this distinction.

Drug laws reflect the decision of some persons that other persons who wish to consume certain substances should not be permitted to act on their preferences. Nor should anyone be permitted to satisfy the desires of drug consumers by making and selling the prohibited drug. For our purposes, the most important characteristic of the legal approach to drug use is that these consumptive and commercial activities are being regulated *by force*.[8] Drug-law users wish to decide what substances others may consume and sell, and they want their decision to be imposed on others by force.

The forcible aspect of the legal approach to drug use is one of two factors that combine to create the serious side effects of drug-law use. The other contributing factor is the nature of the conduct that drug laws attempt to prohibit.

Clarifying the Type of Conduct Under Consideration.   Only by understanding the kind of conduct that is the subject of drug laws and how it differs from other kinds of conduct regulated by law can we begin to see why the legal order is the inappropriate sphere in which to pursue our objectives.

No one claims that the conduct sought to be prohibited is of a sort that, if properly conducted, inevitably causes death or even great bodily harm.[9] Smoking tobacco is bad for your health. It may shorten

8. See Dale A. Nance, "Legal Theory and the Pivotal Role of the Concept of Coercion," *University of Colorado Law Review* 57 (Fall 1985): 1–43. While force is a neglected element of a proper moral evaluation of law, it may not be a *necessary* characteristic of law. Some institutions that may be characterized as genuinely legal in nature may do their work without using force. See, for example, Lon Fuller, *The Morality of Law* (New Haven: Yale University Press, 1965), pp. 108–10; *id. The Principles of Social Order,* ed. Kenneth I. Winston (Durham, N.C.: Duke University Press, 1981), pp. 67–246. What is important here is that the *particular* kind of law advocated by drug control enthusiasts is that kind that *does* involve the use of force. Therefore, in this chapter I will be using the term "law" in this limited sense, and although I will not repeatedly qualify this use in the manner suggested by Fuller's analysis, such a limited use is intended and should be implied.

9. The State of Illinois classifies or "schedules" controlled substances according to their varying characteristics from most serious (Schedule I) to least serious (Schedule V). That drugs can cause death or great bodily harm is not a requirement for prohibition. For drugs under schedules II–V, potential for causing death or great bodily harm is not even a factor to be considered in determining the classification of a controlled substance. See *Illinois Revised Statutes,* ch. 56½, §§ 1205, 1207, 1209, 1211 (1984). Schedule I drugs are those drugs that have a "high potential for abuse" and have "no currently accepted medical use in treatment in the United States *or* [lack] accepted safety standards for use in treatment under medical

your life considerably. But it does not immediately or invariably kill you. The same is true of smoking marijuana.[10] Of course, prohibited drugs can be improperly administered and cause great harm indeed, but even aspirin can be harmful in certain cases. Further, the conduct that drug laws prohibit is not inevitably addicting.[11] Some users become psychologically or physically dependent on prohibited substances. Others do not.[12]

What then characterizes the conduct being prohibited by statutes illegalizing drugs? It is conduct where persons either introduce certain intoxicating substances into their own bodies, or manufacture or sell these substances to those who wish to use them. The prime motivation for the drug user's behavior is to alter his state of mind—

---

supervision," *Illinois Revised Statutes,* ch. 56½, §§1203 (1984), (emphasis added). In other words, if a drug has no accepted medical use in treatment in the United States, all that is required for it to be scheduled is that it have a "high potential for abuse."

10. In discussing the effects of marijuana, the legislative declaration of the Cannabis Control Act of the State of Illinois states only that "the current state of scientific and medical knowledge concerning the effects of cannabis makes it necessary to acknowledge the physical, psychological and sociological damage incumbent upon its use," *Illinois Revised Statutes* ch. 56½, §701 (1984). But see, for example, Munir A. Khan, Assad Abbas, and Knud Jensen, "Cannabis Usage in Pakistan: A Pilot Study of Long-Term Effects on Social Status and Physical Health," in Vera Rubin, ed., *Cannabis and Culture* (The Hague: Morton Publishers, 1975), pp. 349–50: "The most significant point which emerged was that in a society such as Pakistan where cannabis consumption is socially accepted, habituation does not lead to any undesirable consequences. . . . Our study appears to show that cannabis does not produce any serious long-term effects."

11. "For most heavy users the syndrome of anxiety and restlessness seem to be comparable to that observed when a heavy tobacco smoking American attempts to quit smoking." National Commission on Marijuana and Drug Abuse, *Marijuana: A Signal of Misunderstanding* (Washington, D.C., 1972), p. 43. See also, the President's Commission on Law Enforcement and the Administration of Justice, *The Challenge of Crime in a Free Society* (Washington, D.C., 1967), p. 13 ("Physical dependence does not develop"); Khan, Abbas, and Jensen, "Cannabis Usage in Pakistan," p. 349 ("We have deliberately used the word habituation rather than addiction because we did not find either increased tolerance or withdrawal symptomatology, which are the essential prerequisites for addiction"); and Kaplan, *Marijuana—The New Prohibition,* pp. 157–84.

The Illinois statute prohibiting certain substances exemplifies the fact that drug laws are not aimed exclusively at addictive drugs. The criteria of Schedule I drugs, quoted in note 9 above, requires only that the substance have a high potential for abuse. The other schedules make it clear that "abuse" is not the same as potential for "psychological or physiological dependence," by consistently listing them as separate factors that must be found before a drug that does have a legitimate medical usage in the United States may be legally controlled. See *Illinois Revised Statutes,* ch. 56½, §§1203, 1205, 1207, 1209, 1211 (1984).

12. For a recent summary of the latest research on the pharmacology of opiates and their effects on the street user, see Kaplan, *The Hardest Drug,* pp. 3–22.

to get "high."[13] The harmful effects of the substances are not normally the effects being sought by the user—thus they are usually termed "*side* effects." People could introduce all sorts of harmful substances into their bodies, but do not generally do so unless they think that it will have a mind altering effect. Anyone who wishes to ingest substances to cause death or great bodily harm will always have a vast array of choices available to him at the corner hardware store. A widespread black market in poisons has not developed to meet any such demand.

One can speculate about the underlying psyche of those who would engage in such risky behavior. One can argue that such persons must be "self-destructive"—that is, out to harm themselves in some way. It is doubtful, however, that such generalizations are any truer for drug users than they are for alcohol users or cigarette smokers, for whom the adverse health effects may be both more likely and more severe than those of many prohibited substances,[14] or for skydivers or race car drivers—not to mention the millions of people who (for reasons that totally escape me) ardently refuse to wear their seat belts.[15]

We can conclude, then, that the two salient characteristics of drug

13. One objection to the definition offered in the text for the subject of drug laws is that it would apply to alcohol and caffeine consumption and for this reason must miss some special purpose of drug laws. On the contrary, the manufacture and sale of alcohol were once made illegal for similar reasons. Only the disastrous consequences that resulted from alcohol prohibition and the social acceptability of both alcohol and coffee have kept both substances legal to date. However, at least with alcohol, regulation and even prohibition is constantly being advocated by some and implemented in certain locales.

14. See John C. Ball and John C. Urbaitis, "Absence of Major Medical Complications among Chronic Opiate Addicts," in *The Encyclopedia of Opiate Addiction in the United States,* pp. 301–6; World Health Organization Special Committee, "Problems Related to Alcohol Consumption: The Changing Situation," *Contemporary Drug Problems* 9 (1981): 185. Since the much heralded appearance of the *Report of the Surgeon General's Advisory Committee on Smoking and Health* (1964), the adverse health effects of tobacco smoking have been much studied and are quite well known.

15. If anything, drug consumption that causes one to get high seems a bit more rational than the unwillingness to use seat belts in that there is a tangible benefit gained in return for the risk incurred. In this respect only it is more difficult to argue against mandatory seat-belt laws than drug laws, for it is unclear what benefit the nonuser of a seat belt gains from the risk that he runs. And yet, because such laws affect nearly everyone, the liberty interest involved is easier to see and more widely trumpeted.

Moreover, for those who may be sanguine about seat-belt laws, the *mixture* of drug laws and mandatory seat-belt laws will create widespread and very potent social side-effects of its own. See note 44.

laws are the *end* or purpose of such laws and the *means* by which they attempt to fulfill this end. The end of drug laws is to discourage people from engaging in (risky) activity they wish to engage in either because they desire the intoxicating effects they associate with the consumption of a drug or because they desire the profit that can be realized by supplying intoxicating drugs to others. The means that drug laws employ to accomplish this end is to use force against those who would engage in such activities, either to prevent them from doing so or to punish those who nonetheless succeed in doing so.

THE HARMFUL EFFECTS OF DRUG LAWS ON DRUG USERS

At least part[16] of the motivation for drug prohibition is that drug use is thought to harm those who engage in this activity.[17] A perceived benefit of drug prohibition is that fewer people will engage in self-harming conduct than would in the absence of prohibition.[18] While this contention will not be disputed here, there is another dimension of the issue of harm to drug users that may seem obvious to most when pointed out, but nonetheless is generally ignored in policy discussions of drug prohibition. To what degree are the harms of drug use caused not by intoxicating drugs, but by the fact that such drugs are illegal?

16. The other important motivation for drug prohibition is the perceived effects of drug use on the rest of society. This will be considered below at pp. 86–97. The countervailing costs imposed on society by drug laws will also be discussed.

17. In its "Legislative declaration," the legislature of the State of Illinois expressed this typical sentiment as its end in passing the "Dangerous Drug Abuse Act" of 1965: "It is the public policy of this State that the human suffering and social and economic loss caused by addiction to controlled substances and the use of cannabis are matters of grave concern to the people of the State. It is imperative that a comprehensive program be established . . . to prevent such addiction and abuse . . . and to provide diagnosis, treatment, care and rehabilitation for controlled substance addicts to the end that these unfortunate individuals may be restored to good health and again become useful citizens in the community" (*Illinois Revised Statutes,* ch. 91½, §§ 120.2 [1981]).

18. "It is the intent of the General Assembly, recognizing the rising incidence in the abuse of drugs and other dangerous substances and its resultant damage to the peace, health, and welfare of the citizens of Illinois, to provide a system of control over the distribution and use of controlled substances which will more effectively: . . . (2) deter the unlawful and destructive abuse of controlled substances; (3) penalize most heavily the illicit traffickers and profiteers of controlled substances, who propagate and perpetuate the abuse of such substances with reckless disregard for its consumptive consequences upon every element of society" (*Illinois Revised Statutes,* ch. 56½, §§ 1100 [1984]).

Drug Laws Punish Users

The most obvious harm to drug users caused by drug laws is the legal and physical jeopardy in which they are placed. Imprisonment must generally be considered a harm to the person imprisoned or it would hardly be an effective deterrent.[19] To deter certain conduct it is advocated that we punish—in the sense of forcibly inflict unpleasantness upon—those who engage in this conduct.[20] In so doing it is hoped that people will be discouraged from engaging in the prohibited conduct.

But what about those who are not discouraged and who engage in such conduct anyway? Does the practice of punishing these persons make life better or worse for them? The answer is clear. As harmful as using drugs may be to someone, being imprisoned makes matters much worse.

Normally when considering matters of legality, we are not concerned about whether a law punishes a lawbreaker and makes him worse off. Indeed, normally such punishment is deliberately imposed on the lawbreaker to protect someone else whom we consider to be completely innocent—like the victim (or potential victim) of a rape, robbery, or murder.[21] We are therefore quite willing to harm the lawbreaker to protect the innocent. In other words, the objects of these laws are the victims; the subjects of these laws are the criminal.

Drug laws are different in this respect from many other criminal laws. With drug prohibition we are supposed to be concerned with the well-being of prospective drug users. So the object of drug laws—the persons whom drug laws are supposed to "protect"—are often the same persons who are the subject of drug laws. Whenever

19. Imagine if we told people that if we caught them using drugs, we would send them to the Riviera for a few years, all expenses paid.

20. "Characteristically punishment is unpleasant. It is inflicted on an offender because of an offense he has committed; it is deliberately imposed, not just the natural consequence of a person's action (like a hangover), and the unpleasantness is essential to it, not an accidental accompaniment to some other treatment (like the pain of a dentist's drill)." Stanley I. Benn, "Punishment," in Paul Edwards, ed., *The Encyclopedia of Philosophy* (New York: Macmillan, 1967), vol. 7, p. 29.

21. Punishment is also favored on the grounds that the lawbreaker deserves to be punished. See, for example, John Hospers, "The Ethics of Punishment," in Randy E. Barnett and John Hagel III, eds., *Assessing the Criminal: Restitution, Retribution, and the Legal Process* (Cambridge, Mass.: Ballinger, 1977), pp. 181–209. For an opposing view, see Walter Kaufmann, "Retribution and the Ethics of Punishment," in ibid., pp. 211–30.

the object of a law is also its subject, however, a problem arises. The means chosen for benefiting prospective drug users seriously harms those who still use drugs and does so in ways that drugs alone cannot: by punishing drug users over and above the harmful effects of drug use. And the harm done by drug prohibition to drug users goes beyond the direct effects of punishment.

Drug Laws Raise the Price of Drugs to Users

Illegalization makes the prices of drugs rise. By increasing scarcity, the confiscation and destruction of drugs causes the price of the prohibited good to rise. And by increasing the risk to those who manufacture and sell, drug laws raise the cost of production and distribution, necessitating higher prices that reflect a "risk premium." (Price increases will not incur indefinitely, however, because at some level higher prices will induce more production.) Like the threat of punishment, higher prices may very well discourage some from using drugs who would otherwise do so. This is, in fact, the principal rationale for interdiction policies. But higher prices take their toll on those who are not deterred, and these adverse effects are rarely emphasized in discussions of drug laws.

Higher prices require higher income by users. If users cannot earn enough by legal means to pay higher prices, then they may be induced to engage in illegal conduct—theft, burglary, robbery—that they would not otherwise engage in.[22] The increased harm caused to the victims of these crimes will be discussed below as a cost inflicted by drug laws on the general public. Of relevance here is the adverse effects that drug laws have on the life of drug users. By raising the costs of drugs, drug laws breed criminality. They induce some drug users who would not otherwise have contemplated criminal conduct to develop into the kind of people who are willing to commit crimes against others.

22. The traditional linkage between drug use and crime can be accounted for in three ways. The first way, just suggested in the text, is that the higher prices caused by illegality induce many drug users to commit profitable crimes to pay for the drugs. The second way, presented below at pp. 85–86, is that the criminalization of drug users can force them out of legitimate employment and into criminal employment. The third way, not mentioned in the text, is that some persons who, for whatever reason, are criminally inclined are just the sort of persons who are also inclined to use drugs. What is important is that even if the third account is true for some (which it undoubtedly is), the first and second will be true for others; this means that drug laws are causing a comparative increase in the number of persons who are criminally inclined—an effect of drug laws that hardly benefits those drug users so affected.

Higher prices can also make drug use more hazardous for users. Intravenous injection, for example, is more popular in countries where the high drug prices caused by prohibition give rise to the most "efficient" means of ingesting the drug. In countries where opiates are legal, the principal methods of consumption are inhaling the fumes of heated drugs or snorting.[23] While physical dependence may result from either of these methods, neither is as likely as intravenous injections to result in an overdose. And consumption by injection can cause other health problems as well. For example: "Heroin use causes hepatitis only if injected, and causes collapsed veins and embolisms only if injected intravenously."[24]

Drug Laws Make Drug Users Buy from Criminals

Drug laws attempt to prohibit the use of substances that some people wish to consume. Thus because the legal sale of drugs is prohibited, people who still wish to use drugs are forced to do business with the kind of people who are willing to make and sell drugs in spite of the risk of punishment. Their dealings must be done away from the police. This puts users in great danger of physical harm in two ways.

First, they are likely to be the victims of crime.[25] I would estimate that approximately half the murder cases I prosecuted were "drug

23. "Before the Harrison Act [1914], when opiates were cheap and plentiful, they were rarely injected. Moreover, injection is rare in those Asian countries where opiates are inexpensive and easily available. For instance in Hong Kong until recently, heroin, though illegal, was cheap and relatively available, and the drug was inhaled in smoke rather than injected. In the last few years, however, law enforcement has been able to exert pressure on the supply of the drug, raising its price considerably and resulting in a significant increase in the use of injections" (Kaplan, *The Hardest Drug,* p. 128).

24. Ibid., p. 9. In support of this, Kaplan cites Jerome H. Jaffe, "Drug Addiction and Drug Abuse," in Alfred Goodman Gilman, Louis S. Goodman, and Alfred Gilman, eds., *Goodman and Gilman's The Pharmacological Basis of Therapeutics,* 6th ed. (New York: Macmillan, 1980). Kaplan argues that intravenous injection can also increase dependence by producing strong conditioning effects. See Kaplan, *The Hardest Drug,* p. 44. In support of this he cites Travis Thompson and Roy Pickens, "Drug Enforcement and Conditioning," in Hannah Steinberg, ed., *Scientific Basis of Drug Dependence* (New York: Grune & Stratton, 1969), pp. 177–98. Finally, it should be noted that the spread of AIDS (Acquired Immune Deficiency Syndrome) has been caused in part by the sharing of unsterilized needles by drug users.

25. I make the same observation in Barnett, "Public Decisions and Private Rights," which was a review of John Kaplan's *The Hardest Drug.* In that discussion I mistakenly stated that Kaplan had "missed" this phenomenon in "his otherwise exhaustive treatment" (p. 53). In fact, it was I who missed Kaplan's discussion of this most serious problem for drug sellers and users, which appears at pp. 81–83 of his book.

related" in the sense that the victim was killed because it was thought he had either drugs or money from the sale of drugs. Crimes are also committed against persons who seek out criminals from whom to purchase prohibited drugs.[26] These kinds of cases are brought to the attention of the authorities when the victim's body is found. A robbery of a drug user or dealer is hardly likely to be reported to the police.

Second, users are forced to rely upon criminals to regulate the quality and strength of the drugs they buy. No matter how carefully they measure their dosages, an unexpectedly potent supply may result in an overdose. And if the drug user is suspected to be a police informant, the dosage may deliberately be made potent by the supplier.

Drug Laws Induce the Invention of New Intoxicating Drugs

Drug laws make some comparatively benign intoxicating drugs—like opiates—artificially scarce and thereby create a powerful (black) market incentive for clandestine chemists to develop alternative "synthetic" drugs that can be made more cheaply and with less risk of detection by law enforcement. The hallucinogen, phencyclidine hydrochloride—or "PCP"—is one drug that falls into this category.[27] Some of these substitute drugs may turn out to be far more

26. In 1979 I obtained the confessions that were ultimately used in a prosecution involving the savage murder of three young men. See *People* v. *Cabellero,* 102 Ill.2d 23, 464 N.E.2d 223 (1984) (relating the factual details of the case). One of the three had approached four street-gang members to purchase marijuana. When his initial attempt to do business with the gang members was rebuffed, he mistakenly believed that this was due to a lack of trust (rather than a lack of marijuana, which was the case). To ingratiate himself with the gang members, he boasted (falsely) about his gang-affiliated friends and his gang membership. Unfortunately the persons he named were members of a *rival* street gang. The gang members then told him that they could supply marijuana after all and asked the three to accompany them to an alley. There they were held at gun point and eventually stabbed to death. These young men were not members of a street gang. These are drug-*law*-related deaths. Three young men are dead because drug laws prevented them from buying marijuana cigarettes as safely as they could buy tobacco cigarettes. Smoking either kind of cigarette may be hazardous to their health. Unfortunately that issue is now quite moot. Where and how are their deaths registered in the cost-benefit calculation of drug-law users?

27. Although originally developed by Parke-Davis, "the PCP that is now on the streets is illegally manufactured. Unfortunately, it is very easy and very inexpensive to make, and you don't even need a chemistry background." Oakley Ray, *Drugs, Society, & Human Behavior,* 3d ed. (London: Mosby, 1983), p. 414.

dangerous than the substances they replace, both to the user and to others.[28]

Drug Laws Criminalize Users

Prohibition automatically makes drug users into "criminals." While this point would seem too obvious to merit discussion, the effects of criminalization can be subtle and hidden. Criminalized drug users may not be able to obtain legitimate employment. This increases still further the likelihood that the artificially high prices of illicit drugs will lead drug users to engage in criminal conduct to obtain income. It is difficult to overestimate the harm caused by forcing drug users into a life of crime. Once this threshold is crossed, there is often no return. Such a choice would not be nearly so compelling if prohibited substances were legal.

Further, criminalization increases the hold that law enforcement agents have on drug users. This hold permits law enforcment agents to extort illegal payments from users or to coerce them into serving as informants who must necessarily engage in risky activity against others. Thus illegalization both motivates and enables the police to inflict harm on drug users in ways that would be impossible in the absence of the leverage provided by drug laws.

In sum, drug laws harm users of drugs well beyond any harm caused by drug use itself, and this extra harm is an unavoidable consequence of using legal means to prevent people from engaging in activity they deem desirable. While law enforcement efforts typically cause harm to criminals who victimize others, such effects are far

28. Because of the "reefer madness" phenomenon that surrounds early reports by drug-law addicts of the ill-effects of drug use, such reports should be heavily discounted until time permits more objective researchers to do more extensive studies. The jury appears to still be out on PCP: "Some reports in the scientific literature associate violence with PCP use. Users, however, do not. . . . When violence occurred it was either against property or a panic reaction to restraint attempts. . . . PCP can appeal to those looking for: euphoria (low dose); a wasted, body-wide anesthetic effect with supersensitivity to sensations—the out-of-the-body stage (a moderate dose); or an incoherent, immobile, conscious state (a high dose). If you're having trouble getting a feel for PCP, you're in good company. Even users can't agree what the experience is like. One third of PCP users say it's unique, another third say it's like the hallucinogens or marijuana, and the last third isn't sure. When neither the users, the researchers, nor the clinicians can agree on the experience, the mechanisms, or the symptoms, you know that more research is needed." Ray, *Drugs, Society, & Human Behavior*, pp. 415–16.

more problematic with laws whose stated goals include helping the very people that the legal means succeed in harming. Support for drug laws in the face of these harms is akin to saying that we have to punish, criminalize, poison, rob, and murder drug users to save them from the harmful consequences of using intoxicating drugs.

To avoid these consequences, some have proposed abolishing laws against personal use of certain drugs, while continuing to ban the manufacture and sale of these substances.[29] However only the first and last of the five adverse consequences of drug prohibition just discussed result directly from punishing and criminalizing users. The other three harms to the user result indirectly from punishing those who manufacture and sell drugs. Decriminalizing the use of drugs would undoubtedly be an improvement over the status quo, but the remaining restrictions on manufacturing and sale would continue to cause serious problems for drug users beyond the problems caused by drug use itself.

As long as force is used to minimize drug use, these harms are unavoidable. They are caused by (1) the use of force (the legal means) to inflict pain on users, thereby directly harming them; and (2) the dangerous and criminalizing black market in drugs that results from efforts to stop some from making and selling a product others wish to consume. There is nothing that more enlightened law enforcement personnel or a more efficient administrative apparatus can do to prevent these effects from occurring. But, as the next section reveals, enlightened law enforcement personnel or an efficient administrative apparatus will not come from employing legal force to prevent adults from engaging in consensual activity.

THE HARMFUL EFFECTS OF DRUG LAWS ON THE GENERAL PUBLIC

The harmful side effects of drug laws are not limited to drug users. This section highlights the various harms that drug laws inflict on the general public. There is an old saying in the criminal courts that is particularly apt here: "What goes around, comes around." In an

---

29. For such a proposal concerning heroin, see for example, Kaplan, *The Hardest Drug,* pp. 189–235.

effort to inflict pain on drug users, drug laws inflict considerable costs on nonusers as well.

Resources Spent on Drug Law Enforcement

The most obvious cost of drug prohibition is the expenditure of scarce resources to enforce drug laws—resources that can thus not be used to enforce other laws or be allocated to other productive activities outside of law enforcement.

Every dollar spent to punish a drug user or seller is a dollar that cannot be spent collecting restitution from a robber. Every hour spent investigating a drug user or seller is an hour that could have been used to find a missing child. Every trial held to prosecute a drug user or seller is court time that could be used to prosecute a rapist in a case that might otherwise have been plea bargained. These and countless other expenditures are the "opportunity costs" of drug prohibition.

Increased Crime

By artificially raising the price of illicit drugs and thereby forcing drug users to obtain large sums of money, drug laws create powerful incentives to commit property and other profitable crimes. And the interaction between drug users and criminally inclined drug sellers presents users with many opportunities to become involved in all types of illegal conduct.

Finally, usually neglected in discussions of drugs and crime are the numerous "drug-related" robberies and murders (sometimes of innocent parties wrongly thought to have drugs) that the constant interaction between users and criminal sellers creates. Drug dealers and buyers are known to carry significant quantities of either cash or valuable substances. They must deliberately operate outside the vision of the police. They can rely only on self-help for personal protection.

Many drug-law users speculate quite freely about the intangible "adverse effects of drug use on a society." They are strangely silent, however, about how the fabric of society is affected by the increase in both property crimes and crimes of violence caused by drug laws.

Harms Resulting from the "Victimless" Character of Drug Use

The best hidden and most overlooked harms to the general public caused by drug prohibition may also be the most significant. These are harms that result from efforts to legally prohibit activity that is "victimless." It was once commonplace to call drug consumption victimless, but not anymore. Therefore, before proceeding, it is very important to explain carefully the very limited concept of "victimless" crime that will be employed in this section.

To appreciate the hidden costs of drug law enforcement, it is not necessary to claim that the sale and use of drugs are "victimless" in the *moral* sense—that is, to claim that such activity harms only consenting parties and therefore that it violates no one's rights and may not justly be prohibited.[30] For this limited purpose it is not necessary to question the contentions that drug users and sellers "harm society" or that drug use violates "the rights of society."

To understand the hidden costs of drug laws, however, it is vitally important to note that drug laws attempt to prohibit conduct that is "victimless" in a strictly *nonmoral* or descriptive sense, that is, there is no victim to complain to the police and to testify at trial. This will be explained at greater length in the next section, and the implications of this dimension of drug law enforcement will then be explored.

The Incentives Created by Crimes without Victims.   When a person is robbed, the crime is usually reported to the police by the victim. When the robber is caught, the victim is the principal witness in any trial that might be held. As a practical matter if the crime is never reported, there will normally not be a prosecution because the police will never pursue and catch the robber. From the perspective of the legal system, it will be as though the robbery never took place. So also, if the victim refuses to cooperate with the prosecution after a suspect has been charged, the prosecution of the robber will usually not go forward.[31]

---

30. I will discuss later the issue of whether drug laws are just. See pp. 97–102 below.

31. To enforce his decision of noncooperation, the victim always has available the threat of unhelpful testimony at trial. "I don't remember if that is the man who robbed me" is all

As a theoretical matter, however, the victim of a robbery is not a party to a criminal prosecution.[32] The victim is considered to be a witness—sometimes called a "complaining witness"—to the crime; the government could prosecute the defendant without the cooperation of the victim, as it prosecutes those accused of murder.[33] What special law enforcement problems result from an attempt to prosecute crimes in the absence of a victim (or "complaining witness") who will assist law enforcement officials?

To answer this question, let us imagine that robbery—a crime that undoubtedly has a victim[34]—was instead a "victimless" crime in this very limited sense, and that the police set out to catch, and prosecutors to prosecute, all robbers whose victims refused to report the crime to the police and cooperate with the prosecution. How would the police detect the fact that a crime had occurred? How would they go about identifying and proving who did it? How would the case be prosecuted?

To detect unreported crimes, the police would have to embark on a program of systematic surveillance. Because they could not simply respond to a robbery victim's complaint as they do at present, the police would have to be watching everywhere and always. Robberies perpetrated in "public" places—on public streets or transportation, in public alleys or public parks[35]—might be detected with the aid of sophisticated surveillance equipment located in these public places.

---

the victim need say to end the case—and (notwithstanding the theoretical availability of perjury charges) prosecutors know this.

32. The parties to every criminal case are the government (variously referred to as the State, the Commonwealth, the People, or the United States of America) and the defendant(s).

33. Of course, for this reason murder is one of the hardest of all (victim) crimes to prosecute successfully.

34. I have chosen robbery as my example because I wish in this section to separate the issue of who is affected by a crime (who is and who is not a "victim" in this sense) from the issue of how certain crimes must be enforced in the absence of a cognizable victim-witness-complainant. Robberies undoubtedly "affect" the persons who are robbed—and other persons as well. But notwithstanding these effects, if robberies were "victimless" in the sense used in the text—that is, if there was no victim complaining to the police and testifying at trial—certain unavoidable enforcement problems would develop.

35. Breaking and entering into a home or store when no one is present is most everywhere called a "burglary." When someone is home, the crime is sometimes called "home invasion." The most common form of robbery not committed on streets or trains, in alleys or parks is robbery of businesses.

Those robberies committed in private places—homes and stores—would require even more intrusive practices.

If the police did detect a robbery, they would be the principal witnesses against the defendant at trial. It would be their word against that of the alleged robber. As a practical matter, it would be within their discretion to go forward with the prosecution or not. There would be no victim pressing them to pursue prosecution and potentially questioning any decision they might make to drop the charges or withhold a criminal complaint.

We can easily imagine the probable results of such a policy of victimless crime enforcement. To the extent that they were doing their job and that money permitted, the police would be omnipresent. One could not do or say anything in public without the chance that police agencies would be watching and recording. The enormous interference with individual liberty that such surveillance would cause is quite obvious. And putting robbery prosecutions entirely in the hands of the police would create lucrative new opportunities for corruption in at least two ways, depending on whether or not a crime had in fact occurred.

When a crime had occurred, if the effective decision of whether or not to prosecute is solely in the hands of the police, police officers would be far more able to overlook a criminal act than they are when a cognizable victim exists. As a result, the opportunities for extortion of bribes and the incentives for robbery suspects to offer bribes are both tremendously increased. When a crime had not occurred, the fact that the courts would be accustomed to relying solely on police testimony in such cases would give the police a greater opportunity to fabricate (or threaten to fabricate) cases to punish individuals they do not like, to coerce someone into becoming an informant, or to extort money from those they think will pay it.

All of the increased opportunity for corruption would result directly from an attempt to prosecute robberies when robbery victims do not come forward to report and prosecute the crime themselves. If robbery were victimless in this way, the natural counterweight to these corrupt practices—the potential outrage of the victim of the robbery and the normal reliance by courts on victim testimony—would be absent.[36]

36. As those who have prosecuted criminal cases know, some percentage of robbery victims are bought off in a similar way. When this occurs, however, it can fairly be said that the

Of course we know that this is not how robbery victims normally behave. Victims do routinely report instances of robbery, creating a case that the police department must "clear" in some way. And they are usually willing to cooperate with the prosecution, giving the police far less ability to influence the success of a given prosecution.[37] Where a victim exists, the problem of corruption is enormously reduced; this is true even for the crime of murder where the victim cannot be a witness.[38]

Now suppose that in addition to not reporting the crime and not testifying at trial, robbery victims were willing to pay to be robbed; that they actively but secretly sought out robbers, deliberately meeting them in private places so that the crime would be perpetrated without attracting the attention of the police; that billions of dollars in cash were received by robbers in this way.

Such a change in the behavior of robbery victims would dramatically affect law enforcement efforts. First, as will be discussed in the next section, the secrecy engendered by the consensual nature of this "victimless" transaction would make necessary far more intrusive kinds of investigative techniques than we at first supposed. Second, the victims' willingness to pay robbers to be robbed would make robbery more lucrative than it would otherwise be and would thus increase the ability of robbers to bribe the police when they are caught.

Police who are willing to fabricate evidence against someone they knew to be a robber would expect that such a person would probably be able to afford a substantial payoff. Of course, corrupt police officers would be risking detection by honest officers and prosecutors. So we can expect that corrupt officers will attempt to minimize their

---

robber is, at least in part, satisfying his "debt" to the victim. See Randy E. Barnett, "Restitution: A New Paradigm of Criminal Justice," *Ethics* 87 (1977): 279–301 (discussing a restitutive theory of criminal justice).

37. Even with the presence of victims, police still have an ability to influence the outcome of a prosecution. They might, for example, admit to circumstances that would justify the suppression of vital evidence in a case. We thus see some corruption with almost every category of crime. The analysis in the text, however, is a comparative one. The point is that, all things being equal, far more corruption is likely to take place in the absence of a victim.

38. With the crime of murder, there may still be occurrence witnesses. If there are no witnesses to the murder, it is the discovery of the body under circumstances indicating foul play—and the normal procedures that then ensue—that gives rise to the investigation and ultimate prosecution. Murder cases, in the absence of occurrence witnesses or a confession, however, remain the toughest cases (with victims) to solve or to prosecute.

risk by entering into a regular prepayment arrangement with professional robbers to ensure that they would not be arrested when they
commit a robbery. Such an illicit arrangement could be enforced by
the corrupt officer's credible threat to prosecute a legitimate case or,
if necessary, to fabricate a case.

The sale and use of illicit drugs are like victimless robberies, with
the final twist I added. Drug users not only fail to report violations
of the drug laws, they actively seek out sellers in ways that are designed to avoid police scrutiny. Drug use is a private act that, unlike
most robberies, does not take place in public places. And, because
drugs users desire to consume drugs, they are quite willing to pay
for the product.

Because drug use and sale are "victimless" in the special descriptive sense employed here, the hypothetical consequences of policing
victimless robberies result, all too regularly and unavoidably, from
drug law enforcement. The next three sections will discuss some of
the more serious of these consequences.

Drug Laws and Invasion of Privacy.   The fact that drug use takes
place in private, and that drug users and sellers conspire to keep their
activities away from the prying eyes of the police, means that surveillance must be extremely intrusive to be effective. It must involve
gaining access to private areas to watch for this activity.

One way to accomplish this is for a police officer, or more likely
an informant, to pose as a buyer or seller. This means that the police
must initiate the illegal activity and run the risk that the crime being
prosecuted was one that would not have occurred but for the police
instigation.[39] And, since possession alone is also illegal, searches of
persons without probable cause might also be necessary to find
contraband.

Such illegal conduct by police is to be expected when one seeks to
prohibit activity that is deliberately kept away from *normal* police
scrutiny by the efforts of both parties to the transaction. This means
that the police must intrude into private areas if they are to detect
these acts. The police would be overwhelmed if they actually obtained evidence establishing probable cause for every search for illicit
drugs, no matter how small the quantity. But if no constitutional

39. See, for example, Hellman, *Laws Against Marijuana,* pp. 60–88.

grounds exist for such an intrusion, then a police department and its officers are forced to decide which is more important: the protection of constitutional rights or the failure to get results that will be prominently reported by the local media.

The Weakening of Constitutional Rights.   The fact that such privacy-invading conduct by police may be unconstitutional and therefore illegal does not prevent it from occurring. Some of those who are most concerned about the harm caused by drug laws are lawyers who have confronted the massive violations of constitutional rights that drug laws have engendered.[40] Such unconstitutional behavior is particularly likely, given our bizarre approach to policing the police.[41]

At present we attempt to rectify police misconduct mainly by preventing the prosecution from using any illegally seized evidence at trial. While this would generally be enough to scuttle a drug law prosecution, it will not prevent the police from achieving at least some of their objectives. They may be more concerned with successfully making an arrest and confiscating contraband than they are with obtaining a conviction. This is especially true when they would have neither confiscation nor conviction without an unconstitutional search.[42]

In most instances, the success of a suppression motion depends on whether the police tell the truth about their constitutional mistake

40. Ibid., pp. 103–31 ("A large proportion of . . . [marijuana] arrests result from police conduct that violates the spirit if not the letter of the Fourth Amendment's prohibition against unreasonable searches and seizures," p. 103); Kaplan, *The Hardest Drug,* pp. 95–97 ("Many of the techniques used to enforce heroin laws do end up violating the constitutional rights of individuals," p. 96).

41. The discussion that immediately follows in the text is only suggestive of a detailed analysis of this problem and a possible solution I have presented elsewhere. See Randy E. Barnett, "Resolving the Dilemma of the Exclusionary Rule: An Application of Restitutive Principles of Justice," *Emory Law Journal* 32 (1983): 937–85, especially pp. 980–85 where I specifically discuss victimless crimes.

42. "A policeman who is unwilling to lie about probable cause or to conceal a prior illegal search may still be inclined to make an arrest for possession of marijuana, even if he is aware that it will not stand up under judicial scrutiny. At a minimum he will have confiscated a supply of an illegal drug. The defendant will be jailed and have to post bail, and in many cases will have to hire a lawyer; these alone serve as forms of punishment. Finally, there is always the possibility that the defendant will plead guilty to a lesser offense rather than risk a felony conviction." Comment, "Possession of Marijuana in San Mateo County: Some Social Costs of Criminalization," *Stanford Law Review* 22 (1969): 115.

in their report and at trial. They may not do so if they think that their conduct is illegal. "There is substantial evidence to suggest that police often lie in order to bring their conduct within the limits of the practices sanctioned by judicial decisions."[43] The only person who can usually contradict the police version of the incident is the defendant, and the credibility of defendants does not generally compare favorably with that of police officers.

Those who have committed no crime—who possess no contraband—will have no effective recourse at all. Because no evidence was seized, there is no evidence to exclude from a trial. As a practical matter, then, the police only have to worry about unconstitutional searches if something illicit turns up; but if something turns up and they can confiscate it and make an arrest, they may be better off than if they respect constitutional rights and do nothing at all. Moreover, by encouraging such frequent constitutional violations, the enforcement of drug laws desensitizes the police to constitutional safeguards in other areas as well.

The constitutional rights of the general public are therefore threatened in at least two ways. First, the burden placed on law enforcement officials to enforce possessory laws without victims virtually compels them to engage in wholesale violations of constitutional prohibitions against unreasonable searches and seizures.[44] For every search that produces contraband there are untold scores of searches that do not. And given our present method of deterring police misconduct by excluding evidence of guilt, there is little effective recourse against the police available to those who are innocent of any crime.[45]

Second, the widespread efforts of police and prosecutors to stretch the outer boundaries of legal searches can be expected, over time, to contribute to the eventual loosening up of the rules by the courts. The more cases that police bring against obviously guilty defendants

43. Hellman, *Laws Against Marijuana,* p. 105.

44. I predict that the current infatuation with mandatory seat-belt laws will, in consort with drug laws, create a new and potent social side-effect: Violations of seat belt laws will supplant taillight and other traffic offenses as the most popular justification—or "probable cause"—for automobile stops that are really made to find drugs and guns. And it takes no great imagination to predict which neighborhoods will bear the brunt of this type of "law" enforcement. (Incidentally, I also predict that automobile accident injuries to those who transport illegal drugs will be greatly reduced, owing to a marked increase of seat belt usage amongst members of this group who will seek to minimize their risk of being stopped.)

45. See Barnett, "Resolving the Dilemma of the Exclusionary Rule," p. 962.

(in drug prosecutions, the evidence being suppressed strongly supports the conclusion that the defendants are guilty), the more opportunities and incentives the appellate courts will have to find a small exception here, a slight expansion there.[46] And instead of prosecuting the police for their illegal conduct, the prosecutor's office becomes an insidious and publicly financed source of political and legal agitation in defense of such illegal conduct.[47]

One point should be made clear. The police are not the heavies in this tale. They are only doing what drug-law users have asked them to do in the only way that such a task may effectively be accomplished. It is the drug-law users who must bear the responsibility for the grave social problems caused by the policies they advocate. By demanding that the police do a job that cannot be done effectively without violating constitutional rights, drug-law users ensure that more constitutional rights will be violated and that the respect of law enforcement personnel for these rights will be weakened.

The Effect of Drug Laws on Corruption. While most people have read about corrupt law-enforcement officials who are supposed to be enforcing drug laws, few people are fully aware how this corruption is caused by the type of laws being enforced. Drug laws allow police to use force to prevent voluntary activities. Unavoidably, the power to prohibit also gives the police a power to (de facto) franchise the manufacture and sale of drugs, in return for a franchise fee.

The increased corruption caused by prohibiting consensual activity is further increased by the ease with which law enforcement officers can assist criminals when there is no complaining victim. As was seen in the discussion of "victimless robberies," without a victim to file an official complaint, it is easier for police to overlook a crime that they might see being committed. When there is no victim to contradict the police version of the event, it is much easier for police to tailor their testimony to achieve the outcome they desire—whether good search/bad search or guilt/innocence. It is usually their

46. Ibid, p. 959–965.

47. As I have said elsewhere: "Institutionally, the arm of the government whose function is to prosecute illegal conduct is called upon, in the name of law enforcement, systematically to justify police irregularities. If these arguments are successful, the definition of illegal conduct will be altered. . . . Refusal to consider the long run effect of this phenomenon on the stability of constitutional protections would be dangerous and unrealistic." Ibid., p. 967. These effects are greatly heightened by the demand that prosecutors successfully prosecute drug laws.

word against the defendant's, and in such a contest the defendant usually loses. With no victim pressing for a successful prosecution, the police, prosecutor, or judge may scuttle a prosecution with little fear of public exposure.

Owing to the victimless character of drug offenses (in the limited sense discussed above) and the fact that drug users are willing to pay for drugs, the incentives created by making drug use illegal are quite perverse when compared to a victim crime like robbery. When robbery is made illegal, robbers who take anything but cash must sell their booty at a tremendous discount. In other words, laws against robbery reduce the profit that sellers of illegally obtained goods receive and thereby discourage both robbery and the potential for corruption.[48]

Drug laws have the opposite effect. The actions of drug law enforcement create an artificial scarcity of a desired product. As a result sellers receive a *higher* price than they would without such laws. While it is true that drug prohibition makes it more costly to engage in the activity, this cost is partially or wholly offset by an increased return (higher prices) and by attracting individuals to the activity who are less risk-averse (criminals)—that is, individuals who are less likely to discount their realized cash receipts by their risk of being caught.[49] For such persons, the subjective costs of providing illicit drugs are actually less than they are for more honest persons.

As I have observed elsewhere,[50] the social consequences of the wholesale corruption of our legal system by the large amounts of black-market money to be made in the drug trade have never been adequately appreciated. The extremely lucrative nature of the illicit

48. Organized burglary and auto theft remain profitable (victim) crimes, in spite of the fact that they are legally prohibited, and the profits earned from these crimes are used in part to pay for the services of corrupt law-enforcement officials. Note however that—as compared with robbery—these crimes typically occur when the victim is not around, making them effectively "victimless" with respect to having occurrence witnesses available. And property insurance policies greatly cool the victim's enthusiasm to cooperate in the prosecution—another quality of a truly victimless crime.

49. For a discussion of the "time horizons" of criminals that may affect their internal rate of discount, see Edward C. Banfield, "Present-Orientedness and Crime," in Randy E. Barnett and John Hagel III, eds., *Assessing the Criminal: Restitution, Retribution, and the Legal Process* (Cambridge, Mass.: Ballinger, 1977), pp. 133–42. See also, Gerold P. O'Driscoll, Jr., "Professor Banfield on Time Horizon: What Has He Taught Us About Crime," ibid., pp. 143–62; Mario J. Rizzo, "Time Preference, Situational Determinism, and Crime," ibid., pp. 163–77.

50. Barnett, "Public Decisions and Private Rights."

drug trade makes the increased corruption of police, prosecutors, and judges all but inevitable. And this corruption extends far beyond the enforcement of drug laws.

Since the prohibition of alcohol we have witnessed the creation of a multibillion dollar industry to supply various prohibited goods and services. The members of this industry are ruthless profit-maximizers whose comparative market advantage is their ability and willingness to rely on violence and corruption to maintain their market share and to enforce their agreements.

The prohibition of alcohol and other drugs has created a criminal subculture that makes little of the distinction between crimes with victims and those without. To make matters worse, to hide the source of their income from tax and other authorities requires these criminals to become heavily involved in "legitimate" or legal businesses so that they may launder their illegally obtained income. They bring to these businesses their brutal tactics, which they employ to drive out the honest entrepreneur.

The fact that law enforcement personnel are corrupted by drug laws should be no more surprising than the fact that many people decide to get high by ingesting certain chemicals. The tragic irony of drug laws is that by attempting to prevent the latter, they make the former far more prevalent. Drug-law users must confront the question of whether the increased systemic corruption that their favored policies unavoidably cause is too high a price to pay for whatever reduction in the numbers of drug users is achieved.

THE INJUSTICE OF DRUG LAWS

In this chapter I have described some people as being "addicted" to drug laws. Just as many people use drugs in spite of the serious harms such conduct can cause, many people advocate the use of drug laws in spite of the savage social and personal harms these laws can inflict. The argument to this point has dwelled exclusively on exposing the hidden costs of drug prohibition—costs that unavoidably result from the fact that drug use is consensual and victimless in a nonmoral or descriptive sense.

There is, however, a more principled or philosophical lesson to be drawn from this discussion of drug laws. How is it that such policies are so popular? True, many of the costs of drug laws are very well hidden and many drug-law supporters directly gain from these policies. Yet the widespread support of such laws may be a symptom of a deeper or more fundamental malady.

We have grown accustomed to thinking that claims of justice are subjective and personal—that such claims are largely extrinsic to "objective" public policy discussions or matters of legality. Some respond to a contention that drug laws are unjust because they violate the *rights* of drug users by characterizing rights claims as "merely assertions. They do not carry any argument with them."[51] To others, any claim about drug laws based on the rights of the drug user is a non sequitur, since they view rights as claims that a legal system will actually respect rather than as claims that a legal system ought to respect.[52] Finally, some would respond to a claim that the drug user's rights render drug laws unjust with the argument that "society" also has rights and that we must look beyond rights to resolve this "conflict between rights."[53]

Each of these commonplace arguments fails to fully grasp the crucial role that moral claims and general principles of justice based on individual rights should play in legal decision making. One can fully appreciate the vital role played by principles of justice only by comparing alternative ways of reaching decisions about such an important issue as which conduct should or should not be illegal. And the main alternative to resolving claims by appealing to rules based on general principles of justice is to resolve claims by determining the specific exigencies of particular policies.

Policy makers, however, are inherently much more limited in their ability to construct good policy than is normally acknowledged. First,

51. Kaplan, *The Hardest Drug,* p. 103.

52. See note 4 above. For a discussion of the reemergence of normative legal philosophy, see Randy E. Barnett, "Contract Scholarship and the Reemergence of Legal Philosophy (book review)," *Harvard Law Review* 97 (1984): 1223–36; Jeffrie G. Murphy and Jules L. Coleman, *The Philosophy of Law: An Introduction to Jurisprudence* (Totowa, N.J.: Rowman & Allanheld, 1984), pp. 7–68.

53. A legal system based on rights cannot knowingly countenance conflicting rights. A theory of rights is adopted as a means of resolving conflicting claims. A claim of a person who has a right prevails when it conflicts with a claim made by a person without a right. A particular system of rights that generated two conflicting but "legitimate" rights would be defective because it would not be capable of resolving the conflicting claims being made by the parties. Such a system would not, then, be truly rights-based, or a "higher" principle that is employed to resolve the dispute would dictate the true legitimate right when this kind of conflict occurs. See Hillel Steiner, "The Structure of a Set of Compossible Rights," *Journal of Philosophy* 74 (1977): 767–75; Randy E. Barnett, "Pursuing Justice in a Free Society: Power v. Liberty," *Criminal Justice Ethics* 4 (Winter/Spring 1985): 58.

policy makers suffer from a pervasive ignorance of consequences.[54] In advance of implementing certain kinds of social programs, it is difficult, if not impossible, to predict the precise effects they will have. The foregoing discussion of the hidden costs of drug laws illustrates that it is often very difficult even to detect and demonstrate the adverse effects of policies that have *already occurred.*

Second, the judgment of policy makers and other "experts" is often influenced by self-interest (as all judgment can be). Careers are often based on an articulated commitment to certain kinds of programs, which then become difficult to reject when the consequences of the programs are not as expected. Jobs will be lost if programs are seen as counterproductive or harmful. In rendering opinions, such influences can be hard (though, of course, not impossible) to resist.

To minimize decisions made in ignorance or out of self-interest, legal policy makers must somehow be constrained. And the most practical way to constrain them is to craft general principles and rules—*laws*—reflecting a conception of individual rights that rests on fundamental principles of justice.[55]

A sound legal system requires a firmer foundation for analyzing questions of legality than ad hoc arguments about the exigencies of particular policies. It requires general principles crafted to minimize—without resorting to an endless series of explicit cost-benefit analyses—the hidden costs of the sort we have identified as attaching to drug laws. It requires principles of general application that can be defended as basically just and right, despite the fact that occasions will arise when adherence to such principles *appears* to be causing harm that a deviation from principle would be able to rectify.

A legal system based on such principles—if such principles can actually be identified—would not be as vulnerable to the shifting winds of opinion and prejudice as are particularistic public-policy discussions. I have discussed the vital social role and the appropriate substance of individual rights at greater length elsewhere and shall not repeat the analysis here.[56] The conclusion of such an analysis

54. For an excellent summary of the literature that discusses the "knowledge problem" facing public policy analysts, see Don Lavoie, *National Economic Planning: What Is Left?* (Cambridge, Mass.: Ballinger, 1985), pp. 51–92.

55. See Randy E. Barnett, "Foreword: Why We Need Legal Philosophy," *Harvard Journal of Law and Public Policy* 8 (1985): 6–16.

56. See Barnett, "Pursuing Justice in a Free Society," pp. 56–63.

when applied to drug laws is that such laws are not only harmful, they are unjust.

Recognizing the rights of individuals to control their external possessions and their bodies—traditionally known as property rights—free from the forcible interference of any other person is the only practical way of facilitating the pursuit of happiness for each individual who chooses to live in a social setting. If the pursuit of happiness is the Good for each person, then property rights are the prerequisites for pursuing that Good while living in close proximity to others. And the social prerequisites of the Good are the tenets of justice that all must live by. To deny these rights is to act unjustly.

The inalienable rights of individuals to live their own lives and to control their own bodies are, according to this analysis, essential to human survival and fulfillment in a social setting.[57] Drug laws undermine this control by seeking to subject the bodies of some persons to the forcible control of other persons. Such laws seek forcibly to prevent persons from using their bodies in ways that they desire and that do not interfere with the equal liberty of others.

A proper rights analysis would render most legal cost-benefit calculations superfluous and would avoid tragically wasteful (and often irreversible) social experimentation. The two factors that were seen above to generate the hidden costs of drug laws—the *end* of controlling consensual conduct by forcible *means*—are the very factors that together identify drug laws as violations of individual rights and therefore as unjust interferences with individual liberty.

Just as you do not need to try PCP to know it is, on balance, bad for you, a rights analysis tells us that we do not have to try using drug laws to know they are, on balance, bad for all of us. And this is one important reason why a system of rights is ultimately preferable to a system of ad hoc public-policy determinations. If a system of properly crafted individual rights had been adhered to, we would have avoided incurring these serious harms in the first place.

In his essay *Utilitarianism,* John Stuart Mill provides a defense of the distinction between matters of justice or rights that are properly subject to legal enforcement and matters of morality or vice that are not:

---

57. I discuss the distinction between alienable and inalienable rights and the inalienable right one has to one's body in Randy E. Barnett, "Contract Remedies and Inalienable Rights," *Social Philosophy and Policy* 4 (Autumn 1986): 179-202.

Justice is a name for certain classes of moral rules, which concern the essentials of human well-being more nearly, and are therefore of more absolute obligation, than any other rules for the guidance of life; and the notion which we have found to be the essence of the idea of justice, that of a right residing in the individual, implies and testifies to this more binding obligation. . . .

The moral rules which forbid mankind to hurt one another (in which we must never forget to include wrongful interference with each other's freedom), are more vital to human well-being than any maxims, however important, which only point out the best mode of managing some department of human affairs.[58]

A rights analysis that shows the fundamentally unjust and misguided nature of drug laws does not deny that persons who use drugs are capable of violating, and do in fact violate, the rights of others. Such rights-violating conduct is, however, properly illegal whether or not one is using drugs at the time.[59] Nor does it deny that drug use can adversely "affect" the lives of others. Many kinds of con-

---

58. John Stuart Mill, "Utilitarianism" in *Utilitarianism, Liberty, and Representative Government* (New York: Dutton, 1951), p. 73. The position that the law should not attempt to regulate all vices is, of course, much older than Mill. See, for example, Thomas Aquinas, *Summa Theologica.* There he poses the question, "Whether It Belongs to Human Law to repress All Vices?" and answers in part:

> The same thing is not possible to a child as to a full-grown man, and for which reason the law for children is not the same as for adults, since many things are permitted to children which an adult would be punished by law or at any rate open to blame. In a like manner, many things are permitted to men not perfect in virtue, which would be intolerable in a virtuous man.
> Now human law is framed for the multitude of human beings, the majority of whom are not perfect in virtue. Therefore human laws do not forbid all vices, from which the virtuous abstain, but only the more grievous vices, from which it is possible for the majority to abstain; and chiefly those which are *injurious to others, without the prohibition of which human society could not be maintained.* Thus human law prohibits murder, theft and the like.

Ibid., p. 11 (emphasis added). The absence of tangible "injuries to others" led some modern writers to characterize laws regulating matters of vice as "victimless crimes." See, for example, Edwin M. Schur, *Crimes Without Victims* (Englewood Cliffs, N.J.: Prentice-Hall, 1965), pp. 120–80.

59. It is a curious, if not yet again a perverse, offshoot of attitudes toward "good" and "bad" that give rise to a criminal justice system based on punishment, that the use of mind altering substances while committing a crime can *reduce* the legal consequences for that act, because it either affects the ability to prove *mens rea* or special statutes have been created to deal with the "addict" offender. The perversity comes from punishing drug users more harshly than alcohol users—in part because of a fear that they will commit crimes—but if they do commit a crime they are not punished at all or may not be punished as severely as other persons who commit the same crime.

duct—from quitting school to having sex with strangers—can adversely affect the lives of those close to the persons who engage in such activity.[60]

Legal institutions are not capable of correcting every ill in the world. On this point most would agree. Serious harm results when legal means are employed to correct harms that are not amenable to legal regulation. An individual rights analysis is a way of distinguishing harms that are properly subject to legal prohibition from those that are not.

CONCLUSION: CURING THE DRUG-LAW ADDICTION

An addiction to drug laws is caused by an inadequate understanding of individual rights and the vital role such rights play in deciding matters of legality. As a result, policies are implemented that cause serious harm to the very individuals whom these policies were devised to help and to the general public.

If the rights of individuals to choose how to use their person and possessions are fully respected, there is no guaranty that they will exercise their rights wisely. Some may mistakenly choose the path of finding happiness in a bottle or in a vial. Others may wish to help these people by persuading them of their folly. But we must not give in to the powerful temptation to grant some the power to impose their consumptive preferences on others by force. This power—the "essence" of drug laws—is not only "addictive" once it is tasted, it carries with it one of the few guaranties in life: the guaranty of untold corruption and human misery.

---

60. As Herbert Spencer points out:

Some may argue that it is not allowable to assume any essential difference between right conduct toward others and right conduct toward self, seeing that what are generally considered private actions do eventually affect others to such a degree as to render them public actions, as witness the collateral effects of *drunkenness* or suicide.
   In [this allegation] . . . there is much truth, and it is not to be denied that under a final analysis all such distinctions as those above made must disappear. But it must be borne in mind that similar criticisms may be passed upon all classifications whatever. . . . [Spencer then gives several examples of scientific distinctions.] The same finite power of comprehension which compels us to deal with natural phenomena by separating them into groups and studying each group by itself may also compel us to separate those actions which place a man in direct relationship with his fellows from others which do not so place him, although it may be true that such a separation cannot be strictly maintained.

Herbert Spencer, *Social Statics: The Conditions Essential to Human Happiness Specified and the First of Them Developed* (New York: Robert Schalkenbach Foundation, 1970), pp. 64–65 (emphasis added).

3

THE NEED FOR REFORM OF INTERNATIONAL NARCOTICS LAWS

Arnold S. Trebach

INTRODUCTION

The world is in the midst of a drug epidemic. Literally millions of people now use heroin, opium, morphine, cocaine, and marijuana regularly, in flagrant defiance of national and international law. Hundreds of thousands, perhaps millions, are engaged in supplying their illicit needs and desires. The response of most national and international leaders has been rigid support of the existing system of abstinence and prohibition, often through harsh criminal sanctions involving long prison terms and, in at least thirteen countries, even the death penalty. As a result of all this, drug-related crime and official corruption are rising wherever the epidemic spreads. International drug control organizations, such as the U.N. Commission on Narcotic Drugs, blindly support the existing system and the increasingly harsh domestic laws that prop it up. However, compromises

AUTHOR'S NOTE: An earlier draft of a portion of this chapter originally appeared in the *Journal of Drug Issues*, Fall 1983, pp. 379–97. © Arnold S. Trebach, 1982, 1986.

and adjustments must be made to meet new realities. These are not radical thoughts but essentially conservative ones. Unless rational and humane changes are made soon, the entire structure of international drug control may collapse completely.

If this were simply the case of a multitude of evil people doing bad things to the rest of us, it would be easier to cope with. We would gird our loins, make alliances, and World War II–style, carry the fight to the enemy, accepting whatever casualties were necessary to win final victory. It is, however, infinitely more complicated than that. The international framework of control on drugs, as supported and amplified by domestic legal systems, seeks not to repel foreign invaders. Rather, it seeks to prevent our neighbors, most of whom are basically decent and good at heart, from obtaining chemicals and leaves that they wish to use on themselves to feel better. There are, of course, many bad people involved in the process of supplying these drugs. Some of the users, moreover, take the drugs unwisely and hurt themselves, sometimes fatally.

It is, however, very difficult to save people from themselves and their own habits. The Hague Convention of 1912 and the laws of more than a hundred nations say that dangerous drugs are to be restricted to medical and scientific uses. Vast stores of national treasure and armies of police and soldiers have been devoted over the years to supporting that overarching legal restriction. After seven decades, it would seem that this international principle would have had its impact on the habits of the world. This is simply not the case—at least not for millions upon millions of illegal drug users.

THE WORLDWIDE DRUG EPIDEMIC

The most dramatic new fact in the drug abuse field is the growth of heroin use in America and throughout the rest of the world. Many other drugs are involved in this epidemic, but heroin operates almost as a chemical marker, delineating the development of new drug problems that overwhelm traditional approaches and assumptions.[1] For most of this century, the conventional assumptions were that the United States was the center of heroin abuse in the world, that various countries in the Far and Middle East produced the raw material,

---

1. Arnold S. Trebach, *The Heroin Solution* (New Haven: Yale University Press, 1982), pp. 1–21.

and that manufacturing and trafficking often went on under various European auspices. For some reason, the use of heroin did not seem to occur, to any great extent, in those countries involved in production, manufacturing, and trafficking. Indeed, there was almost a smugness among some experts in Europe and the Third World about the failings of American society (capitalism, racism, lack of cultural cohesiveness, and so on) that inevitably produced such social pathologies as mass heroin addiction among its citizens. But times and heroin use patterns are changing; so are fundamental concepts about the drug's impact. Use is no longer equated invariably with abuse, even of heroin.

The changes started in the late sixties, beginning, as far as we know, in America. From all over the country came scattered evidence showing a dramatic upswing in heroin dependence, accompanied by a related huge rise in street crime. Because newly elected President Nixon made an antiheroin campaign the central part of his anticrime strategy, some liberal commentators have attacked the core statistical reality of the existence of the new epidemic itself—even though there were some seemingly reliable official reports that charted a rise from 50,000 to 500,000 heroin addicts between 1965 and the early seventies.[2] (Despite the official nature of these statistics, caution should be used respecting the reliability of the precise number of drug users. Other researchers have focused their attention on the enormous difficulty of obtaining high levels of reliability for any estimates of drug use. For a more thorough analysis of this problem, see Robert Michaels' chapter in this volume.)

Thus, the formulation of solutions to the heroin problem is confounded by the fact that some leading American thinkers have gone to great pains to document that the heroin problem in America really does not exist, at least not in dimensions worth getting bothered about, and that the very emphasis on heroin in enforcement and treatment programs arises either from ignorance or a shoddy desire to manipulate the public for purely political ends. Grave doubts about the "war on drugs" of the Nixon administration were expressed, for example, in "A Statement of Concerns" by the 1972–73 Fellows of the Drug Abuse Council, a prestigious private study group then operating in Washington. That statement objected to the

---

2. Domestic Council Drug Abuse Task Force, *White Paper on Drug Abuse* (Washington, D.C.: Government Printing Office, 1975), p. 14.

fact that "the drug problem in America has often been simplified by portraying it as essentially a *heroin* problem." The Fellows went on to point out that many other drugs are more commonly used and abused, that the impact of heroin on crime is often hysterically overstated, and that there may be greater danger to American society and human rights from antiheroin programs spawned by the government than from heroin addiction itself.

These themes have been carried forward and magnified by political scientist and investigative reporter Edward Jay Epstein, who was also a Fellow of the Drug Abuse Council. In his book *Agency of Fear*, published in 1977, Epstein attempted to make the case that the American heroin epidemic simply did not exist but was manufactured by the Nixon administration.[3] The purpose of this manufactured epidemic was not simply to win votes and reelection for President Nixon but, according to the dust jacket blurb, "to subvert the American system through a kind of *coup d'état*." It is difficult to determine the exact nature of that *coup d'état*. However, it is clear that the strategy, whatever it was, rested on the creation of a heroin epidemic.

Some highly respected voices have expressed agreement with the Epstein thesis. Charles E. Silberman, for example, in his widely acclaimed book *Criminal Violence, Criminal Justice*, made it clear that he accepted the manufactured epidemic theory: The tenfold growth in addiction from the late sixties to the early seventies was a statistical artifact purposely created by the Bureau of Narcotics and Dangerous Drugs, the immediate bureaucratic ancestor of the Drug Enforcement Administration (DEA).[4] Silberman wrote: "What happened, as discovered by Edward Jay Epstein . . . was that the BNDD applied a new formula to the old 1969 data. . . . From beginning to end, as Epstein has documented in great detail, the crusade against heroin was nothing but a cynical public relations device to create the illusion that the Nixon administration was cracking down on crime."[5] There seems no doubt that the Nixon administration used the heroin issue for political ends. But this is quite another matter from creating a heroin epidemic.

3. Edward Jay Epstein, *Agency of Fear* (New York: Putnam, 1977).
4. Charles E. Silberman, *Criminal Violence, Criminal Justice* (New York: Random House, 1978) pp. 173–78.
5. Ibid., pp. 175–76.

Unfortunately, the Epstein-Silberman thesis has led a number of people to view any governmental action in this arena as suspect. A major article on drug policy in the April 1972 issue of *Playboy* magazine, for example, which reflects the opinions of more thinking Americans than care to admit it, repeated the Epstein theory uncritically and in addition dismissed the current existence of a major problem of heroin abuse in America.[6] One cannot be sure of the precise dimension, but there seems good evidence to suggest an overall increase in heroin use in the United States and throughout the world in the last fifteen years.

One official who openly expressed alarm about the worldwide dimensions of the problem was Dr. Peter G. Bourne, who wrote the following when he was candidate Jimmy Carter's chief adviser on drug policy in 1976: "What was once the 'American Disease' has become a worldwide affliction. Heroin addiction has become a major problem in a dozen new countries, with the number of addicts continuing to increase by several thousand every month. Not only are those who are becoming addicted for the most part the children of the social and intellectual elite of these countries, but the massive amounts of money now involved in trafficking have corrupted many high level officials and undermined already unstable economies."[7] The years that have passed since 1976 have shown, sadly enough, that while the substance of Bourne's statement was accurate, even prescient, the dimensions may have been understated.

Unfortunately, there are no reliable official international compilations on the real extent of drug abuse. However, a unique international survey was published in 1977 by three experts who had obtained information, based on a uniform design, from research scientists or physicians in twenty-five countries. As is usually the case, there was a variance between the reports provided by local experts for this survey and other estimates by still other experts regarding such facts as the precise number of opiate addicts in each country, but there was nothing in the report inconsistent, *in terms of broad trends*, with other reports I have reviewed relating to the mid-seventies. The country with the largest estimated number of "opiate

---

6. Lawrence Gonzales, "The War on Drugs: A Special Report," *Playboy*, April 1982, pp. 134, 204.

7. Peter G. Bourne, "The New International Heroin Trade," *Addictions* (Summer 1976): 32.

addicts" was the United States with 620,000, followed by Iran with 400,000, Thailand with 350,000, Hong Kong with 80,000, Canada with 18,000, Singapore with 13,000, Australia with 12,500, Italy with 10,000, and the United Kingdom with 6,000. The principal opiate of abuse in Iran and Singapore was listed, by the domestic experts reporting to the survey, as opium itself, but in all of the other six leading countries it was heroin. The other remaining countries in the sample of twenty-five reported minor opiate abuse problems at the time, the calendar year 1975.

The directors of this survey—Drs. John C. Ball and Harold Graff of the Department of Psychiatry, Temple University, and Jean Paul Smith of the National Institute on Drug Abuse (NIDA)—concluded, "One of the major findings to emerge from the present study is the contemporary increase and spread of heroin dependency throughout most of the nations surveyed. . . . The predominance of heroin abuse is even more marked than this tabulation indicates, as traditional patterns of morphine and opium use are shifting to heroin; this shift is especially notable in Europe and Asia for morphine and opium respectively."[8] Even on the basis of this valuable survey, however, it is impossible to determine with any degree of certainty the number of heroin addicts in the world, or even in the twenty-five countries covered. However, if the opinions of the drug abuse specialists who designed the study and who wrote the country reports are listened to, then this provides more evidence that the numbers of heroin addicts are increasing dramatically throughout the world. My estimate for the world—and it is only a guess based on scattered pieces of data—is that there are at least 2 million heroin addicts and perhaps as many as 4 million.

There continues to be much debate in drug abuse circles over the exact definition of the terms "addicts," "users," and "abusers"—and over the reliability of the count in each country. I chose not to get involved in these debates, except to make the judgment that I have seen enough evidence to become convinced that the problems of heroin use and related crime are terribly serious ones. The problems arise not only from the simple use of the drug, but from the criminal conditions created in large part by their illegality. Moreover, it would make little difference to my position if there had

8. John C. Ball, Harold Graff, and Jean Paul Smith, "International Survey," *Addictive Diseases: An International Journal* 3, no. 1 (1977): 130.

been no great rise in the number of addicts or users—terms I use here interchangeably—from the sixties to the seventies so long as it was accepted that their numbers are now large and that, under current prohibition laws, many of those addicts or users constitute a major social problem.

Because the United States has been viewed for so many years as the nation with the answers to modern problems, many countries are looking to us for answers on how to cope with what appears to be an epidemic of heroin use. Sadly, these countries seem to be learning only the harsh aspects of our drug history—prohibition, law enforcement, punishment, severe sentences—and ignoring the more humane features of drug treatment. Even more distressing, the lessons that can be learned from Great Britain, the other major model of drug abuse control (which operated in accord with more tolerant rules), are almost totally ignored elsewhere. Thus, much of the world seems intent on repeating—indeed, enlarging upon—those chapters of American drug abuse history that, at best, deserve only to be quickly learned, then just as quickly rejected.

In the discussion concerning international drug use that follows, it should be kept in mind that estimates concerning the number of users are not always completely reliable, nor can they be considered comparable. As all researchers who work in the field know, it is often impossible to compare figures respecting drug use from one country to another. This is especially true given the differences in methods of data collection and in the definitions used.

Witness the difference in language used to refer to the number of deaths due to drug use: "heroin-related deaths," "heroin overdose deaths," "drug overdose deaths," "drug-related deaths," "narcotic overdose deaths," etc. The disparity in numbers of deaths from drug use in Italy and France, as compared with Denmark, Switzerland, and West Germany, is particularly striking. The reader will note that while France and West Germany are estimated to have approximately the same number of narcotics addicts, the number of overdose deaths in West Germany is seemingly five times as great. This is not a comment on the more deadly nature of drugs in West Germany but on the imprecision and incomparability of the data. I should repeat that the exact amount of drug use is not central to my thesis. What is beyond question, however, is the substantial increase in drug use throughout the world that has occurred since the early 1970s.

THE FAR EAST

We can appreciate this phenomenon by looking at the spread of heroin addiction and the attendant problems often created by its illegality, even in a faraway tropical island like Borneo. To most Occidentals, Borneo would seem to have nothing to do with a discourse on heroin and crime. But such is not the case. Located in the northern part of the island is the state of Sarawak, which in turn is part of a relatively new country, the Federation of Malaysia. The capital city of Sarawak is Kuching.

The *Borneo Bulletin* of April 29, 1978, carried a story in which Vincent Kho, First Division police chief in Kuching, reported that heroin addiction among the youth of the city had grown considerably in the last three years. "Addicts short of money have been resorting to stealing, extortion, and other crimes to find the cash needed to buy their 'fixes,' " the *Bulletin* reported. The police chief stated that he wanted a rehabilitation center, which Sarawak lacks; moreover, "As with other senior lawmen, Mr. Kho says he is also anxiously awaiting the extension of the amended Dangerous Drugs ordinance to Sarawak—which will mean the death sentence can be applied for drugs possession as is the case in Peninsular Malaysia."

That ordinance was applied in the prosecution of convicted heroin trafficker Hong Hoo Chong, 40, in Peninsular Malaysia, which borders Thailand, in early December 1979. Hong Hoo Chong had been arrested by the police in 1978 with 1,550.1 grams of heroin in his possession. The Penang High Court, the equivalent to the Supreme Court of a state or province, had imposed the penalty of life imprisonment as well as 14 strokes of the *rotan*. In the first appeal ever by the government against a life sentence in a drugs case, the Director of Public Prosecutions, Encik Mohamed Noor bin Haji Ahmad, pointed out to the court of appeals, an intermediate appellate court, that the defendant was a convicted armed robber and burglar who had gone on to trafficking; the DPP then observed, "We should regard him as public enemy No. 1 who is a danger and menace to society and, therefore, the death sentence should be the only way to exterminate him from society." In rendering his decision, Chief Justice Raja Azlan Shah of the court of appeals lectured the trial judges of the country by telling them that they should not develop a phobia against inflicting the death penalty, because "we feel the time has come for some more vigorous element of deterrence to be brought upon those trafficking in drugs.'' Finding "no redeeming features" in Hong Hoo Chong's case, the chief justice took the extraordinary step, supported by his learned colleagues on the court of appeals, of overturning the life term and imposing in its place a sentence of death.[9]

Criminal justice officials apparently took the chief justice's lecture to heart. Two years later, in December 1981, a leading law enforcement official, Datuk Abdul Rahman, was able to report that since 1975, when the new death penalty ordinance went into effect, 530 people had been charged with drug trafficking; 112 were found guilty; 18 were sentenced to death, and 94 to life imprisonment; 4 were hanged; and 14 had appealed but remained under sentence of death.[10]

During the month before, Deputy Prime Minister Datuk Musa Hitam announced that the government was contemplating the enactment of even more amendments to existing law, especially one that would allow detention for the simple fact of being an addict (a status offense declared unconstitutional in America) and would provide for banishment of detained users and pushers to a new island penal colony (a now-discarded invention of advanced European nations). Even before this new legislation was put into effect, however, the police launched *Operasi Berkas* (Operation Detain) and in a few days had picked up approximately a thousand suspected drug addicts. There was an almost immediate negative response from some jail keepers, one of whom complained, "We are full house." It appeared likely that many of the detained suspects would soon be released because the authorities simply had not planned treatment or control facilities to deal with them.[11]

Despite all these Draconian measures, the authorities reported in late 1981 widespread use of illicit drugs. While their methods of counting, it must be assumed, suffer from all the usual methodological defects in this area, officials have made alarming claims about the dimensions of use and abuse. At least 300,000 youth in this small country (population in 1980: 13,435,588) were using illegal chemicals regularly during school days. Moreover, there were 61,334 known

9. *New Straits Times* (Kuala Lumpur), 6 December 1979, p. 1.

10. Ibid., 16 December 1981, p. 2.

11. Ibid., 1 January 1982, p. 3.

drug addicts in the country, 80 percent of whom were men below 30 years of age. Most of these were heroin addicts and many were engaged in crime to support their habits.[12] The point is not that Malaysia is so bad by comparison with other nations; it is, rather, that Malaysia is very probably quite typical of what is happening in many countries from which less information is available. Much of this problem, moreover, has surfaced within the space of a few years, mirroring epidemic heroin addiction eruptions in the United States and other nations.

Similar events have occurred in neighboring Singapore, which also emerged from colonial status to independence in the 1960s. Singapore seems to have learned little from its former British rulers. As in England there is a law labeled the Misuse of Drugs Act, but there the essential resemblance seems to end. In 1975, the Singapore law was amended to impose the death penalty for the illicit manufacture of any quantity of morphine or heroin and for trafficking 30 grams or more of these drugs. Corporal punishment in the form of whipping was brought back in 1973 as a mandatory sentence in several dozen crimes. In a story on the new, harsh discipline of the law, *Wall Street Journal* reporter Barry Newman wrote on July 6, 1977, "While some people here oppose beating and say it doesn't reduce crime, they are a definite minority and have little influence. So Singapore is flexing its 'rotan'—a thin rod of rattan that, when brought down hard against the buttocks, splits the skin, draws blood and scars for life." But later that month, a leading police official said he doubted that these new harsh measures had much effect on controlling heroin traffic or use. The director of the Central Narcotics Bureau in Singapore, John Hanam, observed, "On the contrary, heroin seems to be more widely used than ever before."

Moreover, treatment of known heroin addicts seems, in some cases, to be rather abrupt. Addicts are withdrawn "cold turkey" as a first step in treatment at the Telok Paku rehabilitation center. Home Affairs Minister Chua Sian said that the "suffering experienced by the addict in 'cold turkey' will long be remembered by that person. We hope it will deter him or her from ever going back to drugs." But while heroin abuse was virtually unknown in Singapore ten years ago, the recent worldwide heroin epidemic has also arrived there. As

12. Ibid., 10 December 1981, p. 6.

late as 1973, only ten arrests involved heroin; by 1976, over 4,500. As of 1975 in Singapore there were an estimated 2,000 heroin addicts, 3,000–4,000 morphine addicts, and 7,000–8,000 opium smokers out of a population of 2,249,900.[13] By March 1977 the number of heroin addicts was estimated at 13,000. Singapore invoked the death penalty for drug trafficking five times between 1976 and early 1980. Three Malaysians and two Singaporeans have been hanged under this statute. One official explained the generally harsh governmental response in this way: "The message to the heroin user was either opt out of drugs or opt out of society." By July 1979 there was some evidence that the epidemic was slowing down, but the problem of heroin addiction still deeply troubled the small city-nation.[14] At a six-day meeting of Asian drug experts in December 1981 in Singapore, a call was made to nations of the region to consider preventive detention laws for drug traffickers, manufacturers, financiers, and addicts. It was pointed out that Singapore and Malaysia already had such laws for detaining drug offenders without trial. A joint press release declared, as reported in the Kuala Lumpur *New Straits Times*, that "illicit drug trafficking and abuse pose a threat to national security, stability, and resilience."[15]

The pattern is similar throughout a large part of the world: increasing heroin addiction, destructive crime by addicts, and a social response that is dominated by the criminal sanction in its most awesome forms, even though treatment facilities of one kind or another are to be found in virtually every country affected by the epidemic. The capital of heroin addiction in the world may no longer be New York, as many had heretofore imagined, but Bangkok, Thailand. It has been estimated that 6 to 8 percent of that city's 6 million inhabitants are addicted to hard drugs. According to a Reuters story of August 23, 1978, Dr. Khachit Chupanya, the director of drug rehabilitation in the city, estimated that there were 300,000–400,000 addicts there. "Most of them were addicted to heroin number four, the purest grade sold on the street," the report said. Khachit earlier had estimated that there were 500,000 drug addicts in Thailand. If these estimates are anywhere near the truth, then it is quite conceiv-

13. Ball, Graff, and Smith, "International Survey," pp. 94–95.
14. W. H. McGlothlin, "The Singapore Heroin Control Programme," *Bulletin on Narcotics* 32, no. 1 (1980): 1.
15. *New Straits Times*, 9 December 1981, p. 15.

able that Thailand, considered in its entirety, with its 41 million people (approximately 1 percent addicted) has a much worse heroin problem than the United States, which may have 500,000 heroin addicts and regular users out of a population of approximately 220 million (0.23 percent addicted). The spectacle, moreover, of an opium producing country with a major heroin addiction problem is also part of the new reality of the world.

Another part of that emerging and distressing reality is the perceived need at times for military force to control the activities of some of the most powerful manufacturers and traffickers. Think of the implications of this fact: Because of the huge gap that national and international leaders have allowed to develop between the habits of millions of the world's people and the fabric of the laws, some of those who cater to the illicit demand for drugs become so rich and powerful as to become impervious to ordinary law enforcement measures. Thus, military formations must be deployed against them. For example, in late January 1982, eight companies of Thai border patrol military units launched a major attack against the Shan United Army, headed by the notorious drug warlord Khun Sa in a Thailand province near the Burmese border. Airplanes, including helicopter gunships, were thrown into pitched battles by the government forces. Losses on the SUA side amounted to approximately one hundred dead. A few days after the carnage, however, Thai reporters saw that life in the border areas under control of SUA and other rebel groups, heavily involved in heroin production, was returning to normal. One reporter observed, "The major operation has died down. Casualties have been heavy on both sides. But Khun Sa's influence is far from over. . . . The heroin connection remains relatively unaffected."[16]

In the deep southeastern United States, law, order, and domestic tranquility are being disrupted to a frightening extent by the activities of smugglers from South America, especially from Colombia, sometimes called Cocaine Cowboys. In Dade County alone, 135 murders were attributed to drug traffickers during 1980. The mass movement of smugglers' ships and planes from South America into the Florida Keys, the Florida mainland, and other parts of the American South has brought U.S. naval and air units into coordinated operations with the Coast Guard.[17] In a very real sense, the American nation is

16. *The Nation Review* (Bangkok), 13 February 1982, p. 13.
17. The Navy has provided sophisticated E-2C fixed wing aircraft, with sensitive electronic equipment, to detect the planes of drug smugglers. These Navy planes have been directly as-

now conducting a small war not against foreign invaders but against those who smuggle into this country chemicals that millions eagerly part with billions of dollars to obtain. The ironies are obvious, stunning, and usually ignored.

To return to the addiction situation in the Far East, the problem in the British Crown Colony of Hong Kong would seem to rival that of Thailand. By some standards, it is worse. Authorities claimed that in 1975 an estimated 80,000–100,000 addicts inhabited the crowded colony, whose total population is 4.3 million. Thus, approximately 2 percent of the entire population was dependent on narcotics, perhaps the highest rate for any country in the world. Most of these addicts were smoking or sniffing the fumes of heroin-tipped cigarettes. However, data for 1978, generated by a new computerized Central Registry of Drug Addicts, established with help from the American National Institute on Drug Abuse, made Hong Kong officials a bit more optimistic. It appeared that the number of addicts might be in the range of 35,000–50,000. Even with such lower figures, Hong Kong officials were still deeply concerned.[18]

United States territory in the Far East, moreover, has not been immune. The island of Guam, a remote corner of this planet if there ever was one, has its own Drug Enforcement Administration post, staffed by five special agents. The surprising nature of a major heroin addiction problem in this bucolic and idyllic setting was described by Peter Rieff, the resident agent-in-charge of the DEA office there. "As late as 1968, even experienced police officers were unaware of the presence of drugs on Guam; it was not until 1970 that police became aware of the presence of hard drugs. Felony crimes during the 1968 to 1970 period were low and increased only minimally. During the early months of 1973, the drug abuse problem on Guam reached alarming proportions. The rise in crime from the two preceding years was unprecedented (up 34 percent). Unfortunately, the Guamanian community at large was unaware of this burgeoning interrelated problem of crime and drugs." In 1977 it dawned

---

signed to coordinated operations with the Coast Guard. In addition, those Navy ships which happen to be in the area have been alerted to be aware of drug smuggling activity, especially by surface craft, and to take appropriate action. Interview, Commander Richard Bennett, U.S. Navy, Washington, D.C., April 23, 1982.

18. Action Committee Against Narcotics, *Hong Kong Narcotics Report 1978* (Hong Kong: The Government Printer, 1978), p. 25.

on the community that Guam had an estimated 782 heroin addicts, approximately one for every 143 people.

Almost no part of the Pacific region seems immune from the rapid increase in heroin abuse and its attendant problems. On July 13, 1979, Detective Chief Superintendent Mal Churches reported that the amount of heroin seized in New Zealand, as well as the number of criminal charges made relating to heroin, could double the 1978 figures. In the first six months of 1979, Mr. Churches stated that there had been 302 criminal charges involving heroin, compared to 303 for all of 1978. Also, 1,752 grams had been seized by police and customs officers in the first six months of 1979, compared to 1,945 grams for all of 1978—insignificant by American standards, but alarming to New Zealanders.[19]

Similar reports emanated from neighboring Australia. They told a familiar story: major increases in heroin trafficking and use, related increases in the marijuana arena, allegations of police corruption, and recommendations by many officials, including the police, to get tough in the fight against drugs. A rare, frank glimpse into the mind of one Australian drug enforcement official was provided in 1979 when the retired commander of the southern region of the Australian Bureau of Narcotics, Bernard Delaney, wrote a book about his experiences. Mr. Delaney claimed that drug law enforcement in Australia had been a miserable failure; that corruption in police forces, especially in New South Wales, was making it impossible to catch the "Mr. Bigs" of the illegal trade; that civil libertarians and other do-gooders were hindering the battle against drugs; and that politicians must approve the greater use of wiretapping and electronic surveillance in order to catch the pushers and the dealers. Mr. Delaney openly told how he illegally tapped telephones in order to carry out drug investigations and criticized officials in the Posts and Telegraphs Department for attempting to stop him. He justified his actions by stating, "The only way Narcotics Bureau officers could succeed in their difficult area was by cheating the system.[20]

Typical of the new and difficult problems faced by the Australians—but almost traditional for Americans and becoming so for the people of many other countries—was a report in August 1979 by Melbourne police Detective Chief Inspector Paul Delianis, head of

19. *Evening Post* (Wellington), 13 July 1979, p. 1.
20. *Courier-Mail* (Brisbane), 31 August 1979, p. 5.

the homicide squad. He stated that two New Zealanders recently had been murdered by a New Zealand–based syndicate that had just smuggled nearly a ton of 90 percent pure heroin into Australia. The value of the drugs was estimated at more than $45 million; once the heroin was cut and adulterated, the street value would, of course, increase many times beyond that figure. Thus, Australia is afflicted not only with increased heroin abuse and trafficking but also by the usual attendant violent criminal activity.[21]

Another familiar aspect of the Australian scene was a call to consider new approaches to treating drug addiction. Speaking in the Senate on August 28, 1979, the leader of the Australian Democratic Party, Senator Donald L. Chipp, asked for the "legalization" of heroin on a limited basis to help in the campaign against heroin abuse. Stating that he did not want to make the drug available for anyone to try, he asked, "But if there is a person who has been diagnosed as a heroin addict, why can't a medical practitioner prescribe heroin on a limited basis?"[22] Nevertheless, the criminal sanction continues to dominate official response to drug problems Down Under.

WESTERN EUROPE

According to a variety of official reports and newspaper accounts, western Europe is also experiencing a massive increase in heroin use. On January 9, 1977, the *Sunday Times* of London estimated that in 1971 there had been no more than 11,349 heroin addicts in western Europe, including England; by 1976, the *Times* estimated that the number might have reached as high as 180,000. By late 1978, the American DEA placed the number of heroin users in western Europe at approximately 200,000, with seizures by European police in the previous year exceeding those in the United States. Heroin-related deaths have been officially reported as having reached 1,000 in western Europe during 1978. If these figures are correct, then the rate of growth of heroin addiction in the area might well have outpaced that in the United States during the 1970s.

Health authorities in West Berlin estimated that the number of addicts rose from 2,000 in 1972 to approximately 20,000 in 1977, with 84 heroin overdose deaths in the city for that year. The number

---

21. *The Age* (Melbourne), 28 August 1979, p. 28.
22. *Courier-Mail* (Brisbane), 31 August 1979, p. 5.

of heroin overdose deaths for all of West Germany reached 334 in 1976, and then increased to over 380 in 1977, during which years the United States respectively recorded 1,597 and 596 such fatalities. By 1978, the two countries were drawing even closer together on this unhappy statistic—430 heroin overdose deaths in West Germany and 471 in the United States.

Reports from West Germany in 1979 indicated that the trends were worsening. Journalist Hartmut Palmer wrote on May 4, 1979, in the *Sueddeutsche Zeitung* of Munich, that only "bad news" was to be found in the latest reports from the "drug commissioners" of the Laender (German states or provinces) because these reports revealed "that the efforts made until now by state and private institutions have not succeeded in banishing the danger, in stopping the trend, and much less in reversing it. In the past 6 months, especially for young people, susceptibility to the so-called 'hard drugs' seems to have increased alarmingly. According to the estimates of the drug commissioners, the 'hard core' of chronic users has increased from 40,000 to between 44,000 and 46,000." The West Germans also were facing familiar conflicts over philosophy and policy. Palmer wrote: "In all Laender—no matter of what political color its government—there exists an almost traditional conflict of objectives between local authorities in charge of police and crime control on the one hand, and health and welfare authorities on the other hand. The first see repressive control of drug abuse as the most pressing task; for the others, therapeutic, preventive measures are the most pressing. Both claims are [well] founded, but they are difficult to reconcile." There is some evidence, however, that the tilt in Germany, as in so many other countries, as in the direction of "repressive control."

The West German Minister of the Interior, Gerhart Baum, stated, according to a report in the September 1, 1979, issue of *Die Welt* of Bonn: "As far as I am concerned, the fight against the international narcotic trade has the same priority as the fight against terrorism. We are therefore intent on exhausting every possibility in the police sector. . . . " Mr. Baum went on to explain that a new national system of narcotic information, in cooperation with Laender narcotic offices, would be created; new techniques of police surveillance and investigation would be inaugurated; and hopefully, the legislature would follow his request for harsher criminal penalties for narcotic trafficking. While thus emphasizing the archetypical law enforcement approach to the narcotic problem, Interior Minister Baum also stated that he placed a high priority on the demand side of the equation—on the treatment of drug abusers. At the same time, he said that treatment facilities seemed inadequate to meet the increasingly heavy need. Of particular concern also to Mr. Baum was the possibility of an American-style drug scene growing on West German soil, for not only was heroin abuse growing rapidly, but South American cocaine was also starting to appear.

Preliminary reports for 1979 showed that heroin overdose deaths in West Germany, approximately 611, might have exceeded those in the United States, approximately 566. With 61 million people, West Germany has only one quarter of the population of the United States. If these figures are accurate, they are of major significance, because this would represent the first time that any country had recorded more heroin overdose deaths than the United States. But a host of qualifications are necessary: (1) It is difficult for any pathologist to tell precisely what drug killed a person; (2) not all drug deaths are reported; and (3) it is not known if the methods of collecting data in the two countries are precisely comparable. These are statistical qualifications, however, which apply to all such drug abuse statistics. In substantive terms, there is every reason to believe that heroin use has increased significantly in the Federal Republic of Germany.

Reports from West Germany in 1981 showed that the demand for all kinds of illegal drugs was growing and along with it a vast increase in traffic. A good deal of these drugs was coming through the border from the Netherlands, where, German observers claim, hashish, marijuana, cocaine, heroin, and LSD are freely peddled on the streets and in the pubs. Similar claims were also made about West German streets and pubs. A sense of resignation and a belief that the control system was breaking down was expressed by Chief Customs Inspector Curt Obaron of Dusseldorf's inland revenue office on October 28, 1981: "My people are just about to keel over; I must state unequivocally that we can no longer deal with the drug problem."[23]

The disease has also appeared in neighboring France. Increased and alarming heroin use was described by Monique Pelletier, who was appointed by the president of the French Republic to monitor the development of the drug phenomenon in the country. She estimated the drug-dependent population of the country at 30,000 to

23. *Frankfurter Allgemeine* (Frankfurt), 28 October 1981, p. 12.

50,000, according to a story in *Le Figaro* of January 14, 1980, with clear indications of an upward trend. Five drug overdose deaths were counted for the entire country in 1970; 37 in 1975; and 117 in 1979.

The smaller European countries, including those with reputations for idyllic life-styles and low levels of social disruption, have not been immune. Large quantities of illicit heroin and morphine are now being imported into Denmark, for example. A Copenhagen newspaper reported in January 1980 that the number of narcotic-related deaths had risen from three in 1970 to over 100 in 1979.[24]

Many of the other familiar "side effects" of large-scale narcotic abuse, such as official corruption, are beginning to appear in countries unaccustomed to their presence and deeply disturbed by their discovery. In late January 1980, Belgium was shocked by the arrest of Major Léon François, head of the National Narcotics Bureau, the equivalent of the American DEA, on charges that he cooperated in a narcotics smuggling conspiracy that moved some mysterious suitcases through Brussels National Airport. The case was shrouded in mystery and confusion, although it appears that heroin was involved, and it is certain that M. François and other Belgian drug officials were incarcerated for some time, although they were later released, again under rather mysterious circumstances.[25]

The number of heroin abusers in Switzerland was reported by authorities to have been 10,000 in 1978, only 300 of whom were in treatment. On February 16, 1980, the *Neue Zuercher Zeitung* commented that "despite intensive education, Switzerland's drug scene is becoming increasingly brutal." Heroin, the story noted, was being widely traded in the country. It was also the major cause of narcotic overdose deaths. In 1974, there were 13 drug-related deaths; by 1977, there were 78. Then in 1979, the number topped 100 for the first time, when it reached 102. Other indicators of drug abuse and related crime were equally depressing: Reports to the police of violations of the controlled substances law rose from 6,299 in 1978 to 7,045 in 1979; the number of convictions from 4,465 to 5,466. Large quantities of heroin, hashish, and amphetamines were also seized by the police.

In mid-1981, Laura Wicinski, of the Heroin Section, DEA Office of Intelligence, reported that Europe was "awash" with Southwest

24. *Berlingske Tidende* (Copenhagen), 6 January 1980, p. 17.
25. *Le Soir* (Brussels), 25 January 1980, p. 1.

Asian heroin, more potent than the type from Southeast Asia, which was being replaced in the illegal marketplace. Wicinski placed the number of heroin addicts in western Europe between 190,000 and 330,000. The problem seemed worst in West Germany, where the heroin-addict population had reportedly risen to between 68,000 and 80,000. The final heroin overdose figure for 1979 was now calculated at 623. Italian authorities estimated the heroin addict population in that country at 40,000–50,000 with heroin-related overdose deaths rising from 40 in 1977 to 129 in 1979.[26] The apparent dramatic rise in heroin use throughout the world as well as changes in national patterns of addiction were reflected in comparative data (Table 3–1), which revealed heroin overdose deaths per million of population in a few key countries.

There is more and more evidence of growing official impatience in Europe with those who use and sell drugs, and of increasing resort to harsher legal controls and criminal sanctions. In December 1981, moreover, the Swedish parliament adopted a law providing for the compulsory treatment of drug abusers. This placed drug addicts in the same category with alcoholics in that country and allowed social welfare authorities the power to detain addicts within closed institutions for years, if necessary. A usual period of forced treatment, however, was estimated at two months.[27] While such measures in Sweden and elsewhere in western Europe are totally incompatible with a free society, there is at least no use of capital punishment for drug trafficking, as is the case in some other parts of the world.

Table 3–1. Heroin Deaths per Million Population.

	1978	*1979*
France	2.01	2.17
Italy	1.09	2.26
United States	3.00	3.20
West Germany	6.90	10.04

SOURCE: Derived from Laura M. Wicinski, "Europe Awash with Heroin," *Drug Enforcement,* 8 no. 1 (Summer 1981): 14.

26. Laura M. Wicinski, "Europe Awash With Heroin," *Drug Enforcement* 8, no. 1 (Summer 1981): 14–16.

27. *Dagens Nyheter* (Stockholm), 16 December 1981, p. 2.

IRAN

In the midst of the worldwide spread of heroin abuse in the late seventies, there came the Iranian revolution, known for its fanatical rejection of all things American. That upheaval destroyed the limited control the shah's police had on the export of heroin and thus allowed a vast increase in the international market. But there was an incredibly ironic twist to the story. In the land leading the retreat to Moslem fundamentalism and the rejection of the vices of the modern world, heroin use suddenly became so widespread and open that in early 1980 American television audiences were introduced by name to Iranian heroin smokers and saw them in their homes, with friends and families. Iranian heroin thus seemed to be replacing the more traditional Persian opium.

By the summer of 1980, reports on the Iranian heroin situation, like so much else in that tortured country, took on breathtakingly cruel proportions. The official government statistics indicated that there were 3 million heroin addicts, approximately one for every twelve Iranians. It appears that a large number of opium addicts were included in that clearly improbable figure. A high school teacher in Teheran, dismayed over the widespread addiction among his students, observed, "Heroin and opium were the only commodities that became inexpensive and plentiful after the revolution."[28] The cheap, high potency heroin of Iran's clandestine laboratories was flooding into many other countries, including the United States and those in western Europe. Although at first slow to respond, officials of the revolutionary government finally intervened with what may be, if the stories can be believed, the harshest response to drug selling in the annals of modern history. The roving executioner of the revolution, Ayatollah Sadegh Khalkhali, held brief trials of alleged drug traffickers; shouted, "I shall exterminate you vermin!"; and ordered summary executions, which were carried out within minutes. During a seven-week period, the *Washington Post* Foreign Service reported, 176 people had been executed for heroin and opium offenses. On July 8, while licking an ice cream cone, the revolutionary executioner held a press conference in a deserted mosque where he displayed

28. *Time*, 30 June 1980, p. 39.

goods confiscated primarily from the condemned, including approximately a hundred kilo bags (220 pounds) of heroin.

Even though he seemed ruthlessly efficient in his chosen field, the Ayatollah Khalkhali was stung by criticism that he had not acted swiftly or harshly enough to curb rising drug traffic and addiction. Defensively, he explained that there were practical limits even to his direct method of controlling drug abuse: "If we wanted to kill everybody who had five grams of heroin, we'd have to kill 5,000 people, and this would be difficult."[29]

While he had probably not intended to, the Ayatollah Khalkhali provided the rudiments of a most instructive lesson in criminology and drug abuse control policy for those who would listen carefully to his words. Think of the power he had and of how it must have appealed to at least a few officials in more democratic nations, who, beset by hordes of addicts and traffickers, in their worst moments want to take very direct action—action that, of course, is forbidden by laws, constitutions, and their oaths of office. The ayatollah, however, could and did take that direct action. His word was the supreme law. Not only dealers but simple addicts were sometimes lined up against a neighborhood wall and shot. This policy proved ineffective, not so much because of the stirrings of tender mercy in the hearts of the executioners but rather because of the existence of such huge numbers of Iranian citizens who were flagrantly violating the drugs laws, *even in the face of the imminent possibility and reality of immediate death sentences.* This is what must amount to the ultimate documentation of the proposition that no law can be enforced if a sufficient number of citizens are determined to violate it. At that point, the authorities have the choice of ameliorating their enforcement of the law or of embarking on a course tantamount to fighting a civil war. That is a proposition which applies, of course, to other nations and to the world situation regarding the current drug epidemic. We do not know what has happened in Iran recently, of course, because of unreliable news service. But while there have been reports that thousands of addicts have been rounded up, I have encountered no mention of the execution of a drug offender for many months. Perhaps officials in Iran have learned the ayatollah's lesson.

29. *Washington Post*, 9 July 1980, p. A19.

CAPITAL PUNISHMENT OF DRUG OFFENDERS

There is no reliable compilation of the extent to which capital punishment has actually been used to punish drug offenders in other nations throughout the world in recent years. However, there is a partial listing of countries that provide for the use of the ultimate sanction in their drug laws. This information is contained in a report, *The Global Legal Framework for Narcotics and Prohibitive Substances*, issued by the U.S. Department of State in 1979. Of the 153 countries surveyed, full information was obtained on 80 countries, partial on 44, and none on 29. According to this report, the most severe sanctions in the countries surveyed are for trafficking in opiates. The laws of nine countries provide for the extreme penalty in such cases: Burma, Taiwan, Guinea, Indonesia, Iran, South Korea, Malaysia, Thailand, and Turkey.[30] Admittedly, this list is incomplete. We have already seen that Singapore provides the death penalty for some drug offenses. Moreover, Algeria provides, under the terms of an ordinance of February 18, 1975, that a capital sentence may be imposed for offenses that jeopardize the moral health of the people, which applies to some drug crimes. Also, the Philippines Dangerous Drugs Act of 1972 (Article III, Section 4) provides for the death penalty for traffickers when a particular drug has been "the proximate cause of death of a victim thereof." It would also appear that the use of the death penalty for serious drug offenders has the support of law in China.[31]

---

30. U.S. Department of State, *The Global Legal Framework for Narcotics and Prohibitive Substances* (Washington, D.C.: Government Printing Office, 1979), p. 13.

31. The statements in the text about the death penalty in drug cases in Communist China are made with deliberate caution. Stories abound about the execution of drug dealers and of some addicts in mainland China, especially during the period of revolutionary ferment of the late forties. However, no legal provision has been found, as of the date of this writing, that attaches the death penalty specifically to drug offenses. This may be due to the fact that the Chinese are very sensitive and secretive about the topic. They often claim that the problem of drug addiction was conquered by the advent of the new revolutionary order. Yet, the law does provide the death penalty for economic crimes against the state and for counterrevolutionary activity. Chinese have been executed under these provisions, for example, on charges of smuggling gold; thus, it would appear that drug smuggling might well qualify, in some cases, for the extreme penalty. Drug offenses are dealt with in articles 164 and 171 of the Substantive Criminal Code, People's Republic of China, as approved by the 5th National People's Congress, July 1, 1979, effective January 1, 1980. Article 171 provides for a maximum penalty of five years' imprisonment for "anyone who manufactures, sells or ships opium, morphine or other narcotic drugs." Counterrevolutionary activities, which carry the death penalty, are dealt

Thus, at least thirteen nations provide for the death penalty for some drug offenses. At this point in the progress of civilization, this may seem to be a shocking overreaction to an activity that is, in at least some senses, voluntary on the part of willing purchasers of the contraband. Even more surprising is that at least five countries are known to provide for the extreme penalty in *marijuana* trafficking cases: Burma, Taiwan, Guinea, South Korea, and Malaysia.[32]

The existence of the death penalty in a relatively few countries, however abhorrent it may be in its own right in such cases, is not the main point here. *That penalty is a symbol of a much broader set of problems*: the rock-hard persistence of the major international organizations and national governments in supporting rigid adherence to the old system of international narcotic control. Many countries, other than those with capital punishment, support that system with a vast network of criminal laws, often including life imprisonment; with huge allocations from the national treasury, amounting in the worldwide aggregate to many billions of dollars; and with the efforts of many thousands of enforcement officials. But, as the Ayatollah Khalkhali could teach even the most sophisticated and intelligent police and narcotic control officials, there are simply practical limits to the enforcement art in the face of massive, flagrant violations of the law.

The ultimate meaning of the lesson of Ayatollah Khalkhali is more difficult to fathom. Some will argue that it documents the need to drop all legal controls on the recreational use of addicting chemicals. This extreme alternative, however, is likely to strike many as simplistic and most as impractical. It is necessary, therefore, to work out a new system for the control of dangerous drugs, and such a system must begin on the middle ground between the extremes, where few matters are black and white, where most are gray, and where a

---

with in Part II, Chapter 1, Articles 90–104 of the criminal law. A recent enactment providing for the death penalty for serious economic crimes was a resolution of the 22nd Session, Standing Committee, 5th National People's Congress, entitled Resolution for Severely Punishing Criminals Who Do Great Damage to the Economy, passed March 29, 1982, effective April 1, 1982. For assistance in dealing with the law of the PRC, I am indebted to Jeanette Pinard, Far Eastern Law Division, Library of Congress, Washington, D.C., and to my dean at the American University, School of Justice, Richard A. Myren, who recently returned from a criminal justice study trip to that country. See also Albert P. Blaustein, ed., *Fundamental Legal Documents of Communist China* (South Hackensack, N.J.: Rothman, 1962), p. 220.

32. U.S. Department of State, *Global Legal Framework*, p. 8.

patient sense of humane balance is crucial. In other words, ingenious compromise, cautious experimentation, and readjustments in the face of new experience must become the tools of creating that new system.

THE NEED FOR FLEXIBILITY

What balanced adjustments and compromises can the nations of the world now make? To start with, they can begin to admit what is happening before their very eyes: The system of international control has been almost completely undermined by the desires and actual day-to-day behavior of millions of the world's citizens. Next, they can start thinking in terms of specific compromises and adjustments rather than rigid support of a system that has no relevance to present reality.

It is crucial that some of these changes start soon in the personnel and attitudes of the international drug control bodies, such as the United Nations Commission on Narcotic Drugs. Robert Pisani's description of the seemingly benign attempt of the International Cannabis Alliance for Reform to be granted Non-Governmental Organization status with the U.N. lends support to the need for change. The U.N. bureaucrats who turned down this request were not in touch with the real nature of the drug situation in the world today. Even speaking on a regular basis to those quite respectable professionals who are openly working for reform of marijuana laws was considered to be too radical for the United Nations. The U.S. delegate on the subcommittee of the Economic and Social Council hearing the application for NGO status observed that the actions of the International Cannabis Alliance might be incompatible with the Single Convention on Narcotic Drugs, the omnibus treaty that is the keystone of international legal control.[33] Such rigid reactions in in-

---

33. For a description of the manner in which established international organizations rebuffed the cautious attempts at dialogue by the International Cannabis Alliance for Reform, see Robert L. Pisani, "International Efforts to Reform Cannabis Laws," *Journal of Drug Issues* 13, no. 4 (Fall 1983): 401–15.

For details of the Single Convention on Narcotic Drugs, see Kettil Bruun, Lynn Pan, and Ingemar Rexed, *The Gentlemen's Club—International Control of Drugs and Alcohol* (Chicago: University of Chicago Press, 1975). As explained on page 16 of that book, the Single Convention of 1961 was aimed at replacing virtually all of the international treaties on drugs, starting with the Hague Conference treaty of 1912. It thus provided a major codification of international drug law and also provided some wholly new laws, such as that prohibiting cannabis.

ternational bodies, which should be leading the way to realistic reforms, are recipes for disaster. Any future scheme of control must provide for a great deal of flexibility allowing for many national and regional variations based on local cultures and also on the type of drug involved. After many years of reviewing the evolution of heroin policy in Britain and America, for example, I concluded that my recommendations for dealing with that drug could be specific to it (as well as to related opiates) and did not necessarily apply to other drugs such as cannabis, alcohol, or barbiturates.[34] All countries, moreover, should reassess their drug laws and methods of enforcement so as to bring these laws and enforcement practices closer into line with the wishes of their citizens, with local cultures, and with evolving new practices.

Does this mean I am recommending that all drugs should be legalized? Far from it. I am suggesting rather that national leaders seek out the acceptable middle ground that might save the venerable Hague system, which in its essence maintained that addicting drugs should not be treated as ordinary articles of commerce but should be controlled by special laws. Thus, drugs were not to be available to anyone who simply wanted to try them. Doctors, on the other hand, had relatively free use of them in the practice of their profession. It is possible to seek to preserve the essential elements of that scheme by suggesting amendments, exceptions, and modern redefinitions. The essence of that future scheme must be flexibility and realistic adjustment, not surrender.

An *amendment* might include major changes of existing controls; such reforms would be framed in innovative packages that accordingly might be socially and politically more appealing than in the past. Why not, for example, encourage nations to consider coupling reform of laws controlling both marijuana and tobacco? The latter substance is not even recognized as a drug by the international control system and is totally without regulation in most countries. Yet, it seems fair to say that tobacco smoking may well cause far more organic damage to more human beings than any illicit drug, such as heroin or marijuana. On March 11, 1982, the U.S. Public Health Service flatly declared cigarette smoking to be "clearly the single most preventable cause of premature illness and death in the United

34. Trebach, *Heroin Solution*, pp. 3–6, 291–95.

States," with estimated deaths of over 300,000 annually traceable to this drug.[35]

A modern control scheme might move both tobacco and marijuana into a newly defined middle ground where both would be governed by roughly the same rules. Tobacco would be placed under greater controls, marijuana fewer. These new common rules would include allowing both drugs to be used legally but with restrictions on advertising, distribution, and sale. This policy is more in touch with the real nature of drug taking today than the current system.

A *modern redefinition* might well deal with the meaning of "legitimate medical practice." Of the two major national models of addiction control in the world, that of the United States has had, unfortunately, the greatest impact on establishing the meaning of that phrase. While in this country, addicts are now treated as diseased and thus deserving of medical treatment, the most onerous controls have been placed on American doctors in terms of their dealing with addicts. These controls are particularly harsh in regard to the prescription of addicting drugs in nondiminishing doses over extended periods of time. Indeed, for forty years, from the early twenties to the early sixties, it was absolutely forbidden under pain of criminal prosecution for a doctor to provide any narcotic to an addict except for a brief period to aid detoxification. Since 1974, it has been legal, although haltingly so, for doctors to prescribe oral methadone to narcotic addicts for long-term maintenance. Heroin addicts are not allowed to receive that drug legally from doctors; nor for that matter may codeine addicts receive codeine from their physicians. It is oral methadone or no narcotic. Even so, this system has helped a great many people, which is testimony to the courage and wisdom of some American doctors and other addiction treatment specialists.

While many countries have adopted methadone and other American methods, they and their addicts would do much better by learning from the more reticent British. British physicians have the power to choose from a wide variety of modalities in dealing with their addict-patients. In some cases, as in America, they may choose psychotherapy and oral methadone, and often do. In others, injectable

35. Edward N. Brandt, Jr., "Statement by Edward N. Brandt, Jr., M.D., Assistant Secretary for Health, Before the Subcommittee on Health and the Environment, Committee on Energy and Commerce, March 11, 1982."

methadone; in still others, injectable heroin and cocaine. This holds true in spite of the changes made to British regulations and medical practice since 1968. The original British model could well help a great many nations to a much greater extent than the more rigid and repressive American system.

To those, however, who see the British approach as a total surrender, I hasten to point out why it is a moderate approach, which allows rational adjustments to meet local conditions. The British approach applies only to the opiates and cocaine. It does not apply to a whole host of other drugs, such as marijuana or smoking opium. The British take an American approach to both. Recreational users cannot apply to a doctor for their drugs. Be that as it may, the British have created a humane system that we would do well to emulate.

Such qualities have been found in humane models of drug abuse control and treatment located elsewhere than in Britain—in Shreveport, Louisiana, for example, from 1919 to 1923 in the renowned clinic of Dr. Willis Butler.[36] Still other models of change may be found in even the most unlikely places, if we will but look with open eyes. Before Khalkhali and Khomeini, the law of Iran allowed regular doses of opium to patients designated as addicts by licensed physicians. The law favored older smokers, but younger ones conceivably could have been registered by a physician under provisions of the regulations.[37]

The foregoing are but a few illustrations of the types of moderate reforms that are possible in many countries, aided and encouraged by new international control agreements and by a more flexible international control climate. Each country, moreover, must carefully weigh the consequences of inaction in the face of the current epi-

---

36. Trebach, *Heroin Solution*, pp. 148–67.

37. The full text of Article 4 of the amendment, approved on March 4, 1969, to the Iranian Law on Limited Poppy Cultivation and Export of Opium reads as follows:

For those addicts of opium and its derivatives who may be over 60 years of age, or whose withdrawal from addiction is considered impossible for the time-being because of old age or illness, the procedure shall be as follows:

(a) the attending physician shall issue, in his handwriting and signature, a special certificate according to a pro-forma to be prepared and announced by the Ministry of Health;

(b) after confirmation of the certificate by one of the centres, to be announced by the Ministry of Health, the said centre shall issue a card, bearing the photograph of the addict, for the purchase of his quota, in which shall be set out full details of the addict, the daily dose, the address of the selling centre, and the period of validity of the card, which in any event shall not exceed six months. Note. Any quota card shall be valid only for the selling centre, the address of which shall be mentioned on the card.

demic. For example, unless the United States makes adjustments at home soon, we may have to consider an even greater commitment of naval and air forces to keep drugs from our shores. In that military situation, an American president might someday consider it perfectly logical to order a marine incursion into Colombia. The same might be true of army search-and-destroy missions within this country, say in California where, some authorities claim, the number-one cash crop is now marijuana.

Of course, the demand for heroin has not yet reached that of marijuana, but that demand is escalating and is coming from all segments of American society now. To meet that demand, those in the trade have had to import their product from outside the country, because in the past there have been no domestic crops. But the hardy opium poppy, *Papaver somniferum*, like the virtually indestructible marijuana plant, will grow almost anywhere. Indeed, the poppy once grew all over the United States, and mass cultivation could easily be reintroduced. Under present world conditions, that horticultural event seems foreordained, unless, of course, it has already occurred.

THE UNLEARNED LESSON

The lesson remains unlearned by most policy makers and social leaders around the globe. That is the sad conclusion we must draw as we reflect on the course of events during the few years since an earlier version of this chapter was originally written. Not only are governmental leaders becoming more insistent in their demands for greater force in dealing with drug problems, but traffickers are also commencing to strike back, for the first time in modern history, directly against drug abuse officials.

In March of 1986 the bodies of American DEA Special Agent Enrique Camarino Salazaar and his Mexican pilot, Alfredo Zavalar Avelar, were found near a rural road in Mexico. It appeared probable that the pilot had been buried while still alive. U.S. Ambassador to Mexico John Gavin declared that the murders, apparently by Mexican drug traffickers aided by corrupt police officers, represented "losses in an ongoing war." Defense Minister General Juan Arevalao Gardoqui had already responded to criticism of his country's commitment to the drug war by pointing out that many Mexican drug enforcement agents had been killed recently.[38]

38. *Washington Post*, 27 February 1985, p. A15.

Urgent calls for more military force and other retaliatory actions came from political leaders of both major political parties. Congressman Charles Rangel (D-N.Y.), Chair of the House Select Committee on Narcotics Abuse and Control, declared that the Joint Chiefs of Staff were dragging their feet and preventing a full commitment of the military in the war on drugs. He asked for greater involvement of the armed forces. Senator Dennis DeConcini (D-Ariz.) introduced legislation that would authorize $100 million to create a new air command equipped with advanced radar for easier detection of planes smuggling drugs into the country. Senator Paula Hawkins (R-Fla.), chair of the Senate Subcommittee on Alcoholism and Drug Abuse, demanded that President Reagan enforce the so-called Hawkins Amendment of 1983, a law that empowers the president to suspend foreign aid to those countries that do not cooperate with the United States in the war against drugs. "What will it take for us to uphold the law?" the junior senator from Florida asked. "Another kidnapping? Another death?"[39]

On May 4, 1984, Senator Hawkins had dispatched a highly publicized letter to President Reagan urging him to use "whatever resources necessary including U.S. troops . . . helicopters, flame throwers . . . and firearms" to aid Colombia in its war against drugs. Her letter was sent in the wake of the murder by drug traffickers of Colombia's Minister of Justice, Rodrigo Lara Bonilla.[40] On April 25, 1984, Senator Hawkins had introduced a bill that would have made murder in connection with the drug trade a federal crime carrying the possibility of a death sentence.[41]

A vocal group of leading American officials and drug abuse experts have been calling in recent months for even harsher criminal sanctions, including the death penalty in cases of simple trafficking where no violence was involved. Such a bill was introduced into the House of Representatives in early 1985. Moreover, Congressman Henry Hyde (R-Ill.) called for the firing squad in those cases where narcotics agents were found corruptly involved in trafficking.[42] Commentator Patrick Buchanan, during my appearance on the television show "Crossfire" on the Cable News Network in late November 1984, vehemently disagreed with my arguments for drug law

---

39. *U.S. News and World Report*, 25 March 1985, pp. 16–17.
40. "News From Paula Hawkins, United States Senator," 4 May 1984.
41. Ibid., 25 April 1984.
42. *Washington Post*, 20 March 1985, p. A3.

reform and declared that he much preferred the Singapore method for dealing with drug traffickers, especially those who sold to children. A rope around the neck and spring the trapdoor, that will stop them, Mr. Buchanan stated definitively.[43] Several months later Mr. Buchanan was appointed to the powerful position of director of communications in the Reagan White House.

The experience of Singapore seems to have become a shining example for those who refuse to learn, or are ignorant of, the lesson of Ayatollah Khalkhali. Dr. Gabriel G. Nahas, for example, has for years argued for harsher measures to deal with users and sellers of illicit drugs. Dr. Nahas is a professor of anesthesiology at the College of Physicians and Surgeons of Columbia University and a consultant to the United Nations Commission on Narcotics. In a guest editorial in the *Wall Street Journal* of February 13, 1985, the physician explained what America must do in order to revive the cultural taboos against illicit drug use that ''were shattered 20 years ago by the false prophets and social nihilists of the drug culture.'' Dr. Nahas explained that the United States did not have to go as far as Eastern bloc countries and China, which have succeeded in controlling ''illicit drugs with repressive measures against traffickers and addicts alike.'' Rather, we should follow the advice of the World Health Organization and ''suppress the drugs as much as possible, as if they were infectious agents, and . . . rehabilitate addicts through quarantine until they are able to lead drug-free lives.''

The medical school professor stated that a number of Asian countries had succeeded in controlling illicit drug use through these methods, especially Singapore. Dr. Nahas described the situation in positive, even glowing, terms. The number of traffickers hanged increased from five, several years ago, to fifteen. Over 2,000 people suspected of being traffickers had been arrested in recent years, and many were retained in preventive detention, without benefit of trial. Thousands of suspected users were arrested, given a urine test, and committed for forcible treatment in drug rehabilitation centers—again all without the messy formality of a trial. The jewel in the crown of this argument was that the number of addicts had allegedly dropped from 13,000 in 1977 to 6,000 in 1983.

If this reduction in the number of addicts did actually take place, and if it was achieved even partly because of these harsh govern-

43. ''Crossfire'' television program, Cable News Network, 26 November 1984.

mental measures, the experience of Singapore might represent an important exception to the lesson being expounded here. However, caution must be used in accepting claims of such success in the face of simple common sense. What happened to the other 7,000 addicts? Did they simply stop taking drugs as a result of fear of death or as a result of treatment? Did they leave the country? Such questions are difficult to answer since drug users live in a world hidden from the view of most governmental officials. A reduction of such magnitude in a few years is, however, highly unlikely. In time we may learn, as more evidence becomes available, that the reductions were not real. We know already that Dr. Nahas's claims about the success of the Eastern bloc countries are not true, at least about Poland, which has recently admitted to a significant increase in heroin use. Perhaps the most important question is, Why would any citizen educated in the traditions of democracy knowingly support such harsh programs that so curtailed the rights of all its people, including those who allegedly used and sold drugs? Yet large numbers of our fellow citizens do exactly that.

Among advocates of these harsh measures are people holding influential government and academic positions, including Mr. Buchanan and Dr. Nahas. They say they are quite prepared to trade American freedoms, hewn out of centuries of hard battle with sometimes well-intentioned zealots, in order to win total victory over the drug menace. Even if the success of Singapore were real, which is doubtful, the lessons of other countries make it more likely that in the long run repressive measures to control drug use will produce a loss of freedom for all of the nation's people, not simply those in the drug scene; violent reactions from drug users and traffickers; and no reliable evidence of a significant drop in drug use.

That seems to be the case now in Iran. In a statement made at a recent United Nations meeting on narcotic drugs, the Islamic Republic of Iran explained the "strict and decisive campaign since the revolution in 1979. . . . Many major international traffickers had been convicted and sentenced to capital punishment by Islamic Revolutionary Courts. This, however, had not stopped the traffic which entered . . . Iran almost exclusively across the country's eastern frontiers. A total of 84 Iranian drug law enforcement officers had been killed in this area during [the first six months of 1984]. The brutality of the organized and heavily armed trafficking gangs was shown by the fact that those members of the drug law enforcement agencies who were captured or wounded had their faces burned and disfigured by the traffickers, either before or after death." At this meeting, the representative of the Islamic Republic of Iran circulated a number of photographs of the bodies of police officers who had been so brutally disfigured.[44]

It is distressing that influential opinion leaders in one of the countries that lies on those eastern frontiers read the lessons of Iran and of the United States so differently from their presentation here. The chairman of the Pakistan Narcotics Control Board stated in early 1985 that heroin use was first observed in the country during 1980, and by the end of 1984 heroin abuse had spread to all major cities. The board estimated a total of 270,000 heroin addicts, all of whom had appeared in this short time. There were another million addicts of other drugs. In a long editorial of January 23, 1985, the Karachi *Morning News* observed that even in the United States with all its vast resources, almost every strategy to control drug use has failed. The reason for this failure, the Pakistani editors declared, "is because the U.S. laws are rather 'soft' for dealing with criminals engaged in the dope traffic. And so are the laws of Pakistan dealing with this crime."

And what about the success of Iran in dealing with this mysterious and stubborn problem? Remarkably, in light of published official reports on the drug traffic across the common border, the editorial declared, "In Iran which has enforced the death penalty for drug traffickers, these criminals are fighting a losing battle. A large number of them have already been hanged in that country." Accordingly, the logical next step in this typically illogical chain of reasoning was to call for the extreme criminal sanction, which did not really work in the neighboring country, to be applied at home. The *Morning News* recommended strongly that "Pakistan must enforce the death penalty for all criminals engaged at any stage of the heroin trade, from production and distribution to smuggling and retail trade on the streets. Because in the light of past experience it is obvious that physical destruction of the heroin dealers is the only appropriate

44. The United Nations Commission on Narcotic Drugs, "Situation and Trends in Drug Abuse and the Illicit Traffic, Including Reports of Subsidiary Bodies Concerned With the Illicit Traffic in Drugs. Subcommission on Illicit Drug Traffic and Related Matters in the Near and Middle East," Report on the Eighteenth Session, 1–3 October 1984 (Vienna: United Nations, 1985), pp. 4–5. (Mimeographed.)

measure that would discourage these fiends out to destroy the whole future of the nation.''

Thus, the irrational refrain continues. Trafficking in and consumption of addicting drugs persist in the face of criminal laws, armed force, and the death penalty. The entire structure of international drug control moves more and more toward complete collapse. The necessary compromises and adjustments are not being made because so many powerful officials view those humane innovations as surrender. When humane instincts are driven from the arena of an emotional conflict, the executioners among us reign supreme. Enlightened progress then becomes impossible.

By the summer of 1986, the drug-war situation became even more threatening. Leading officials sought to convince the public of their devotion to uncompromising measures to control the drug menace—and that they were tougher in this regard than their political competitors. In the process, they took measures that, in earlier sections of this chapter, I have suggested as absurd examples of what might happen if the war logic were pushed to foolish extremes. One such example was the idea of sending American troops into South America. In July Army troops were actually dispatched to the cocaine fields of Bolivia. At the same time it was revealed that troops had previously been sent on secret missions of a similar nature to Colombia.

Then the president and leading White House officials volunteered to take urine tests for drugs—to set an example for the nation. Soon, candidates for election in the fall campaign were volunteering themselves for urine tests and daring their opponents to provide a jar themselves. It if were not so tragic it might have been good comic opera.

Also tragic was an action taken by 13-year-old Deanna Young of Los Angeles in August. For the first time in recent history, to my knowledge, a child turned her parents in to the police for using drugs. Deanna took drugs and paraphernalia from her home to the local police station after hearing an antidrug lecture by a deputy sheriff at a church meeting. Joyce Nalepka, leader of the White House-endorsed National Federation of Parents for Drug-Free Youth, declared, ''This child did exactly the right thing.'' Within a few weeks three other children around the country had imitated Deanna and done that right thing.

By September, the frenzy hit Congress with full force as the fall elections loomed in the face of rising public fears about drugs. Several billions of dollars were pledged by the legislators to support an irrational series of measures that increased criminal penalties and invaded freedoms. It was proposed again to apply the death penalty to murders committed in the drug trade; only this time the measure seemed close to passage. Also thrown in the legislative hopper were provisions for restricting the exclusionary rule on evidence in drug cases. The use of the military in an increased drug-war role was a central part of this congressional steamroller.

All of this took place in disregard of the data coming out of NIDA which seemed to indicate that the drug epidemic in America had leveled off by the mid-80s. While this plateau may only have been temporary, the data showed either decreases or only slight rises in recorded drug use for a period of several years. This flattening of data applied to cocaine, even its recent new form prepared for smoking, known as "crack." When the media was reporting an epidemic of crack abuse in 1986, there was little official data to support the cries of disaster. But the cries from the media continued and had an impact on the government.

Even though the epidemic seemed to have abated, the demand for illicit drugs remained strong and continued to produce a market measured in the multiple billions of dollars. As a result of all the contradictory pressures, another unthinkable event began unfolding: mass production of opium poppies on American soil. Huge fields have been discovered by lawmen in remote areas of the country.

In Britain, the model system of addiction treatment began to get tougher in the face of American pressure and rising crime. The core of the relatively gentle system seemed still intact, but there was cause to worry among those who were accustomed to using the British approach as a lodestar for humane and effective treatment policies.

The only silver lining in this dark cloud is that a small group of drug-law reformers has been gaining strength in the United States and in other countries recently. If they can achieve some political stature as a centrist and moderate force, then rational reform is possible. If enough good people from all segments of the political spectrum—but especially from the dominant middle—come forward soon enough, the disastrous consequences of our current war against drugs can be averted and the war itself ended.

4

DRUGS AND UNITED STATES FOREIGN POLICY

Jonathan Marshall

Like ordinary consumers of ketchup or toothpaste, millions of Americans smoke marijuana, snort cocaine, or shoot up heroin without considering the long chain of manufacturers and middlemen who bring to their communities the quality products they demand. The supply lines are tortuous, threading from foreign fields, across seas, and through fissures in the wall of domestic law enforcement. But the drugs do get through, despite the herculean efforts of the police, courts, and prisons to deter the traffic in mood-altering chemicals.

Supply-side drug enforcement has failed. Tens of thousands of federal, state, and local police have been trying to block a deluge with a drain stopper. The General Accounting Office estimates that authorities intercept no more than 10 percent of drugs smuggled across U.S. borders.[1] This country is simply awash in substances to inject, swallow, snort, or smoke.

---

1. *New York Times,* 9 September 1984. For other representative evidence of the failure of enforcement, see *San Francisco Chronicle,* 29 May 1984; Associated Press, 28 September 1983; Mathea Falco, "The Big Business of Illicit Drugs," *New York Times Magazine,* 11 December 1983, pp. 108–12.

Narcotics officials know their only possible hope lies in stopping the flow at its origin abroad, where supplies are still concentrated in a few hands. As Jim Smith, Florida's attorney general, told a congressional committee, "I don't believe traditional law enforcement can ever effectively deal with the problem. . . . Enough people are involved in it that unless we get to the point we have a military standing shoulder to shoulder around our coastline, I don't think we will get it done with traditional law enforcement methods. We have to get to the source countries to do it."[2]

International cooperation has been a concern of U.S. narcotics enforcement ever since Congress passed the Harrison Act outlawing narcotics in 1914. But the challenge is awesome: In just three years, despite drug control agreements with such major supplier nations as Bolivia, Colombia, Pakistan, and Peru, worldwide production of opium poppies has increased by more than 50 percent, coca by 40 percent, and marijuana by 20 percent.[3]

Almost invariably federal officials adopt military metaphors to describe their ceaseless efforts to combat this international trade. Yet just as war is the continuation of politics by other means, so the "war on drugs" has become an extension of foreign policy by other means. Drug control has become "a new and subtle form of U.S. intervention abroad," observed the president of Colombia's National Association of Financial Institutions.[4] The ideology of drug control has become a front, and the apparatus of enforcement a tool, for counterinsurgency, Cold War propaganda wars, and covert action campaigns in the Third World.

GOING TO THE SOURCE

As in most other markets, world supply-and-demand patterns for drugs have traditionally been led by the West—from Britain's promotion of the opium trade in China to more recent pressures from the United States and European consuming nations through the League of Nations and United Nations to ban drug production for any but limited medicinal purposes. Today the Western taboo against

2. U.S. Congress, House, Select Committee on Narcotics Abuse and Control (hereafter HSCNAC), hearings, *Financial Investigation of Drug Trafficking* (Washington, D.C.: Government Printing Office, 1981), p. 28.

3. *New York Times,* 15 September 1984.

4. *High Times,* January 1979, p. 27.

drugs other than alcohol and tobacco has become the standard by which nearly all countries measure their own legal codes.

That fact underpins the central pretense of international narcotics control: that in assisting foreign governments to carry out their formal law enforcement missions, the United States can win victories in its own battle against drugs.

The reality is all too different. The very governments and foreign police agencies Washington supports more often than not shield the big-time drug producers and smugglers—if they don't monopolize the traffic themselves. As exposure of the "French Connection" showed, the profits of the drug trade attract and corrupt intelligence and police officials even in nations with strong traditions of professionalism.

Drug-related corruption often follows a progression as it becomes entrenched. Over time police realize that taking bribes offers fewer rewards than dealing the drugs themselves—while using drug laws as a pretext to eliminate their independent competitors. In extreme cases, drug profits may strengthen police or military elites vis-à-vis other government institutions to the point where they seize state power, as the Bolivian military did in the 1980 "cocaine coup."

In the Third World particularly, where government institutions have short histories and questionable legitimacy, officials charged with national security may rationalize their takeover of lucrative drug rackets as preempting independent, antistate syndicates.

Failure to contain the traffickers, with the power they draw from unlimited finances, can lead to internal chaos, civil war, or warlordism—as the current plight of Bolivia, Colombia, and Burma attests. As the United Nations International Narcotics Control Board noted in its 1984 annual report, "Illegal drug production and trafficking financed by organized crime is so pervasive that the economies of entire countries are disrupted, legal institutions menaced and the very security of some states threatened."[5] If even Italy had to send an antiterrorist commander (Gen. Carlo Alberto Dalla Chiesa) to combat secessionist pressures from Mafia strongholds in Sicily, the threat to newer regimes should be clear.

In such countries suppression works no better than in the United States. Antidrug campaigns guarantee instability, not security. Government elites find state control of the drug traffic a more attractive

5. *San Jose Mercury,* 17 January 1985.

solution than continual war against it. Using drug laws and armed force as weapons against independent competitors, governments can create de facto drug monopolies that enhance their larger ambition to consolidate power within the national territory.

That was precisely the tactic of Chiang Kai-shek in his campaign to unify Nationalist China under his party, the Kuomintang (KMT). By seizing opium fields and drug marketing channels in the name of opium "suppression," he strengthened his own position at the expense of independent warlords whose finances depended on skimming drug profits.[6]

Similar symptoms can be found in every country where drugs are produced or transshipped in quantity. In country after country, official corruption makes a mockery both of local laws and international narcotics enforcement.

Bolivia

Suffering from disastrous political instability, rampant inflation, and a staggering foreign debt, Bolivia survives only by the grace of cocaine. Coca leaf production, a staggering 55,000 metric tons annually, accounted for fully 21 percent of gross domestic product in 1981.[7]

Official complicity in the traffic was cemented during the reign of Gen. Hugo Banzer from 1971 to 1978. Banzer seized power with the help of a countryman arrested a decade later in Florida for smuggling 530 kilos of cocaine. Among Banzer's relatives implicated in the drug trade were a brother, a stepbrother, a son-in-law, and a nephew. One of his ranches housed a plant for processing coca paste into cocaine.[8] Ironically, in 1976 Secretary of State Henry Kissinger offered Banzer millions of dollars to train Bolivia's narcotics police and fund coca eradication programs.[9]

After a brief democratic interlude, Bolivia's military once again

6. Jonathan Marshall, "Opium and the Politics of Gangsterism in Nationalist China, 1927–1945," *Bulletin of Concerned Asian Scholars* 8 (July–September 1976): 19–48.

7. HSCNAC, report, *International Narcotics Control Study Missions to Latin America and Jamaica* (Washington, D.C.: Government Printing Office, 1984), p. 51; U.S. Congress, Senate Committee on Government Operations, Permanent Subcommittee on Investigations (hereafter SPSI), hearings, *International Narcotics Trafficking* (Washington, D.C.: Government Printing Office, 1981), p. 195.

8. *New York Times,* 31 August 1981; *Le Monde,* 2 October 1980.

9. *New York Times,* 14 February 1979; HSCNAC, report, *International Narcotics Control Study Missions to Latin America and Jamaica,* note 7 above, p. 49.

seized power, but not before top officers sat down with six of the country's leading traffickers in June 1980 to negotiate protection payments. Gen. Luis García Meza came away $1 million richer. His coup a month later brought to power a small army of uniformed drug profiteers. The Carter administration withdrew its ambassador to protest the regime's human rights abuses and drug record.[10]

Now liberated from the grip of its brutal cocaine colonels and generals, Bolivia has yet to make any progress toward suppression of the traffic. If anything, production has grown. The military remains as corrupt as ever, and the traffickers have retreated into virtually impregnable fiefdoms where government police dare not enter. A congressional study concluded in 1985 that "not one hectare of coca leaf has been eradicated since the United States established the narcotics assistance program in 1971."[11]

Colombia

Drugs are hardly less important to Colombia's economy, where they approach even coffee as earners of foreign exchange. Flamboyant drug kings have purchased soccer teams, opened zoos to the public, and financed city slum rehabilitation schemes. They also spend $115 million a year to buy public officials, according to Colombia's National Association of Financial Institutions.[12]

Under heavy pressure from Washington, successive Colombian governments have granted extraordinary powers to police and military to wage the drug war. In 1978 a presidential decree granted those authorities a virtual license to kill in the line of duty. "The new law makes us appear to want to stop smuggling," observed one Colombian judicial official. "But it also places more power in the hands of those already receiving huge payoffs to permit marijuana and cocaine to leave the country. Either those dealing in these products pay off or they are killed."[13]

Colombian police are indeed extraordinarily corrupt. The Depar-

10. *Sunday Times* (London), 10 August 1980; *New York Times,* 3 August 1981; *St. Louis Post-Dispatch,* 27 May 1984.

11. Report of a Staff Study Mission . . . to the Committee on Foreign Affairs, House of Representatives, *U.S. Narcotics Control Programs Overseas: An Assessment,* 22 February 1985, p. 17; *High Times,* May 1984, p. 19; *New York Times,* 21 July 1984; *San Francisco Examiner,* 26 August 1984.

12. *New York Times,* 11 September 1984; Penny Lernoux, "Corrupting Colombia," *Inquiry,* 30 September 1979, p. 15.

13. *High Times,* July 1978.

tamento Administrativo Seguridad, a sort of militarized FBI, was particularly notorious under the leadership of Gen. Jorge Ordoñez Valderrama. His ruthless subordinates robbed independent cocaine dealers, then resold their stashes. Three provincial DAS chiefs were arrested on drug charges before Ordoñez Valderrama himself was finally jailed for embezzlement.[14]

Other units also had their hands in the trade. Greedy customs agents even did battle with DAS forces for control of a major drug shipment.[15] And in 1976 the entire top command of the national police narcotics unit was implicated in drug crimes by a former agent.[16]

Again at Washington's instigation, Colombia sent its military to combat drug traffickers in the remote Guajira Peninsula in late 1978. But smugglers had corrupted the defense ministry, which prevented honest police actions against known traffickers.[17] Noted one U.S. congressional delegation, "The Guajira campaign appears to have been a great deterrent to the small unorganized trafficker; however, there is still a significant amount of marijuana available for the major trafficking networks."[18]

The murder of the country's attorney general in May 1984 aroused a national furor. Political leaders vowed to punish the drug mafia. Many bosses were indeed driven underground, but few drug caches were seized. All of which led one cynical newspaper to discover a new disease, "mafia blindness," that had infected police investigating teams.[19]

Mexico

Mexico accounts for about two-fifths of all heroin consumed in the United States, is the number one exporter of controlled barbiturates and amphetamines, and transships a quarter of all cocaine crossing

14. Antonil, *Mama Coca* (London: Hassle Free Press, 1978), pp. 79–81; *Latin America Political Report,* 5 May 1978.

15. Antonil, *Mama Coca,* p. 81.

16. Ibid., p. 80; *NACLA Report,* May–June 1983, p. 20.

17. *NACLA Report,* May–June 1983, p. 20; Penny Lernoux, "Corrupting Colombia," p. 16.

18. HSCNAC, report, *Oversight on Federal Drug Strategy—1979* (Washington, D.C.: Government Printing Office, 1980), p. 5.

19. *Latin America Weekly Report,* 20 July 1984.

U.S. borders. In late 1984, police discovered one 10,000-ton marijuana cache, enough to satisfy the entire U.S. market for a year.[20]

Corruption indisputably explains the persistent inability of Mexican law enforcement officials to catch the culprits. "Mexico hasn't arrested a major drug trafficker in eight years," former DEA Administrator Francis Mullen, Jr., charged after authorities failed to make any progress in solving the kidnap-murder of a U.S. narcotics agent in early 1985. "They let the suspects get away. Then they start the raids."[21]

One of President Miguel de la Madrid's first official acts was to fire Mexico City's chief of police, Arturo Durazo-Moreno, who had amassed a fortune estimated at several hundred million dollars. U.S. and Mexican intelligence files reportedly named him as a protector of the illegal heroin trade, as well as a brutal murderer of rival traffickers.[22]

In 1985, admitting to "criminal links between narcotics traffickers and police agents," the government of de la Madrid fired hundreds of agents from the Federal Judicial Police and Directorate of Federal Security. Members of both organizations, along with police units from several states, had acted as virtual bodyguards for some of Mexico's top drug criminals.[23]

But the most notorious traffickers and their agents continue to receive favored treatment despite these purges.[24] One U.S. intelligence assessment concluded in 1979 that corruption so permeated the government that "any wholesale housecleaning would cause cracks in the power structure."[25] That judgment still holds.

Peru

Responsible for producing about half the cocaine shipped to the United States, Peru almost ranks with Bolivia in the extent of drug-related corruption. The military has had its hand in the cocaine trade

20. *Los Angeles Times,* 13 February 1985; *San Jose Mercury,* 15 February 1985; *New York Times,* 23 November 1984; *Washington Post,* 12 May 1985.

21. *Oakland Tribune,* 26 February 1985. Cf. Report of a Staff Study Mission . . . to the Committee on Foreign Affairs, House of Representatives, *U.S. Narcotics Control Programs Overseas: An Assessment,* 22 February 1985.

22. *Chicago Tribune,* 1 April 1984; *Latin America Weekly Report,* 3 February 1984.

23. *New York Times,* 16 March 1985, 21 April 1985, 30 April 1985; *San Francisco Chronicle,* 17 May 1985; *Los Angeles Times,* 19 March 1985; *Washington Post,* 17 February 1980.

24. *San Francisco Chronicle,* 1 December 1985.

25. *Washington Post,* 24 July 1979.

ever since 1949, when the government established a state coca monopoly and set aside all profits for the construction of military
barracks.[26]

Peru's urban police force, PIP, has had more than its share of
drug scandals. In 1971 the acting chief of its narcotics division was
exposed as head of the leading drug ring.[27] Two PIP directors in a
row were forced out of office under a cloud in the late 1960s and
early 1970s.[28] In 1981, an entire PIP squad was accused of stealing
cocaine from dealers for its own profit.[29]

In 1982 a former Peruvian air force general was sentenced to fifteen years in prison after being caught with 5 kilos of cocaine on his
way to Miami.[30] The same year the war minister accused two former
ministers of interior with conspiring to undertake a major cocaine
deal.[31]

In 1985, a series of drug scandals prompted President Alan García
to dismiss at least 100 air force personnel, more than 200 top officers
from Peru's three national police forces, and well over 1,000 policemen. Several hundred judges also came under investigation for suspected corruption.[32]

Lebanon

Hashish and opium are the chief currency and financial prop of the
various competing political factions and warlord families in Lebanon. Hashish is grown in Syrian-controlled Moslem regions, shipped
through a Christian Phalangist town, on to territory controlled by
the Franjieh family (Christian but pro-Syrian), and finally out via
the Syrian-controlled port of Tripoli.[33]

The Phalangist Gemayel family—which supplied Lebanon's current president and dominates the national army—is deeply implicated in the trade. "We had hard evidence that (the hashish trade)
was tied into the Christian Front and the Gemayel family is a major

26. Antonil, *Mama Coca*, p. 96.
27. *Latin America*, 10 September 1971.
28. Ibid.
29. *Latin America Weekly Report*, 16 October 1981.
30. *Boston Globe*, 24 January 1982.
31. *Latin America Weekly Report*, 5 March 1982.
32. *Newsweek*, 25 February 1985; *Oakland Tribune*, 2 June 1985; *Los Angeles Times*, 1
December 1985.
33. Jonathan Randal, *Going All the Way* (New York: Viking Press, 1983), pp. 136–37.

part of the front," said former Congressman Lester Wolff (D-N.Y.), who chaired the House Select Committee on Narcotics Abuse and Control.[34]

And like all other contestants for power, Palestine Liberation Organization forces apparently have not abstained from raising money through the drug trade.[35]

Thailand

Though not itself a major heroin producer, Thailand is the primary outlet for heroin produced by border laboratories inside Burma. The drugs are handled by ethnic Chinese syndicates in Bangkok. Thai law enforcement officers have never seriously cracked down on them, perhaps because as much as 50 percent of the economy is dependent on drug money, according to one informed estimate.[36]

Congressman Lester Wolff reported in 1977 that one of Bangkok's top drug wholesalers had "a knack for making friends in Thai government circles. He has close connections with the Thai army and the Thai police as well as officials of the former government."[37]

Corruption and politics have also kept the government from touching drug traffickers in the remote hill country of the opium-rich "Golden Triangle." There, remnants of the KMT armies forced out of China in 1949 settled and made a livelihood out of smuggling. In return for Bangkok's sanction, they provided intelligence and even counterinsurgency assistance against leftist revolutionaries in the region.

As a result, noted one congressional report, "Thai police are permitted to mount operations against minor smugglers [but] not al-

34. *San Jose News,* 18 May 1983.

35. *Baltimore Sun,* 10 July 1982; U.S. Senate Judiciary Committee, Subcommittee on Internal Security, hearings, *World Drug Traffic and Its Impact on U.S. Security* (Washington, D.C.: Government Printing Office, 1972), part 4, pp. 138, 187–88. PLO: "The PLO, in part, finances its activities from drug trafficking. That organization has been involved to some degree in drug trafficking, but so have other terrorist or insurgent groups in Lebanon." Statement of Francis Mullen, Director of DEA, Senate Committee on Labor and Human Resources, Subcommittee on Alcoholism and Drug Abuse, hearing, *Drugs and Terrorism, 1984* (Washington, D.C.: Government Printing Office, 1984), p. 53.

36. Eleanore Hill, staff report in SPSI, hearings, *International Narcotics Trafficking* (Washington, D.C.: Government Printing Office, 1981), p. 441.

37. HSCNAC, report, *Study Mission on International Controls of Narcotics Trafficking and Production, January 2–22, 1978* (Washington, D.C.: Government Printing Office, 1978), pp. 36–37.

lowed to interfere at the higher levels of opium politics which provide
the armies with their financial support. The result is a charade for
international consumption in which roughly 3 percent of the narcotics are seized and several score of traffickers arrested yearly, while
the principal organizations of the trade continue unimpeded."[38]

DRUG ENFORCEMENT AS COUNTERINSURGENCY

In spite of this appalling record of official corruption and hypocrisy,
the United States only rarely challenges the governments responsible
for the international drug trade. Higher interests of state take precedence. In particular, narcotics enforcement has always taken second
place to communist containment as an objective of U.S. foreign policy. As one DEA official remarked when challenged about the Jamaican government's open toleration of the marijuana trade, "The
issue is, should we press them to do things which could result in the
election and installation of a leftist government, as they've had in
the previous administration. Drugs are a serious problem. But Communism is a greater problem."[39]

By turning a blind eye to the real drug situation abroad, the United
States often extends assistance to the very forces most implicated in
the traffic, helping them indeed to snuff out their competition and
reinforce their criminal monopoly. Perhaps the earliest and most blatant example was the Federal Bureau of Narcotics' World War II
training program for the Chinese secret police under Gen. Tai Li—
who had ganged up with the head of the Shanghai underworld to
run the largest opiate trafficking syndicate in the world.[40]

Police aid may have another consequence: strengthening the forces
of order—or repression—vis-à-vis dissident groups and other government bureaucracies, sometimes to the point of promoting a country's transition to a police state.

Such outcomes may be the inadvertent results of a misapplied drug
strategy. Sometimes, however, U.S. drug enforcement programs have
been used as a conscious tool of Cold War foreign policy, both as a

38. HSCNAC, report, *Opium Production, Narcotics Financing and Trafficking in Southeast Asia* (Washington, D.C.: Government Printing Office, 1977), p. 39.
39. *New York Times*, 10 September 1984. For more on Jamaican corruption, see Report
of a Staff Study Mission . . . to the Committee on Foreign Affairs, House of Representatives,
U.S. Narcotics Control Programs Overseas: An Assessment, 22 February 1985, p. 28.
40. *New York Times*, 14 September 1945.

pretext for bypassing congressional restrictions on foreign police assistance and (in collusion with local security forces) as a pointed counterinsurgency weapon justified by accusing local insurgents of smuggling narcotics.

U.S. programs to train and equip foreign police, established in the Eisenhower administration, were greatly extended when President Kennedy established the Office of Public Safety (OPS) in 1962. OPS encouraged foreign police to expand beyond their traditional role to embrace paramilitary, counterinsurgency, and sophisticated intelligence functions. This police push was a Camelot experiment in containing domestic unrest before it reached the stage of guerrilla warfare. Washington also hoped to guide "nation-building" in the Third World by exposing influential foreign security elites to American personnel, methods, and institutions.[41]

As Attorney General Robert Kennedy told the first graduating class of the Washington, D.C.–based International Police Academy in 1964, "These are critical days for law enforcement. . . . In the world today, most wars are 'police actions.' Law enforcement officials are a very real first line of defense, and the fate of governments and nations hangs in the balance."[42]

Up through 1974, when Congress disbanded the OPS, the International Police Academy trained more than 7,500 officers from seventy-seven countries. Its courses ranged from crowd control to coping "with high level violence brought about by externally supported subversion, guerrilla activities in rural areas, and warfare." More than a million more policemen were trained abroad.[43]

Proud OPS officials boasted that as of 1972 they had trained the heads of thirteen foreign police forces, taught police from Nicaragua to Uruguay to "identify and apprehend urban terrorists," and boosted the size of the paramilitary Thai Border Patrol Police by 50 percent.[44]

But legislators saw matters differently. Horror stories of the OPS-

41. A. J. Langguth, *Hidden Terrors* (New York: Pantheon, 1978), pp. 48ff.

42. *Brazilian Information Bulletin,* no. 1, p. 9.

43. Testimony of Byron Engle, OPS director, in U.S. Congress, House Committee on Appropriations, Subcommittee on Foreign Operations and Related Agencies, hearings, *Foreign Assistance and Related Agencies, Appropriations for 1973* (Washington, D.C.: Government Printing Office, 1974), p. 791; Michael Klare and Cynthia Arnson, *Supplying Repression* (Washington, D.C.: Institute for Policy Studies, 1981), p. 23.

44. Engle testimony, note 43 above, pp. 792–95, 814–17.

backed Phoenix assassination program and prison "tiger cages" in South Vietnam and of ubiquitous torture committed by military regimes in South America prompted Congress in 1974 to prohibit foreign police assistance—except for combating the drug traffic. A small enough loophole, that might have seemed. But it proved large enough to drive much of the old OPS program through.

OPS had long had responsibility for specialized narcotics enforcement training and support, though such activities had previously been a small part of its mission. Taking up the slack after 1973 was the State Department's International Narcotics Control program.

INC has supplied foreign governments with all manner of aid, including shotguns, submachine guns, jeeps, night vision devices, helicopters, and communications equipment. Much of it has gone to notorious dictatorships in such countries as Bolivia, Paraguay, Chile, and Argentina—the very countries whose abuses had moved Congress to limit police aid in the first place.

In 1975 the Senate Appropriations Committee complained that "it is not the purpose of the narcotics program to give the participating government access to a continuous supply of free police equipment, much of which is possibly being used for purposes unrelated to control of drug traffic."[45]

A General Accounting Office study the next year confirmed the committee's worst fears, citing "circumstances that we believe are contrary to the intent of the prohibitions limiting assistance to foreign police." These included a sixfold increase in INC commodity assistance from fiscal year 1973 to fiscal year 1974, and the fact that "commodities previously furnished to police units under the public safety program are now being provided to the same units under the narcotics program"—amounting to a blatant end run around Congress.[46]

Along with the equipment came advisers. The GAO pointed out that "overseas narcotics advisers perform essentially the same functions that public safety advisers used to perform." Nothing had changed; as of 1978, former OPS officials staffed all INC posts in Latin America.[47]

---

45. U.S. Congress, Senate report 94–39, 94th Congress, 1st Session (Washington, D.C.: Government Printing Office, 1975), p. 88.

46. U.S. General Accounting Office, *Stopping U.S. Assistance to Foreign Police and Prisons,* 19 February 1976, pp. 22–23.

47. Klare and Arnson, *Supplying Repression,* p. 29.

Narcotics training programs filled the gap left by the demise of the International Police Academy. INC funded the training of 11,763 foreign police between 1973 and 1976 alone.[48] Courses continued to emphasize such topics as intelligence, surveillance, and interrogation; many graduates of the DEA's Advanced International School applied their new expertise in lines of police work other than drug control.[49]

U.S. policy makers are chiefly interested in the ancillary benefits of such programs. Besides "exposing . . . key visitors to United States agencies and procedures," said one State Department officer in 1981, they develop "personal ties of communication and cooperation between United States and foreign government officials."[50]

Narcotics training also serves key intelligence objectives, the DEA says, by creating a "brotherhood of foreign police officers who cooperate with each other in conducting investigations and exchange information regularly"—an unexceptional goal in theory, but chilling in the context of Third World realities.[51]

As Amnesty International and other human rights groups have documented, torture remains a regular, institutionalized practice in close to a hundred countries throughout the world. The United States may not approve such practices, but the police it trains and the equipment it supplies under the narcotics program are often essential tools of police repression against dissident students, labor leaders, and politicians. In Bolivia, a U.S.-trained drug enforcement unit, the Leopards, even staged an abortive coup in June 1984 against the democratic regime of Siles Zuazo.[52]

In short, under the guise of drug enforcement, the United States continues to advance the original missions of police assistance: counterinsurgency, countersubversion, and indirect political control.

Argentina

A classic case of narcotics assistance serving repressive political ends rather than its stated purpose occurred during the mid-1970s in Ar-

---

48. Argentine Commission for Human Rights, Washington, D.C. Information Bureau, memorandum, "US Narcotics Enforcement Assistance to Latin America," 10 March 1977.

49. Klare and Arnson, *Supplying Repression,* pp. 33–37.

50. Statement of Joseph Linnemann, acting assistant secretary of state for international narcotics matters, in SPSI hearings, *International Narcotics Trafficking,* p. 559.

51. Statement of DEA Administrator Peter Bensinger before HSCNAC, 13 July 1977, DEA print.

52. *New York Times,* 2 July 1984.

gentina. There the INC commodity budget zoomed from $3,000 in FY 1973 to $347,000 in FY 1974, filling the vacuum left by the phasing out of OPS. The jump coincided with the October 1973 return from exile of Juan Perón, who brought with him a former policeman and Rasputin-like confidant, José Lopez Rega, to supervise the police from his new post as minister of social welfare.

In March 1974 the State Department requested $200,000 for FY 1975 narcotics assistance and announced that $295,000 still clogged in the pipeline from past years would be spent in the next eighteen months for vehicles, aircraft, communications, and photographic equipment.

Two months later, Lopez Rega appeared in a nationally televised press conference with the U.S. ambassador to announce, "We hope to wipe out the drug traffic in Argentina. We have caught guerrillas after attacks who were high on drugs. Guerrillas are the main users of drugs in Argentina. Therefore the antidrug campaign will automatically be an antiguerrilla campaign as well."[53]

That neat formula would become a standard operating procedure of foreign leaders: Implicate the enemy in drug crimes, then collect U.S. police aid without any unpleasant questions from Washington.

The consequences in Argentina weren't long in coming. In May 1974, one month after Lopez Rega took delivery of automatic weapons and other equipment under INC, the Argentine Anticommunist Alliance, a shadowy death squad formed under his direction, began its campaign of assassination with the murder of a leftist priest.[54] Composed in part of off-duty police, the AAA likely benefited from training, communications, and transportation equipment provided by the U.S. taxpayer.

Lopez Rega fled the country in the fall of 1975 after Argentina's Congress pinned dozens of political murders on him. Soon military intelligence sources were leaking the facts about Lopez Rega's own responsibility for the drug traffic: Cocaine, it seemed, had been a main underpinning of his secret empire. Lopez Rega was reportedly tied in with notorious smugglers high in the Paraguayan regime.[55]

The military coup of March 1976 strengthened the hand of se-

53. Argentine Commission for Human Rights, "U.S. Narcotics Enforcement Assistance to Latin America"; *Sevendays,* 19 April 1976, p. 16.

54. *Latin America Political Report,* 18 May 1979.

55. *Latin America,* December 19, 1975.

curity forces that already had their hands deep into the drug traffic. Lopez Rega's charge of guerrilla involvement in drug smuggling still proved opportune. In February 1977 the junta's foreign minister declared war against subversion: "We attack its body through the war against guerrillas, and its spirit through the war against the drug traffic, both carriers of nihilistic and collectivist ideas."[56]

Colombia

U.S. drug enforcement functionaries spearheaded a drive to turn Colombia into an armed camp. Following a helicopter tour of the Guajira Peninsula in 1978, DEA Administrator Peter Bensinger urged the military to occupy the region, citing the marijuana industry as a "national security" threat to the nation. His words caused a storm of protest. DAS chief Dr. Guillermo León Linares called them an "imprudent interference in the affairs of this country which we should reject. Neither he nor any other foreign official should tell us, the Colombian government, what to do—and much less what our armed forces should do."[57]

Nonetheless President Julio Turbay Ayala placed the entire peninsula under martial law—possibly to protect his political flanks against reports leaked from Washington that had implicated him in the drug traffic. With $2.4 million in special U.S. funding, 6,500 soldiers swept through the wild area in Operación Fulminente, to little practical effect against the big traffickers.[58]

The government empowered the military under a special security statute that also gave it special authority against kidnappers and instigators of illegal strikes and other "social crimes." Some Supreme Court justices called the new regime a "constitutional dictatorship."[59] Most of the arrestees were held on subversion charges, not for drug crimes. Critics charged that military investigators relied extensively on torture.[60]

Happy with the military's vigor, Washington proposed extending martial law to the entire country under the rubric of narcotics en-

56. Antonil, *Mama Coca,* p. 106.
57. *High Times,* December 1978, p. 35.
58. *Washington Post,* 20 June 1979.
59. Penny Lernoux, "Corrupting Colombia," p. 16; *NACLA Report,* May–June 1983, p. 20.
60. *New York Times,* 26 November 1978; Penny Lernoux, "Corrupting Colombia," p. 18.

forcement. Joseph Linnemann, the State Department's narcotics expert, exulted that "involvement of the military's greater material and personnel resources has created the potential for similar campaigns in other regions of the country, such as the Llanos, the Choco, and along the southern border, all of which are real or potential producing or transit areas."[61]

Instead the army was withdrawn in December 1980 to stem further corruption of its ranks.[62] But the military, with U.S. encouragement, remains a force in the antidrug program by its very role in the antiguerrilla fight: Like Lopez Rega in Argentina, Colombian security officials blame both subversion and drugs on the same "narcoguerrillas." As Defense Minister Gen. Gustavo Matamoros warned, "This alliance is a new threat to our democracy and we will continue to act rapidly and energetically to stop this danger."[63]

The military used such charges to undermine President Belisario Betancur's attempts to arrange a cease-fire with several guerrilla factions. When the government declared a state of emergency following the April 1984 murder by the drug mafia of the minister of justice, the army sabotaged cease-fire negotiations. "The government said the state of siege was aimed at the traffickers and not at the guerrillas," one Colombian journalist explained, "but the army doesn't see it like that. As a result, we're now seeing the fiercest fighting between army and guerrillas in several years."[64]

The U.S. embassy in Bogotá has encouraged talk of a guerrilla-mafia alliance. Its briefing paper on the "FARC/Narc Connection" linked the Moscow-line Fuerzas Armadas Revolucionarias de Colombia with high-level cocaine producers. Some critics accused Ambassador Lewis Tambs of grinding an ideological ax; a close political ally of Senator Jesse Helms (R-N.C.), he once called for an invasion or blockade of Cuba and Nicaragua to rid the Caribbean of the "Cuban-Sandinista cancer."[65]

Journalists and congressional investigators report that only the

61. HSCNAC, hearings, *Oversight Hearings on Federal Drug Strategy—1979,* (Washington, D.C.: Government Printing Office, 1979), p. 404.

62. Narcotics enforcement fell to the paramilitary National Police (F-2), with $13 million in U.S. funds and equipment. *New York Times,* 11 September 1984; HSCNAC, report, *International Narcotics Control Study Missions to Latin America and Jamaica,* note 7 above, p. 72.

63. *San Francisco Chronicle,* 21 March 1984.

64. *New York Times,* 22 May 1984; cf. *New York Times,* 21 March 1984; *Seattle Times,* 26 March 1984.

65. *NACLA Report,* May–June 1983, pp. 31–32.

ideologically muddled M-19 movement ever had any clear involvement with drugs.[66] Indeed, in late 1981, several notorious smugglers and their allies in the army set up a death squad targeted against leftist guerrillas who preyed upon the drug chieftains by kidnapping family members in return for enormous ransoms. "Muerte a Secuestradores" (Death to Kidnappers) murdered more than 300 suspected leftists at the direction of the cocaine kingpins.[67]

Mexico

Often considered the classic success story of cooperative drug eradication programs, the Mexican example showed the consequences of giving U.S. aid to corrupt police who turned it against the peasantry.

During the 1970s, the critical decade of opium poppy and marijuana eradication, the INC program pumped more than $95 million into Mexico.[68] Aid included 64 helicopters, 24 airplanes, submachine and shotguns, tear gas projectiles, and at least 30 full-time DEA agents working in conjunction with the Federal Police.[69]

Critics have charged that narcotics enforcement was used as a pretext to crush peasant land occupations and peasant-worker alliances in the countryside. Some of the worst incidents occurred in the southern state of Guerrero, home of Acapulco Gold and poor dirt farmers who sheltered a modest guerrilla movement until the army stamped it out in 1974. "Guerrero today remains in a state of military occupation," one American journalist observed two years later, "and many of its people view the current campaign against drugs, carried out by Mexican soldiers and judicial police who march in from their own encampments or drop from helicopters, as a veneer of legitimacy for an ongoing campaign to terrorize the populace and keep down an incipient anti-government movement." The head of the State Judicial Police in northern Guerrero, meanwhile, was reportedly himself a heroin dealer.[70]

---

66. *Miami Herald,* 21 May 1984; Report of a Staff Study Mission . . . to the Committee on Foreign Affairs, House of Representatives, *U.S. Narcotics Control Programs Overseas: An Assessment,* 22 February 1985, p. 22.

67. Penny Lernoux, "The Minister Who Had to Die," *Nation,* 16 June 1984, pp. 734–35; *NACLA Report,* May–June 1983, pp. 22–23.

68. U.S. Department of State, "International Narcotics Control Strategy," 13 November 1981, *Current Policy* series, no. 345.

69. Klare and Arnson, *Supplying Repression,* p. 38; *Newsweek,* 10 April 1978.

70. M. J. McConahay, "Mexico's War on Poppies—and Peasants," *New Times,* 3 September 1976, pp. 33–38.

In early 1978, 7,000 Mexican soldiers backed by DEA advisers waged a "special war" against marijuana cultivators in the northern states of Durango, Sinaloa, and Chihuahua. The real targets of Operation Condor, according to the organ of the U.S. Catholic Conference, were Indian peasants. Tanks and helicopters intimidated the local population; herbicide sprayings poisoned their land and starved them out.[71]

A six-month investigation of Federal Judicial Police practices in this operation, published by an American reporter in 1979, found that "torture, extortion, self-incrimination, forced confession, incommunicado detention and excessive detention without sentencing" were "regular practices." The worst incidents occurred in Sinaloa, where DEA agents coordinated field training and actual operations by their Mexican counterparts. Witnesses, including Mexican police, accused American agents of standing by during torture sessions. The Sinaloa Bar Association compiled no fewer than 567 prisoner affidavits attesting to torture in connection with "Operation Condor."

Victor Gomez Vidal, the highest-ranking state security official in Sinaloa, charged that "Operation Condor is a way for some federal authorities to make themselves very rich. They have their own jail—nobody knows who comes and goes but them. It's a closed system. And once inside they torture people to see who has the money and who doesn't and it's their word against ours." When the notoriously brutal commander of the Federal Police was gunned down in late 1978, he left an estate valued at $10 million.[72]

Ironically, recent congressional studies of the drug eradication program and admissions by DEA agents in the field contradict Washington's former boasts of success—which in turn were based on unverified Mexican claims. Apparently, corrupt Mexican authorities pocketed some of the aid, used the program as an excuse to

---

71. *NACLA Report,* March–April 1978, p. 41. Regarding recent repression against peasant organizations by army and state police, including extrajudicial executions, torture, and "disappearances," see Amnesty International Report, 1984, 174–177 and AI memorandum, "Unacknowledged detention/Health concern," 10 August 1984, AI Index AMR 41/22/84. Gustavo Zarate, an Amnesty Prisoner of Conscience, was a 29-year-old professor of social studies at the Autonomous University of Chiapas who was arrested 24 July 83 "based on planted police evidence" of marijuana and explosives See AI memo, "Hunger strike," 31 August 1984, AI Index AMR 41/24/84 and Amnesty International Report, 1984, p. 176.

72. Craig Pyes, "Legal Murders," *Village Voice,* 4 June 1979, pp. 1, 11–15.

shake down drug producers, and sprayed the same fields over and over to give the pretense of action while protecting those traffickers with political clout. "We're perpetuating a fraud just by being there," one frustrated DEA official told *Newsweek*.[73]

Peru

The U.S. push for narcotics enforcement in Peru, as in Mexico, has evolved into a counterinsurgency campaign. The targets in this case are the fanatical Maoist guerrillas of Sendero Luminoso (Shining Path).

In 1981 the State Department programmed $15 million for cocaine eradication and enforcement programs over five years; the Agency for International Development kicked in another $18 million for crop substitution programs to give peasant cultivators of coca an alternative livelihood.[74]

Crop substitution was doomed to fail. Coca plants are grown not in the prime agricultural land of the valleys but on steep slopes unsuited to other crops.[75] Previous experiments with rubber, bananas, coffee, tobacco, rice, sorghum, and cacao all failed; peasants grow coca because it is a traditional crop, attracts a high price, and enjoys a relatively stable market.[76]

Coca eradication programs have forged ahead nonetheless. The United States spent more than $1.7 million to train and equip an antidrug rural mobile police unit (Umopar) based in Tingo María, a center of the coca growing region northeast of Lima.[77] Umopar has conducted joint operations with the air force and counterinsurgency-trained civil guard.[78]

But a series of devastating guerrilla raids, including police station bombings, forced a cancellation of field operations. Shining Path guerrillas have taken advantage of peasant anger toward the anticoca

73. *Newsweek*, 16 December 1985; Report of a Staff Study Mission . . . to the Committee on Foreign Affairs, House of Representatives, *U.S. Narcotics Control Programs Overseas: An Assessment*, 22 February 1985, p. 37–38; *Peninsula Times Tribune*, 18 February 1980.

74. HSCNAC report, *International Narcotics Control Study Missions to Latin America and Jamaica*, pp. 24, 41.

75. Testimony of Richard F. Weber, AID, in SPSI hearings, *International Narcotics Trafficking* (Washington, D.C.: Government Printing Office, 1981), pp. 201–2.

76. *Wall Street Journal*, 20 March 1984.

77. *Latin America Weekly Report*, 17 August 1984; *New York Times*, 13 September 1984.

78. *Latin America Weekly Report*, 22 June 1984.

drive, which uprooted more than 4,000 acres of cultivated land. "No doubt we have created an environment for anti-government and anti-American operations," a U.S. official told the *New York Times*.[79]

The *Times* also reported that with antidrug programs shut down "the strike force is now almost fully occupied in the counterinsurgency campaign. This new role has raised questions among United States officials in Peru and in Washington about the spending of United States Government funds that are earmarked for narcotics control, not for counterinsurgency."[80]

Though U.S. officials say there is no evidence of an alliance between the smugglers and the guerrillas,[81] Peru's security forces use the drug issue as an excuse to go after the greater evil. In July 1984 President Fernando Belaunde Terry declared a "holy war" against what he called the "narcotics-terrorism threat," extending a state of national emergency for thirty days to give the armed forces a chance to use "new methods" against the guerrillas.[82]

Washington continues to support the notoriously brutal civil guard and military in rural counterinsurgency. It has discussed plans to open a new eradication front in the upper Apurímac area. The real aim can only be to fight guerrillas; the region is a major center of Sendero Luminoso activity but not of coca cultivation.[83]

Burma

Opium production in the Golden Triangle is concentrated in the wild Shan states of northeastern Burma. The poppy crop, high in value but low in weight, is well suited for transport over rugged mountain

---

79. *New York Times*, 13 August 1984; cf. *Wall Street Journal*, 10 August 1984.
80. Ibid.
81. *Wall Street Journal*, 10 August 1984; testimony of Hon. Edwin G. Corr, former ambassador to Peru, in SPSI hearings, *International Narcotics Trafficking*, p. 199; statement of Clyde Taylor, acting assistant secretary of state for INM, Senate Committee on Labor and Human Resources, Subcommittee on Alcoholism and Drug Abuse, hearing, *Drugs and Terrorism, 1984* (Washington, D.C.: Government Printing Office, 1984), p. 25; cf. 46–49. Congressional investigators cite "disturbing—though unconfirmed—reports that the military has actually collaborated with drug traffickers to identify guerrilla strongholds." (Report of a Staff Study Mission . . . to the Committee on Foreign Affairs, House of Representatives, *U.S. Narcotics Control Programs Overseas: An Assessment*, 22 February 1985, p. 20.
82. *San Francisco Examiner*, 7 July 1984; *Norfolk Virginian-Pilot*, 29 July 1984.
83. *Latin America Weekly Report*, 17 August 1984.

terrain to evade the price controls and heavy taxes the socialist government of Rangoon imposes on legitimate goods.[84]

Opium has become the financial mainstay of separatist political movements in the Shan states, which rebelled against Rangoon in the late 1950s. "It's like a cottage industry," said one guerrilla commander. "Every army has its own lab at the border (of Thailand), just like homes in Europe used to have their own ovens to bake bread. We take care of our own needs. . . . We must fight the Rangoon government and we must have weapons."[85]

Some of these groups are really freebooting smuggling gangs with only a thin nationalist veneer; others have a genuine political agenda. Of the latter, the Burmese Communist Party controls the largest opium-poppy-growing territory. In the early 1970s the BCP encouraged crop substitution.[86] In recent years, since the People's Republic of China cut back its support, the BCP reportedly had taken up opium smuggling and even heroin refining.[87]

But long before the BCP began dealing opium, U.S. and Burmese authorities targeted it and other rebel groups for suppression under the guise of drug enforcement. Rangoon tolerated and even armed several large-scale, anti-Communist traffickers until they developed political ambitions of their own.[88] But it cracked down mercilessly on the real Shan nationalists.

American support to the People's Police Force has included 26 helicopters, 5 aircraft, communications equipment, and associated training and support.[89] In a letter to Congressman Lester Wolff in 1977, Lt. Gen. Bo Mya, commander-in-chief of the Karen National Liberation Army, charged that "the helicopters given to the Burmese . . . Government for use in Narcotic Suppression is nothing but a farce and a misused gift of honor. Over a month old fighting in

84. William Delaney, "On Capturing an Opium King," *Society,* September–October 1975, p. 64.

85. *San Francisco Chronicle,* 21 March 1984.

86. *Far Eastern Economic Review,* 14 September 1979, p. 39; *Washington Post,* 11 April 1976; Delaney, "Capturing an Opium King," p. 68.

87. HSCNAC, report, *International Narcotics Control Study Missions to Latin America and Jamaica,* p. 143.

88. William Delaney, "Capturing an Opium King," p. 66; *Far Eastern Economic Review,* 18 June 1982; Interview with Walter Mackem, former CIA drug analyst, 19 December 1978.

89. Klare and Arnson, *Supplying Repression,* p. 39; *New York Times,* 4 August 1975; Eleanore Hill report, in SPSI, hearings, *International Narcotics Trafficking,* p. 425.

Wankha a place on the Burma-Thailand border was a good proof. Not a poppy was or is grown in the area. They used helicopter you have given them as a combat transport. This kind of method has been adopted not to the Karen Freedom Fighter alone, but to all the Kachin, Shan, Men, Kayah etc., the minority groups who are fighting for their freedom as we are" (sic).[90]

Wolff's House narcotics committee reported "convincing evidence that Burma's anti-narcotics campaign is a form of economic warfare aimed at the subjugation of its minority peoples. . . . A policy which encourages attacks on farmers, the destruction of fields and livestock, and the contemplated use of herbicides is incompatible with any civilized conception of human rights."[91]

The guerrillas themselves proposed an attractive alternative: The United States could simply buy from them the entire opium crop, some 250 tons with a street value estimated by the DEA at $16 billion, for a mere $6 million to $12 million.[92] There was even a precedent in the U.S. purchase of 26 tons of opium from the KMT for $1 million in 1972.[93]

The reasons given by the White House for opposing the idea highlight the political underpinnings of the entire international narcotics control program: A preemptive buy would "work directly counter to our foreign policy objectives in that area" by aiding separatist parties and even "Communist insurgencies against the friendly governments of Burma and Thailand."[94] The unspoken but central fact was that assistance to central government paramilitary narcotics units would serve U.S. foreign policy interests by undermining those same insurgencies.

90. HSCNAC, hearings, *Southeast Asian Narcotics* (Washington, D.C.: Government Printing Office, 1978), pp. 45–46.

91. HSCNAC, report, *Opium Production, Narcotics Financing and Trafficking in Southeast Asia* (Washington, D.C.: Government Printing Office, 1977), p. 37.

92. U.S. Congress, House, International Relations Committee, Subcommittee on Future Foreign Police Research and Development, hearings, *Proposal to Control Opium From the Golden Triangle and Terminate the Shan Opium Trade* (Washington, D.C.: Government Printing Office, 1975); HSCNAC, hearings, *Cocaine and Marijuana Trafficking in Southeastern United States* (Washington, D.C.: Government Printing Office, 1978); cf. analysis by Robert Schwab in HSCNAC, hearings, *Southeast Asian Narcotics,* pp. 185–221.

93. U.S. Congress, Senate, Committee on the Judiciary, Subcommittee on Internal Security, hearings, *World Drug Traffic and Its Impact on U.S. Security,* part 1 (Washington, D.C.: Government Printing Office, 1972), pp. 33ff; *Washington Post,* 31 July 1972.

94. Mathea Falco, coordinator for international narcotics matters, Department of State, 13 July 1977 (State Department release).

NARCOTICS AND COMMUNISM

The dreaded "heroin epidemic" of 1969 and 1970, along with the rise of rec-reational drug use throughout the 1960s, drove millions of voters into the law-and-order camp by giving them a bogeyman far more virulent, despicable and immediate than the classical godless communist of yore: the pusher. . . . It was the answer to a central dilemma: the exhaustion of the cold war.

Robert Singer[95]

Drug enforcement as a counter to leftist insurgencies requires friendly governments to receive U.S. police assistance. Against hostile governments, on the other hand, the drug issue has become a significant propaganda weapon, a rationale for U.S.-sponsored destabilization campaigns abroad and the mobilization of public opinion at home.

The popular image of communist subversion—its poisoning of minds with enticing propaganda—has a counterpart in the image of the drug pusher enslaving America's youth with alluring poisons of the body. Both entail a fall from grace, a loss of reason and will, a disruption of social bonds.

Viewed this way, narcotics enforcement is an essential element of the nation's defense against hostile attempts to undermine the physical and moral strength of our population. As President Ford once declared, "All nations of the world—friend and adversary alike—must understand that America considers the illegal export of opium to the country a threat to our national security."[96]

Harry Anslinger, founder and longtime head of the Federal Bureau of Narcotics, championed this outlook. "Reefers and propaganda," he declared, " . . . go hand in hand." He warned Americans to "be on guard against the use of drugs as a political weapon by the Communists" who "may try to make narcotics a new 'sixth' column to weaken and destroy selected targets in the drive for world domination."[97]

His favorite bête noir was Red China, which he accused of planning a "long range dope-and-dialectic assault on America and its leaders." The first charges against that regime seem to have come from

95. Robert Singer, "The Rise of the Dope Dictators," *High Times* (March 1977): 57.
96. Ibid., p. 58.
97. Harry Anslinger, *The Murderers* (New York: Farrar, Straus and Cudahy, 1962), pp. 294-95.

Gen. Douglas MacArthur's military intelligence chief, Charles Willoughby, and from a CIA-funded labor organization.[98]

The quality of Anslinger's evidence, however, may be illustrated by the publicity surrounding a San Francisco drug bust in January 1959. The agent in charge called it "the biggest Chinese narcotics operation that we've ever come across."[99] Anslinger later cited it as proof that "Red China" was the primary source of heroin entering the United States.[100] Buried in news accounts was the fact that one of the ring leaders was an official of the Chinese Anti-Communist Committee, whom U.S. officials permitted to flee to Taiwan.[101]

Fourteen years later, when a large bust in New York City turned up a plastic bag of pure heroin labeled (in English) "People's Republic of China," Washington didn't bite. A State Department spokesman remarked drily, "There would seem to be a potential for counterfeit here."[102]

What had happened in the interim, of course, was the opening to China and the concerted American effort to bring it into the anti-Soviet camp.

Political expediency governed Washington's public position on Chinese complicity in the drug traffic. Thus as late as 1970 the BNDD stated flatly that "opium is cultivated in vast quantities in the Yunnan Province of China."[103] Yet by 1971, following President Nixon's announcement of his forthcoming mission to China, the State Department was claiming, "There is no reliable evidence that the Communist Chinese have *ever* engaged in or sanctioned the illicit export of opium or its derivatives."[104] (Emphasis added.) Indeed, the White

98. Ibid., p. 228; Richard Deverall, *Red China's Dirty Drug War* (Tokyo, 1954). Deverall was working for the AFL's Free Trade Union Committee.

99. *New York Times,* 15 January 1959.

100. Harry Anslinger, "The Red Chinese Dope Traffic," *Military Police Journal,* February–March 1961.

101. Peter Dale Scott, "Foreword," in Henrik Kruger, *The Great Heroin Coup* (Boston: South End Press, 1980), p. 15.

102. *New York Times,* 18 January 1973, quoting Nelson Gross, the State Department's special advisor on narcotics; cf. *Los Angeles Times,* 18 January 1973.

103. BNDD Fact Sheet 2—"Illegal Traffic in Narcotics and Dangerous Drugs" (Washington, D.C.: Government Printing Office, 1970), p. 6.

104. October 27, 1971 statement of Louis J. Link, chief of the Public Inquiries Division of the Department of State, cited in *Congressional Record,* 29 March 1972, p. 10880. George Belk, former assistant administrator of DEA, confirmed that "we never really had any firm intelligence that the Red Chinese were ever involved in or sanctioned drug trafficking." Interview with Belk, 18 February 1986.

House instructed executive agencies to beware of communist dope stories, alleging that they originated in the propaganda mills of Taiwan.[105]

Despite the reversal on China, the Communist-drug connection remains a potent propaganda theme against the Soviets' "evil empire."[106] Secretary of State George Shultz, pointing to "the complicity of some Communist governments in the drug trade," has charged that "smuggling massive amounts of drugs into Western nations may serve their broader goal of attempting to weaken the fabric of Western democratic society."[107]

The Reagan White House, preoccupied with stemming the spread of Soviet influence in Central America and the Caribbean, has repeatedly alleged Cuban and Nicaraguan complicity in drug smuggling.

In July 1984, for example, Reagan administration officials leaked to the conservative *Washington Times* lurid stories linking top Nicaraguan leaders to notorious Colombian cocaine traffickers. Among those implicated were Interior Minister Tomas Borge and Defense Minister Humberto Ortega.[108]

Since then opponents of the Sandinista regime have milked the charges for all they are worth. The 1984 GOP presidential platform condemned "the Sandinista government's smuggling of illegal drugs into the United States as a crime against American society and international law." Senator Paula Hawkins (R-Fla.), whose constituents include large numbers of anti-communist Cuban exiles, said, "The partygoer in Georgetown 'doing up' a line of coke, the Wall Street broker 'copping a snort' in the men's room on lunch break, the junior high school kid at recess—they must realize that they are tools in a geopolitical movement designed to perpetuate totalitarianism in Nicaragua and to spread Marxist insurgency throughout Latin America."[109]

105. Jack Anderson in *Washington Post,* 26 May 1972. For a balanced assessment, see Andrew Tully, *The Secret War Against Dope* (New York: Coward, McCann & Geoghegan, 1973), p. 247.

106. Conservatives also accused Salvador Allende's Chilean socialist government of earning foreign exchange through the cocaine traffic. See *Congressional Record,* 15 July 1974, p. 23285; *Washington Post,* 19 January 1975.

107. *New York Times,* 15 September 1984; *New York Post,* 15 September 1984.

108. Joel Millman, "False Connection," *Nation,* 22 September 1984, p. 228-29.

109. Transcript of hearing before Senate Subcommittee on Alcohol and Drug Abuse, 19 April 1985.

Her case, minus the rhetoric, is partially supported by testimony from former participants in the drug trade.[110] The charges may ultimately stick. Yet DEA officials admit having little evidence to implicate Sandinista leaders. Stanley Marcus, the U.S. attorney in Miami who indicted one former Nicaraguan official on cocaine charges, also confessed the weakness of administration claims against the regime.[111]

Curiously, conservative accusers of the Sandinistas were less troubled when the CIA reported in 1972 that Gen. Somoza's Nicaragua was a "transit point for heroin shipped north from South America via Panama to the United States" or when the strongman was revealed to be a business partner of two major traffickers who smuggled drugs via Nicaragua.[112]

Nor have administration officials had much to say about reports from U.S. government investigators and others that some anti-Sandinista Contra leaders, in league with CIA-connected Cuban exiles, have financed their guerrilla struggle with proceeds from the cocaine traffic.[113]

The Cuban government, too, has long been the target of narcotics-related propaganda. Anti-Castro sources leveled such preposterous charges as that Fidel Castro personally discussed guns-for-drugs trades with Jack Ruby, the Dallas killer of Lee Harvey Oswald.[114]

In 1976 a Cuban exile leader, Manuel de Armas, who defected to Havana after working for the CIA, declared that his former employer was planning to blacken Cuba's image with disinformation linking the communist government to drugs.[115]

Nonetheless, serious evidence points to possible Cuban complicity in the drug trade. U.S. prosecutors and drug agents had long heard from reliable informants in the drug trade that Havana takes a share of profits in return for providing traffickers a haven and transfer

110. Ibid.
111. *New York Times,* 28 July 1984; *Los Angeles Times,* 28 July 1984.
112. *Washington Post,* 6 May 1972; *Tampa Tribune,* 9 June 1974; *Atlanta Constitution,* 11 November 1981.
113. *Dallas Morning News,* 21 December 1985; *San Francisco Examiner,* 16 March 1986, 18 March 1986, and 23 June 1986; *UPI,* 26 April 1986; "CBS Evening News," 12 June 1986; *Washington Post,* 11 April 1986 and 17 April 1986; *Christian Science Monitor,* 9 May 1986.
114. Interview with Frank Sturgis, *High Times,* April 1977, p. 26.
115. *Granma Weekly Review,* 2 May 1976.

station for drug shipments originating in Colombia.[116] Finally, in 1982, a federal grand jury in Miami indicted four senior Cuban officials and ten others for conspiring "to use Cuba as a loading station and source of supplies for ships transporting" Quaaludes and marijuana to the southeastern United States.[117]

The DEA assistant special agent-in-charge of the case was careful, however, to tell the press, "We are not saying this is the policy of the Cuban government. We don't know and we have not suggested there is a conspiracy by the Cuban government in general."[118] The State Department's top narcotics officer similarly cautioned that "while individual Cuban officials have been indicted, there is no solid evidence of Cuban Government involvement, nor do reports confirm a connection between international terrorism and Cuban involvement in narcotics trafficking."[119] But the fact that fugitive financier and suspected drug trafficker Robert Vesco took refuge in Cuba suggests that Castro does protect some smugglers.[120]

Once again the truth appears less clear-cut than some partisans allow. But serious drug experts agree that whatever communist-drug connection does exist has little impact on the availability of drugs in the United States.[121] And no less clear is that official outrage over foreign complicity in the drug trade has been highly selective, with

116. Interview with a former assistant U.S. attorney, 11 February 1986; with former Dade County Metro Police Lt. Raul Diaz, 12 February 1986; and with former Alcohol, Tobacco and Firearms agent Ed Seibert, 27 February 1986. The first two believe that Fidel Castro uses the profits to finance an intelligence network parallel to and independent of the KGB-dominated Cuban DGI. See also Ernest Volkman, "The Odd Couple," *Family Weekly,* 29 April 1984.

117. See joint hearings before the U.S. Senate, Committee on the Judiciary, Subcommittee on Security and Terrorism; Committee on Foreign Relations, Subcommittee on Western Hemisphere Affairs; and U.S. Senate Drug Enforcement Caucus, *The Cuban Government's Involvement in Facilitating International Drug Traffic* (Washington, D.C.: Government Printing Office, 1983).

118. *San Jose Mercury,* 6 November 1982.

119. Statement of Clyde Taylor, acting assistant secretary of state for international narcotics matters, Senate Committee on Labor and Human Resources, Subcommittee on Alcoholism and Drug Abuse, hearing, *Drugs and Terrorism, 1984* (Washington, D.C.: Government Printing Office, 1984), p. 25. See also Francis Mullen's statement in *Miami Herald,* 24 April 1982, 1 May 1982; and FBI Director William Webster in *Los Angeles Times,* 14 February 1986.

120. *San Jose Mercury,* 4 May 1984; *New York Times,* 10 May 1984; for a general treatment of the evidence against the Cuban government, see *Wall Street Journal,* 30 April 1984.

121. Statement of Francis Mullen, DEA administrator, Senate Committee on Labor and Human Resources, Subcommittee on Alcoholism and Drug Abuse, hearing, *Drugs and Terrorism, 1984* (Washington, D.C.: Government Printing Office, 1984), p. 13.

U.S. politicians quick to exploit the issue as a potent emotive vehicle for pursuing other political agendas.

NARCOTICS ENFORCEMENT AND THE CIA

Propaganda and counterinsurgency are the most "overt" foreign policy aims of U.S. international drug programs. But the covert side has not been neglected; for the Central Intelligence Agency, drugs and drug enforcement have proved a vital key to undercover missions during the Cold War.

Though the CIA is officially a relative newcomer to the drug field—having only joined the drug war in 1971, by order of President Nixon—it has long had a keen interest in the doings of the criminal underworld.

Its parent and sister organizations, the Office of Strategic Services and the Office of Naval Intelligence, both cultivated Mafia leader Charles "Lucky" Luciano during World War II. His racketeering army patrolled the eastern seaboard docks on the lookout for enemy sabotage; they also supplied intelligence that facilitated the invasion of Sicily. OSS and the Navy collaborated with the most notorious narcotics smugglers in Republican China, Tai Li and Tu Yueh-sheng, to organize a far-flung intelligence network against the Japanese.[122]

The CIA carried on the same tradition in its infancy, sending funds to the heroin-smuggling Corsican underworld of Marseilles to assist its battle with Communist unions for control of the city's docks in 1947.[123]

The same strategy worked to gory effect in Sicily, where U.S. intelligence officers in 1947–48 allegedly aided the long-suppressed Mafia (and their Christian Democratic political allies) regain power on the island at the expense of several hundred murdered leftists. Claims former CIA operative Miles Copeland, "Had it not been for the Mafia the Communists would by now be in control of Italy."[124]

It is not too much to say that, with its assistance to the opium-

122. Rodney Campbell, *The Luciano Project* (New York: McGraw-Hill, 1977); Jonathan Marshall, "Opium and the Politics of Gangsterism in Nationalist China, 1927–1945."

123. Alfred McCoy, *The Politics of Heroin in Southeast Asia* (New York: Harper & Row, 1972), chaps. 1, 2.

124. Peter Dale Scott, "Foreword," in Henrik Kruger, *The Great Heroin Coup*, p. 14; Miles Copeland, *Beyond Cloak and Dagger* (New York: Pinnacle Books, 1975), pp. 240–41.

smuggling KMT troops in Burma in the early 1950s, the CIA had reestablished the three pillars of the postwar heroin traffic: the Sicilian, the Corsican, and the Chinese organizations. Without critical American aid they might have remained limited, regional gangs; with it, they forged a truly international production and smuggling network.

Since then, drug smugglers have regularly turned up as CIA "assets." For example, in the late 1960s the agency had to quietly wind down its major Cuban counterintelligence operation when police learned that it was fronting for a heroin and cocaine syndicate. During the Vietnam War, the CIA's complicity with opium-growing tribesmen of the "Golden Triangle" and with heroin-smuggling generals of Thailand, Laos, and South Vietnam became a notorious embarrassment.[125] At home, the CIA immunized Latin American smugglers in no fewer than twenty-seven federal drug cases.[126]

Today the potential for embarrassment is hardly less great in Afghanistan, where CIA-armed tribesmen produce enormous quantities of opium to finance their rebellion against the Soviet occupation. In 1983 Afghan peasants harvested about 400 tons of opium, much of which they smuggled into Pakistan for refining. Heroin from that region accounts for about half of all U.S. consumption.[127]

At least two considerations seem to have dictated the CIA's close relationship with traffickers, even at the expense of official U.S. antidrug policies. At a minimum, it has always behooved the agency to infiltrate and keep under surveillance underworld networks whose financial resources, tradecraft, and access to intelligence (often with

125. Cuba (Operation 40): *New York Times,* 4 January 1975. Southeast Asia: McCoy, note 123 above; Catherine Lamour, *The International Connection* (New York: Pantheon, 1974); Richard Kunnes, *The American Heroin Empire* (New York: Dodd, Mead, 1972), pp. 11–13.

126. Unsigned, undated DEA memorandum, probably by Lucien Conein in 1975, *CIA Narcotic Intelligence Collection.* Released by DEA under the Freedom of Information Act and supplied to the author by John Hill.

127. See statement of David Melocik, DEA congressional liaison, quoted in *San Francisco Chronicle,* 16 December 1983; cf. U.S. Congress, House, Select Committee on Narcotics Abuse and Control, report, *International Narcotics Control Study Missions* (Washington, D.C.: Government Printing Office, 1984), p. 161; Konrad Ege, "CIA Rebels Supply U.S. Heroin," *Counterspy,* November 1980, p. 16; *Oakland Tribune,* 2 June 1985. A DEA report noted in 1981 that "Soviet forces have taken over antismuggling operations from the Afghan nationals as part of overall military operations against the insurgents." *Washington Post,* 2 January 1981.

blackmail potential) make them a significant political force.[128] As one leading State Department official noted in 1985, drug profits "can buy an election, finance a supply of arms for insurgency and, in sum, destabilize legitimate governments and subordinate democratic processes."[129]

Beyond that, however, such organizations, usually militantly hostile to communism, can make excellent allies: They provide conduits for money laundering, agents for covert operations, and valuable intelligence on the dirty underside of politics in the countries where they operate. "The fact is," remarked Gen. Paul F. Gorman, former head of the U.S. Southern Command, "if you want to go into the subversion business, collect intelligence and move arms, you deal with the drug [movers]."[130]

Consider briefly one such informal network of CIA assets and drug-related operatives, starting with the late Florida attorney Paul Helliwell. As head of OSS wartime intelligence in China, he was close to the notorious Chinese secret police chief and narcotics smuggler Tai Li. Helliwell also made a regular practice of buying information from tribesmen in the China-Burma-India theater with five-pound shipments of opium. Returning to civilian life in Florida, he continued to work for the CIA. In 1951 he helped set up Sea Supply Corp., a front the agency used to run supplies to the KMT troops stranded in northern Burma after the Chinese revolution; it also ran the KMT's opium out of the hill country to Bangkok. Later Helliwell laundered CIA funds through the Bahamas-based Castle Bank.[131]

Castle Bank catered to the tax-evasion set—notably several leading American gangsters with interests in Las Vegas. But it also did mysterious transactions with a Cayman Islands firm, ID Corp. Its sole owner, the American Shig Katayama, became notorious as one of the key facilitators of Lockheed Corp.'s huge payoffs to Japanese politicians in return for airplane contracts. Of Katayama one Jap-

128. Drug enforcement officials foster this view within the government for their own bureaucratic ends. Thus DEA Administrator Francis Mullen, Jr., insisted, "International politics and economics hinge on the balance of power and trade controlled by narco-dollars." See SPSI, hearings, *International Narcotics Trafficking*, p. 562.

129. Clyde D. Taylor, deputy assistant secretary of state for international narcotics matters, quoted in *San Diego Union*, 12 January 1986.

130. *Latin America Weekly Report*, 23 March 1984.

131. *Wall Street Journal*, 18 April 1980; Peter Dale Scott, *The War Conspiracy* (Indianapolis: Bobbs-Merrill, 1972), p. 210; Edward Hymoff, *The OSS in World War II* (New York: Ballantine, 1972), p. 277; interview with Stanley Karnow, 7 March 1986.

anese journalist has charged, "His real job (in the early 1950s) was to handle narcotics for the U.S. intelligence work."[132]

Lockheed disbursed money to Japanese politicians through the notorious rightist "wire-puller" Yoshio Kodama, who enjoyed unsurpassed contacts within the ruling Liberal Democratic Party. During World War II Kodama proved himself a gifted smuggler and procurement specialist for the Japanese navy, on whose behalf he traded opium and heroin for scarce raw materials.[133] Arrested after VJ-day as a class-A war criminal suspect, Kodama was released from prison in 1948 and quickly recruited by the CIA, which used him, among other purposes, when it needed leverage over politicians in Tokyo. Investigators of the corporate bribes trail have concluded that the CIA "orchestrated much of Lockheed's financial operations in Japan pursuant to covert U.S. foreign policy objectives . . . particularly in support of ultraconservative groups."[134]

Lending weight to that deduction was the role of another intermediary in the bribery conduit, the international currency dealer Deak & Co., founded by OSS veteran Nicholas Deak and reportedly used by the CIA for the financial end of covert operations, including the 1953 overthrow of Iranian Prime Minister Mohammed Mossadegh.[135]

Deak & Co. was also said to be the channel by which the CIA's Saigon station traded millions of dollars on the black market to supplement its appropriation—at the expense of American taxpayers who propped up Vietnam's currency.[136] The firm also moved money for at least one notorious underworld figure who also played the black market in Saigon. He in turn was visited in 1968 by a powerful American Mafia boss (and veteran of CIA plots to assassinate Fidel Castro), who apparently was looking for new sources of heroin fol-

132. ID Corp. and Castle: U.S. Congress, House, Committee on Government Operations, hearings, *Oversight Hearings into the Operations of the IRS* (Washington, D.C.: Government Printing Office, 1976), pp. 907-9. Lockheed: Yamakawa Akio, "Lockheed Scandal," *Ampo,* April-September 1976, p. 3; cf. Jim Hougan, *Spooks* (New York: William Morrow, 1978), p. 456.

133. "Report on the Showa Trading Company" by Lt. Eric W. Fleisher, Investigative Division, U.S. Army, 25 July 1947, National Archives.

134. Tad Szulc, "The Money Changer," *The New Republic,* 10 April 1976, pp. 10-11; Anthony Sampson, *The Arms Bazaar* (New York: Viking, 1977), pp. 218-21.

135. Szulc, "The Money Changer," pp. 10-11.

136. Ibid.; *Washington Post,* 9 June 1976.

lowing the disruption of traditional European suppliers.[137] No wonder Deak & Co. was called the "Black Bank of Asia."[138]

Finally, the Deak firm came under fire in 1984 by the President's Commission on Organized Crime, which accused it of laundering millions of dollars (perhaps unwittingly) on behalf of Colombian cocaine traffickers.[139]

If intelligence and drug trafficking have often been intertwined, so have intelligence and drug enforcement—or at least the pretense of drug enforcement. From the days of the Federal Bureau of Narcotics to the DEA, the CIA has taken cover in antidrug organizations even as its field operations undercut their law enforcement function.

The police training and assistance programs taken over from the Office of Public Safety by DEA and the State Department's narcotics section, for example, functioned as CIA fronts from their inception. The longtime head of OPS was former CIA counterintelligence specialist Byron Engle. The CIA used OPS to supply credentials to its overseas agents and simplify liaison with local police, an ideal source of intelligence on dissident politics and personalities. The CIA was also happy to further the OPS's counterinsurgency mission—even to the point of assigning Green Beret instructors to teach foreign police students how to build and set off bombs.[140]

The CIA used its opium-and-arms-smuggling front Sea Supply Corp., among other things, to train the paramilitary Thai Border Patrol Police under Gen. Phao Sriyanon. Washington aimed to build the BPP into a force beholden to the CIA rather than the Thai government. CIA assistance enabled Phao "to build the police force into a powerful military organization which was better led, better paid and more efficient than the army," according to a former CIA analyst, until Thailand had "one of the highest ratios between policemen and citizens of any country in the world."[141]

137. McCoy, *The Politics of Heroin in Southeast Asia,* pp. 214–16; SPSI, hearings, *Illegal Currency Manipulations Affecting South Vietnam* (Washington, D.C.: Government Printing Office, 1969), pp. 276–79.

138. Interview with Stanley Karnow, 7 March 1986.

139. *The Tribune* (Oakland), November 30, 1984.

140. A. J. Langguth, *Hidden Terrors* (New York: Pantheon, 1968), pp. 48–49, 57, 72, 124, 138, 242–43; Thomas Lobe, *United States National Security Policy and Aid to the Thailand Police* (University of Denver, 1977), p. 9; Commission on CIA Activities Within the United States, *Report to the President* (New York: Manor Books, 1975), p. 235 (hereafter Rockefeller report).

141. Frank C. Darling, cited in Noam Chomsky and Edward S. Herman, *The Washington Connection and Third World Fascism,* vol. 1 (Boston: South End Press, 1979), pp. 221–22.

But Phao was also the most notorious Thai drug smuggler of his era. The contacts he established through Sea Supply Corp. with the KMT opium traffickers allowed him to sew up a near-monopoly on Burmese opium exports. His border police escorted opium caravans from the frontier and managed the transport of drugs to Bangkok by train or official planes.[142]

A 1957 coup unseated Phao, but the CIA continued to aid the BPP under OPS cover. The program continued at least into the early 1970s, when a CIA employee was caught smuggling a load of opium into the United States. The Justice Department dropped charges in order to protect the operation's cover.[143]

That embarrassment didn't prevent U.S. narcotics aid from flowing to the BPP to make up for some of the loss of OPS support in 1974. The political fruits of the program ripened in the bloody military coup of October 6, 1976, when BPP units, backed by OPS-trained and INC-supplied elements of Bangkok police, burst into Thammasat University to crush student demonstrators. "Their revenge [against the students] was taken in meting out humiliations, in mutilizations brutally inflicted, in burning a student alive and in simple wholesale murder," according to one academic account of the coup. "Thousands of unarmed students were killed, injured or arrested, and a few days later, most of the liberal to left journalists, scholars and intellectuals were also rounded up and put in prison or 'rehabilitation camps.'"[144]

U.S. intelligence reports indicated that several years later the Border Patrol Police were still protecting leading traffickers and using official vehicles to transport heroin from the north into Bangkok.[145]

The CIA's undercover use of narcotics agencies and programs did not become a significant public issue until 1975, when the Rockefeller Commission revealed that the CIA had infiltrated agents into the BNDD on an improper domestic counterintelligence mission.[146]

142. McCoy, *The Politics of Heroin in Southeast Asia,* pp. 136–45.

143. Lobe, *United States National Security Policy,* pp. 30–31, 38, 41–42, 80; Hougan, *Spooks,* pp. 142–43; John Burgess, "The Thailand Connection," *Counterspy* (Winter 1976): 31–33.

144. Lobe, *United States National Security Policy,* p. 117; cf. William Shawcross, "How Tyranny Returned to Thailand," *New York Review of Books,* 9 December 1976, pp. 59–62; interview with Norman Rossner, Bureau of International Narcotics Matters, Department of State, 13 December 1984.

145. DEA weekly intelligence digest, WDNI-79-14, 13 April 1979.

146. *New York Times,* 11 July 1975; *Washington Post,* 19 February 1975; Rockefeller report, pp. 233–34.

Long before, however, Harry Anslinger had permitted his narcotics bureau agents to assist in foreign covert operations.

Thus Garland Williams, the first agent ever sent overseas by the narcotics bureau, became chief of the Army's Counter-Intelligence Corps in 1940 and then Director of Special Training for the OSS, where he taught hundreds of agents the arts of "espionage, sabotage and guerrilla tactics." In the Korean War he commanded a military intelligence group. In the early 1960s he retired from the FBN to help African nations set up police and intelligence services.[147]

After the war FBN agents collaborated with OSS's successor. One doubled as a CIA agent in Rome; another, Sal Vizzini, took on a special undercover assignment for the agency in Beirut. "As a narcotics agent I'd have a certain immunity from government surveillance," he explained. "I'd have a cover within a cover, which was more than you could say for the CIA regulars on the scene."[148] Vizzini also worked with the CIA station in Bangkok in the early 1960s in a plot to bomb a notorious KMT heroin manufacturer in Burma.[149]

George White, a lieutenant colonel in OSS and one of Anslinger's top men, also had a cover-within-cover. Because of what the CIA called his "good access to criminal types,"[150] the agency recruited him in 1952 to set up apartments where secret drug tests could be conducted on unwitting subjects. Helping White to set them up was another narcotics agent and OSS veteran, Charles Siragusa.[151]

"The particular advantage of these arrangements with the Bureau of Narcotics officials has been that test subjects could be sought and cultivated within the setting of narcotics control," the CIA explained in one memo. "Some subjects have been informers or members of suspect criminal elements from whom the bureau has obtained results of operational value through the tests."[152]

The CIA's drug tests, according to another memo, were meant to "develop means for the control of the activities and mental capacities of individuals whether willing or not." Operation ARTI-

147. Harry Anslinger, *The Protectors* (New York: Farrar, Straus, 1964), pp. 24, 107.
148. Sal Vizzini, *Vizzini* (New York: Pinnacle Books, 1972), pp. 31–32, 166.
149. Author's interview with Vizzini, 20 December 1978.
150. *Washington Post,* 11 January 1976.
151. *New York Times,* 20 September 1977; U.S. Congress, Senate, Committee on Human Resources, Subcommittee on Health and Scientific Research, hearings, *Human Drug Testing by the CIA* (Washington, D.C.: Government Printing Office, 1977), p. 117.
152. *New York Times,* 8 November 1975.

CHOKE, in particular, asked whether an individual could "be made to perform an act of attempted assassination, involuntarily" and suggested testing possible methods "against a prominent (deleted) politician or if necessary against an American official. . . . " After the Manchurian Candidate did his job, the CIA assumed he would be "taken into custody . . . and 'disposed of.' "[153]

The CIA officer responsible for this tightly held program also recruited Mafia drug traffickers for the murder plots against Fidel Castro in 1960.[154]

The FBN was no stranger to those plots, either. In the summer of 1960 a CIA officer approached Charles Siragusa, by then deputy director of the FBN and official liaison with the CIA, with the news that the agency was forming an "assassination squad." "Since you have a lot of contacts with the underworld," he told Siragusa, "we'd like you to put together a team to conduct a series of hits. . . . There's some foreign leaders we'd like dead."[155]

The FBN official declined—it was peacetime, after all—but the CIA found another back channel for its purpose.

The CIA recruited potential assassins through a reliable intermediary, known by his code-name QJ/WIN. A European criminal hired first to help kill Patrice Lumumba in the Congo, QJ/WIN had first been contacted "in connection with an illegal narcotics operation into the United States" and "in behalf of the Bureau of Narcotics." That QJ/WIN was in fact an important cog in the Corsican "French Connection" is suggested by the notes of a CIA conspirator who specified *"No* American citizens or American residents for direct action. Corsicans recommended. Sicilians could leak to Mafia."[156]

For advice on the Corsican underworld and narcotics, the CIA

153. CIA document dated 22 January 1954, released under Freedom of Information Act on 4 January 1979.

154. David Wise, "The CIA's Svengalis," *Inquiry,* 18 September 1978; *San Francisco Examiner,* 18 September 1977.

155. Dan Moldea, *The Hoffa Wars* (New York: Paddington Press, 1978), p. 127; *Washington Post,* 4 January 1978. The CIA officer was almost certainly Col. Sheffield Edwards of the Office of Security. Interview with a former House and Senate staff investigator, 7 March 1986.

156. "Project ZR/RIFLE," CIA document released to the Center for National Security Studies under the Freedom of Information Act; cf. U.S. Congress, Senate, Select Committee to Study Governmental Operations With Respect to Intelligence Activities, report, *Alleged Assassination Plots Involving Foreign Leaders,* pp. 43–48, 181–90.

could turn to its in-house expert, Lucien Conein. The French-born covert operator had worked with the Corsicans during World War II as an OSS agent in France and Indochina (with Paul Helliwell), and later in Vietnam where he became the CIA's liaison with the generals who murdered President Ngo Dinh Diem in 1963. U.S. Senate investigators heard allegations—which Conein apparently did not deny—that he paid off friendly Vietnamese hill tribesmen with drugs they later sold to American troops.[157]

In 1971 Conein hired on with his CIA buddy and Castro-assassination plotter E. Howard Hunt to help the Nixon White House with political dirty tricks. After the Watergate break-in made Hunt's operation too hot to handle, the White House disposed of Conein by finding him a consulting job with the BNDD.[158] He stayed on after BNDD's reorganization into the DEA, and became its chief of special operations.

Conein recruited to his staff twelve former CIA agents to undertake what he called "clandestine operations." That was a euphemism for something much bigger. "When you get down to it," one of his colleagues explained, "Conein was organizing an assassination program. He was frustrated by the big-time operators who were just too insulated to get to. . . . He felt we couldn't win, the way things were going."[159]

Official reports of this project, first code-named BUNCIN and later DEACON, indicate that its object was to create "an international network of deep cover assets" to "immobilize or eliminate international sources of illicit drugs and significant narcotic traffickers." All its recruits were "former Central Intelligence Agency assets who operated in the Miami area during the 1960s." (The CIA secretly supported the project until at least the fall of 1973.) Cover was so tight that "if necessary" the operation could "be 'blamed' on other governmental agencies, or even on the intelligence services of other nations." Although ostensibly aimed at drug traffickers, the

157. Taylor Branch, "Raising a Glass to *Beau Geste*," *Esquire*, August 1976, pp. 30–34; interview with Stanley Karnow, 7 March 1986; interview with a former House and Senate staff investigator, 7 March 1986. On Conein-Helliwell connection, see E. Howard Hunt, *Undercover* (London: W. H. Allen, 1975), p. 42. On Conein and Montagnards, interview with former Senate Permanent Investigations Subcommittee staffer William Gallinaro, 19 February 1986.

158. Interview with former BNDD director John Ingersoll, 12 February 1986.

159. *Washington Post*, 13 June 1976.

intelligence gathered by DEACON included reports on "violation of neutrality laws, extremist groups and terrorism, and information of a political nature" as well as material "of an internal security nature." This political orientation may explain why, in the three-year existence of the project, DEACON produced only a single drug bust.[160]

In direct connection with DEACON, Conein in 1974 went shopping for assassination equipment from a firm connected with his OSS colleague Mitchel WerBell III. A Georgia-based arms dealer who did business with alleged drug financier Robert Vesco, WerBell was later indicted (and acquitted) on drug smuggling charges. "He would never get involved in a conspiracy to import marijuana," his attorney protested. "Guns, revolutions, maybe even assassinations, but he's not being tried on that." The attorney said WerBell had worked with a secret antidrug unit directed out of the White House and had assisted Conein in "putting together assassination devices for the DEA."[161]

Conein could hardly be considered a lone wolf within bureaucracy. On May 27, 1971, President Nixon ordered that $100 million be secretly budgeted for clandestine BNDD assassinations. Officials of the narcotics agency began talking of the need to establish "hit squads" and of aiming to disrupt the heroin trade with "150 key assassinations." The CIA, apparently, was willing to assist.[162]

So, too, was the National Security Agency, which along with the CIA began monitoring the telephone calls of U.S. citizens on behalf of the BNDD, probably in violation of the Communications Act of 1934. In 1973 the NSA destroyed records of this operation after its

---

160. *"Project BUNCIN - Operational Plan"* 29 November 1972; *Project Buncin: Summary, September 1972–March 1973.* Date: 12 March 1973; Lucien Conein memorandum, 25 May 1976, re Government Operations Subcommittee Hearings; *Overall Assessment of Project DEACON I,* 2 December 1974. These and other documents on BUNCIN/DEACON were released by the DEA under the Freedom of Information Act and generously supplied to the author by John Hill. One DEA agent who may have been recruited by Conein from the CIA for special DEACON-type operations was Hugo Murray, former CIA station chief in Bolivia at the time of the Che Guevara operation. Murray worked out of the DEA's office in Tucson. One of his drug informants charged under oath that Murray used him to launder bribes to members of the Lopez Portillo cabinet in Mexico. See *Arizona Daily Star,* 13 April 1984, 5 September 1984, 7 September 1984; interview with reporter Guillermo García, 8 February 1986.

161. Conein: *Washington Post,* 23 January 1975; Report of 18 June 1975 to the Attorney General, Subject: Additional Integrity Matters, submitted by Michael A. Defeo, et al., pp. 8–9. WerBell: *Miami Herald,* 4 September 1976; interview with Edwin Marger, 20 February 1986.

162. Edward J. Epstein, *Agency of Fear* (New York: Putnam, 1977), pp. 143–46.

general counsel learned of the "flap potential associated with reports going into the BNDD mechanism, particularly since they may well become the basis for executive action"—an intelligence euphemism for assassination.[163]

The plots reached deep within the White House itself, which organized a secret unit under Howard Hunt and Gordon Liddy with the ostensible mission of prosecuting the administration's "war on drugs." Hunt, the CIA veteran-turned-"Plumber" who employed Conein in 1971, recruited CIA-trained Cuban exiles in late 1971 and the spring of 1972 to murder Panamanian leader Gen. Omar Torrijos. Though the strongman's alleged protection of heroin traffickers supplied the rationale, Torrijos was almost certainly targeted because of his independent, leftist political stance and his opposition to the administration's demand for a new fifty-year lease on the Panama Canal. Only the Watergate break-in, mounted by the Hunt-Liddy team, prevented the plot from coming to fruition.[164]

CONCLUSION

Any serious consideration of the costs and benefits of international drug enforcement cannot ignore certain key factors in the equation.

First is the dismal return on the dollar investment, a fact that even enthusiasts of the concept admit. The enormous resources expended abroad on crop eradication and substitution programs have made hardly a dent either in world production or American consumption of drugs.[165] An eighteen-month study by the Rand Corporation concluded that "the most basic point is that the supply of drugs can never be eliminated." Attorney General William French Smith reluctantly had to agree that "unless you can eliminate the demand for drugs, the amount of money is so large that the dealers will continue to take whatever risk is necessary."[166]

163. U.S. Senate, Select Committee to Study Governmental Operations with Respect to Intelligence Agencies, *Supplementary Detailed Staff Reports on Intelligence Activities and the Rights of Americans,* Book 3 (Washington, D.C.: Government Printing Office, 1976), pp. 752–56; memorandum for NSA general counsel, 26 January 1973, obtained by Jay Peterzell of the Center for National Security Studies under the Freedom of Information Act.

164. Jonathan Marshall, "The White House Death Squad," *Inquiry,* 5 March 1979, pp. 15–21.

165. *New York Times,* 9 and 13 September 1984.

166. *New York Times,* 16 September 1984.

But no less important, citizens and policy makers must begin to weigh less obvious though sizable costs attributable at least in part to current international drug policy. These range from the disruption of traditional economies in Peru and Bolivia, where peasant leaders have warned that "pressures from the United States are about to provoke a bloodbath,"[167] to the corruption of entire societies in Latin America and Asia, where drug profits, artificially boosted by legal constraints, have lured members of the political, judicial, police, and even church establishments.

Though Washington's overwhelming political and economic presence stifles most dissent, a few brave voices in the Third World have spoken out against the consequences of these programs. "Colombia cannot afford to go on obeying the orders of the United States to solve a U.S. drug problem at the cost of our institutions," said Fabio Echeverri, president of the National Association of Industrialists. "Our problem is different. The economy is at stake, and we have the obligation to seek solutions that serve our own interests."[168] But Colombia is now more than ever a partner in U.S.-sponsored anti-drug programs.

In Colombia, as in Peru, Bolivia, Mexico, Thailand, and Burma, the effect of drug enforcement, police aid, and related programs has been to militarize the society, put enormous pressure on fledgling liberal institutions, and divert resources from more productive endeavors.

To a lesser but still dangerous degree, those same effects are felt here at home. The militarization of south Florida following amendment of the Posse Comitatus Act is symptomatic. So is the opportunistic use of the public's deep-seated antidrug ideology by Cold War practitioners to disguise programs that subvert the stated aims of United States foreign policy—whether by aiding repressive police states or even assassinating foreign leaders.

The prospect for any reevaluation of these programs is not promising, at least in the short run. Few politicians dare question the prevailing orthodoxy. And even among some who admit the failures of drug control, the need to expand tried-and-failed government pro-

---

167. *Latin America Weekly Report,* 17 August 1984.

168. Bolivia: *Latin America Weekly Report,* August 17, 1984. Colombia: Penny Lernoux, "Corrupting Colombia," p. 19.

grams remains an unshakable dogma. "To deal with this problem, we have to blanket the world," insisted Attorney General Smith. "We have no other choice."[169]

This profound failure of imagination stems from an equally profound failure to look at the facts. They may not tell a story policy makers want to hear, but they tell it clearly to all who listen.

169. *New York Times,* 16 September 1984.

SELECTED BIBLIOGRAPHY—
Part I

Antonil. *Mama Coca*. London: Hassle Free Press, 1977.

Berridge, Virginia, and Griffith Edwards. *Opium and the People: Opiate Use in Nineteenth-Century England*. New York: St. Martin's, 1981.

Bonnie, Richard J. *Marijuana Use and Criminal Sanctions: Essays on the Theory and Practice of Decriminalization*. Charlottesville, VA: Michie/Bobbs Merrill Company, 1980.

Bonnie, Richard J., and Charles H. Whitebread II. *The Marihuana Conviction: The History of Marihuana Prohibition in the United States*. Charlottesville, Va.: University of Virginia Press, 1974.

Brecher, Edward M., and Consumer Reports Editors. *Licit and Illicit Drugs: The Consumers Union Report on Narcotics, Stimulants, Depressants, Inhalants, Hallucinogens & Marijuana—Including Caffeine, Nicotine and Alcohol*. Boston: Little, Brown, 1972.

Courtwright, David T. *Dark Paradise: Opiate Addiction in America Before 1940*. Cambridge: Harvard University Press, 1982.

Domestic Council Drug Abuse Task Force. *White Paper on Drug Abuse*. Washington, D.C.: Government Printing Office, 1975.

Drug Abuse Council. *The Facts About "Drug Abuse."* New York: Free Press, 1980.

Epstein, Edward Jay. *Agency of Fear.* New York: Putnam, 1977.

Judson, Horace Freeland. *Heroin Addiction in Britain: What Americans Can Learn from the English Experience.* New York: Harcourt Brace Jovanovich, 1974.

Kruger, Henrik. *The Great Heroin Coup: Drugs, Intelligence and International Fascism.* Boston: South End Press, 1980.

Lindesmith, Alfred R. *The Addict and the Law.* New York: Vintage Books, 1965.

McCoy, Alfred. *The Politics of Heroin in Southeast Asia.* New York: Harper & Row, 1972.

McGlothlin, William H. "The Singapore Heroin Control Programme." *Bulletin on Narcotics* 32, no. 1 (1980): 1.

Mills, James. *The Underground Empire.* Garden City, N.Y.: Doubleday, 1986.

Morgan, H. Wayne. *Drugs in America: A Social History, 1800–1980.* Syracuse, N.Y.: Syracuse University Press, 1981.

Musto, David F. "Lessons From the First Cocaine Epidemic." *Wall Street Journal,* 11 June 1986, p. 30.

———. "Iatrogenic Addiction: The Problem, Its Definition and History." *Bulletin of the New York Academy of Medicine* 61, 2d Series (October 1985): 694–705.

———. *The American Disease: Origins of Narcotic Control.* New Haven: Yale University Press, 1973.

Musto, David F., and William Fischer. "A Cruel Deception—Heroin for the Terminally Ill." *New York Times,* 1 August 1984, p. 24.

President's Commission on Organized Crime. *America's Habit: Drug Abuse, Drug Trafficking, and Organized Crime.* Washington, D.C.: Government Printing Office, 1986.

Raphael, Ray. *Cash Crop: An American Dream.* Mendocino, Calif.: Ridge Times Press, 1985.

Silberman, Charles E. *Criminal Violence, Criminal Justice.* New York: Random House, 1978.

Sonnedecker, Glenn. *Kremers and Urdang's History of Pharmacy.* 4th ed. Philadelphia: Lippincott, 1976.

Taylor, Arnold H. *American Diplomacy and the Narcotics Traffic, 1900–1939.* Durham, N.C.: Duke University Press, 1969.

Trebach, Arnold S. *The Heroin Solution.* New Haven: Yale University Press, 1982.

———. "Time to Declare a Drug Truce." *Wall Street Journal,* 2 August 1982, p. 24.

———. "Peace Without Surrender in the Perpetual Drug War." *Justice Quarterly* 1, no. 1 (March 1984): 125–44.

———. "The Trusted Physician in a Humane Drug Control System." *Journal of Psychoactive Drugs* 16, no. 2 (April–June 1984): 141–60.

———. "Heroin and Pain Relief." *Journal of the Addiction Research Foundation of Ontario* 13, no. 5 (May 1, 1984): 5–6.

———. *The Great Drug War.* New York: Macmillan, 1987.

U.S. Department of State. *The Global Legal Framework for Narcotics and Prohibitive Substances.* Washington, D.C.: Government Printing Office, 1979.

MEDICAL RESEARCH CONCERNING ILLICIT SUBSTANCES

5

MEDICAL USES OF ILLICIT DRUGS

Lester Grinspoon
James B. Bakalar

INTRODUCTION

Most of the psychoactive drugs banned or severely restricted by law
in modern industrial societies have had significant medical uses at
some places and times. In the case of natural plant drugs like opium,
coca, cannabis, mescaline, and psilocybin, this medical history usually reaches back thousands of years and through a variety of cultures. The general tendency has been to restrict the uses of these
drugs as their dangers are more strongly emphasized and substitutes
become available. Although the trend toward greater precision in the
use of drugs and greater concern for safety is a medical advance,
there is a danger that legal and social restrictions will prevent the
realization of some genuine medical potential. As we suggest in this
chapter, establishing the balance is a difficult process that has not
yet been worked out adequately. (The use of illicit drugs also raises
other issues, such as individual freedom of choice, that are outside
the scope of this essay.)

Different drugs are assigned to different social categories in different cultures. The spectrum includes magic, religion, medicine, recreation, disease, vice, crime, and madness. In modern industrial societies, we put great emphasis on keeping these categories separated, and that is one reason why psychoactive drugs are so difficult for us to deal with. For industrial societies, medicine or therapy is one thing, fun another, religious ritual still another—an attitude reflected in separate formal and informal institutions. The distinctions among magic, religion, and medicine have not always been so clear as we make them, or at least profess to make them. The words health and holiness have a common root meaning "whole." In preindustrial societies medical diagnosis and prognosis have an aura of the occult, something resembling divination, and disease is usually considered an instrument of gods or evil spirits.

By the early nineteenth century, healers in Europe and in the United States no longer attributed illness to spirits or consciously identified the power of drugs as magical. The scientific revolution had convinced physicians that most diseases had physical and chemical causes, but a medical science created in the image of physics remained only a hope. This uncertain situation, together with the growth of manufacturing, capitalist entrepreneurship, and the spirit of liberal individualism, made the nineteenth century a great age of self-medication and competing medical authorities. The patent medicine industry therefore flowered in the late nineteenth century United States. Many of the proprietary medicines contained psychoactive drugs—alcohol, opium, cocaine, or cannabis. Orthodox physicians used them extensively as well; as late as 1910, morphine was the fourth most commonly used drug, and alcohol was the fifth.[1] These drugs were not specific cures for specific diseases, and little was known of their mechanism of action, but they provided relief from suffering in varied situations. They were the classic panaceas. Opium, alcohol, or cocaine, like faith in some pharmacologically inactive proprietary nostrum, actually reduced the pain while nature took its course, often toward a restoration of health.

It was a familiar fact that psychoactive drugs, like most strong medicine, could also be powerfully poisonous. Alternative, often synthetic drugs, with less apparent abuse potential, were developed in the late nineteenth century, and consciousness of the dangers of

1. Mickey C. Smith and David Knapp, *Pharmacy, Drugs, and Medical Care* (Baltimore: Williams and Wilkins, 1972), p. 161.

the familiar natural drugs became more intense. Problems were magnified by the isolation of drug substances in pure form and the development of such technologies as the hypodermic syringe. But the public and medical professionals also began to mistrust psychoactive drugs because of their indeterminate and apparently uncontrollable powers. Alcohol, for example, lost its status as a medicine in the first two decades of the twentieth century.

Psychoactive drugs had been used too freely in the nineteenth century, and often the distinction between use for health and use for pleasure was not carefully made. This ambiguity now began to seem dangerous, just as the primitive ambiguity between health and holiness had long been obsolete. Taking opium to relax or cocaine to feel vigorous would no longer be regarded as a cure or treatment. The common man's right to make choices about these substances (even, for a time, alcohol) was repudiated. The government and organized medicine took control over their manufacture and distribution, carefully restricting their medical uses and rejecting almost all other uses. This was part of the process by which nineteenth century liberal capitalism transformed itself into a more "orderly" state-corporate system; at the same time, the organized medical and pharmaceutical professions and the larger drug companies consolidated their power. In what is now known as the Progressive Era, the Pure Food and Drug Act, the Harrison Narcotic Act, and the Volstead Act were as much characteristic legislation as the Federal Reserve Act.

The impulse to clean up society and reduce disorder was hostile to free self-medication and chaotic small-scale entrepreneurial competition. Professional hygiene required new standards for medical and pharmaceutical practice, and intellectual hygiene required clear and enforceable categories for psychoactive drugs. Changes in medicine itself were also important. Synthetic chemistry, experimental physiology, and bacteriology advanced. The promise of a materialist medicine based on the recognition of specific agents for specific diseases seemed about to be fulfilled. Psychoactive drugs, with their nonspecific and merely palliative effects, became more suspect.

The system established during the Progressive Era has persisted until the present. As the medical and allied professions expand, divide, and send out new branches, they incorporate more and more social functions. This has sometimes been called "moral entrepreneurship" or "medical imperialism." More recently, the right of medical professionals to interpret the meaning of psychoactive drug use has been challenged by scholars and social critics as well as illicit drug users. In some cases they have advocated an openly religious conception of psychoactive drug use, a recommendation that we apply the standards of preindustrial cultures. The practical merit of this idea may be dubious, but it does raise two interesting issues: the dangers of technological advance and the protective function of ritual.

Technical advances in science and manufacturing have increased the danger of drug abuse by producing chemicals in pure form and permitting their production on a vast scale. On the other hand, these products of modern industry have powers commensurate with their dangers: the face of Dr. Jekyll as well as Mr. Hyde. It could be argued that in modern industrial societies the medical profession has to provide the same kind of ritual or quasi-religious context that makes drug use relatively safe in primitive cultures. The priestly role of doctors in prescribing occasions for drug use and warning against possession by the demons in these drugs may sometimes seem arrogant, but it is doubtful whether nineteenth century individualism or a return to preindustrial cultural and technological forms would be better, even if they were possible.

Physicians are now in a good position to examine rationally how and when to use their authority in controlling psychoactive drugs. They do not have to regard the complex powers of these drugs as a challenge to their own domination of territory they have legitimately staked out. Psychoactive drugs are still an important part of the medical armamentarium, although most of those in use today are synthetic. The doctrine of specific etiology, based on infectious and dietary deficiency diseases, is the source of modern medicine's great triumphs, and yet it remains inadequate. For the vaguely defined functional problems that still account for many visits to doctors, we often still have no clear explanations and no better remedies than drugs that affect the mind. This situation naturally causes much unease. Doctors are accused by lay people and accuse one another of using pills to resolve problems of living that demand more complex and difficult adjustments. These fears are reasonable. On the other hand, there remains a large area in which diseases and problems of living overlap. What a doctor does in prescribing a tranquilizer is not always different in a fundamental way from what lay persons do in prescribing a beer or marijuana cigarette for themselves.

Twentieth century societies have kept increasing government control of therapeutic drugs on the ground that authoritative knowledge about their efficacy and safety makes free individual choice illusory. Psychoactive substances used as pleasure drugs were the first to be restricted, but all prescription medicines now have to go through an elaborate procedure of testing and certification before they are approved for medical use. Of all federal drug laws, only the Pure Food and Drug Act (1906) was designed to encourage free choice by consumers, because it was aimed at simple fraud—false statements about the contents of the package. Since the passage of the Food, Drug and Cosmetics Act of 1938, the power to decide the availability of most drugs has gradually been transferred, first from consumers to doctors and then from doctors to the government. Before allowing a drug on the market, the federal government must now judge whether it is effective as well as whether it is safe.

Although most drugs are now illicit except when taken by prescription, the common understanding of the term "illicit drugs" includes only psychoactive drugs used for pleasure, most of which are covered by the federal criminal provisions of the Controlled Substances Act of 1970 and similar state laws. It would be impossible to discuss all of them here. Some are among the most commonly used drugs and have a variety of medical applications—notably the benzodiazepine tranquilizers, the barbiturates, and the synthetic and natural opioids. We will concentrate here on four classes of drugs that have much more limited medical acceptability. All four are placed in the two most restricted schedules under the Controlled Substances Act. Cocaine and amphetamines have currently accepted medical uses; marijuana and psychedelic drugs do not. We will explore the past and present, potential and actual, experimental and established, legal and illegitimate therapeutic uses of these drugs.

COCA AND COCAINE

Cocaine is an alkaloid extracted from the leaves of the shrub *Erythroxylon coca,* which has long been cultivated in Bolivia and Peru as a stimulant and for medicinal purposes. For thousands of years, inhabitants of the Peruvian and Bolivian highlands and the western

Amazon region have been mixing coca leaves with ash or lime, putting the wad in a cheek, and letting the juice trickle into their stomachs. In many parts of the Amazon and the Andes today, coca is the everyday stimulant drug, used more or less as coffee, tea, chewing tobacco, and khat are used in other areas of the world.

In one study of a mountain village in Peru, coca was found to be the standard remedy for symptoms of hunger and cold and for two folk illnesses: *el soka,* a condition of weakness, fatigue, and general malaise; and *el fiero,* a chronic wasting illness. Coca was also the treatment of choice for stomach upset and stomachache and for colic, or severe gastrointestinal distress including diarrhea, cramps, and nausea.[2]

In the form of leaf powder or tea, coca is taken for toothache, ulcers, rheumatism, asthma, and even malaria. Coca tea is often served to tourists arriving in hotels and inns in the high Andes as a remedy for the nausea, dizziness, and headache of *soroche* (altitude sickness). Unlike other stimulants, coca is also a local anesthetic. The juice of the leaf can be applied to soothe eye irritations or gargled for hoarseness and sore throat. Coca leaves are also used as a topical anesthetic for mouth sores. Coca contains minerals, vitamin C, and some B vitamins, and it is sometimes said to be an important source of these nutrients in the Andean diet.

An American physician, Andrew Weil, has recently been trying to revive interest in the therapeutic uses of coca, which he believes have been neglected because of the medical profession's fascination and subsequent disillusionment with the pure alkaloid cocaine. He has found coca useful in the symptomatic relief of indigestion, gastritis, constipation, motion sickness, laryngitis, and other ailments. He believes that it could serve as a substitute for coffee in persons who find that their stomachs are upset by that stimulant. He also proposes its use as an appetite-reducing drug and as an energizer for physical labor, and he suggests that it might serve as a relatively safe substitute in treating amphetamine and cocaine dependence. He points out that coca differs from cocaine in several ways. It contains a number of related alkaloids rather than a single one, and it is less subject to abuse because it enters the body by the normal gastrointestinal route rather than intranasally, intravenously, or through the

2. Horacio Fabrega and Peter K. Manning, "Health Maintenance Among Peruvian Peasants," *Human Organization* 31 (1973): 243–56.

lungs. He believes that coca might best be administered in the form of a chewing gum.[3]

Ever since the Spanish conquest there has been controversy about the health effects of habitual coca use. The evidence is unreliable, contradictory, and heavily colored by the political and social biases of observers. A number of studies have suggested that coca chewers are apathetic, subnormal in intelligence, or subject to various physical illnesses because they are weakened by the drug.[4] But even these results are ambiguous and inconclusive.[5] The biggest problem is separating cause from effect. If coca users in the high Andes seem undernourished, demoralized, and unhealthy, that is easily explained by the miserable physical and social conditions under which many of them live—conditions for which coca use apparently gives them some relief. It is significant that many Indians in the Amazon who use coca are reported to be strong and healthy.[6] In any case, the people of the Andes themselves, including those who do not use coca, usually reject the suggestion that it is a drug problem, a threat to health, or a danger to their community.

Cocaine was isolated from the coca leaf in 1860. Throughout the late nineteenth century, both coca itself (that is, an extract from the leaf including all of its alkaloids) and the pure chemical cocaine were popular as medicines in Europe and North America. In 1863 Angelo Mariani, a Corsican chemist, patented a preparation of coca extract and wine, which he called Vin Mariani; it became one of the most popular prescription medicines of the era, and was used by such celebrities as Thomas Edison, Ulysses Grant, Henrik Ibsen, Pope Leo XIII, Emile Zola, Jules Verne, and the Prince of Wales. Mariani wrote several articles and monographs on coca in which he combined

---

3. Andrew Weil, "The Therapeutic Value of Coca in Contemporary Medicine," *Journal of Ethnopharmacology* 3 (1981): 367–76.

4. Carlos Gutiérrez-Noriega, "El Cocaísmo y la Alimentación en el Perú," *Anales de la Facultad de Medicina* 31 (1948): 1–90; J. C. Negrete, "Psychological Deficit in Chewers of Coca Leaf," *Bulletin on Narcotics* 19, no. 4 (1967): 11–13; H. B. M. Murphy, O. Rios, and J. C. Negrete, "The Effects of Abstinence and Retraining on the Chewer of Coca Leaf," *Bulletin on Narcotics* 21, no. 2 (1969): 41–47; Alfred A. Buck et al., "Coca chewing and Health: An Epidemiological Study Among Residents of a Peruvian Village," *American Journal of Epidemiology* 88 (1968): 159–77.

5. Lester Grinspoon and James B. Bakalar, *Cocaine: A Drug and Its Social Evolution* (New York: Basic Books, 1976), pp. 120–29; Andrew T. Weil, "Coca and Brain Damage," April 1978 (unpublished).

6. Weil, "Therapeutic Value of Coca," p. 374.

historical, botanical, and medical information with the promotion of his company's product; he could list thousands of physicians who recommended it.[7]

By 1878 coca was being promoted in advertisements in the United States for young persons suffering from shyness and as a stimulant. In the same year, an American physician, W. H. Bentley, began to recommend coca as a cure for morphine addiction. Extract of coca was admitted to the United States Pharmacopoeia in 1882. In July 1884, Sigmund Freud published a famous paper, "On Coca," in which he recommended cocaine or coca extract for a variety of illnesses including the syndrome of fatigue, nervousness, and minor physical complaints then known as neurasthenia.[8] Referring to Freud's writings, the Parke-Davis Company declared in its pamphlet "Coca Erythroxylon and Its Derivatives": "If these claims are substantiated . . . [cocaine] will indeed be the most important therapeutic discovery of the age, the benefit of which to humanity will be incalculable."[9]

This article and later articles by Freud were influential, but the rediscovery of cocaine's local anesthetic properties by his colleague Karl Koller proved to be of more permanent importance. Koller introduced topical cocaine in eye operations, and soon cocaine was being used in many other forms of surgery. William Halsted of Johns Hopkins University invented nerve block or conduction anesthesia by injecting cocaine into nerve trunks. Soon regional anesthesia and spinal anesthesia were introduced. It was not until the early twentieth century that synthetic local anesthetics without the stimulant properties of cocaine were developed.

Meanwhile, cocaine was triumphing as what would now be disparagingly called a panacea. It was recommended for exhaustive and irritative conditions of the central nervous system, seasickness, trigeminal neuralgia, hay fever, head colds, and what was then called "catarrh." In 1901 the American physician W. Golden Mortimer published an encyclopedic volume, *History of Coca,* in which he recommended coca wine, coca extract, or cocaine for a great variety of purposes. In an appendix he cited the responses to a letter he had

7. Angelo Mariani, *Coca and Its Therapeutic Applications* (New York: Jaros, 1890).

8. Sigmund Freud, "On Coca," in Robert Byck, ed., *The Cocaine Papers* (New York: Stonehill, 1974), pp. 49–73.

9. Parke Davis and Company, "Coca Erythroxylon and Its Derivatives," in Byck, *Cocaine Papers,* p. 144.

sent to "a selected set" of more than 5,000 physicians asking for their observations on coca. Of the 1,206 replying, 369 said that they had used coca in their own practices. They commonly observed that it increased appetite, raised blood pressure, stimulated circulation, strengthened the heart, improved digestion, stimulated the mind, and worked as an aphrodisiac. The most popular therapeutic uses were for exhaustion, overwork, and neurasthenia. Few thought there was a dangerous tendency to form a coca habit.[10]

One of the most popular drinks containing cocaine was Coca-Cola, first concocted in 1886 by a Georgia pharmacist. The Coca-Cola Company was founded in 1892, and throughout the 1890s Coca-Cola was advertised as a headache remedy and stimulant as well as an enjoyable drink. In 1903 coca extract was removed from Coca-Cola and replaced with caffeine. A de-cocainized extract of the coca leaf is still used for flavoring.

In the medical use of coca and cocaine, it is hard to separate the central stimulant from the digestive, respiratory, and local anesthetic effects. A singer or actor who drank Mariani's wine could hardly know how much of the improvement he or she noticed was caused by local anesthesia or constriction of blood vessels in the throat and how much by euphoria and a feeling of mastery. As for stomach and intestinal problems, the gastrointestinal system is probably the most common site of psychosomatic symptoms. The use of coca or cocaine in convalescence from long-lasting debilitating diseases represents a similar combination of central and peripheral effects.

Abuse and dependence became problems almost as soon as cocaine was introduced into medicine. Cocaine dependence first appeared in morphine addicts who took the cocaine cure recommended by Bentley and Freud. Halsted, the inventor of nerve block anesthesia, appears to have cured himself of a craving for cocaine by taking up morphine and paying the price of physical addiction. In his last paper on cocaine, published in 1887, Freud admitted that the cocaine habit could be more dangerous to health than morphine addiction.[11] Later in life he seldom referred to cocaine.

The growing fear of cocaine changed attitudes toward coca. Advocates of coca then began to fight a rear-guard action in its defense,

10. W. Golden Mortimer, *History of Coca* (New York: Vail, 1901), pp. 491–509.

11. Sigmund Freud, "Craving For and Fear Of Cocaine," in Byck, *Cocaine Papers,* pp. 171–76.

insisting that coca never caused the kinds of problems that were ruining the reputation of cocaine, and even saying that the effects of coca might be caused primarily by other chemicals in the leaf. But by 1900 public and medical opinion had begun to turn against both coca and cocaine. In 1906 the Pure Food and Drug Act banned food and drinks containing cocaine, and further legal restrictions soon followed, culminating in the Harrison Act of 1914, which regulated cocaine as well as opiates. Cocaine and the coca leaf were still prescribed occasionally through the 1920s for many of the same purposes as in the late nineteenth century, although criminal laws and other restraints made it less easily available. But its use gradually declined until, by 1930, it was rarely being used except as a surgical anesthetic and an illicit pleasure drug.

Today cocaine is used in medicine mainly as a topical anesthetic in eye, ear, nose, and throat surgery and fiber tube optical examinations of the upper respiratory and digestive tracts. It has a combination of properties that cannot be duplicated by any of the synthetic local anesthetics: intense constriction of blood vessels (important whenever bleeding must be prevented), long duration of anesthesia (one hour), and low toxicity. Cocaine is no longer used in infiltration anesthesia (subcutaneous injection), in nerve block anesthesia, or in spinal anesthesia.[12] Recently topical application of cocaine to the upper palate has been recommended as a way of aborting the severe pain of cluster headaches.[13]

Other medical uses are rare. Cocaine is an ingredient in Brompton's mixture, a preparation used in Great Britain for treating the chronic pain of terminal cancer, but controlled studies at a hospice in England have suggested that the cocaine in this drink provides no advantage over morphine alone.[14] Cocaine was never tested seriously as a treatment for severe depression, but this idea is unlikely to be revived because the pharmacologically similar amphetamines have proved a failure for that purpose. Today substitutes have been found for most therapeutic uses of cocaine, and in most cases its dangers

12. Grinspoon and Bakalar, *Cocaine,* pp. 161–63; Nicholas L. Schenk, "Local Anesthesia in Otolaryngology: A Reevaluation," *Annals of Otology, Rhinology and Laryngology* 84 (1979): 65–72.

13. Felix Barre, "Cocaine as an Abortive Agent in Cluster Headache," *Headache* 22 (1982): 69–73.

14. R. G. Twycross, "Value of Cocaine in Opiate-containing Elixirs," *British Medical Journal* 2 (1977): 1348.

are believed to outweigh its potential benefits. Despite the recent and so far uncertain signs of reviving interest, coca and cocaine will never again be so widely used in medicine as they once were.

Legally, the coca leaf and all its derivatives containing cocaine are classified under the Controlled Substances Act as Schedule II drugs: This means that there is a currently accepted medical use but also a high potential for abuse and dependence. Schedule II drugs may be prescribed under special restrictions; hospitals and pharmacies are required to keep them in a locked place.

AMPHETAMINES

Amphetamines and amphetamine congeners are a large group of chemically related central stimulant drugs; among the best known are dextroamphetamine (Dexedrine), methamphetamine (Methedrine) and methylphenidate (Ritalin). Racemic amphetamine sulfate (Benzedrine) was first synthesized in 1887, but it was not introduced as a medicine until 1932, when the Benzedrine inhaler became available over the counter in drugstores as a treatment for nasal congestion and asthma. In late 1937 the new drug was introduced in tablet form to treat narcolepsy and postencephalitic parkinsonism. It was also recommended for depression and to heighten energy and capacity for work. Soon amphetamine was receiving sensational publicity with numerous references to "brain," "pep," and "superman" pills. Even when phrased as warnings, these reports served mainly to arouse curiosity.

But amphetamine use spread mainly because the medical profession was so enthusiastic about the drugs. Many doctors regarded amphetamines as remedies with extraordinary scope, efficacy, and safety. By 1943 more than half the sales of Benzedrine went to fill prescriptions written for people who wanted to lose weight, obtain a temporary lift in spirits, or stay awake for extended periods. In 1946 W. R. Bett asserted that amphetamine had thirty-nine clinical uses, including treatment for epilepsy, postencephalitic parkinsonism, schizophrenia, alcoholism, behavior problems in children, migraine, muscular rigidity and spasm, head injuries, dysmenorrhea, and hypotension.[15]

---

15. W. R. Bett, "Benzedrine Sulfate in Clinical Medicine: A Survey of the Literature," *Postgraduate Medical Journal* 22 (1946): 205–18.

Although not all these uses were generally adopted, by 1971 the total production of amphetamines had reached the equivalent of more than 10 billion 5 mg tablets. Until 1971, amphetamines were sold freely over the counter without prescription in the form of inhalers such as the Dristan inhaler. They were also easy to obtain in the form of pills, capsules, or injectable liquids, with or without a visit to the doctor for a prescription. The Army used amphetamines heavily during the Vietnam War, and amphetamine abuse became a problem among the troops.[16] From the mid-1960s on there was also a growth in both illicit bathroom laboratory synthesis of amphetamines and black market diversion of legitimately produced drugs.

Since 1970 use and abuse of amphetamines have declined because of legal restrictions and a better understanding of their dangers, which include weight loss, psychosis, severe dependence, and depression on withdrawal. It is as though the career of amphetamines from 1940 to 1970 recapitulated the career of cocaine in the late nineteenth century. Not having learned from history, we were condemned to repeat it. Although chemically different from cocaine, the amphetamines have similar stimulant effects and similar liabilities. After the first flush of enthusiasm, the range of accepted medical uses for amphetamines narrowed, just as it had for cocaine a generation earlier. The only present widely accepted medical uses for amphetamines are in treating narcolepsy and attention deficit disorder. They are occasionally used as an adjunct to tricyclic antidepressants in the treatment of depression. They are also still prescribed for weight loss, but this practice is becoming less and less common because of well-founded doubts about their safety and effectiveness.

The amphetamines used in medicine are placed in Schedule II under the Controlled Substances Act of 1970 as later amended. Like cocaine, they are regarded as drugs having a currently accepted medical use but a high potential for abuse, which may lead to severe psychological or physical dependence. An applicant to manufacture such drugs must register with the attorney general. The attorney general establishes production quotas, and there are special restrictions on prescriptions.

---

16. See Lester Grinspoon and Peter Hedblom, *The Speed Culture: Amphetamine Use and Abuse in America* (Cambridge: Harvard University Press, 1975), pp. 19–20.

Weight Loss

Until the early 1970s, amphetamines were overwhelmingly the drug of choice in treating overweight by appetite reduction. Their anorectic effect is apparently secondary to the stimulating effect. Controlled studies have found that amphetamines increase weight loss, at least in the first few months, by making it easy to adhere to a diet. But the user rapidly grows tolerant to the anorectic effect, and it can rarely be sustained more than a few months without an increase in the dose.[17] It also appears that most patients, once they stop using amphetamines or become tolerant to them, go back to their former eating habits and regain the weight they have lost.

The favorable results of clinical studies on the appetite reducing effects of amphetamines must also be balanced by a consideration of adverse effects, including the danger of abuse. Even if the intention is to expose the patient to amphetamine only for a short period, compulsive eaters who have a need for constant gratification may find it hard to put aside a medication that makes them feel good. They may also discover, when they no longer have the magic potion that protects them from themselves, that a psychological vacuum has developed that needs to be filled with food.

Appetite is governed by physiology, habit, and emotional state. Tension and depression, inability to delay gratification, and the substitution of food for other forms of pleasure, all of which are common in cases of overweight, increase the danger of drug dependency. A drug that reduces appetite without requiring any solution to emotional problems may seem to be a reasonable alternative at first, but the short-term weight loss may cause patients to avoid the issue of changing their eating and exercise habits. (The same problem, of course, often occurs when drugs are administered for other emotional problems and habitual behavior.)

It is doubtful whether amphetamines should be used for weight reduction under any circumstances. All anorectic drugs, and especially amphetamines, have a limited value in the treatment of obesity; because of their potential for dependence and abuse, they should

---

17. D. Adlersberg and M. E. Mayer, "Results of Prolonged Medical Treatment of Obesity with Diet Alone, Diet and Thyroid Preparations, and Diet and Amphetamine," *Journal of Clinical Endocrinology* 9 (1949): 275–84.

be used with extreme care, if at all. The prescription of amphetamines for weight loss has properly declined in the last decade.

Narcolepsy

Narcolepsy, first described ninety years ago, is a disorder marked by an uncontrollable desire for sleep or sudden attacks of sleep during the daytime. It usually begins in adolescence, and it never completely remits. Narcolepsy is considered rare, but it is not clear just how common it is, and in any case, it is a complicated problem. It may involve either REM (dreaming) sleep or non-REM sleep, and it may be complicated by cataplexy (loss of muscle tone), sleep paralysis, or hypnagogic hallucinations. Tricyclic antidepressants are used to treat these symptoms, but they do not eliminate the sleep attacks themselves. There is no evidence of brain pathology in narcolepsy, but heredity may be a factor.

Amphetamine was first introduced as a treatment for narcolepsy in 1935, and one or another amphetamine congener continues to be the drug treatment of choice. Dextroamphetamine or methylphenidate may be necessary for a narcoleptic person whose work is dangerous, but most victims of narcolepsy can perform satisfactorily without drugs if they take at least one nap a day. The risk of dependence, toxic reactions, and psychosis must be weighed against the advantages of drug-induced wakefulness.

Depression

Depression is probably the most common complaint of adults. Its symptoms are both physical and emotional: loss of appetite and energy, insomnia, fatigue, difficulty in concentration, feelings of worthlessness and self-reproach, thoughts of death and suicide, anxiety and irritability. Amphetamines were one of the first classes of drugs to be used in the treatment of depression, beginning in 1936. Early studies sometimes led to excessive enthusiasm, because they were not controlled and the clinical symptoms of depression show a strong tendency to spontaneous remission. Even in the early stages, amphetamines were generally found to be ineffective in severe depressions and in treating the depressed phase of bipolar (manic-depressive) illness. Early studies of less serious depressions demonstrated some effectiveness but raised questions about possible dangers. Even at that time researchers mentioned the possibility of increasing the risk of suicide by heightening energy and mobility. Suicide attempts may also occur during the severe depression that sometimes follows withdrawal. Nevertheless, as late as 1958, C. D. Leake strongly recommended amphetamines for depression in an authoritative book.[18]

As the dangers of insomnia and anxiety became more apparent, interest developed in using amphetamines together with sedatives such as the barbiturate sodium amytal. Each drug, it was thought, would counteract the unfortunate side effects of the other. Although doubt soon developed about the effectiveness of these combinations, they were marketed for years under various trade names and soon became sources of a new kind of drug abuse.

By the 1950s, new amphetamine congeners with fewer side effects, such as methylphenidate, had been developed, but they proved to be no more effective in treating depression. Eventually two new groups of drugs, the monoamine oxidase (MAO) inhibitors and the tricyclics, revolutionized the field. Tricyclic derivatives, along with lithium for manic-depressive illness, are now believed to be the most effective drug treatment for depression. Controlled studies comparing tricyclic antidepressants to amphetamines or placebo have found amphetamines ineffective in the treatment of all types of depression.[19] But amphetamine-related stimulants may potentiate the effects of the tricyclics by slowing their metabolism in the body; and they may also evoke an immediate response that encourages the depressed patient to keep taking a tricyclic whose effects do not become apparent for a few weeks.[20]

A few other uses for amphetamines in the treatment of depression are still occasionally recommended. Methylphenidate has been proposed to treat depression in patients who are medically ill or re-

18. C. D. Leake, *The Amphetamines: Their Actions and Uses* (Springfield, Ill.: Thomas, 1958), pp. 67–69.
19. E. H. Hare, J. Dominian, and L. Sharpe, "Phenelzine and Dexamphetamine in Depressive Illness: A Comparative Trial," *British Medical Journal* 1 (1962): 9–12; J. E. Overall et al., "Drug Therapy in Depressions: Controlled Evaluation of Imipramine, Isocarboxazine, Dextroamphetamine-Amobarbital, and Placebo," *Clinical Pharmacology and Therapeutics* 3 (1962): 16–21.
20. Eric J. Drimmer, Michael J. Gitlin, and Harry E. Gwirtsman, "Desipramine and Methylphenidate Combination Treatment for Depression: Case Report," *American Journal of Psychiatry* 140 (1983): 241–42; R. N. Wharton, et al., "A Potential Clinical Use for Methylphenidate with Tricyclic Antidepressants," *American Journal of Psychiatry* 127 (1971): 1619–25.

covering from surgery and therefore unable to tolerate the side effects of tricyclic antidepressants. This is especially true of heart patients and elderly people with organic brain disease.[21] Amphetamines taken intravenously in combination with morphine have also been recommended in the treatment of postoperative pain.[22] In some studies amphetamines seem to be effective in obsessive-compulsive disorder, but other drugs are available for this purpose as well.[23]

Drugs should not be used as a substitute for reassurance and exploration of the patient's concerns in cases of mild depression, fatigue, or anxiety. If amphetamines are used to relieve symptoms that are often indistinguishable from the tensions of everyday life, they may make the patient feel good but they will only mask the underlying problem. A patient complaining of fatigue, nervousness, anxiety, or insomnia may be asking for a kind of short-term psychotherapy from a person believed to be trustworthy. When a doctor responds with a stimulant pill, he or she may be depriving the patient of a service that should be provided and may perpetuate a pattern of drug use as a substitute for coping with the problems of daily life. Fortunately, most physicians have come to recognize this, and amphetamines are no longer commonly used in treating depression.

Attention Deficit Disorder

The most controversial remaining medical use of amphetamines is the treatment of the syndrome known variously as hyperactivity, hyperkinesis, minimal brain dysfunction, and, most recently, attention deficit disorder. It is probably the most common behavioral disorder of childhood; boys are affected five to ten times as often as girls. The main symptoms are extreme physical restlessness (hyperactive children move more, even in sleep) and short attention span; other symptoms are poor coordination, intolerance for frustration, aggressive and impulsive behavior, and learning disabilities. The prob-

21. M. W. Kaufmann et al., "The Use of Methylphenidate in Depressed Patients After Cardiac Surgery," *Journal of Clinical Psychiatry* 45 (1984): 82–84; Wayne Katon and Murray Raskind, "Treatment of Depression in the Medically Ill Elderly with Methylphenidate," *American Journal of Psychiatry* 137 (1980): 963–65.

22. W. H. Forest et al., "Dextroamphetamine with Morphine for the Treatment of Postoperative Pain," *New England Journal of Medicine* 296 (1977): 712–15.

23. Thomas R. Insel et al., "Amphetamine in Obsessive-Compulsive Disorder," *Psychopharmacology* 80 (1983): 231–35.

lem usually begins in infancy, but it becomes especially troublesome in the classroom. Hyperactive children do not usually outgrow their problems, although the symptoms may change. In adolescence they are often academic underachievers with poor social skills and low self-esteem, who may become juvenile delinquents. Many of the symptoms also persist in adult life.

Attention deficit disorder overlaps in its symptoms with disorderly behavior and more serious developmental disorders of childhood. Symptoms found in hyperactive children are also found in some children with known brain injuries and are often associated with neurological signs of central nervous system malfunction. The term "minimal brain dysfunction" suggests an organic cause, but so far no specifically characteristic neurological disorder or brain pathology has been found. The current term "attention deficit disorder" suggests that the problem reflects the way activity is organized in response to social demands as much as it involves physical motion. Hyperactivity is probably a mixture of symptoms with different origins in different children; in many cases a genetic factor may be involved.

The use of amphetamines in treating hyperactive children began in 1937, when Charles Bradley observed that it produced striking effects on a number of schoolchildren showing various kinds of disturbance. Their problems, aside from hyperactive behavior, included specific learning disabilities, aggressiveness associated with epilepsy, and schizoid withdrawal. The drug reduced their motor activity and impulsive behavior, improved their attention, diminished mood swings, increased their interest in the surroundings, made them less anxious and irritable, and improved their school achievement.[24] Studies on the amphetamine treatment of disturbed children with a variety of diagnoses reported a substantial improvement in behavior and school performance as judged by parents, teachers, and caregivers.[25]

There is still much confusion about what symptoms respond to

24. Charles Bradley, "The Behavior of Children Receiving Benzedrine," *American Journal of Psychiatry* 94 (1937): 577–85.

25. C. K. Conners et al., "Dextroamphetamine Sulfate in Children with Learning Disorders: Effects on Perception, Learning, and Achievement," *Archives of General Psychiatry* 21 (1969): 182–90; Gabrielle Weiss et al., "Studies on the Hyperactive Child: V. The Effects of Dextroamphetamine and Chlorpromazine on Behavior and Intellectual Functioning," *Journal of Child Psychology and Psychiatry* 9 (1968): 148–53.

amphetamines. Some studies suggest that children who show signs of a neurological disorder do better on amphetamines than other restless children who do not show such signs. Others find that amphetamines contribute to relieving the symptoms of disturbed children in general, whether or not there is evidence of a learning disorder or brain injury.[26] The apparent calming effect of these stimulant drugs on hyperactivity in children has been called paradoxical, with the implication that the effect is specifically related to the disorder. But it turns out that single doses of amphetamine affect normal boys the same way they affect hyperkinetic boys—increasing attention span and reducing motor activity.[27]

Amphetamines have serious limitations and dangers. The results of treatment are more variable and less spectacular than they may appear. Amphetamines probably do not help hyperkinetic preschool children or improve specific learning disorders such as reading problems.[28] The symptoms usually return when the drug is withdrawn, and in any case its benefits seem to occur mainly in the first few months; long-term treatment does not lead to a better outcome.[29] Attention problems, impulsiveness, and academic failure persist in adolescence among children diagnosed as hyperactive whether or not they have taken amphetamines.

Some hyperactive children even get worse on amphetamines; in one study, 16 percent of the children showed an exaggeration of the original symptoms.[30] A few serious adverse reactions have also been reported, including an amphetamine psychosis and movement dis-

26. Peggy T. Ackerman et al., "Methylphenidate Effects on Cognitive Style and Reaction Time in Four Groups of Children," *Psychiatry Research* 7 (1982): 199–213; Roscoe A. Dykman, Peggy T. Ackerman, and David S. McCray, "Effects of Methylphenidate on Selective and Sustained Attention in Hyperactive, Reading-Disabled, and Presumably Attention-Disordered Boys," *Journal of Nervous and Mental Disease* 168 (1980): 745–52.

27. J. L. Rapaport et al., "Dextroamphetamine: Cognitive and Behavioral Effects in Normal Prepubescent Boys," *Science* 199 (1978): 560–63.

28. C. K. Conners, "Controlled Trial of Methylphenidate in Preschool Children with Minimal Brain Dysfunction," *International Journal of Mental Health* 4 (1975): 61–74; Rachel Gittelman, "Indications for the Use of Stimulant Treatment in Learning Disorders," *Journal of the American Academy of Child Psychiatry* 19 (1980): 623–36.

29. Linda Charles and Richard Schain, "A Four-Year Follow-Up Study of the Effects of Methylphenidate on the Behavior and Academic Achievement of Hyperactive Children," *Journal of Abnormal Child Psychology* 9 (1981): 495–505.

30. Charles Bradley, "Benzedrine and Dexedrine in the Treatment of Children's Behavior Disorders," *Pediatrics* 5 (1950): 24–36.

orders.[31] Even children who are benefited by amphetamines may suffer from loss of appetite, dizziness, pallor, and digestive troubles. These symptoms usually diminish or disappear after the first week, and they can usually be minimized by adjusting the dose. (Methylphenidate has fewer toxic side-effects than do other forms of amphetamine.) A more serious problem is that some amphetamine-treated hyperactive children fail to achieve expected gains in weight and height. The effect is statistically significant but generally not large. It might be neutralized by the spurt in growth that begins in adolescence; the evidence is not yet available. In any case, the growth of children taking stimulant drugs must be carefully monitored.[32]

For educational psychologists who found that many disturbed children did not respond to psychotherapy and for educators interested in the relationship between learning disabilities and behavior problems, amphetamines have suggested new approaches to treatment. But children should not be given drugs as soon as they become restless or unruly. Often the problem lies in the school or home as much as in the child. Children need an educational environment that will help them come to grips with their problems without using pharmacological shortcuts unless they are absolutely necessary. Teachers, parents, and physicians should try other methods before resorting to amphetamines. Physicians must be certain that their diagnoses are accurate. At one time amphetamines may have been used excessively in treating hyperactivity because of imprecise diagnosis and overzealous promotion by drug companies and educators, but it is our impression that physicians and educators now have a better understanding of the limitations as well as the advantages of amphetamines and are using them with more care.

PSYCHEDELIC DRUGS

The psychedelics or hallucinogens are a large group of drugs, some natural and some synthetic, with a variety of chemical structures. The best known are mescaline, derived from the peyote cactus; psil-

31. R. H. Mattson and J. R. Calverly, "Dextroamphetamine Sulfate-Induced Dyskinesias," *Journal of the American Medical Association* 204 (1968): 400-2; P. G. Ney, "Psychosis in a Child Associated with Amphetamine Administration," *Canadian Medical Association Journal* 97 (1967): 1026-29.

32. Jeffrey A. Mattes and Rachel Gittelman, "Growth of Hyperactive Children on Maintenance Regimen of Methylphenidate," *Archives of General Psychiatry* 40 (1983): 317-21.

ocybin, found in over a hundred species of mushrooms; and the synthetic drug lysergic acid diethylamide (LSD), which is chemically related to certain alkaloids found in morning glory seeds, the lysergic acid amides. This class of drugs also includes the natural substances harmine, harmaline, ibogaine, and dimethyltryptamine (DMT), as well as a large number of synthetic drugs that are chemically described as tryptamines or methoxylated amphetamines. A few of these are diethyltryptamine (DET), 3,4,-methylenedioxyamphetamine (MDA), and 2,5-dimethoxy-4-methylamphetamine (DOM, also known as STP).

The natural hallucinogens have long been used by preindustrial cultures, especially in Mexico and South America, for magical, religious, and healing purposes, and today the peyote cactus is the sacrament of the Native American Church, a religious organization with branches in all western states of the United States. Peyote became known in industrial society toward the end of the nineteenth century, and many other plant hallucinogens have been discovered since. LSD was first synthesized in 1938 and its psychoactive properties were discovered in 1943; since then many other synthetic psychedelic drugs have been developed in laboratories.

The psychedelic drugs differ somewhat in their subjective effects and greatly in the effective dosage. LSD is the most potent and produces the widest range of effects; it can be taken as a prototype. Although the response to LSD varies with personality, expectations, and setting, it almost always produces profound changes in perception, mood, and thinking. Perceptions become unusually brilliant and intense; normally unnoticed details capture the attention and ordinary things are seen with wonder. Synesthesia, changes in body image, and alterations in time and space perception are common. Vivid dreamlike imagery appears before closed eyes. True hallucinations are rare, but visual distortions and pseudohallucinations are common. Emotions become unusually intense and may change abruptly and often. Suggestibility is greatly heightened. The experience is suffused by a heightened sense of reality and significance, and it often produces feelings of religious and philosophical insight. The sense of self is greatly changed, sometimes to the point of merging with the external world, separation from the body, or dissolution in mystical ecstasy.

The most common adverse effect of LSD and related drugs is the "bad trip," which occasionally produces a true psychotic reaction.

Another common effect is the flashback, a spontaneous transitory recapitulation of drug-induced experience in a drug-free state. Prolonged adverse reactions, which are considerably less common, include anxiety reactions, depressive reactions, and psychoses. They are most likely to occur in schizoid and prepsychotic personalities with barely stable egos who cannot cope with the mind alterations produced by the drug trip. There is a close resemblance between people hospitalized for LSD reactions and those hospitalized for psychoses not produced by drugs.[33]

A persistent issue has been possible genetic damage and birth defects. The available evidence suggests that LSD produces no chromosome damage in reproductive cells of a kind that is likely to cause birth defects; the same is true of other psychedelic drugs to the extent that they have been tested. There is also no evidence that LSD is teratogenic in human users at normal doses.[34]

Ever since experimentation with psychedelic drugs began, some users and psychotherapists have maintained that a single psychedelic experience or several such experiences can provide religious insight, heightened creative capacity, psychological insight, or relief from neurotic symptoms. From 1950 to the mid-1960s, psychedelic drugs—especially LSD, mescaline, and psilocybin—were used extensively in experimental psychiatry. The drugs were studied as a chemical model for natural psychoses and also used extensively in psychotherapy. More than a thousand clinical papers were published discussing forty thousand patients; there were several dozen books and six international conferences on psychedelic drug therapy. It was recommended at one time or another for a wide variety of problems, including alcoholism, obsessional neurosis, and childhood autism. Beginning in the mid-1960s, with the increase of illicit use, it became difficult to obtain the drugs or get funding for research, and professional interest declined. There is now only one legally approved project in the United States involving the therapeutic use of psychedelic drugs; it is located at the Maryland Psychiatric Research Institute in Baltimore. Maybe those two decades of psychedelic research will even-

33. Lester Grinspoon and James B. Bakalar, *Psychedelic Drugs Reconsidered* (New York: Basic Books, 1979), pp. 163–66, 168–71.

34. Norman I. Dishotsky et al., "LSD and Genetic Damage," *Science* 172 (1971): 431–40; Sally Y. Long, "Does LSD Induce Chromosomal Damage and Malformations? A Review of the Literature," *Teratology* 6 (1972): 75–90.

tually be written off as a mistake that has only historical interest, but it might be wiser to see if something can be salvaged from them.

One source of the therapeutic interest was the belief of some experimental subjects after taking a psychedelic drug that they were less depressed, anxious, and guilty, and more self-accepting, tolerant, or sensually alert. Interest also arose from the possibility of making therapeutic use of the powerful psychedelic experiences of regression, abreaction, intense transference, and symbolic drama to improve the results of psychodynamic psychotherapy. Two kinds of therapy emerged, one making use of the mystical or conversion experience and the other exploring the unconscious in the manner of psychoanalysis. Psychedelic therapy, as the first kind was called, involved the use of a large dose (200 micrograms of LSD or more) in a single session; it was thought to be potentially helpful in reforming alcoholics and criminals as well as improving the lives of normal people. The second type, psycholytic (literally, mind-loosening) therapy, required relatively small doses and several or even many sessions; it was used mainly for neurotic and psychosomatic disorders. In practice, many combinations, variations, and special applications with some of the features of both psycholytic and psychedelic therapy evolved.

Neurotic Disorders

In a book about her LSD treatment, one woman described the result this way:

> I found that in addition to being, consciously, a loving mother and a respectable citizen, I was also, unconsciously, a murderess, a pervert, a cannibal, a sadist, and a masochist. In the wake of these dreadful discoveries, I lost my fear of dentists, the clicking in my neck and throat, the arm tensions, and my dislike of clocks ticking in the bedroom. I also achieved transcendent sexual fulfillment. . . .
>
> At the end of nine sessions over a period of nine weeks I was cured of my hitherto incurable frigidity, and at the end of five months I felt that I had been completely reconstituted as a human being. I have continued to feel that way ever since.[35]

These passages were written three years after a five-month period during which this woman took LSD twenty-three times. Before that

---

35. Constance A. Newland, *My Self and I* (New York: New American Library, 1962), pp. 20–47.

she had had four years of psychoanalysis, but it was only after LSD that she became convinced of the value of Freud's theories.

The literature contains a number of such impressive case histories, but these anecdotal accounts can always be questioned; placebo effects, spontaneous recovery, special and prolonged devotion by the therapist, and the therapist's and patient's biases in judging improvement must be considered. The most serious deficiencies in psychedelic drug studies were absence of controls and inadequate follow-up. And psychedelic drug effects are so striking that it is difficult to design a double-blind study, in which neither the person administering the drug nor the person taking it knows whether it is the active substance or a placebo. No form of psychotherapy for neurotics has ever been able to justify itself under stringent controls, and LSD therapy is no exception.

Furthermore, psychiatrists did not agree about details. Should the emphasis be on expression of repressed feelings or on working through a transference attachment to the psychiatrist? How much therapy is necessary in the intervals between LSD treatments? Because of the complexity of psychedelic drug effects, there are no general answers to these questions. It appeared that LSD treatment sometimes produced spectacular improvement in neurotic symptoms, but no reliable formula for success was derived from these results. But again, in these respects psychedelic drug therapy seems to be in no better or worse position than most other forms of psychotherapy.

Alcoholism

Psychedelic therapy for alcoholism is based on the assumption that one overwhelming experience sometimes changes the self-destructive drinking habits of a lifetime, and the hope that psychedelic drugs can consistently produce such an experience. In one reported case, a 40-year-old black, unskilled laborer was brought to a hospital from jail after drinking uncontrollably for ten days. He had been an alcoholic for four years, and he was also severely anxious and depressed. He described his experiences during an LSD session as follows:

> I was afraid. I started to run, but something said "Stop! Stop!" . . . then I felt as if ten tons had fallen from my shoulders. I prayed to the Lord. Everything looked better all around me. . . . I changed my mind from alcohol toward Christ and the rose came back into my life. . . . As

I sat up and looked in the mirror I could feel myself growing stronger. I feel now that my family and I are closer than ever before and I hope that our faith will grow forever and ever.

One week later his score on a questionnaire testing neurotic traits had dropped from the 88th to the 10th percentile. Six months later his psychological tests were within normal limits; he had been totally abstinent from alcohol for all that time and despite a temporary relapse when he lost his job, he was still sober after twelve months.[36]

LSD undoubtedly produces powerful effects on alcoholics; the question is whether they can be reliably translated into enduring change. Early studies reported dazzling success. About 50 percent of severe chronic alcoholics treated with a single high dose of LSD were said to be recovered and sober a year or two later.[37] But the early studies proved to be inadequate. When the patients were randomly assigned to drug and control groups it proved difficult to demonstrate any advantage for LSD treatment, even in studies conducted by advocates of the drug.[38] The problem is that many alcoholics will improve, at least temporarily, after any treatment because excessive drinking is often sporadic and periodic relapses are common. The alcoholic who arrives at a clinic or hospital is probably at a low point in the cycle and has nowhere to go but up.

It would be wrong to conclude that a psychedelic experience can never be a turning point in the life of an alcoholic. As William James said, "Religiomania is the best cure for dipsomania." Unfortunately, psychedelic experiences have the same limitations as religious conversions. Their authenticity and emotional power are not guarantees against backsliding when the old frustrations, constraints, and emotional distress have to be faced in everyday life. Even when the revelation does seem to have lasting effects, it might have been merely a symptom of readiness to change rather than a cause of change.

The fact remains that there is no proven treatment for alcoholism.

---

36. Albert A. Kurland, "The Therapeutic Potential of LSD in Medicine," in R. DeBold and R. Leaf, eds., *LSD, Man, and Society* (Middletown, Conn.: Wesleyan University Press, 1967), pp. 20–35.

37. Abram Hoffer, "A Program for the Treatment of Alcoholism: LSD, Malvaria, and Nicotinic Acid," in Harold A. Abramson, ed., *The Use of LSD in Psychotherapy and Alcoholism* (New York: Bobbs-Merrill, 1967), pp. 353–402.

38. Reginald G. Smart et al., "A Controlled Study of Lysergide in the Treatment of Alcoholism," *Quarterly Journal of Studies on Alcohol* 27 (1966): 469–82; Frances E. Cheek et al., "Observations Regarding the Use of LSD-25 in the Treatment of Alcoholism," *Journal of Psychopharmacology* 1, no. 1 (1966): 56–74.

Where so little is known, it may not make sense to give up entirely on anything that has possibilities. In the religious ceremonies of the Native American Church, periodic use of high doses of mescaline in the form of peyote is regarded as, among other things, part of a treatment for alcoholism. Both the Indians themselves and outside researchers believe that those who participate in the peyote ritual are more likely to abstain from alcohol. Peyote sustains the ritual and religious principles of the community of believers, and these sometimes confirm and support an individual commitment to give up alcohol. Even federal alcoholism clinics for Indians now recognize that peyote might have some value.[39] If, for whatever reasons, psychedelic drugs work for at least some Indians some of the time, they might also help some non-Indian alcoholics.

Dying

There is a new consciousness today of the significance of dying as part of life. As we look for ways to change the pattern, so common in chronic illness, of constantly increasing pain, anxiety, and depression, the emphasis is shifted away from impersonal prolongation of physical existence toward a conception of dying as a psychiatric crisis, or even, in older language, a religious crisis. The purpose of giving psychedelic drugs to the dying might be stated as reconciliation: reconciliation with one's past, one's family, and one's human limitations.

Beginning in 1965, the experiment of providing a psychedelic experience for the dying was pursued at Spring Grove State Hospital in Maryland and later at the Maryland Psychiatric Research Institute. Walter Pahnke, the director of the project from 1967 until 1971, was a Doctor of Divinity as well as a psychiatrist, and he first reported on his work in an article in the *Harvard Theological Review* in 1969. When terminal cancer patients received LSD or DPT after appropriate preparations, about one-third were said to have improved "dramatically," one-third improved "moderately," and one-third were unchanged; the tests of improvement were reduced tension, depression, pain, and fear of death.[40] Later experiments with

---

39. Bernard J. Albaugh and Philip O. Anderson, "Peyote in the Treatment of Alcoholism Among American Indians," *American Journal of Psychiatry* 131 (1974): 1247–51.

40. Walter N. Pahnke, "The Psychedelic Mystical Experience in the Human Encounter with Death," *Harvard Theological Review* 62 (1969): 1–21.

terminal cancer patients produced similar results.[41] There were no control groups in these studies, and there is no certain way to separate the effects of the drug from those of the special therapeutic arrangements and increased attention that were part of the treatment. Nevertheless, the case histories are impressive, and it would be interesting to renew the research; the present work at the Maryland Psychiatric Research Institute is an attempt to do that.

Complications and Dangers

Like any probing psychotherapy, psychedelic drug therapy presents the danger that unconscious material will come up and be neither accepted and integrated nor totally repressed; in that case, symptoms will become worse. Psychosis and even suicide have been reported in the course of psychedelic drug treatment. On the other hand, some people who have worked with psychedelic drugs consider them more likely to prevent suicide than to cause it, and most studies questioning psychiatrists about adverse reactions to psychedelic drugs in experimental or therapeutic research have revealed a low rate of serious complications.[42]

All such studies have limitations. Some psychiatrists may have minimized the dangers out of therapeutic enthusiasm or reluctance to admit mistakes; some may have exaggerated the dangers under the influence of bad publicity; long-term risks may have been underestimated if follow-up was inadequate. The studies provide no basis for comparison with patients who were not treated with psychedelic drugs or not treated at all. But the fact remains that psychedelic drugs were used for more than fifteen years by hundreds of psychiatrists who considered them reasonably safe as therapeutic agents.

Conclusion

When a new kind of therapy is introduced, especially a new psychoactive drug, events often follow a pattern of spectacular success

41. Stanislav Grof et al., "LSD-Assisted Psychotherapy in Patients with Terminal Cancer," *International Pharmacopsychiatry* 8 (1973): 129–41.

42. Walter Houston Clark and G. Ray Funkhouser, "Physicians and Researchers Disagree on Psychedelic Drugs," *Psychology Today* 3, no. 11: 48–50, 70–73; Sidney Cohen, "Lysergic Acid Diethylamide: Side Effects and Complications," *Journal of Nervous and Mental Disease* 130 (1960): 30–40; Nicholas Malleson, "Acute Adverse Reactions to LSD in Clinical and Experimental Use in the United Kingdom," *British Journal of Psychiatry* 188 (1971): 229–30.

and enormous enthusiasm followed by disillusionment. But the rise and decline of psychedelic drug therapy took a somewhat unusual course. From the early 1960s on, the revolutionary proclamations and religious fervor of the nonmedical advocates of psychedelic drugs began to evoke hostile incredulity rather than simply the natural skeptical response to extravagant claims backed mainly by intense subjective experiences. Twenty years after their introduction, psychedelics were pariah drugs, scorned by the medical establishment and banned by the law. In rejecting the absurd notion that these drugs were a panacea, we have chosen to treat them as entirely worthless and extraordinarily dangerous. Maybe the time has come to find an intermediate position. If the therapeutic results have been erratic and inconsistent, that is partly because of the complexity of psychedelic drug effects. For the same reason, we may simply not yet have had enough time to sort out the best uses of these drugs.

An informal kind of research continues anyway. Illicit psychedelic drug use is an underground spring that continues to feed the stream of interest in systematic, publicly controlled experimentation. Ironically, the illicit drug use that was one of the reasons for the interruption of legitimate research now serves to keep alive efforts aimed at resuming that research. Interest also persists among some psychologists and psychiatrists. We quote a letter written in 1979 by Hanscarl Leuner of the University of Gottingen:

> Though in several European countries therapists in this field could apply for licenses to continue using the drugs, the government authorities over the years started to make things difficult. . . . I myself was convinced that science does not depend on ideologies. This seems to be an error. The continuation of psycholytic therapy during the last years led us to new techniques and conceptions. The results in practical therapy are even more convincing than before. We would like not to stop doing psycholytic therapy. Optimistically, I hope that in time we can publish these results. For so many patients there is a tremendous need for deep probing and intensity in psychotherapy which psycholytic and related therapies could fill.[43]

There are now dozens of known psychedelic drugs, some of them synthesized only in the last twenty years. Few have been tested seriously in human beings. Their effects are sometimes different from

---

43. Personal communication, 1979.

those of LSD and other familiar substances. These differences may be significant for the study of the human mind and for psychotherapy, but we cannot analyze them properly without more controlled human research. A Chilean psychiatrist, Claudio Naranjo, has pioneered in the use of psychedelic drugs that do not produce the same degree of perceptual and emotional change as does LSD. He has worked especially with MDA and a related shorter-acting amphetamine, MMDA, which give a heightened capacity for introspection and intimacy along with a temporary freedom from anxiety and depression.[44] These and related drugs might be useful in marital counseling, in diagnostic interviews, and in helping patients decide whether they want to go through the process of psychotherapy.[45]

It is a misunderstanding to regard psychedelic drug therapy as a form of chemotherapy, like giving lithium to manic patients. Patients are not maintained for a long time on psychedelic drugs, and these drugs do not produce dependence or addiction. On the other hand, the claims of psychedelic drug therapy are subject to the same doubts as those of psychoanalysis or religious conversions. The mixture of mystical and transcendental claims with therapeutic ones is an aspect of psychedelic drug therapy troubling to our culture. The pronouncements of drug enthusiasts are sometimes too much like religious testimonials to please either psychiatrists or priests and ministers. Preindustrial cultures seem to tolerate more ambiguity in this matter, and there is now a growing interest in the ideas and techniques shared by primitive shamans, Eastern spiritual teachers, and modern psychiatrists. The word "cure," after all, means both treatment for disease and the care of souls.

The role of the guide on a psychedelic drug trip, which has both religious and medical aspects, is spontaneously reproduced in all cultures where psychedelic drugs come to be used. Much of the controversy about psychedelic drugs in the 1960s was in effect concerned with the question of who was qualified to be a guide. For the moment we have made the curious decision that no one in modern industrial society is qualified for this position. Nevertheless, psychedelic drug therapy apparently still goes on underground, in one form or another. Many have regarded it as an experience worth having, some

44. Claudio Naranjo, *The Healing Journey* (New York: Ballantine, 1975).
45. George Greer, "MDMA: A New Psychotropic Compound and Its Effects in Humans," 1983 (unpublished).

as a first step toward change, and a few as a turning point in their lives. They might be deceiving themselves, but we do not know enough to be certain; the field has potentialities that are not being allowed to reveal themselves.

A Note on Legal Status

The publicly familiar psychedelic drugs are classified in Schedule I of the Controlled Substances Act; they are regarded as having a high potential for abuse, no current medical use, and a lack of safety for use under medical supervision. They are available for medical experimentation as investigational drugs, but present research is confined almost entirely to animals. A number of psychedelic drugs that were recently synthesized or that have never been available in any quantity on the illicit market are not scheduled. It is legal for physicians to work clinically with these substances, although experimental research in human beings is not permissible until animal tests have been done.

CANNABIS

Marijuana is derived from the hemp plant (*Cannabis sativa*). Its most important psychoactive chemical, delta-9-tetrahydrocannabinol (delta-1-tetrahydrocannabinol in another nomenclature), is contained in a resin that covers the flower clusters and top leaves of the plant; the resin also contains many chemically related substances with lesser effects. Cannabis preparations vary widely in quality and potency depending on the type of plant, climate, soil, and methods of cultivation and manufacture. The resin can be ingested in the form of a drink or in foods, but usually the leaves and flowering tops are smoked, either in a pipe or in a cigarette called a joint.

History

Like cocaine and other psychoactive drugs derived from natural plant sources, marijuana has been used for thousands of years as a medicine as well as an intoxicant. It was listed in an herbal published by a Chinese emperor that may go back to 2800 B.C. In Jamaica, where it was introduced in the seventeenth century by African slaves, it has become the most popular folk medicine. Cannabis in the form of an alcoholic tincture was commonly used in nineteenth-century Europe and the United States as an anticonvulsant, sedative, and analgesic, and also in tetanus, neuralgia, uterine hemorrhage, rheumatism, and other conditions. It was thought to be a milder but less dangerous sedative than opium, and it was also considered an appetite stimulant. Between 1839 and 1900 more than a hundred articles appeared in scientific journals on the therapeutic uses of marijuana. After the introduction of injectable opiates in the 1850s and synthetic analgesics and hypnotics in the early twentieth century, the medical use of cannabis declined. But even as late as 1937, extract of cannabis was still a legitimate medicine marketed by drug companies. The Marijuana Tax Act of 1937 imposed a registration tax and record-keeping requirements that made medical use of cannabis so cumbersome that it was dropped from the U.S. Pharmacopoeia and National Formulary.

The Marijuana Tax Act was introduced under the influence of a growing concern about the use of marijuana as an intoxicant, especially among blacks and Mexican-Americans in the South and Southwest. The law passed after a strong campaign by the Federal Bureau of Narcotics, despite a lack of empirical evidence on the harmfulness of marijuana. The legislative counsel for the American Medical Association at the time objected to the law, saying that future investigations might show substantial medical uses for cannabis. But the American Medical Association soon changed its stance and for the next thirty years maintained a position on marijuana very similar to that of the Federal Bureau of Narcotics. Recent years have seen some relaxation of legal restrictions and increasing clarification of the medical potential of cannabis and cannabis derivatives, but considerable obstacles remain and considerable research still has to be done.

Safety

The greatest advantage of cannabis as a medicine is its unusual safety. The ratio of lethal dose to effective dose is estimated on the basis of extrapolation from animal data to be about 20,000 to one. Huge doses have been given to dogs without causing death, and there is no reliable evidence of death caused by cannabis in a human being. Cannabis also has the advantage of not disturbing any physiological functions or damaging any body organs when it is used in therapeutic doses. It produces little physical dependence or tolerance; there has never been any evidence that medical use of cannabis has led to habitual use as an intoxicant.

Whole cannabis preparations have the disadvantages of instability, varying strength, and insolubility in water, which makes it difficult for the drug to enter the bloodstream from the digestive tract. Another problem is that marijuana contains so many ingredients with possible disadvantageous effects, including too high a degree of intoxication. This multitude of ingredients is also an opportunity, since it suggests the manufacture of different cannabinoids, synthetic or natural, with properties useful for particular purposes; some of these have now become available.[46]

Depression and Pain Relief

Cannabis and synthetic cannabis derivatives have been tested as treatments for depression, so far without good evidence of effectiveness.[47] It might be possible to develop synthetic cannabis preparations with a higher euphoriant-to-sedative ratio than the drugs that have been tested so far.

There are many anecdotal reports of marijuana smokers using the drug to reduce pain: postsurgery pain, headache, migraine, menstrual cramps, and so on. The disadvantage is its inconsistent effect; sometimes it actually heightens sensitivity to pain. It is possible that cannabis acts by mechanisms different from those of other analgesics, but the literature does not indicate a specific effect of cannabis on pain pathways or suggest that it is likely to be more effective than other analgesics. Again, some new synthetic derivative might prove useful as an analgesic, but this is not an immediate prospect.

Alcohol Dependence

Because of reports that some people use less alcohol when they smoke marijuana, cannabis has been proposed as an adjunct to alcoholism treatment. But so far it has not been found useful.[48] Most alcoholics

---

46. R. Mechoulam and E. A. Carlini, "Toward Drugs Derived from Cannabis," *Naturwissenschaften* 65 (1978): 174–79.

47. J. Kotin, R. M. Post, and F. K. Goodwin, "Delta-9-tetrahydrocannabinol in Depressed Patients," *Archives of General Psychiatry* 28 (1973): 345–48.

48. C. M. Rosenberg, J. R. Gerrein, and C. Schnell, "Cannabis in the Treatment of Alcoholism," *Journal of Studies on Alcohol* 39 (1978): 155–58.

neither want to substitute marijuana nor find it particularly useful. But there might be some hope for use of marijuana in combination with disulfiram (Antabuse), which protects alcoholics by producing uncomfortable symptoms when they drink.[49] Certainly a cannabis habit would be preferable to an alcohol habit for anyone who could not avoid dependence on a drug but was able to substitute one drug for another.

Spasticity and Seizures

About 20 percent of epileptics do not get much relief from conventional anticonvulsant medications. Cannabis has been explored as an alternative, at least since a case was reported in which marijuana smoking, together with the standard anticonvulsants phenobarbital and diphenylhydantoin, was apparently necessary to control seizures in a young epileptic man.[50] Marijuana also reduces muscle spasm and tremors in some people who suffer from cerebral palsy or multiple sclerosis.[51] But the effects of delta-9-tetrahydrocannabinol (hereafter called THC) itself are inconsistent; it can actually heighten susceptibility to some types of seizures. The cannabis derivative that is most promising as an anticonvulsant is cannabidiol. In one controlled study, cannabidiol in addition to prescribed anticonvulsants produced improvement in seven patients with grand mal seizures; three showed great improvement. Of eight patients who received a placebo instead, only one improved.[52]

Asthma

Asthma is a breathing disorder that arises when bronchial muscles go into spasm and the pathway to the lungs is blocked by mucus and swelling. A number of antiasthmatic drugs are available, but they all have drawbacks—limited effectiveness or side effects. Because

49. C. M. Rosenberg, "The Use of Marihuana in the Treatment of Alcoholism," in S. Cohen and R. C. Stillman, eds. *The Therapeutic Potential of Marihuana* (New York and London: Plenum, 1976).

50. Paul F. Consroe, George C. Wood, and Harvey Buchsbaum, "Anticonvulsant Nature of Marihuana Smoking," *Journal of the American Medical Association* 234 (1975): 306–7.

51. D. J. Petro, "Marihuana as a Therapeutic Agent for Muscle Spasm or Spasticity," *Psychosomatics* 21 (1980): 81–85.

52. J. M. Cunha et al., "Chronic Administration of Cannabidiol to Healthy Volunteers and Epileptic Patients," *Pharmacology* 21 (1980): 175–85.

marijuana dilates the bronchi and reverses bronchial spasm, cannabis derivatives have been tested as antiasthmatic drugs. Smoking marijuana would probably not be a good way to treat asthma because of chronic irritation of the bronchial tract by tars and other substances in marijuana smoke, so recent research has sought a better means of administration. THC in the form of an aerosol spray has been investigated extensively.[53] Other cannabinoids such as cannabinol and cannabidiol may be preferable to THC for this purpose. An interesting finding for future research is that cannabinoids may affect the bronchi by a different mechanism from that of the familiar antiasthmatic drugs.

Glaucoma

A promising new medical use for cannabis is in treating glaucoma, the second leading cause of blindness in the United States. In this disease, fluid pressure within the eyeball increases until it damages the optic nerve. About a million Americans suffer from the form of glaucoma (wide angle) treatable with cannabis. Marijuana causes a dose-related, clinically significant drop in intraocular pressure that lasts several hours in both normal subjects and those with the abnormally high ocular tension produced by glaucoma. Oral or intravenous THC has the same effect, which seems to be specific to cannabis derivatives rather than simply a result of sedation. Cannabis does not cure the disease, but it can retard the progressive loss of sight when conventional medication fails and surgery is too dangerous.[54]

It remains to be seen whether topical use of THC or a synthetic cannabinoid in the form of eyedrops will be preferable to smoking marijuana for this purpose. So far THC eyedrops have not proved effective, and in 1981 the National Eye Institute announced that it would no longer approve human research using these eyedrops.[55] Studies continue on certain synthetic cannabis derivatives and other

53. D. P. Tashkin et al., "Effects of Smoked Marijuana in Experimentally Induced Asthma," *American Review of Respiratory Diseases* 112 (1975): 377–86; D. B. Tashkin et al., "Bronchial Effects of Aerosolized Delta-9-tetrahydrocannabinol in Healthy and Asthmatic Subjects," *American Review of Respiratory Diseases* 115 (1977): 57–65.

54. R. S. Hepler, I. M. Frank, and R. Petrus, "Ocular Effects of Marihuana Smoking," in M. C. Braude and S. Szara, eds., *Pharmacology of Marihuana* (New York: Raven Press, 1976).

55. Roger A. Roffman, *Marihuana as Medicine* (Seattle: Madrona, 1982), p. 99.

natural cannabinoids. Smoking marijuana is a better way of titrating the dose than taking an oral cannabinoid, and most patients seem to prefer it. Unfortunately, many patients, especially elderly ones, dislike the psychoactive effects of marijuana.

Cancer Treatment

Cannabis derivatives have several minor or speculative uses in the treatment of cancer, and one major use. As appetite stimulants, marijuana and THC may help to slow weight loss in cancer patients.[56] THC has also retarded the growth of tumor cells in some animal studies, but results are inconclusive, and another cannabis derivative, cannabadiol, seems to increase tumor growth.[57] Possibly cannabinoids in combination with other drugs will turn out to have some use in preventing tumor growth.

But the most promising use of cannabis in cancer treatment is the prevention of nausea and vomiting in patients undergoing chemotherapy. About half of patients treated with anticancer drugs suffer from severe nausea and vomiting. In about 30 percent to 40 percent of these, the commonly used antiemetics do not work.[58] The nausea and vomiting are not only unpleasant but a threat to the effectiveness of the therapy. Retching can cause tears of the esophagus and rib fractures, prevent adequate nutrition, and lead to fluid loss.

The antiemetics most commonly used in chemotherapy are phenothiazines like prochlorperazine (Compazine). The suggestion that cannabis might be useful arose in the early 1970s when some young patients receiving cancer chemotherapy found that marijuana smoking, which was of course illegal, reduced their nausea and vomiting. In some studies, oral THC has proved effective where the standard drugs were not.[59] In other studies the two types of drugs seemed to

56. W. Regelson et al., "Delta-9-tetrahydrocannabinol as an Effective Antidepressant and Appetite-Stimulating Agent in Advanced Cancer Patients," in Braude and Szara, eds., *Pharmacology of Marihuana,* pp. 763–76.

57. A. C. White et al., "Effects of Delta-9-tetrahydrocannabinol in Lewis Lung Adenocarcinoma Cells in Tissue Culture," *Journal of the National Cancer Institute* 56 (1976): 655–58.

58. Roffman, *Marijuana as Medicine,* pp. 82–83.

59. V. S. Lucas and J. Laszlo, "Delta-9-tetrahydrocannabinol for Refractory Vomiting Induced by Cancer Chemotherapy," *Journal of the American Medical Association* 243 (1980): 1241–43; S. E. Sallan, N. E. Zinberg, and E. Frei, "Antiemetic Effect of Delta-9-tetrahydrocannabinol in Patients Receiving Cancer Chemotherapy," *New England Journal of Medicine* 293 (1975): 795–97.

be equally effective.[60] In one study nabilone, a synthetic cannabinoid, was found more effective than a phenothiazine.[61] But nabilone tests have been discontinued because of animal deaths and adverse reactions in human beings.

It is generally agreed that THC is a good antiemetic, but as in the case of glaucoma, many patients reject it because they find the psychoactive effects unpleasant. There is some controversy about whether THC is best taken orally or smoked in the form of marijuana. Marijuana is related to THC in much the same way that coca is related to cocaine; it contains a variety of chemicals instead of one and enters the body by a different route. Smoking generates quicker and more predictable results in both glaucoma and cancer treatment, because it raises THC concentration in the blood more easily to the needed level. Also, it may be hard for a nauseated patient in chemotherapy to take oral medicine. But many patients dislike smoking or cannot inhale.

Conclusion

A committee of the Institute of Medicine of the National Academy of Sciences remarked in a report in 1982:

> Cannabis shows promise in some of these areas, although the dose necessary to produce the desired effect is often close to one that produces an unacceptable frequency of toxic [undesirable] side effects. What is perhaps more encouraging . . . is that cannabis seems to exert its beneficial effects through mechanisms that differ from those of other available drugs. This raises the possibility that some patients who would not be helped by conventional therapies could be treated with cannabis. . . . It may be possible to reduce side effects by synthesizing related molecules that could have a more favorable ratio of desired to undesired actions; this line of investigation should have a high priority.[62]

60. S. Frytak et al., "Delta-9-tetrahydrocannabinol as an Antiemetic for Patients Receiving Cancer Chemotherapy: A Comparison with Prochlorperazine and a Placebo," *Annals of Internal Medicine* 91 (1979): 825–30.

61. T. S. Herman et al., "Superiority of Nabilone Over Prochlorperazine as an Antiemetic in Patients Receiving Cancer Chemotherapy," *New England Journal of Medicine* 300 (1979): 1295–97.

62. Institute of Medicine, *Marijuana and Health* (Washington, D.C.: National Academy Press, 1982), p. 139.

The committee recommended further research, especially in the treatment of nausea and vomiting in chemotherapy, asthma, glaucoma, and seizures and spasticity.

Under federal and most state statutes, marijuana is listed as a Schedule I drug: high potential for abuse, no currently accepted medical use, and a lack of accepted safety for use under medical supervision. It cannot ordinarily be prescribed and may be used only under research conditions.

But public pressure has begun to change the situation. Several individuals have successfully argued the rare defense of medical necessity in response to criminal charges of marijuana possession; in one case glaucoma was involved and in another multiple sclerosis. Now the National Cancer Institute, the Drug Enforcement Agency, and the Food and Drug Administration have agreed to a program whereby the National Cancer Institute is making THC available through the pharmacies of about five hundred teaching hospitals and cancer centers to physicians who want to use it for chemotherapy. The legislatures of twenty-three states have also authorized special research programs that supply cannabis for the management of nausea and vomiting in chemotherapy. In effect these programs provide means for the seriously ill to gain legal access to marijuana. Physicians acting on their own can apply for permission to use marijuana, but the regulations are so complicated that physicians who want help for one or two patients may advise them to get the marijuana on the streets instead. State programs, in effect, assume responsibility for completing the paperwork required by the federal government and relieve the physician of this burden. The states make use of confiscated marijuana or marijuana cigarettes or THC pills supplied by the federal government.

The Food and Drug Administration does not approve of efforts to publicize therapies that have not gone through the standard legal process of new drug testing. Advocates of medical marijuana use want to circumvent not only the Controlled Substances Act but also the Food, Drug, and Cosmetics Act of 1938 and its amendments that establish procedures for testing and marketing new drugs. The FDA says that marijuana will never be an approved medicine because it contains so many chemicals and its composition is so variable. The requirement of a standardized dose alone may prevent the marketing of marijuana in the ordinary way as medicine. This obstacle does not stand in the way of THC in pill form. A special form of THC in a gelatin capsule with sesame seed oil has recently been transferred to Schedule II under the Controlled Substances Act, and hearings are being held to determine whether THC in other forms should also be placed in Schedule II.

The potential of cannabis as a medicine is yet to be realized, partly because of its reputation as an intoxicant, ignorance on the part of the medical establishment, and legal difficulties involved in doing the research. Recreational use of cannabis has affected the opinions of physicians about its medical potential in various ways. When marijuana was regarded as the drug of blacks, Mexican-Americans, and bohemians, doctors were ready to go along with the Bureau of Narcotics, ignore its medical uses, and urge prohibition. For years the National Organization for the Reform of Marijuana Laws (NORML) and other groups have been petitioning the government to change this classification. Although that has not happened, cannabis derivatives have become more available for medical purposes through various devices. Now that marijuana has become so popular among a broad section of the population, we have been more willing to investigate its therapeutic value. Recreational use now spurs medical interest instead of medical hostility.

The struggle over medical marijuana use illustrates some of the issues discussed earlier: self-medication versus government control, pure chemicals versus natural drugs, the historical direction of drug policy and the present minor challenges to it, the need to find a better balance in making rules about drugs. The potential dangers of marijuana when taken for pleasure and its possible usefulness as a medicine are historically and practically interrelated issues: historically, because the arguments used to justify public and official disapproval of recreational use have had a strong influence on opinions about its medical potential; practically, because the more evidence accumulates that marijuana is relatively safe even when used as an intoxicant, the clearer it becomes that the medical requirement of safety is satisfied. Most recent research is tentative, and initial enthusiasm for drugs is often disappointed after further investigation. But it is not as though cannabis were an entirely new agent with unknown properties. Studies done during the past ten years have confirmed a centuries-old promise. With the relaxation of restrictions on research and the further chemical manipulation of cannabis derivatives, this promise will eventually be realized. The weight of past and contemporary evidence will probably prove cannabis to be valuable in several ways as a medicine.

6

COCAINE, MARIJUANA, AND THE MEANINGS OF ADDICTION

Robert Byck

Are cocaine and marijuana addicting? Are some drugs more addicting than others? These two questions, although they seem "scientific," are semantic. In ordinary English the answer to both questions is "yes."

Ordinary English is not the language of pharmacology, medicine, public policy, or law. To answer the questions properly we must first know something about drugs, words, and prejudices. For this reason I will divide this chapter into sections. The first will be an introduction to the variables of pharmacology and descriptions of the pharmacology of cocaine and marijuana. The second section discusses the words pharmacologists, lawyers, policy makers, and the public use in describing drug-taking behavior and its effects. The third section tries to make sensible distinctions about the way we might use terminology to be descriptive and communicative instead of political and obscurative.

VARIABLES OF PHARMACOLOGY

There are standard reference works describing the pharmacology of marijuana and cocaine in some detail.[1] There is a language of pharmacology with circumscribed definitions, used for the most part in a consistent way. One can use primary texts such as *The Pharmacological Basis of Therapeutics* for pharmacological explanations of these terms. Although "drug abuse" occurs only in man, some of the measurable variables relevant to the topic can be measured only in animals. We will be concerned here with the effects of drugs in man, but some reference must be made to the animal behavioral studies that are the systematic scientific base for statements about drug dependency.

Before discussing the pharmacology of the drugs, I will present the pertinent pharmacological variables that are important to consider in evaluating the behavioral and physiological effects of all drugs. The word *drug* itself has acquired a common meaning relating to certain, but not all, abused chemicals. I will try to use the term in the broader sense of a chemical substance that causes physiological changes when administered to a living organism. Although "drugs" are commonly assumed to have unitary and specific effects, this is not the reality. Each drug has a spectrum of effects depending on *form, dosage, route* of administration, and *chronicity*. The human variables of personality structure and circumstance of drug administration are equally important in judging the psychopharmacological results of drug taking.

Using familiar examples, I will illustrate the importance of pharmacological and human variables in the effects of drugs on human behavior. The *form* of a drug is important. For example, "cocaine" is a small percentage of active substance in coca leaf, a substance chewed by 12 million people throughout the world. But "cocaine" might also be cocaine hydrochloride, a refined chemical,

1. J. H. Jaffe, "Drug Addiction and Drug Abuse," and J. M. Ritchie and N. M. Greene, "Local Anesthetics," both in A. G. Gilman, L. S. Goodman, and A. Gilman, eds., *The Pharmacological Basis of Therapeutics,* 6th ed. (New York: Macmillan, 1980), pp. 535–84 and 300–320 respectively. See also, R. Byck and C. Van Dyke, "What Are the Effects of Cocaine in Man?" in R. C. Petersen and R. C. Stillman, eds., *Cocaine 1977,* National Institute on Drug Abuse (NIDA) Research Monograph 13 (Rockville, Md.: DHEW, 1977), pp. 97–117; Institute of Medicine, *Marijuana and Health* (Washington, D.C.: National Academy Press, 1982).

which is used in medical anesthetic practice. The effects of the substances may be different because the form can limit the *route* and the *dosage* of the drug. A pure substance, such as cocaine hydrochloride, can be taken by many routes and in unlimited dosage. Dosage is restricted if one is chewing leaves with a maximum concentration of less than 2 percent cocaine. A large amount of substance must be masticated before any significant amounts of cocaine can accumulate in the blood.

Form limits the route of administration. There is little one can do with leaves except chew them; on the other hand, the hydrochloride could be injected or swallowed or sniffed. The hydrochloride cannot be smoked, a popular method of taking in cocaine, since first it must be converted to the so-called "freebase" of cocaine by a chemical extraction process. Only the freebase or cocaine paste, a raw extract containing free alkaloid, will vaporize in with heat and give an adequate dosage when smoked.

Marijuana, in contrast to cocaine, is almost always the botanical dried leaf form, and the extracted active chemicals are probably never seen in the street drug-abuse market.

Dosage of a drug is a critical variable in determining its effects. It is quite clear that *very* tiny amounts of a potent substance may cause no effects, whereas huge amounts of relatively innocuous material may cause death. For the most part I will consider the dosages ordinarily self-administered by abusers of the drugs. It is a principle of pharmacology that dosage and effect are related. In a single administration, effect is usually linearly related to the log of dose. Various effects may have different dose-effect relationships. It is an ancillary principle of pharmacology that almost all drugs have multiple effects.

Dosage on the street is not always what it seems to be. If cocaine is heavily diluted or "cut," the amount or dosage of real cocaine that can be taken in is limited by the percentage of cut. In today's world most street cocaine is about 30 percent pure substance. The physical volume limits the amount that can be taken in, although the psychological effect of snorting a line of white powder is based on the belief that all of it is really cocaine. In general, street users have unwarranted faith in the unlabeled product they buy. Buyers of street drugs will usually insist that they have particularly good "stuff." Chemical analyses often indicate that street users are often taking small absolute quantities of active substance.

The *route* of administration is also an important factor in how drugs have their effect. Cocaine, for example, can be taken by chewing the leaves, by swallowing the hydrochloride, by snorting or sniffing the powder, by smoking the alkaloidal substance, or by injecting the material intravenously. Each of these routes produces a particular pattern of drug usage that is more determined by the route than it is by the drug itself. For example, chewing the leaves provides a continuous, but low level, exposure to cocaine. Snorting is usually done in a series of small doses at intervals of about twenty minutes. With snorting there is a relatively rapid uptake into the blood stream. That uptake of the drug into the blood from the nasal mucosa is limited by the constriction of blood vessels by cocaine. Because there is less blood flow, large amounts cannot be taken up rapidly. When the drug is swallowed it is more effective than if taken intranasally. Most users ignore this because the traditional method of administration for cocaine is to snort it. The smoking and intravenous routes both provide a rapid and almost unlimited uptake of the drug into the bloodstream and therefore are associated with much more severe forms of abuse. Smoking, a recently popular method of administration, is more acceptable to most drug users because it is accepted as a social method of drug ingestion. Intravenous use is usually reserved for more hardened drug takers. The assembling of the intravenous drug use paraphernalia represents an obvious shift out of normal life-style patterns and into the patterns of heavy drug users. Giving oneself an injection requires skill and a commitment to drug misuse.

The patterns of usage and problems that affect drug users are determined in part by these different routes of administration. The problems associated with intravenous drug use include infection and rapid overdose. Smoking creates lung problems. Snorting can damage the nasal mucosa. Intravenous cocaine users obviously are in the greatest danger, and snorters and chewers in the least.

The *frequency* and *chronicity* of taking drugs is also an important factor in their effects. Oftentimes scientific reports show the effects of only a single dosage of a drug. This is a standard approach to describe the effects of drugs in man. Such reports can only be partially extrapolated to the effects of chronic administration. Because there are limits to human experimentation, we are forced to gather much of our information from observation of street users.

Important data can be obtained from laboratory studies. If the drug is given in a single dosage, one can examine the time to the onset of effect, the plasma levels of the drug, and the specific drug effects from that single administration. If, however, a drug is taken in repeated administrations every fifteen minutes, the effects may be different. The effect may increase with each administration and, if the administration continues for a long period of time, the effects seen with chronic usage can differ markedly from those seen with a single drug dosage.

Each drug has its own typical pattern of usage. For example, cocaine and stimulant users take the drug in "runs": They will use whatever amount is available in continuous usage over hours or a day and then, when the drug runs out, stop using it. This is in contrast to the usage of heroin, which is taken day and night almost continuously. The effects of the drugs and their ability to produce dependence or withdrawal syndromes are often governing factors in how the drug is used. Cocaine is usually used in short runs, but if large amounts of the drug are available, prolonged ingestion of the drug can occur. Whereas single doses of cocaine rarely produce striking psychological effects, chronic and continuous usage of the drug can cause a paranoid state and a state of extreme edginess or nervousness associated, in some instances, with a psychosis.

Marijuana, the other substance to be considered, is often used chronically and daily by the drug users, who thus can remain in almost a continuous state of intoxication. This form of usage would be rare for a cocaine abuser. There are cumulative effects that can be either the result of larger and larger amounts of drugs building up in the body or the result of the nervous system's adaptation to a continuous state of drug effect.

A simple unitary description of a drug is not likely to be accurate. The reader should be aware that drugs can have completely different effects at different dosages. It is possible to look at the effects of a drug as moving through a spectrum as concentrations in the body increase. The most familiar example would be alcohol. In a small dose, alcohol can cause relaxation and a decrease in anxiety. In a somewhat larger dose, alcohol can cause ataxia and drunkenness; and in an even larger dose, it will tend to cause sleep. In a high dose, alcohol can act as a general anesthetic; and in an even higher dose, it can be a lethal poison and cause death. So here we have one of the most commonly used drugs whose effects can differ not only quantitatively but even qualitatively, depending on the dosage ingested. Alcohol can be examined with relation to the other factors given for cocaine above, in that it is obvious that an occasional social drink has a behavioral effect different from that of the continuous drinking of a chronic alcoholic, and the behavior of a chronic alcoholic is markedly different from the behavior of an occasional social drinker.

A reasonable first premise of drug abuse research is that the pharmacological properties of the substance must be known. The description of properties should include a description of the material, its pharmacological effects in man, its distribution and metabolism in the body, measures of its reinforcing properties, and estimates of abuse potential.

Cocaine

Although in the popular mind cocaine is considered an evil, it is a widely used therapeutic substance. Many physicians consider the drug to be indispensable as a vasoconstrictor and local anesthetic. Local anesthetics block nerve conduction when applied directly to nerves or in places where they can diffuse to the site of nervous tissue. They differ from the many compounds that can injure or permanently destroy nerve tissue in that their effect is reversible. All local anesthetics, including cocaine and synthetic drugs such as procaine (novocaine) and lidocaine, work by a similar mechanism.

Nerve conduction proceeds by an ionic mechanism involving the passage of sodium and potassium ions across the nerve membrane. This action is prevented by local anesthetics. The specific details of how local anesthetics change the membrane are not known, but it is now presumed that the effects are the result of both dissolution into the nerve membrane and binding at a receptor site within the sodium channel. Vasoconstrictor drugs, which diminish local blood flow, are often mixed with other local anesthetics to prolong their effect. Cocaine has its own sympathomimetic vasoconstrictor activity and so combines the two effects.

Sympathomimetic, a term coined in 1910 by the English pharmacologists Barger and Dale, refers to a drug action that mimes the effects of activation of the sympathetic nervous system. This sympathomimetic action is partially the result of cocaine's ability to restrict the reuptake of neurotransmitters such as norepinephrine and dopamine into the cells of the sympathetic nervous system.

One way by which the organism stops the action of sympathomimetic drugs is to pump the unused amine back into the cell terminal that released it. If by some mechanism this pumping or reuptake is blocked, the sympathetic effects are both enhanced and prolonged by the continued presence of the transmitter. Reuptake block is a property of many of the antidepressant drugs used in psychiatry that do not have the immediate stimulant and euphorigenic properties of cocaine. This implies that we cannot totally explain the central stimulant effect of cocaine simply by its known sympathomimetic action.

Most of the current interest in cocaine is concerned with its sympathomimetic action and stimulant effects. *Sympathomimetic* refers to peripheral effects on heart and blood vessels, whereas *stimulant* implies activation of the central nervous system. Caffeine, for example, is a stimulant but not a sympathomimetic. Cocaine is a typical sympathomimetic drug in its peripheral effects. It increases blood pressure and heart rate and, in large doses, increases temperature. With high doses or regular use, the pupillary size is increased. Small arterial blood vessels are constricted, thereby restricting the drug's passage into the body when applied topically.

Cocaine, easily soluble in alcohol as the base or in water as the hydrochloride, has high fat solubility. This property makes it likely that it is quickly taken up into the brain from the bloodstream. The effects of cocaine in the brain and on the emotional state of the individual may be in part governed by this rapid transfer. There is some evidence that brain concentrations of cocaine markedly exceed those in plasma.

Cocaine, like all local anesthetics, is a convulsant at high doses. Repeated small doses of cocaine in animals may eventually lead to convulsions. Some have postulated that this "kindling" effect, (i.e., repeated small doses eventually producing the equivalent response of a much larger dose) may account for the sudden appearance of psychosis in chronic users. Except for the heart rate increase, there is no effect on the electrocardiogram after 2 mg/kg cocaine administered intranasally. At this dose there is no reliable dilatation of the pupil but there is a slight temperature increase. Larger doses increase pupillary size. It has been postulated that hyperthermia is a major reason for the deaths that have resulted from massive cocaine overdosage.

The psychological effects of cocaine described by Conan Doyle through Sherlock Holmes as "transcendently stimulating and clarifying to the mind'' are less spectacular when examined in the laboratory.

In a dose effect study of intranasal cocaine (0.20, 0.75, and 1.50 mg/kg), our group found that higher doses produced higher peak plasma levels and more intense psychological effects.[2] The peak psychological effects occurred within fifteen to thirty minutes after the drug was administered. In all our subjects, cocaine produced a ''high'' and pleasant feeling without any dysphoric effects. Javaid et al. in Chicago found that 10 mg of cocaine could not be differentiated from placebo, but doses of 25 and 100 mg produced euphoria.[3] Some of the subjects in these experiments experienced dysphoria forty-five to sixty minutes after the 100 mg dose. The dysphoria was characterized by anxiety, depression, fatigue, and a desire for more cocaine. A crash, or period of extreme discomfort and dysphoria, reliably occurs after intravenous or smoked cocaine but is less common after intranasal use. This crash is not the model opiate withdrawal syndrome but obviously would encourage repeated self-administration of the drug.

Doses of 25 and 100 mg of intranasal cocaine produce increases in heart rate of 10 to 15 beats/minute, and in systolic and diastolic blood pressures of 10 to 20 mm Hg. These effects peak at fifteen to twenty minutes after drug administration. The size of these physiological changes is well within the changes seen in response to fearful or exciting stimuli.

A group at the University of Chicago found that their experimental subjects could not distinguish the immediate effects of intravenous cocaine from amphetamine. At Yale we found that single intranasal doses of lidocaine, a synthetic local anesthetic, could not be differentiated from the same small dose of cocaine. Findings for chronic administration would probably differ.

Psychologists have determined that monkeys in an experimental situation will work for procaine (novocaine) injections (i.e., procaine is a reinforcing drug), and some recent reports indicate that procaine is perceived as a rewarding and pleasurable experimental stimulus by human subjects.

2. C. Van Dyke et al., ''Intranasal Cocaine: Dose Relationships of Psychological Effects and Plasma Levels,'' *International Journal of Psychiatry in Medicine* 12, no. 1 (1982): 1–13.

3. J. I. Javaid et al., ''Cocaine Plasma Concentration: Relation to Physiological and Subjective Effects in Humans,'' *Science* 202 (1978): 227–28.

In the form of the hydrochloride salt, cocaine is readily absorbed through mucous membranes and enters the systemic circulation. The most popular route of administration is through the nasal mucosa, but almost any route is possible for cocaine.

Cocaine is broken down in the plasma by pseudocholinesterase, an enzyme responsible for breakdown of natural substances such as acetylcholine and drugs such as succinylcholine. We found that some individuals who, because of a genetic abnormality, lack pseudocholinesterase activity also do not metabolize cocaine rapidly.

Cocaine has the reputation of being a short-acting drug. Nonetheless the half-life of cocaine in man is about an hour and its psychological effects persist much longer than the five to fifteen minutes that is commonly assumed. When the drug is applied locally in the nose, traces of the material are still present on the membranes hours after application. If the drug is applied repeatedly, damage to the nasal mucosa can occur.

If we look at the psychological effects of cocaine in relationship to plasma levels of the drug, we find that the effects are most marked as the plasma concentration is rising and the effects have almost disappeared on the descending limb of the plasma curve. This effect, seen with other drugs such as alcohol or the benzodiazepines, could be interpreted either as acute tolerance (i.e., the receptors once occupied become less responsive), or as a redistribution phenomenon whereby the large initial plasma concentrations lead to a high brain level, which quickly diffuses out and equilibrates with the circulating drug.

Cocaine causes a "high." This drug effect is akin to euphoria or elation, but also contains elements of a sense of power or clarity of thought. This central effect, seen at moderate doses of cocaine, is accompanied by peripheral sympathetic signs, predominantly a heart rate and blood pressure increase that may in turn enhance the individual's psychic state.

The smoking of cocaine paste, a crude derivative of coca leaves with 30 percent to 90 percent cocaine freebase, has become a new form of abuse among the urban youth of South America. In the United States a material refined from street "cocaine" (i.e., "freebase") is pyrolyzed in "base pipes" and inhaled through the lungs. When burned, cocaine is destroyed, but the hot gases from the smoking device vaporize much of the drug. Cocaine smoking causes a drug dependence with many of the characteristics of intravenous amphetamine use. There is an intense euphoria followed by a crash and an almost irresistible craving for more drug. An equivalently malignant form of abuse is the intravenous injection of cocaine hydrochloride.

Drug dependence on intranasal cocaine shows a pattern similar to other stimulant dependencies. An individual will use the drug in a "run" of continued use until supplies are no longer available. He may then not use the drug for long periods, but when it is available, he will use it. In contrast, smoking or intravenous use leads to almost continuous usage and drug seeking behavior. The strength of the drug dependence is related to the form and method of taking the drug.

Chronic use of cocaine produces sleeplessness, loss of appetite, and after high doses or long use, an uncomfortable anxious paranoid state. The question of whether cocaine produces a true psychosis remains moot, but there is increasing evidence that a hallucinatory paranoid state can result from intense cocaine use.

There is reasonable evidence for tolerance to the cardiovascular effects of cocaine, and it is true that chronic users often take large doses, implying some degree of tolerance to the psychological effects of cocaine. This "tolerance" is, however, short-lived, since even heavy users will start off with small doses after a drug-free day.

It has been difficult to define a withdrawal syndrome from cocaine despite the reported crash involving a depressive state and increased sleep. This either could be a drug effect or simply a physiological response to any prolonged exciting or euphorigenic stimulus. Prolonged wakefulness often results in prolonged sleep when the reasons for the wakefulness are no longer present. This blurring of pharmacological withdrawal from the expected consequences of the drug-induced state makes it difficult to make unequivocal statements about the importance of a withdrawal syndrome after cocaine usage.

Marijuana

Like cocaine, marijuana is a substance that has been known for centuries and used for its psychoactive effects in many societies. The pharmacology of the drug has been the subject of extensive reports and summaries and so only a brief account will be given here.[4]

4. J. H. Jaffe, "Drug Addiction and Drug Abuse"; Institute of Medicine, *Marijuana and Health*.

The source of marijuana is the cannabis plant (*Cannabis sativa*) and the plant form is almost universally used without significant modification. There is some popularity of concentrated extracts such as hashish, but the use of the pure psychoactive ingredients is all but unknown outside the laboratory. Synthetic cannabis-like substances have been produced and some have a limited use in medicine. There are sixty-one cannabinoids unique to the cannabis plant but hundreds of other chemicals are also present. It is generally accepted that the primary psychoactive ingredient is delta-9-tetrahydrocannabinol (delta-9-THC or THC).

The most striking pharmacological effects of marijuana are on mind and behavior, and most of these can be duplicated with delta-9-THC. Marijuana is almost always smoked, usually in home-rolled cigarettes, but animal research depends usually on the administration of more pharmacologically pristine substances.

Smoking is an efficient method of drug delivery. Because of the large absorptive area of the lungs, the drug is quickly taken up into the bloodstream and reaches the brain within seconds. Cannabinoids are very soluble in fat and the brain is largely made up of fatty substances. For this reason the drug is taken up into the brain preferentially. Over time the drug and its metabolites are redistributed throughout the body and slowly eliminated.

Because of the wide variety of marijuana plants and their varying content of THC, the dosage taken by average users is harder to evaluate with marijuana than with cocaine. The smoking route of administration is also highly variable and is dependent on the experience and style of the user. Dosage is, of course, critical in evaluating pharmacological effect, but for marijuana only rough estimations can be made. These factors make it difficult to make meaningful parallels between laboratory experiments with marijuana and street usage.

Certain evidence is clear. Acute use of marijuana is highly unlikely to kill a person. The drug has almost no lethal potential. This makes it similar to tobacco in its acute effects and different from alcohol and heroin. Marijuana does resemble alcohol in some respects. It is a rapid onset intoxicant widely used in social situations, forbidden by some societies and accepted by others.

Marijuana is taken by users for the "high," as is cocaine. The high from marijuana is different from the cocaine high. Marijuana is sedative and cocaine is stimulant. They produce different types of pleasurable experiences and have different specific pharmacological effects and patterns of use.

Marijuana impairs motor coordination and accuracy of the execution of movements. Various skills related to driving are impaired by usual street doses of marijuana. Attention is diminished. Single doses impair short-term memory. Modification of time sense is a reliable effect of marijuana and is often sought by users as part of the drug experience.

In many ways marijuana resembles a mild sedative drug. It reduces anxiety. It produces relative quiescence in users as well as a selective indifference to the environment. Marijuana, however, is different from the sedatives in many respects. The active pharmacological substance is a hallucinogen in high doses. Marijuana and its metabolites tend to remain in the body and have residual effects for days to months. About a third of users report that while under the influence of the drug, they have had panic reactions, hallucinations, changes in body image, and paranoid reactions. First-time users will occasionally have acute anxiety or fearfulness. Some people have an acute dysphoric (unpleasant) reaction to the drug and this has limited its medical usefulness. The reader should recognize that the medical usefulness of a drug is a red herring when one is considering the problems of street use. Many medically useful drugs are abused, and some totally innocuous drugs are "scheduled" as dangerous because of their chemical properties.

A major concern about long-term users of marijuana has been the occurrence of the so called "amotivational syndrome." Clinical reports on chronic users describe a washed-out state with apathy, difficulty in carrying out plans, loss of ambition, and difficulty in concentrating. Acceptable scientific evidence has not established marijuana as a unique cause for such behavior, but one cannot ignore the repeated clinical reports of this syndrome in marijuana users.

The existence of large numbers of chronic daily users, particularly among the young, has led to the conceptualization of marijuana as an "addicting" drug. It does not have the use pattern of the opioids, but nonetheless some of the traditional characteristics of addiction can be shown for marijuana.

In 1946 tolerance to the psychological and physiological effects of marijuana were demonstrated in human subjects. When high doses were given, decreased effects on temperature, pulse, respiration, blood pressure, and mood state were seen after a few days of administration. It turns out that it is much more difficult to show such tolerance after exposure to lower doses, even for considerable periods of time. This is but another demonstration that none of the drug properties are absolute at all doses.

After two weeks or more of administration of delta-9-THC every four hours, a moderate withdrawal syndrome with sweating, salivation, tremor, and irritability occurred.[5] This evidence of dependence is of pharmacological interest but of dubious social policy significance. As with cocaine it is possible to demonstrate repeated self-administration of marijuana by humans in a laboratory as well as a naturalistic setting.

TERMINOLOGY OF "ADDICTION"

Marijuana and cocaine can to some degree fulfill the most rigid requirements for addicting drugs. They are rewarding, they will support self-administration, there is demonstrable tolerance and physical dependence. Why then is there any doubt about their status? For both drugs the tolerance and physical dependence are not the driving forces behind the self-administration. It is also clear that there are many drug users who do not become either drug dependent or addicted to these substances.

To responsibly answer the question about addiction for purposes of setting or defining policy, I will categorize the generally accepted evidence about cocaine and marijuana in respect to their pharmacological properties, chronic and acute threat to individuals, epidemiology, and lastly their social and economic effects.

Although they share some characteristics with the opioid drugs, neither cocaine nor marijuana has a pharmacologically significant withdrawal syndrome that would, by its presence, enforce the continued taking of the drug. This is not to say that withdrawal cannot be demonstrated; it can. Users do not continue involvement with the drugs primarily to avoid withdrawal.

Similarly, although tolerance to pharmacological effects can be demonstrated, neither cocaine nor marijuana creates a tolerance in

---

5. N. L. Benowitz and R. T. Jones, "Effects of Delta-9-tetrahydrocannabinol on Drug Distribution and Metabolism," *Clinical Pharmacology and Therapeutics* 22 (1977): 259–68; R. T. Jones, N. L. Benowitz, and R. I. Herning, "Clinical Relevance of Cannabis Tolerance and Dependence," *Journal of Clinical Pharmacology* 21 (1981): 143s–52s.

human use that forces a significant increase in the amounts of drug taken by individuals. We do not see the form of continuous escalation in dosage characteristic of the opioid drugs.

Tolerance, physical dependence, and withdrawal are properties of many drugs that are not abused and are neither pleasurable nor reinforcing. For example propranolol, a widely prescribed drug for heart problems, can produce each of these phenomena. We should be aware of, but not totally rely on, these characteristics in assessing the chronic human pharmacology of abused drugs. Even if cocaine and marijuana share some of these characteristics, it is important to note that drug seeking and drug taking behavior can be maintained at doses that do not cause noticeable tolerance or physical dependence.

Whether they harm all users, both cocaine and marijuana harm *some* users. The selection of "victims" is not biologically capricious but is dependent upon pharmacological variables; the health, personality, physiology, age, and genetics of the individuals; social circumstance; the chronicity and route of use; and the purity of the substances. Since these are often not quantifiable for an individual, it is possible to consider that a certain percentage of a population at risk will suffer some harm. Epidemiological studies to define that percentage are not yet satisfactory. We must therefore make generalizations based on inadequate studies and often flawed figures. A useful analogy might be to consider that one of every fifty cocaine users will become involved in compulsive use. We have no way of telling which one will become the victim. This means that it will appear that many casual users can "get away with it," but at the same time every first-time user takes a risk that can be quantified. The time course of development of compulsive drug use is such that this dependency may not become apparent for a year or so after initial regular exposure, or it may occur rapidly. The existence of users who have not become overwhelmingly involved with the drug lends credence to the mistaken thought that cocaine is "safe." A similar situation exists for marijuana, but the population at risk is much greater, supplies of the drug are cheaper, and the young population may be more vulnerable because of their developmental stage.

From the above it should be clear that cost of drug and availability of supply are also critical variables in the resultant drug problem. These are economic parameters. Human, social, pharmacological, political, and economic factors determine the importance of a drug problem. The magnitude of that problem decides whether we refer to particular drug use as "addictive." Addiction is viewed by the public as a societally harmful state resulting from an evil property of a drug.

Each of these drugs can, in some populations, produce drug dependencies that meet all the commonly accepted attributes of addiction. In that sense they are addicting. Each of these drugs can produce harm to individuals in particular groups, depending on the characteristics of the individuals, the dosage, the form, and the chronicity of drug usage. In that sense the drugs also meet the implied quality of addiction in that they can cause harm. For both cocaine and marijuana, the societal impact of significant groups of drug dependent persons is considerable. For both drugs, the economic effects and criminal involvement with trade are important factors in using the pejorative "addicting." Despite these congruencies with the term addiction, it is necessary to be aware that there is a behavioral spectrum around every drug of abuse. We must consider the situation of the drug user or abuser before he takes a drug, we must consider the behavior when he is taking a drug, and lastly we must consider the behavior consequent to the drug ingestion.

Some drugs are more reinforcing than others. Some drugs are more pleasurable than others. Some drugs have a higher dependence liability than others. An agreed-upon set of definitions for a society is necessary before one can establish whether, within the spectrum of misused drugs, some drugs are more "addicting" than others.

WORDS DESCRIBING ATTITUDES TOWARD ADDICTION

The National Institute of Drug Abuse in 1982 assembled a group of definitions for drug abuse research.[6] The definition of *addiction* quoted in part below is a starting point for discussion.

> ADDICTION: From the Latin verb "addicere," to give or bind a person to one thing or another. Generally used in the drug field to refer to chronic, compulsive, or uncontrollable drug use, to the extent that a person (referred to as an "addict") cannot or will not stop the use of some drug. Beyond this, the term is ambiguously used with a wide variety of

---

6. J. E. Nelson et al., eds., *Research Issues 26: Guide to Drug Abuse Research Terminology* (Rockville, Md.: USPHS [NIDA], 1982); *Webster's Ninth New Collegiate Dictionary* (Springfield, Mass.: Merriam-Webster, 1983); *Oxford English Dictionary*, s.v. "addiction."

often arbitrary meanings and connotations; sometimes interchangeably with, sometimes in contrast to, two other ill-defined terms, HABIT-UATION and (DRUG) DEPENDENCE, the former imprecisely referring to some lesser form of chronic drug use, the latter capable of being either of psychological or physical origin, often in varying combinations depending on the drug. It usually implies a strong (PSYCHOLOGICAL) DEPENDENCE resulting in a WITHDRAWAL SYNDROME when use of the drug is stopped. Many definitions place primary stress on psychological factors, such as loss of self-control and overpowering desires; i.e., addiction is any state in which one craves the use of a drug and uses it frequently. Others use the term as a synonym for physiological dependence; still others use it as a combination.

The primary popular stereotype, what has been called the "classical definition of addiction," is that it is an extraordinarily debilitating vice or disease—even an evil and sinful state—rooted in the invariable pharmacological effects of a drug on the human body, an irrevocable process that involves the presence of tolerance and results in a withdrawal syndrome that can be avoided only by total abstinence.[7] The classical definition of addiction further links this phenomenon particularly to the OPIATE NARCOTICS. Like the popular concept of narcotics, this classical definition emerged in the 1920s out of a blending of popular and scientific terminology laden with emotional and imprecise meanings. The term "addict" began to be increasingly stigmatized and used by both the scientific and lay communities to express that the compulsive use of opiates was not just a bad habit but was worse both to the individual and society than other forms of habituation, such as to tobacco and alcohol, and resulted in debility, insanity, crime, and death.

Consultation with the *Oxford English Dictionary* shows that in 1597 Shakespeare is the source of the first quote that mentioned a drug (alcohol) in relationship to the word *addicted*. He wrote, "To forsweare thinne Potations and to addict themselves to Sack" (*Second Part of Henry IV,* act 4, sc. 3).[8] Of course the word is much older than that and it is only recently that *addiction* can once again be used to refer to alcohol. Shakespeare was probably using the term in the sense of "to devote to," but he did find ethanol more appropriate than books to team with the verb *addict*.

7. S. Peele, "Redefining Addiction. I. Making Addiction a Scientifically and Socially Useful Concept," *International Journal of Health Services* 7, no. 1 (1977): 103–24. (Cited in Nelson et al., eds., *Research Issues 26.*)

8. Quoted in the *Compact Edition of the Oxford English Dictionary,* vols. 1 and 2 (New York: Oxford University Press, 1971).

Although the first meaning of *addict* in *Webster's Ninth Collegiate Dictionary* is "one who is addicted to a drug," the definition of *addiction* gives "the quality or state of being addicted (to reading)" as a first meaning.[9] Webster gives for the second meaning "compulsive physiological need for a habit forming drug (as heroin)." The analogy is an opiate and the emphasis is on physiological need. One definition of the verb *addict* in the *Oxford English Dictionary* gives "to devote, give up, or apply habitually to a practice. (A person addicts his mind, etc., or his tastes addict him.)" This strikes to the major point that generates wobbly semantics around the word *addiction*. Do drugs addict people or do people addict themselves to drugs? The state of addiction in all senses requires both an activity, or drug, and a population at risk. Are the drug characteristics or the population characteristics more important? This chapter focuses more on drug characteristics than on the many populations who might be considered. Despite this emphasis, addiction is not a problem without addicts.

When we speak of addiction, our interest is in humans and their behavior in their environment. The definition of the term is most meaningful for humans. There are, however, terms used in pharmacology that are associated with addiction and that can best be quantified in animal experimental situations. To make the description of cocaine and marijuana more useful, I will first give definitions of some words used in describing the results of chronic drug-taking behaviors.

Reinforcement is a term most frequently used in animal behavioral pharmacology. In that context it is a measure of whether, and how hard and long, an experimental animal will "work" for administration of a drug. The animal experiments are therefore not subject to the variables of human societal influences. They are, however, both route- and dose-specific. Standard methods for the measurement of reinforcement are well established. The first question is whether a drug will be self-administered by animals or humans. For example delta-9-THC, the pharmacologically active ingredient of marijuana, is a poor reinforcer as measured by the response rates of animals. Despite this the drug's enduring popularity among humans indicates that the animal experiments are missing some important

---

9. *Webster's Ninth New Collegiate Dictionary.*

characteristics of the human situation. Cocaine on the other hand is a powerful reinforcer, and one might conclude that the current extreme popularity of the drug is primarily the result of this property. The historical evidence indicates that there have been times when cocaine was simply not a major drug-abuse problem. It has been available in South American countries for many years and was not perceived as a public health problem. The fact that this is no longer true is obviously not the result of a change in the drug but in the perception of its desirability as a self-administered substance. Reinforcing properties are only one factor in the equation of "addiction."

Tolerance was once considered to be a requirement for addictive drugs but experience has changed this viewpoint. One should remember that the model for addiction has always been the opioid or narcotic drugs. The pharmacological characteristics of this group have been assumed to be a model, and this misconception has led to most of the semantic difficulties around the concept of addiction to other drugs. There are several variants of tolerance, which are described in the following definitions.

Tolerance in general is the phenomenon of decreased responsiveness to a specific effect of the same dose of a drug as a result of prior exposure to the drug. When the same decreased responsiveness is seen after administration of a different drug, the phenomenon is known as cross-tolerance. A parallel terminology is used for dependence, i.e., a dependence on one drug can be supported with another in the same class. For example, methadone shows cross-tolerance and cross-dependence with morphine. Sometimes the reverse phenomenon is seen; there is increased responsiveness to an effect of a drug as a result of prior exposure. This is called reverse tolerance or sensitization. Acute tolerance can be seen on a single administration of a drug and refers to an observation of less effect at the same apparent plasma level of a drug when the drug level is falling compared to the effect when the level was rising. The mechanism that produces the tolerance may be related to the metabolism of the drug or its interaction with receptors. If a drug increases its own metabolism and thereby decreases the effect of successive doses, this is known as dispositional tolerance. If the reason for the decreased responsiveness is not the result of metabolism, it is known as pharmacological tolerance or pharmacodynamic tolerance or adaptive tolerance or functional tolerance. Sometimes there is a change in sensitivity to a behavioral effect of a drug as a result of prior exposure to the drug. This is known as behavioral tolerance and may not become apparent until the behavioral test is given.[10]

Dependence is a separate characteristic from tolerance and, in both pharmacological and common usage, has been combined with many modifying terms. The distinction often made between psychological and physical dependence is hard to define in operational terms. My discussion of this terminology draws heavily from a 1984 document by the Committee on Problems of Drug Dependence.[11] The term itself is used in both biological and behavioral contexts. Biologically the term is used to describe the biochemical and physiological consequences of repeated exposure to a drug and is often intertwined with the concept of tolerance. This biological definition is synonymous with the term *neuroadaptation* as used in the World Health Organization's memorandum on nomenclature and classification.[12] This "neuroadaptation" is, for the most part, inferred from the appearance of a withdrawal syndrome when either the drug is withdrawn or a specific antagonist to the drug is given. "Neuroadaptation" does not involve behavior and it is possible to exhibit dependence when there is no evidence of neuroadaptation. Dependence in this broader sense refers to the physiological and behavioral effects that occur when drug administration is stopped after a period of repeated exposure to the drug.

Neither tolerance nor dependence is a necessary concomitant to "drug abuse." Drug abuse is a societally relative term, which is as unsatisfactory for science as it is necessary for society. The words become tangled in inconsistencies. Expert committees have often attempted without success to reach a universally acceptable definition. The WHO expert committee of 1969 defined drug abuse as " . . . persistent or sporadic excessive drug use inconsistent with or unrelated to acceptable medical practice." The WHO committee of 1981 criticized this and commented, "Since alcohol is not usually prescribed by the medical profession, then any excessive use would be

10. N. A. Krasnegor, ed., *Behavioral Tolerance: Research and Treatment Implications,* NIDA Research Monograph 18 (Washington, D.C.: Government Printing Office, 1977).

11. J. V. Brady and S. E. Lukas, eds., *Testing Drugs for Physical Dependence Potential and Abuse Liability,* NIDA Research Monograph 52 (Washington, D.C.: Government Printing Office, 1984).

12. World Health Organization (WHO), "Nomenclature and Classification of Drug- and Alcohol-Related Problems: A WHO Memorandum," *Bulletin of the World Health Organization* 59, no. 2 (1981): 225–42.

abuse. But then what is excessive?'' They then suggested a division into (a) unsanctioned use, (b) hazardous use, (c) dysfunctional use, and (d) harmful use.[13] Whatever the semantic distinctions, it seems that drug abuse, sanctioned by an institute name, is here to stay, and "addiction" is etymologically incurable.

We must deal with the terms as they are but have a recognition that the ambiguities will always confuse communications. In those instances we can drop back to the more precise definitions of pharmacology as sanctioned by textbooks and the World Health Organization. In our present use of the language, addiction has a pejorative connotation in some—but not all—contexts. It sounds "right" with some subjects and not others. For example a sports addict is all right; a videogame addict is questionable. A cigarette addict sounds wrong, but a marijuana addict sounds more fitting. The natural modifier seems to be heroin. There is nothing semantically distressing about a heroin addict. "He is addicted to good books and fine wine," is in no way a pejorative statement and would be acceptable colloquial American English.

Is there a relationship between the terminology of addiction and the concept of dangerousness? This is the case with public acceptance of undesirable activities, e.g., sports are not dangerous but videogames might "rot the mind." In a consideration of marijuana and cocaine, an examination of danger is in order. "Dangerous Drugs" is an alliterative and acceptable combination of words that comes easily to the typewriters of reporters. What do we think of? Heroin, once again, and cocaine. Not marijuana and probably not cigarettes. Almost certainly not alcohol. In the perception of the reader, neither cigarettes nor alcohol is a drug and so cannot be subsumed under the terms.

The use of the term *drug* should also be examined. In common parlance, a drug is a drug of abuse. Substances like alcohol, clearly drugs to the pharmacologist, are considered to be something else to the public. "Dangerous drugs" is often true when referring to the self-administration of substances. Dangerous behavior with chemicals is more descriptive of the reality.

Danger can be a threat to the individual, to his immediate surroundings, or to society in general. It can be the result of acute or chronic

13. Ibid.

usage of a drug. If an addiction is not considered dangerous in any way, the use of the term is neutral. Sports addicts are not condemned. Heroin, the prototype, can be acutely dangerous to the individual by a direct pharmacological respiratory depressant action. The intravenous route of administration is inherently chronically dangerous because of possibilities of contamination of needles and syringes. Marijuana is acutely dangerous to a much lesser degree. The intoxication by marijuana can impair driving performance, but death by overdosage is not a possibility in ordinary usage. The smoking route of administration and the natural plant form of dosage limit the possibilities of acute harm. There is still a debate on whether marijuana is chronically dangerous to the individual, but the probabilities are that any substance delivered to the lungs by smoking will turn out to have a significant risk. Societal danger from the use of marijuana is related to the population group at risk, the young. We see here that pure pharmacological factors are often not the issue. Who uses what, when, and how—these are the issues that often create the questions of risk. Cocaine, too, exemplifies the population and environmental factors in assessing dangerousness. Its usage, formerly limited, now has spread through all society. The youth of the country are not the major consumers. A high middle-class involvement in the use of the drug causes a different danger to society. The acute effects of the drug in ordinary dosages by the intranasal route are not considered "dangerous" by many authors. The threat to the individual from overwhelming involvement with cocaine use can be considerable. This is more because of psychological and social factors rather than any health effects of the substance. Heavy use can cause health effects, but this is rare. The health effects of smoking and intravenous usage are less properties of the drug than characteristics of anything taken by these routes.

We do not know what percentage of casual users become intensively involved with cocaine use, nor do we know how to identify the population at greatest risk. As with many substances, the risk is statistical; some people get away with it and others don't. Of course the first-time user always assumes he will not become one of those who is damaged by the drug. The most conservative strategy is to condemn all self-administered drug use. Despite this, can we call all self-administered agents "addicting"? The term is so broadly used that this might be an acceptable but probably useless exercise.

A REASONABLE USE OF WORDS

Given the understandable meaning of addiction as equivalent to a pejorative version of WHO's "drug dependence," why has any confusion ever developed about marijuana and cocaine? First, the definition of drug dependence, "a socio-psycho-biological syndrome manifested by a behavioral pattern in which the use of a given psychoactive drug (or class of drugs) is given a sharply higher priority over other behaviors which once had significantly greater value [i.e., drug use comes to have a greater relative value]. . . . A key descriptive element is the priority given to drug-seeking over other behaviors."[14] This is a semantic mouthful but anyone who has ever examined serious marijuana or cocaine users will have no trouble matching them up to the definition.

The difficulty has developed over an ambivalence about certain drug usages that are accepted by society and are thus not appropriately condemned by the harsh word "addiction." When this situation occurs, the definers of words look for loopholes. Tolerance and dependence used to be loopholes for cocaine and marijuana. That was in the late sixties and early seventies, when a generation accustomed to marijuana use and unaware of the dangers of cocaine use felt that these were safe additions to the armamentarium of pleasure. The broad middle-class use of these drugs required that they be labeled as safe in as many ways as possible. The media, certainly including some chemical habitués, made every effort to minimize the risk of drugs. In 1943 *Life* magazine, using the word *narcotics* in a pharmacologically incorrect fashion in its article title, said, "Cocaine, extracted from the leaves of the tropical coca bush, and marijuana, the resin of the ubiquitous hemp weed, are not physiologically habit-forming but they get their users into more immediate trouble. The "snowbird" (cocaine sniffer) and "hay-burner" (marijuana smoker) are carried off into a state equivalent to deep alcoholic intoxication. In this state, which is characterized by irresponsible violence, the swing musician ascends to new peaks of virtuosity and the ordinary criminal becomes a spectacular public enemy."[15]

This quote, typical of the time, is almost entirely incorrect in its

14. Ibid.
15. G. Piel, "Narcotics: War Has Brought Illicit Traffic to All-Time Low but U.S. Treasury Fears Rising Postwar Addiction," *Life*, July 19, 1943, pp. 82–84, 86, 88, 91–92, 94.

description. Even in the early years of the eighties, deliberate or careless misquotations were used to advance the idea that cocaine, for instance, was not "addicting."[16]

We need condemnatory words to speak of behaviors we do not like. We also need descriptive terms that are accurate. It is humanly necessary to have summary terms that give both description and opinion. Addiction is such a term. Drug dependence can be defined with less emotion but still carries the stigma of societal disapproval. Is the diabetic drug-dependent? The answer "no" seems obvious, because diabetes is an accepted disease that is being self-treated by the patient's use of insulin. We have chosen to make the traditional drug dependencies diseases as well, thereby blurring the distinction. The discovery of the enkephalins and endorphins, providing a biological basis for a need for opiates, has further blurred the semantic picture. In the novel *Nineteen Eighty-four* George Orwell described a new set of languages. The "C" language was used by technicians and scientists and contained unambiguous meanings. The pharmacological definitions presented in this paper are in the "C" language, but the word "addiction" has all the characteristics of Newspeak.

The difficulties in understanding can be exemplified by the summary of drug characteristics shown in Table 6-1. I have attempted to compare cocaine and marijuana with two legal but dangerous drugs, cigarettes and alcohol; two older drug-abuse problem centers, barbiturates and the hallucinogens (LSD and similar drugs); the prototype of addicting drugs, heroin; and one of the most widely prescribed prescription drugs, propranolol. The scores given in the table are based on an interpretation of the published literature but probably would be concurred with by most experts. To summarize in this way, I have had to compress some definitions. In the table, "Tolerance" is a sum of all forms of tolerance. "Physical Dependence" is a measure of both the range of effects where physiological withdrawal can be demonstrated and the intensity of the combined withdrawal syndromes. "Self-Administered" is an estimate of the ease of making experimental animals administer the drug to themselves by any route. "Reinforcement" as used in the table is a relative measure of the amount of work animals in an experimental situation will

---

16. R. Byck, "History and Sociology of Cocaine Use and Research: Three Histories of Cocaine," in S. Fisher and U. Ulenhuth, eds., *Cocaine: Clinical and Biobehavioral Aspects* (New York: Oxford University Press, 1986).

Table 6–1. A Comparative Chart of the Pharmacology of Selected Drugs.

	Tolerance	Physical Dependence	Self-Administered	Reinforcement	Acute Toxicity	Chronic Toxicity	Problem Today
Marijuana	+	+	++	++	0	+	++
Cocaine	+	+	++	+++	++	++	++
Cigarettes	++	++	+	++	0	+++	+++
Alcohol	+++	+++	++	+++	+	+++	+++
Heroin	+++	+++	++	+++	+++	+	++
Barbiturates	0	0	+	+	0	++	+
Hallucinogens	++	+	+	+	+	+	+
Propranolol	+	+	?	?	+	+	0

Notes: 0, no significance; +, present but not important; ++, a significant amount; +++, important; ?, data not available.

244

do to receive a single dose of the drug. "Acute Toxicity" is the probability of physical damage to an individual from all causes as the result of less than a single day of self-administered drug. "Chronic Toxicity" is a combination of the probability of and seriousness of the effects of each of these drugs when given or taken for periods of months to many years. "Problem Today" is my estimate of the net social, individual, political, and economic significance of the widespread use of this drug in the United States in 1985.

The reader should note that by summarizing ideas in a table, I have immediately destroyed the concept of accurate definition in describing drugs of abuse. This sort of summation is only an insignificant version of the condensation of the popular press. If you do not have the table, I cannot condense a wide range of information about drugs. If you do have the table, you will to some degree be misled by the information.

Given these shortcomings, what is the substance of the impression created by the table? First, tolerance and physical dependence as drug characteristics have little to do with the magnitude of a drug abuse problem. Second, reinforcement potential also is poorly related to the problem today. Third, acute and chronic toxicities are not related to society's acceptance of drug usage.

Rules, regulations, and laws are based on the degree of condensation of information that can be held in the minds of the rule makers. Unfortunately, there are no simple definitions of drug characteristics that lend themselves to law or policy making. The behavior of individuals in their interaction with drugs makes rule making even more frustrating.

This chapter started with the assertion that cocaine and marijuana are addicting and that some drugs are more addicting than others. It should end with a realization that the question is not clear but the answers are.

7

THE USE AND MISUSE OF INTOXICANTS

Factors in the Development of Controlled Use

Norman E. Zinberg

INTRODUCTION

Careful interviewing has revealed that controlled users—regular occasional users of intoxicants whose use is unquestionably under control—and even abstainers express much more interest in and preoccupation with the use of intoxicants than is generally acknowledged. Whether to use, when, with whom, how much, how to explain why one does not use—these questions are of concern to a great many citizens. Within the American culture lies a deep-seated aversion to acknowledging this preoccupation. As a result, our culture plays down the importance of the many social mores, sanctions, and rituals that enhance our capacity to control the use of intoxicants. Thus the whole issue becomes muddy. The existence of some control on the part of even the most compulsive users, and the interest in drugs and the quality of drug use (the question of with whom, when, and how much to use) on the part of most controlled users, are ignored. We are left with longings for the utopian society where no one would want drugs either for their pleasant or unpleasant effects, or for relaxation and good fellowship, or for escape and torpor.

Since such abstinence is impossible, however, the reigning culture's model of extreme decorum overemphasizes the pharmaceutical powers of the drug or the personality of the user. It inculcates the view that only a disordered person would not live up to the culture's standards or that the power of the drug is so great that the standards cannot be upheld. To consider only the drug itself or the personality of the user tends to ignore the power of the social setting in which the drug use takes place. This oversight requires considerable psychological legerdemain, for as in most areas of living, people in complex social situations can rarely remain indefinitely on an extremely decorous course. Intoxicant use tends to vary with one's time of life, status, and even geographical location. Most adolescents who have used intoxicants heavily slow down appreciably as they reach adulthood and change their social setting (friends and circumstances); there are some adults who, as they become more successful, may increase intoxicant use. A man born and bred in the dry part of Kansas may change his use significantly after moving to New York City. The effects on intoxicant use of such variations in social circumstances have certainly been perceived, but they are usually not incorporated into a sound theoretical understanding of how the social setting influences the use and control of intoxicants.[1]

In this chapter I will consider first some background on historical variations of controlled use before looking at how the reactions to the drugs themselves, the personalities of the users, and the social setting lead to the development of social sanctions and rituals that are the bases for controlled intoxicant use. A section on the powerful influence of social learning on such use is followed by a discussion of the problems for researchers in the field of intoxicant use at a time when there is so much controversy about social policy.

HISTORICAL BACKGROUND

The history of the use of alcohol in America provides a striking example of the variability of intoxicant use and its control.[2] First, it illustrates the social prescriptions that define the social concept of

---

1. N. E. Zinberg, *Drug, Set, and Setting: The Basis for Controlled Intoxicant Use* (New Haven and London: Yale University Press, 1984).

2. G. Ade, *The Old-Time Saloon: Not Wet—Not Dry, Just History* (Detroit: Gale Research Corporation, 1931); S. Bacon, "Introduction," in D. Cahalan, I. H. Cisin, and H. M.

control, and second, it shows that the time span of these control variations can be decades.

Five social prescriptions that define controlled or moderate use of alcohol—and these may apply to other intoxicants as well—have been derived from a study of alcohol use in many different cultures. All five of these conditions encourage moderation and discourage excess.[3]

1. Group drinking is clearly differentiated from drunkenness and is associated with ritualistic or religious celebrations.
2. Drinking is associated with eating or ritualistic feasting.
3. Both sexes, as well as different generations, are included in the drinking situation, whether they drink or not.
4. Drinking is divorced from the individual effort to escape personal anxiety or difficult (even intolerable) social situations. Furthermore, alcohol is not considered medicinally valuable.
5. Inappropriate behavior when drinking (violence, aggression, overt sexuality) is absolutely disapproved, and protection against such behavior is exercised by the sober or the less intoxicated. This general acceptance of a concept of restraint by the controlled intoxicant user usually indicates that drinking is only one of many activities and thus susceptible to reasonable levels of constraints on behavior. It also shows that drinking is not associated with a male or female "rite of passage" or sense of superiority.

The enormous variations in alcohol use that have taken place during three major periods of American history (the 1600s to the 1770s, the 1770s to about 1890, and 1890 to today) illustrate the importance of these social prescriptions in controlling the use of alcohol.[4]

During the first period, the American colonies, although veritably steeped in alcohol, strongly and effectively prohibited drunkenness. Families drank and ate together in taverns, and drinking was asso-

Crossley, eds., *American Drinking Practices: A National Survey of Behavior and Attitudes,* Rutgers Center for Alcohol Studies, No. 6 (New Brunswick, N.J.: Rutgers University Press, 1969).

3. N. E. Zinberg and K. M. Fraser, "The Role of the Social Setting in the Prevention and Treatment of Alcoholism," in J. H. Mendelson and N. K. Mello, eds., *The Diagnosis and Treatment of Alcoholism,* 2d ed. (New York: McGraw-Hill, 1985), pp. 457–83.

4. Ibid.

ciated with celebrations and rituals. Tavern keepers were people of status; keeping the peace and preventing excesses stemming from drunkenness were grave duties. Manliness or strength was measured neither by the extent of consumption nor by violent acts resulting from it. Prerevolutionary society, however, did not abide by all the prescriptions, for certain alcoholic beverages were viewed as medicines: "Groaning beer," for example, was consumed in large quantities by pregnant and lactating women.

The second period, which included the Revolutionary War, the Industrial Revolution, and the expansion of the frontier, was marked by excess. Men were separated from their families and began to drink together and with prostitutes. Alcohol was served without food and was not limited to special occasions, and violence resulting from drunkenness grew. In the face of increasing drunkenness and alcoholism, people began to believe (as is the case with some illicit drugs today) that it was the powerful, harmful pharmaceutical properties of the intoxicant itself that made controlled use remote or impossible.

Although by the beginning of the third period moderation in the use of alcohol had begun to increase, this trend was suddenly interrupted in 1920 by the Volstead Act, which ushered in another era of excess. We are still recovering from the speakeasy ambience of Prohibition in which men again drank together and with prostitutes, food was replaced by alcohol, and the drinking experience was colored with illicitness and potential violence. Although repeal provided relief from excessive and unpopular legal control, the society was left floundering without an inherited set of social sanctions and rituals to control use.

THE BASIS FOR CONTROLLED INTOXICANT USE

In order to understand how sanctions and rituals that help differentiate use from misuse of intoxicants develop, one must think in terms of how three factors or variables interact to affect an individual's decision to use an intoxicant, the degree of effect it has on him, and the ongoing social and psychological reactions to use. These variables are (1) the pharmaceutical properties of the intoxicant, (2) the attitude and personality of the user (the set), and (3) the physical and social setting in which use takes place. Despite apparent acceptance of this theoretical position, which stresses the importance of all three variables (as mentioned in the Introduction), the influence of setting on intoxicant use and the user, and the way in which setting interacts with the other two variables have been little understood.[5]

Even those who make use of this threefold theoretical construct in analyzing the patterns of drug use and treating users fail to realize the exact role played by the setting (including both physical and social setting) as an independent variable in determining the impact of use. When a drug is administered in a hospital setting, for example, the effect is very different from that experienced by a few people sitting around in a living room listening to records. Not only is there a vast difference between the actual physical locations, but different social attitudes are involved. In the hospital the administration of opiates subsumes the concept of the institutional structure of therapy and licitness. In the living room there is a flavor of dangerous adventure, antisocial activity, and illicit pleasure, as well as the considerable anxiety that accompanies all three. It is not surprising that few patients in hospital settings continue to take drugs on their own after the necessity for therapy has passed,[6] whereas many living room users express an intense and continuing interest in the drug experience.

When intoxicant use is considered, it is remarkable how often people attempt to deny the existence of a widespread preoccupation with drugs. In particular, when the "drug revolution" began in the 1960s, public and professionals alike tended to think of any use of substances not only as misuse but as something that was difficult to understand. The question that comes up again and again is, "Why do they use it?"

The obvious reply, "Because they like it," is misleading. First, the question of what constitutes pleasure is extremely hard to answer, and even in a general sense the notion of personal gratification is misunderstood. Such a reply is often used pejoratively to indicate a dangerous relationship with a substance that could lead to dependency or addiction. By implication, this view suggests that controlled users of intoxicants do not get personal satisfaction from ingesting

---

5. N. E. Zinberg, "Addiction and Ego Function," *Psychoanalytic Study of the Child* 30 (1975): 567–78; N. E. Zinberg and W. M. Harding, "Introduction," in N. E. Zinberg and W. M. Harding, eds., *Control over Intoxicant Use: Pharmacological, Psychological, and Social Considerations* (New York: Human Sciences Press, 1982), pp. 13–35.

6. C. O'Brien, Personal Communication (1978); N. E. Zinberg, "The Search for Rational Approaches to Heroin Use," in P. G. Bourne, ed., *Addiction: A Comprehensive Treatise* (New York: Academic Press, 1974).

their drugs. Although there unquestionably are people who use a small amount of a substance merely to be sociable, like the guest who nurses one drink throughout a cocktail party, most users find their use gratifying. In fact, even those who obviously are in careful control of their use respond "yes" to the question, "Would you like to use more than you do?" Besides citing their fear that they might get addicted—a fear expressed most strongly, of course, by those with the least to fear—people who use drugs moderately apparently do so to preserve the pleasure obtained from the substance.

The issue, therefore, is not one of obtaining gratification from substance use, for most users do. The issue is the degree to which an individual can balance and hence control those wishes for substance gratification with other factors, such as moral revulsion, the desire to enhance gratification in the long run, automatic acceptance of peer group standards, or unconscious utilization of available social sanctions and rituals. In other words, the gratification aspect of drug use may not be very different from that aspect of the consumption of everyday things, such as food. Some people who gratify themselves thoroughly and overeat one evening find that the next day food does not appeal to them. Others after a debauch can exercise a balancing control by keeping busy, getting distraught by seeing the numbers on the scale, beginning a careful regimen of exercise, or consciously being where the food is less appetizing or is low in calories. Still others try these same mechanisms but they succeed only intermittently or partially. They gain weight or, in psychodynamic terms, suffer from inhibitions against control. But the difficulty, in the case of both food and intoxicants, lies not in the pleasure factor but in the inhibition of existing controls. And it can be seen easily, if only by watching old movies, how the cultural norm of what an attractive body is, i.e., the social setting, influences the extent of the control exercised.

As to how one fixes on a substance that is pleasurable, I am not sure that the analogy with food altogether holds. With drugs there is far less choice, and that choice is determined by what is socially available. Today respectable, middle-class professionals can easily find marijuana as well as alcohol, but they probably would have to go to some unacceptable lengths to obtain heroin.

Much has been made of the possibility of drug specificity, the view that an individual is so enamored of a particular drug that the pleasure from it overwhelms all other substances and nothing else would have the same appeal.[7] Every once in a while a story emerges, usually from a patient under drug treatment, that tells of multiple and dysfunctional drug use until the user discovered *the* drug, which makes giving up all else easy, and despite its own problems is an overall stabilizing experience. In my clinical experience *the* drug has always been heroin. But this kind of story goes beyond the question of extent of pleasure. One patient, for example, had been using "ups" (usually amphetamines), "downs" (usually barbiturates or diazepam [Valium]), some alcohol, and some marijuana. The combination kept her in a state of chaos, socially, psychologically, and physiologically. Periods of little sleep, food, personal interaction, or euphoria alternated, in no particular sequence, with periods of being constantly on the nod, gregarious, or high. When she finally found a drug with a strong, consistent, regular, and flexible action, it was a great relief. It is strange to think of heroin as being an integrating drug, but in this case it seemed to be just that.

If the idea of a particular drug for a particular person is less generally true than the popular myth implies, then could the reverse of that myth be true? Will any drug do as long as it gets one high? Probably not. There is no doubt that some people like one drug or some drugs better than others. And the converse is even more likely to be the case. Some who very much like to get high are quite negative about one drug or another. Although the split of the 1960s between heads and juicers has long since faded out, there still are regular marijuana users who express a distaste for alcohol, and few heroin users show much appreciation for marijuana. If they use it at all, they use it so heavily that it acts more as a "down" than as an experience enhancer.

Studies suggest that there are two large classes of drugs.[8] One class, for want of a better term, may be called "bread-and-butter" drugs. Within it alcohol, cannabis, and the opiates can be depended upon to give a consistent but relatively flexible effect that can thus be adapted to the situation as desired. A small number of respondents would also include the minor tranquilizers in this class, but so far most clinical experience has not borne this out. The pleasurable effect of the bread-and-butter drugs can generally be depended upon,

    7. H. Milkman and W. A. Frosch, "The Drug of Choice," *Journal of Psychedelic Drugs* 9 (1977): 11–20.
    8. Zinberg, *Drug, Set, and Setting.*

although alcohol, cannabis, and the opiates have quite different subjective qualities and, as already noted, liking one does not necessarily mean liking the others. Despite books with titles such as *It's So Good, Don't Even Try It Once,*[9] I would guess that many people find the opiates dysphoric.

The other class of drugs I call the "exotics." People try them either because they are pleasurable or because they are faddish. The fad factor is of great importance. Since the drug revolution of the 1960s, many people have discovered that they like to get high. If they hear that something new—remember the banana skin craze of 1967—will get them high, a mini drug explosion may occur. But among the exotics, even the pleasurable drugs have a limited application. The psychedelics, for example, are long lasting and have an extremely high impact. Although the content of trips may range widely from euphoria to depression to chaos, and even to an indication of a higher sensibility, the changed state of consciousness in any particular person is invariant and repetitious.[10] Despite the frequent reports of immense delight and discovery upon initial use, the interviewed subjects usually got bored with the experience after a time. This controlled-use study, sponsored by the Drug Abuse Council, confirmed reports from the Haight Ashbury Free Medical Clinic that not one user continued to use psychedelics frequently after a year or two.[11]

Generally the amphetamines belong in the exotic class, as far as their pleasure-seeking use is concerned. Again the initial sense of enormous stimulation from these high-impact, disorganizing drugs seems extremely pleasurable to some, but after a period of regular use the disorganizing qualities become uppermost, and the difficulty of maintaining interpersonal relationships either creates serious troubles for the user or makes him (or her) give up the drug. In the late 1960s when there was a faddish outbreak of amphetamine use all over the country, even the most prodrug underground newspapers ran headlines reading, "Speed Kills."[12] Obviously, drug users of

9. D. E. Smith and G. R. Gay, eds., *It's So Good, Don't Even Try It Once: Heroin in Perspective* (Englewood Cliffs, N.J.: Prentice-Hall, 1972).

10. N. E. Zinberg, *"High" States: A Beginning Study,* Drug Abuse Council Publication No. SS-3 (Washington, D.C.: Drug Abuse Council, 1974).

11. Zinberg, *Drug, Set, and Setting;* Zinberg, *"High" States;* N. E. Zinberg et al., *Controlled Nonmedical Drug Use* (Washington, D.C.: Drug Abuse Council, 1976); D. E. Smith, Personal Communication, 1975.

12. *Avatar,* August 1968, p. 3.

either exotics or bread-and-butter drugs can find that their use and interest in use can change over time, particularly after a period of heavy use.

The dependency-inducing potential of the amphetamines (and the barbiturates) can create a serious problem for another sort of user. Many a woman, and not a few men, who have been given a low dose of amphetamines for mild depression or as a diet aid have later found that they could not get through the day without them. When there was a general crackdown on the overprescribing of amphetamines, many of these people became desperate and protested strongly that they were not taking the drugs for fun. In the words of one woman, "I have four children and a house to clean. I can't get through the day without Dexedrine."[13] To their knowledge, these people never got high from the drug and did not want to. Much of the heavy use of a variety of tranquilizers may fall into the same category rather than into that of pleasure seeking. It is often argued, of course, that this is to some extent true of all chronic substance use, but the research interviews of my control studies support the contention of McAuliffe and Gordon that even the most chronic users continue to report a pleasurable response.[14]

The difficulty of defining pleasure makes it very hard to discuss two other exotic drugs, phencyclidine (PCP) and amyl nitrate. There is no doubt that PCP, which has been readily available on the street for more than ten years, produces some sort of high state.[15] Nevertheless, interviews with many users rarely specify particularly pleasurable experiences. As is the case with any other drug, users learn how to use it so as to avoid the most dysphoric effects; these subjects have reported little of the violence and few of the toxic symptoms that have been emphasized in the recent flurry of frightening reports about PCP.[16] They do, however, report considerable psychological and physiological disorientation as well as the heavy feelings in the

13. N. E. Zinberg and J. A. Robertson, *Drugs and the Public* (New York: Simon and Schuster, 1972).

14. W. E. McAuliffe and R. A. Gordon, "A Test of Lindesmith's Theory of Addiction: The Frequency of Euphoria among Long-term Addicts," *American Journal of Sociology* 79 (1971): 795–840.

15. A. Stickgold, "The Metamorphosis of PCP," *Grassroots* 1, October Supplement (1977).

16. R. C. Petersen and R. C. Stillman, eds., *Phencyclidine (PCP) Abuse: An Appraisal,* National Institute on Drug Abuse (NIDA), Research Monograph 21 (Washington, D.C.: Government Printing Office, 1978).

limbs and body that are characteristic of this drug. Almost without exception they have understood why PCP, which can be sniffed, smoked, or eaten but is, in itself, not usually experienced as pleasurably as the other intoxicants, generally is passed off as another substance, such as delta-9-tetrahydrocannabinol (THC), mescaline, psilocybin, or even LSD. Users of amyl nitrate, too, although mentioning the excitement of the "pop" in the head that comes with ingestion and repeating the traditional story of popping at orgasm, do not sound so interested in or pleased with the drug experience as when they are discussing the bread-and-butter drugs.

In the current climate it is possible for any of the exotic drugs to catch on for a time, but it is hard to imagine them in continuous usage for pleasure. Great media attention, if fueled by the "scare" reports from professional sources that always make a drug sound much more attractive than it actually is to those hungry for a high, can push usage beyond that which the drug would warrant on a simple pleasure scale. Even the constant discovery of one more drug menace probably cannot ensure continued popularity of a substance that is not intrinsically pleasurable (whatever that means), except among a relatively small group with highly specialized and possibly peculiar tastes.

The existence of a small group whose interest in a substance experience may be perverse raises again the familiar question of the set or personality variable. Set and personality are not identical; set subsumes personality but in a basic sense goes beyond personality. For example, as attitudes toward marijuana have changed, many people who had been negative or fearful about it, and whose personality did not polarize toward either adventurousness or righteousness, now find it easy to accept marijuana use or to try it themselves. Here, set has been affected by the interaction with the social setting, while personality has remained constant. In fact, there is increasing evidence that many who did try marijuana under the social conditions of the 1960s and 1970s find that they like it little in the eighties and have stopped using it.[17]

At no point should it be assumed that the social setting is the only active factor at work. Just as the actions of the small group mentioned above—and of other groups who find some special attraction in an otherwise not pleasant experience—are dominated by person-

---

17. NIDA, *Marihuana and Health, Ninth Annual Report to the Congress from the Secretary of Health and Human Services* (Washington, D.C.: Government Printing Office, 1982).

ality factors, there are those whose antipathy on personality grounds to specific intoxicants or intoxicants in general is so great that they would not use them under most circumstances.

In the majority of instances, even the very extreme, it is the interaction of the three variables (drug, set, and setting) that is crucial. This can vary at different times, of course, and the powerful influence of one variable may even obscure the effect of another. The example of heroin use in Vietnam, which will be discussed later to illustrate the power of the social setting, also shows how easy it is to miss the influence of one of the other variables. Because so many servicemen used heroin in Vietnam, the social-setting variable seemed predominant. But what of the group that continued to use the drug after returning to the United States? According to follow-up studies of Vietnam veterans, they are fewer than 8 percent, and the same studies raise the suspicion that their problems with drugs antedated Vietnam and may well have sprung predominantly from personality.[18]

The existence of this group, however, poses serious questions about the nature of addiction and the interaction of the three variables. Did these men really have the sort of addictive personality structure that would have led them to some sort of addiction whether or not they had gone to Vietnam? Perhaps in the United States they might have become alcoholics. But might not some of them have functioned adequately in a more regular social situation where heroin was not so easily available? And might they not, therefore, have avoided addiction, even though they would have had other psychological problems? Unfortunately, it is not possible to devise controlled experiments that can easily answer these questions.

The Vietnam experience, however, teaches us a great many things. The fact that most of those soldiers who became addicted to heroin in Vietnam but did not become readdicted in the United States demonstrates clearly the inhibition exercised by controls under certain social circumstances.[19] That those who became readdicted in the United States chose not to exercise the available controls, which must

18. L. N. Robins, D. H. Davis, and D. W. Goodwin, "Drug Use in U.S. Army—Enlisted Men in Vietnam: A Follow-up on Their Return Home," *American Journal of Epidemiology* 99 (1974): 235–49.

19. Ibid.; L. N. Robins, J. E. Helzer, and D. H. Davis, "Narcotic Use in Southeast Asia and Afterwards," *Archives of General Psychiatry* 32 (1975): 955–61; L. N. Robins et al., "Vietnam Veterans Three Years after Vietnam," in L. Brill and C. Winick, eds., *Yearbook of Substance Abuse* (New York: Human Sciences Press, 1979).

have existed inasmuch as they had not been addicts before going to Vietnam, is not necessarily evidence of inherent personality defects.

The use of any drug involves values and rules of conduct, norms, if you will, which in this essay are called "social sanctions," and patterns of behavior, called "social rituals," which together are known as "social controls." Social sanctions define whether and how a particular drug should be used. They may be informal and shared by a group—as in the maxims applied to alcohol use, "Know your limit" and "Don't drive when you're drunk"; or they may be formal—as in laws and policies aimed at regulating drug use.[20] Social rituals are the stylized, prescribed behavior patterns surrounding the use of a drug and may apply to the methods of procuring and administering the drug; the selection of the physical and social setting for use; the activities undertaken after the drug has been administered; and the ways of preventing untoward drug effects. Rituals thus serve to buttress, reinforce, and symbolize the sanctions. In the case of alcohol, for example, the statement, "Let's have a drink," automatically exerts control by using the singular term "a drink."

Social controls (rituals and sanctions) apply to all drugs, not just to alcohol, and operate in a variety of social contexts, ranging all the way from very large social groups, representative of the culture as a whole, down to small, discrete groups.[21] Certain types of special-occasion use involving widely disparate, culturally diverse groups of people—beer at ball games, drugs at rock concerts, wine with meals, cocktails at 6:00—have become so generally accepted that few if any legal strictures are applied even if such uses technically break the law. For example, a policeman will usually tell young people with beer cans at an open-air concert to "knock it off," but he will rarely arrest them; and in many states the police reaction would be the same even if the drug were marijuana.[22] If the culture

20. D. Maloff et al., "Informal Social Controls and Their Influence on Substance Use," in Zinberg and Harding, eds., *Control over Intoxicant Use*, pp. 53–76; N. E. Zinberg, W. M. Harding, and M. Winkeller, "A Study of Social Regulatory Mechanisms in Controlled Illicit Drug Users," in H. Shaffer and M. E. Burglass, eds., *Classic Contributions in the Addictions* (New York: Brunner/Mazel, 1984), pp. 277–300.

21. W. M. Harding and N. E. Zinberg, "The Effectiveness of the Subculture in Developing Rituals and Social Sanctions for Controlled Drug Use," in B. du Toit, ed., *Drugs, Rituals, and Altered States of Consciousness* (Rotterdam, Neth.: Balkema, 1977), pp. 111–33.

22. J. Newmeyer and G. Johnson, "Drug Emergencies in Crowds: An Analysis of 'Rock Medicine,'" in Zinberg and Harding, eds., *Control over Intoxicant Use*, pp. 127–37.

as a whole thoroughly inculcates a widespread social ritual, it may eventually be written into law, just as the socially developed mechanism of the morning coffee break has been legally incorporated into union contracts. But small group sanctions and rituals tend to be more diverse and more closely related to circumstances. Nonetheless, some caveats may be just as firmly upheld, for example, "Never smoke marijuana until after the children are asleep," "Only drink on weekends," "Don't shoot up until the last person has arrived and the doors are locked."

The existence of social sanctions or rituals does not necessarily mean that they will be effective, nor does it mean that all sanctions or rituals were devised as mechanisms to aid control. "Booting" (the drawing of blood into and out of a syringe) by heroin addicts seemingly lends enchantment to the use of the needle and, therefore, opposes control. But it may once have served as a control mechanism that gradually became perverted or debased. Some old-time users, at least, have claimed that booting originated in the (erroneous) belief that by drawing blood in and out of the syringe, the user could tell the strength of the drug that was being injected.

More important than the question of whether the sanction or ritual was originally intended as a control mechanism is the way in which the user handles conflicts between sanctions. With illicit drugs the most obvious conflict is that between formal and informal social controls, that is, between the law against use and the social group's condoning of use. The teenager attending a rock concert is often pressured into trying marijuana by his peers, who insist that smoking is acceptable at that particular time and place and will enhance his musical enjoyment. The push to use may include a control device, such as, "Since Joey won't smoke because he has a cold, he can drive," thereby honoring the "don't drive after smoking" sanction. Nevertheless, the decision to use, so rationally presented, conflicts with the law and may make the user anxious as to whether the police will be benign in this instance. Such anxiety interferes with control. In order to deal with the conflict, the user will probably come forth with more bravado, exhibitionism, paranoia, or antisocial feeling than would be the case if he or she had patronized one of the little bars set up alongside the concert hall for the selling of alcohol during intermission. Perhaps with some drugs such as marijuana, it is this kind of mental conflict, even more than their illegality, that makes control of illicit drugs more complex and difficult than the control of licit drugs.

The existence and application of social controls, particularly in the case of illicit drugs, does not always lead to moderate, decorous use, and yet it is the reigning cultural belief that controlled use is or should be always moderate and decorous. This requirement of decorum is perhaps the chief reason why the power of the social setting to regulate intoxicant use has not been more fully recognized and exploited. The cultural view that the users of intoxicants should always behave properly stems from the moralistic attitudes toward such behavior that pervade our culture, attitudes that are almost as marked in the case of licit drugs as in the case of illicit drugs. Yet on some occasions—at a wedding celebration or during an adolescent's first experiment with drunkenness—less decorous behavior is culturally acceptable. Although we should never condone the excessive use of any intoxicant, it has to be recognized that when such boundary-breaking occurs, it does not necessarily signify a breakdown of overall control. Unfortunately, these occasions of impropriety, particularly after the use of illicit drugs, are often taken by the advocates of abstinence to prove what they see as the ultimate truth: that in the area of drug use there are only two possible types of behavior—abstinence or unchecked excess leading to addiction. Despite massive evidence to the contrary, many people remain unshaken in this belief.

Such a stolid stance inhibits the development of rational understanding of controlled use. As mentioned earlier, the fact is overlooked that the most severe alcoholics and addicts who cluster at one end of the spectrum of drug use exhibit some control in not using as much of the intoxicating substance as they could. Next, and of great importance, at the other end of the spectrum of drug use, as the careful interviewing of ordinary citizens has shown, highly controlled users and even abstainers, as noted earlier, express much more interest in and preoccupation with the use of intoxicants than is generally acknowledged.

In most sectors of our society, informal alcohol education, which conveys the culture's informally developed sanctions and rituals, is readily available. Few children grow up without an awareness of a wide range of behaviors associated with the use of alcohol, learned from that most pervasive medium, television. They see cocktail parties, wine at meals, beer at ball games, homes broken by drink, drunks whose lives are wrecked, along with all the advertisements that present alcohol as lending glamour to every occasion.

Buttressed by movies, the print media, observation of families and family friends, and often by a sip or watered-down taste of the grown-ups' potion, young people gain an early familiarity with alcohol. When, in a peer group, they begin to drink and even, as a rite of passage, to overdo it, they know what they are about and what the sanctions are. Finding a "limit" is the direct implementation of the injunction, "Know your limit." Once that sanction has been experientially internalized—and our culture provides mores of greater latitude for adolescents than for adults—they can move on to such sanctions as "it's not nice to be drunk" and "it's O.K. to have a drink at the end of the day, or a few beers on the way home from work or in front of the television, but don't drink on the job."[23]

This general description of the learning or internalization of social sanctions, although neat and precise, does not take account of the variations from individual to individual that result from differences in personality, cultural background, and group affinity. Specific sanctions and rituals are developed and integrated in varying degrees with different groups.[24] Certainly a New York child from a rich, sophisticated family, brought up on a Saturday lunch with a divorced parent at the 21 Club, will have a different attitude toward drinking from that of the small-town child who vividly remembers accompanying a parent to a sporting event where alcohol intake acted as fuel for the excitement of unambivalent partisanship. Yet one common denominator shared by young people from these very different social backgrounds is the sense that alcohol is used at special events and belongs to special places.

This kind of education about drug use is social learning, absorbed inchoately and unconsciously as part of the living experience.[25] The learning process is impelled by an unstated and often unconscious recognition by young people that this is an area of emotional importance in American society and, therefore, knowledge about it may be quite important in future social and personal development. At-

23. Zinberg, Harding, and Winkeller, "A Study of Social Regulatory Mechanisms in Controlled Illicit Drug Users."

24. G. F. Edwards, "Drugs, Drug Dependence, and the Concept of Plasticity," *Quarterly Journal of Studies on Alcohol* 35 (1974): 176-95.

25. Zinberg, *"High" States.*

tempts made in the late 1960s and early 1970s to translate this informal process into formal drug education courses, chiefly intended to discourage any use, have failed.[26] Formal drug education, paradoxically, has stimulated drug use on the part of many young people who were previously undecided, and at the same time has confirmed the fears of those who were already excessively concerned. Is it possible, one might ask, for formal education to codify social sanctions and rituals in a reasonable way for those who have somehow been bypassed by the informal process? Or does the reigning cultural moralism, which has pervaded all such courses, preclude the possibility of discussing reasonable informal social controls that may, of course, condone use? So far, these questions remain unanswered. It will be impossible even to guess at the answers until our culture has accepted the use not only of alcohol but of other intoxicants sufficiently to allow teachers to explain how they can be used safely and well. A course in the safe use of alcohol is not intended to encourage use: Its main focus is the prevention of abuse. Similarly, the primary purpose of the few good sex education courses in existence today is to teach the avoidance of unwanted pregnancy and sexually transmitted disease, not to encourage or discourage sexual activity.

Whatever happens to formal education in these areas, the natural process of social learning will inevitably go on, for better or for worse. The power of this process is illustrated by two recent and extremely important social events: the use of psychedelics in the United States in the 1960s and the use of heroin during the Vietnam War.

Following the Timothy Leary "Tune In, Turn On, and Drop Out" slogan of 1963, the use of psychedelics became a subject of national hysteria—the "drug revolution." These drugs, known then as psychotomimetics (imitators of psychosis), were widely believed to lead to psychosis, suicide, or even murder.[27] Equally well publicized were the contentions that they could bring about spiritual rebirth, mystical oneness with the universe, and the like.[28] Certainly there were nu-

26. H. N. Boris, N. E. Zinberg, and M. Boris, "Social Education for Adolescents," *Psychiatric Opinion* 15 (1978): 32–37.

27. R. E. Mogar and C. Savage, "Personality Change Associated with Psychedelic (LSD) Therapy: A Preliminary Report," *Psychotherapy: Theory, Research and Practice* 1 (1954): 154–62; E. S. Robbins, W. A. Frosch, and M. Stern, "Further Observations on Untoward Reactions to LSD," *American Journal of Psychiatry* 124 (1967): 393–95.

28. A. Huxley, *The Doors of Perception* (New York: Harper and Row, 1954); A. T. Weil, *The Natural Mind* (Boston: Houghton Mifflin, 1972).

merous cases of not merely transient but prolonged psychoses after the use of psychedelics. In the mid-1960s psychiatric hospitals like the Massachusetts Mental Health Center and Bellevue were reporting that as many as one-third of their admissions resulted from the ingestion of these drugs.[29] By the late 1960s, however, the rate of such admissions had declined dramatically. At first, many observers concluded that this decline was due to fear tactics—the warnings about the various health hazards, the chromosome breaks and birth defects, which were reported in the media (and which were later proved to be false). In time, although psychedelic use continued to be the fastest growing drug use in America through 1973, the dysfunctional sequelae virtually disappeared.[30] What then had changed?

It has been found that neither the drugs themselves nor the personalities of the users were the most prominent factors in those painful cases of the 1960s. The retrospective McGlothlin and Arnold study of the use of such drugs before the early 1960s has revealed that although responses to the drugs varied widely, they included none of the horrible, highly publicized consequences of the mid-1960s.[31] Another book, *LSD: Personality and Experience,* describes a study, made before the drug revolution, of the influence of personality on psychedelic drug experience.[32] It found typologies of response to the drugs but no one-to-one relationship between untoward reaction and emotional disturbance. And Howard S. Becker, in his prophetic article of 1967, compared the then current anxiety about psychedelics to anxiety about marijuana in the late 1920s, when several psychoses were reported.[33] Becker hypothesized that the psychoses came not from the drug reactions themselves but from the secondary anxiety generated by unfamiliarity with the drug's effects and ballooned by media publicity. He suggested that such unpleasant reactions had disappeared when the effects of marijuana became more widely known, and he correctly predicted that the same thing would happen with the psychedelics.

29. Robbins, Frosch, and Stern, "Further Observations on Untoward Reactions to LSD."

30. National Commission on Marihuana and Drug Abuse, *Drug Use in America: Problem in Perspective* (Washington, D.C.: Government Printing Office, 1976).

31. W. H. McGlothlin and D. O. Arnold, "LSD Revisited: A Ten-Year Follow-Up of Medical LSD Use," *Archives of General Psychiatry* 24 (1971): 35–49.

32. H. L. Barr et al., *LSD: Personality and Experience* (New York: Wiley-Interscience, 1972).

33. H. S. Becker, "History, Culture, and Subjective Experience: An Exploration of the Social Bases of Drug-induced Experiences," *Journal of Health and Social Behavior* 8 (1967): 163–76.

The power of social learning also brought about a change in the reactions of those who expected to gain insight and enlightenment from the use of psychedelics. Interviews have shown that the user of the early 1960s, with his great hopes or fears of heaven or hell and his lack of any realistic sense of what to expect, had a far more extreme experience than the user of the 1970s, who had been exposed to a decade of interest in psychedelic colors, music, and sensations. The later user, who might remark, "Oh, so that is what a psychedelic color looks like," had been thoroughly prepared, albeit unconsciously, for the experience, and responded accordingly, within a middle range.

The second example of the enormous influence of the social setting and of social learning in determining the consequences of drug use comes from Vietnam. Current estimates indicate that at least 35 percent of enlisted men used heroin, and 54 percent of these became addicted to it.[34] Statistics from the U.S. Public Health Service hospitals active in detoxifying and treating addicts showed a recidivism rate of 97 percent, and some observers thought it was even higher. Once the extent of the use of heroin in Vietnam became apparent, the great fear of Army and government officials was that the maxim "once an addict, always an addict" would operate, and most of the experts agreed that this fear was entirely justified. Treatment and rehabilitation centers were set up in Vietnam, and the Army's slogan that heroin addiction stopped "at the shore of the South China Sea" was heard everywhere. As virtually all observers agree, however, those programs were total failures. Often people in the rehabilitation programs used more heroin than when they were on active duty.[35]

Nevertheless, as the study by Robins et al., cited earlier, has shown, most addiction did indeed stop at the South China Sea.[36] For addicts who left Vietnam, recidivism was approximately 10 percent after they got home to the United States—virtually the reverse of the previous U.S. Public Health Service figures. Apparently the abhorrent social setting of Vietnam led men who ordinarily would not have considered using heroin to use, and often become addicted to, the drug. But evidently they associated its use with Vietnam, much as

34. Robins et al., "Vietnam Veterans Three Years after Vietnam."
35. N. E. Zinberg, "Heroin Use in Vietnam and the United States: A Contrast and a Critique," *Archives of General Psychiatry* 26 (1972): 486–88.
36. Robins et al., "Vietnam Veterans Three Years after Vietnam."

hospital patients who are receiving large amounts of opiates for a painful medical condition associated the drug with the condition. The returnees were like those patients who, having taken opiates to relieve a physiological disturbance, usually do not crave the drug after the condition has been alleviated and they have left the hospital.

Returning to the first example—psychedelic drug use in the 1960s—it is my contention that control over use of drugs was established by the development in the counterculture of social sanctions and rituals very like those surrounding alcohol use in the culture at large. "Only use the first time with a guru" was a sanction or rule that told neophytes to use the drug the first time with an experienced user who could reduce their secondary anxiety about what was happening by interpreting it as a drug effect. "Only use at a good time, in a good place, with good people" was a sanction that gave sound advice to those taking a drug that would sensitize them intensely to their inner and outer surroundings. In addition, it conveyed the message that the drug experience could be simply a pleasant consciousness change, a good experience, instead of either heaven or hell. The specific rituals that developed to express these sanctions—just when it was best to take the drug, how, with whom, the best way to come down, and so on—varied from group to group, though some rituals spread from one group to another.

It is harder to document the development of social sanctions and rituals in Vietnam. Most of the early evidence indicated that the drug was used heavily in order to obscure the actualities of the war, with little thought of control. Yet later studies showed that many enlisted men used heroin in Vietnam without becoming addicted.[37] More important, although 95 percent of heroin-addicted Vietnam returnees did not become readdicted in the United States, 88 percent did take heroin occasionally, indicating that they had developed some capacity to use the drug in a controlled way.[38] Some rudimentary rituals, however, do seem to have been followed by the men who used heroin in Vietnam. Gently rolling the tobacco out of an ordinary cigarette, tamping the fine white powder into the opening, and then replacing a little tobacco to hold the powder in before lighting up the O.J. (opium joint) seemed the ritual followed all over the country, even though the units in the north and in the highlands had no direct

37. Robins, Davis, and Goodwin, "Drug Use in U.S. Army—Enlisted Men in Vietnam."
38. Robins et al., "Vietnam Veterans Three Years after Vietnam."

contact with those in the delta.[39] To what extent this ritual aided control is, of course, impossible to determine. Having observed it many times, however, I can say that it was almost always done in a group and thus formed part of the social experience of heroin use. While one person was performing the ritual, the others sat quietly and watched in anticipation. It would be my guess that the degree of socialization achieved through this ritual could have had important implications for control.

Still, the development of social sanctions and rituals probably occurs more slowly in the secretive world of illicit drug use than with the use of a licit drug like alcohol. The furtiveness, the suspicion, the fears of legal reprisal, as well as the myths and misconceptions that surround illicit drug use, all make the exchange of information that leads to the development of constraining social sanctions and rituals more difficult. It is particularly hard to imagine that any coherent social development occurred in the incredible pressure cooker of Vietnam. Today the whole experience has receded so far into history that it is impossible to nail down what specific social learning might have taken place. But certainly Vietnam illustrates the power of the social setting to induce large numbers of apparently ordinary people to engage in drug activity that was viewed as extremely deviant and to limit the activity to that setting. Vietnam also showed that heroin, despite its tremendous pharmaceutically addictive potential, cannot in any sense be regarded as universally or inevitably addictive.

Further study of various patterns of heroin use, including controlled use, in the United States confirms the lessons taught by the history of alcohol use in America, the use of psychedelics in the 1960s, and the use of heroin during the Vietnam War. The social setting, with its legal and institutional formal controls and its informal social controls, its capacity to develop new informal social sanctions and rituals, and its transmission of information in numerous informal ways, is a crucial factor in the controlled use of any intoxicant. This does not mean, however, that the pharmaceutical properties of the drug or the attitudes and personality of the user count for little or nothing. As I stated early in this chapter, all three variables—drug, set, and setting—must be included in any valid theory

---

39. N. E. Zinberg, "GIs and OJs in Vietnam," *New York Times Sunday Magazine,* 5 December 1973.

of drug use. In every case of use it is necessary to understand how the specific characteristics of the drug and the personality of the user interact and are modified by the social setting and its controls.

THE POWER OF SOCIAL LEARNING

It may be that society is facing not only the powerful impact of widespread drug use on individual behavior but also a striking change in the influence of social learning itself. Technological change is one of the most important elements affecting society today. Philosophers of science point out that the rate of growth of knowledge has increased exponentially, as judged by rates of publication, patents, and other measurements. Before 1945, it took more than a hundred years for the sum of knowledge to double; then, amazingly, it doubled between 1945 and 1960, and again between 1960 and 1970.[40] What is more, as of the early 1980s, the totality of human knowledge is expected to double every twelve years.

This rapid change means, for one thing, that parents have a different social environment from that of their children. Parents born in the 1920s or 1930s often find computers and their accessories strange and forbidding. When first confronted with computers, they found it difficult to restrain themselves from disobeying the injunction not to "fold, spindle, or mutilate." By contrast, people born in the 1960s or later regard the computer, whether pocket, desk-top, or any other model, as just one more familiar article they have learned about and used in school.

The splendid works of Thomas Hardy describe a society in which most learning took place vertically from one generation to the next. In Hardy's Wessex, children learned from their parents about work, relationships, and customs, and they followed the family pattern. Leaving one's village was a major step. When Jude left home to live in far-off Oxfordshire, he broke away from the family pattern, and his life broke up in consequence.[41] For most people in such a society, social learning hardly went on outside the family or the close social group.

Today much learning and perhaps most social learning is horizontal, that is, intragenerational. The peer group is largely respon-

40. T. S. Kuhn, *The Structure of Scientific Revolutions,* 2d ed. (Chicago: University of Chicago Press, 1970).
41. T. Hardy (1895), *Jude the Obscure* (New York: W. W. Norton, 1978).

sible for spreading information about work, relationships, and customs. Certainly most information about drug use, including particularly sanctions and rituals, is transferred through peer groups, although the specific informational content may vary enormously from one group to another. It seems likely that this growing familiarity will permit future generations to make distinctions among drugs and forms of use that are not being made today by either parents or policy makers. It is also possible that social learning relating to drug use will in the future be transmitted within the family, as is the case with alcohol use now, and that the role of the peer group will be less important. A change in that direction seems to be taking place already in relation to certain illicit drugs, in particular marijuana.

The first generation of illicit drug users in the general society is always regarded as deviant. They have strong personal motives for seeking out such a drug as marijuana, and they use it with great anxiety. Gradually, as the deviant activity catches on (as marijuana use did in the mid-1960s), knowledge increases, misconceptions are corrected, and the users become more confident and tend to stop thinking of themselves as deviants.

The second generation of users tries the illicit drug not primarily because it wants to rebel against the straight society (the larger social setting) but out of curiosity or because they are interested in its effects. When the second generation supports the arguments of the first generation and opposes the cultural stereotypes about marijuana use and users, it is more likely to be heard: There are more of them; they are more diverse in background; and their motives, which seem less personal and less antagonistic to the reigning culture, are more acceptable to society.

By this time even the straight society has moved away from its formerly rigid position toward marijuana and has become mainly confused. Such confusion encourages others in the larger social setting who are not primarily motivated by either drug hunger or social rebellion to experiment with the drug. Their reports have an even greater effect on the larger society; and in addition, the new diversity of the using population makes it possible to develop various styles of use that work better and cause less trouble.

Although advances in drug technology have enormously increased the availability and use of both licit and illicit substances, they have at the same time inhibited the development of rituals and sanctions like those that accompany the social use of many natural drugs. Before the American Indians use peyote, they all take part in the ritual of preparing the drug. This ritual puts them into the right frame of mind for use, gives them a knowledge of the drug, and emphasizes the quality of use, thus providing social learning and social control of the drug. But when, as in our culture, drug preparation is transferred to the technical expert or manufacturer, the natural social method of control is lost. The first-time user can suddenly be confronted with a substance he does not understand, one for which rituals, sanctions, and other social controls have not been developed or disseminated.

In addition to providing society with new, more powerful drugs that lack built-in social controls, technology has supplied the means of publicizing the worst effects of these new drugs. In the 1960s, at the beginning of the drug revolution, the reading and viewing public suddenly learned from widely disseminated media reports, principally on television, about the disastrous results of a psychedelic trip. The discovery of this new experience, experimentation by a few individuals who had a variety of reactions, and further experimentation by others were all kaleidoscoped into a few searing media presentations. These presentations gave the impression, accepted by most of the public, that such disastrous effects were the normal response to psychedelic drug use. Those whose personal experiences or observations had shown them otherwise were forced into a sharply opposing position, as has often happened in the field of illicit drugs. Neither of these positions allowed room for reasonable social learning about the range of responses to the drug and how best to cope with them or for the development of social sanctions and rituals that might prevent many of the dysfunctional reactions.

Personality Theory and Social Integration

Most proponents of strictly psychological theories, such as the original Freudian instinct theory, do not deny that technological change brings about social change, but they do question the view that social change contributes to continued personality development. They say instead that the two dominant drives, sex and aggression, are aroused in all individuals and that society works out ways for those impulses to achieve a degree of discharge under acceptable circumstances. For example, when an individual uses alcohol to remove his inhibitions, society accepts his flirtatiousness and his argumentativeness within limits that are subtly but differently defined by various ethnic groups and social classes. But why do such Freudian theorists not apply the same reasoning to the individual who uses marijuana in a *controlled* way in order to focus attention on a particular event or to reduce the boundary between himself and his sensations? Both the alcohol user and the marijuana user find reassurance in being able to express or gratify their feelings in a socially acceptable, albeit somewhat primitive, way.

Unlike those, including Andrew Weil,[42] who believe that the search for intoxication and consciousness change is instinctual, I believe that much interest in intoxicants is an integral function of the more structured part of the personality, the ego. The ego has the potential to achieve discharge of primitive affects and fantasies in various ways, including that of consciousness change. Thus, in this and many other societies, the use of intoxicants, which may well be closely linked with impulse discharge, is integrated so as to be under ego control. The group ceremonies and other elaborate social mechanisms developed by primitive societies not only define these discharges as acceptable but also structure and regulate them, often under conditions of religious exemption. Those South American Indian societies that use psychedelic drugs on special occasions have for centuries managed to control their use in this fashion. It is interesting to note, however, that such societies have not been able to cope with a new, technologically advanced intoxicant—distilled alcohol.

No society can hold back technological and social change. New substances, along with ideas about their use, are continually being introduced, and it takes time for society to find out which of them affect personality development and personal relationships. Not only the drug and the personal needs of the user but also the subtleties of history and social circumstances must be taken into account. No one has understood this more clearly than Griffith Edwards, director of the intoxicant research center at the Maudsley Hospital in England. He once remarked, in pointing out the fallacy of trying to separate the specific incident of drug taking from its social matrix, "One could not hope to understand the English country gentleman's foxhunting simply by exploring his attitude toward the fox."[43]

42. Weil, *The Natural Mind*.
43. G. F. Edwards, "Drugs, Drug Dependence, and the Concept of Plasticity."

The view that intoxicant use depends only on the drug or on a disturbed personality may seem attractive to those who accept the moral condemnation that society has visited upon illicit drug use. But for experts to use psychoanalytic theory to further such a view would be to belittle their own clinical and theoretical aims as well as the capacity of personality theory to incorporate social structural variables and the social learning process.

THE PROBLEM FOR RESEARCH IN AN ARENA OF SOCIAL CONTROVERSY

Doing research on intoxicants, particularly illicit drugs, invariably raises the question as to whether the findings will act to increase use. As our current formal social policy is aimed unabashedly at attempting to decrease use of illicit substances,[44] the question also arises whether research efforts, if they are to be judged ethical, must adhere to this social policy. Then, if research is so judged, and there is little doubt that to a large extent it is, what effect does that have on which research projects get funded, how the research is done, and how the findings are treated by the public, as represented by both professionals and the media?

Almost everyone engaged in drug research would agree that it is extremely difficult in this field to have one's work perceived as objective and relatively neutral. Not only do the popular radio and television shows try to "balance" their presentations by including someone considered "antidrug" on a program that negates the specific harmfulness of drug use, but scientific programs have often felt obliged to follow a similar procedure. In this climate almost any work or worker is quickly classified as for or against use, and halfway positions are not acknowledged. It is virtually equivalent to the political litmus test of the Communist Party. To a diehard advocate of the National Organization for the Reform of Marijuana Laws (NORML), any indication that marijuana can be disruptive is disputed, just as any claim that Communists were inhumane was disputed in the 1930s. When it was suggested at a recent scientific meeting that marijuana users should not drive when intoxicated, floor discussants were quick to point out that some experienced users

44. M. H. Moore, "Limiting Supplies of Drugs to Illicit Markets," in Zinberg and Harding, eds., *Control over Intoxicant Use,* pp. 183–200.

claim to drive better while intoxicated. Conversely, at the same meeting the statement that there had been no deaths attributed to marijuana during the last fifteen years, when over 51 million people had used the drug, was greeted by a retort from the floor that marijuana was not water-soluble and, therefore, was retained in the body. This non sequitur was not intended to counter the original statement but merely to show that no one could get away with saying something about marijuana that did not stress its dangers.

Although it is easy to ridicule the extremes of this litmus testing, the ethical issues themselves are serious, and the implications of publicizing and exploiting drug effects so as to make drug use glamorous, as in Timothy Leary's case, have given rise to grave concerns. There is little doubt that the explosion of LSD use in the 1960s was propelled by the wide publicity given such use. It certainly could be argued that this explosion around Timothy Leary was not principally the result of the presentation of actual drug research. But the drug hysteria aroused by that drug use very quickly spread to research, so that one previously objective inquirer apparently saw little wrong in stating that he was setting out to prove the drug's potential for harm.[45] With the appearance and widespread acceptance of this attitude by, among others, the National Institute on Drug Abuse,[46] the official research-funding body, every researcher has had to concern himself with whether his work would meet a standard based more on discouraging the use of drugs than with uncovering the truth.

In a basic sense, it is doubtful if anyone in the field, no matter how misguided he might be considered, has set out to falsify the facts. Rather, within a certain frame of values—say, the outlook that any illicit drug is so bad that efforts to prove it so are legitimate and for the greater good—the search for truth can become deductive rather than inductive. And, indeed, because to a certain extent all scientific inquiry begins with an operating hypothesis, what we are worrying about in relation to the aims of research is hardly a 100-percent-or-nothing matter. The issue is rather the subtle one of feeling sufficiently righteous about the culture's current policy or value

45. M. M. Cohen, M. Marinello, and N. Bach, "Chromosomal Damage in Human Leukocytes Induced by Lysergic Acid Diethylamide," *Science* 155 (1967): 1417–19.

46. See the following NIDA publications, all available from the Government Printing Office (Washington, D.C.) and dated 1977, 1977, and 1978, respectively: *Cocaine—1977*, Research Monograph 13; *The Epidemiology of Heroin and Other Narcotics*, Research Monograph 16; *Drug Use in Industry*.

of reducing illicit drug use to allow that to outweigh objectivity. Researchers who treasure objectivity and neutrality and present the data, whatever they are, may end up carrying on work that contravenes dearly held cultural beliefs. These beliefs are not only dearly held in their own right but are believed to be sacrosanct in that they help to prevent a bad thing, that is, more illicit drug use.

In 1968, when Andrew Weil and I began the first controlled experiments in giving marijuana to naive subjects in order to study the effects of acute intoxication, we were much criticized.[47] If marijuana proved to be as dangerous as many people thought at that time, we ran the risk of addicting or otherwise damaging our innocent volunteer subjects. If it should prove that marijuana was not so deadly as was assumed, then, we were told by many, our findings could be morally damaging to the country by removing the barrier of fear that was assumed to prevent drug use. It is, of course, impossible to say whether these experiments and others that replicated the findings were significant in increasing the popularity of drug use. Even by 1968 it was becoming clear that marijuana was not the devil drug of "Reefer Madness." During that period of criticism, I believed, and continue to believe, that supplying credible, responsible, and objective information about the drug was essential.

Because the issue is so polarized, however, withholding or distorting information in order to support the current social policy of reducing use runs a great risk of causing possible users, whose information about the substance in question is different and more experiential, to disbelieve any reports of potential harmfulness.[48] This situation makes it extremely difficult to separate use from misuse and to help people avoid the destructive and dysfunctional consequences of misuse. On the other hand, in this same climate the presenting of information indicating that all use need not be misuse, thus contravening formal social policy, runs the equally grave risk that the work will be interpreted and publicized as condoning use.

It is a frightening dilemma for a researcher, particularly for one who cannot believe that "the truth will set you free" in some mystical sense. Of course, neither can one believe that hiding facts, hid-

47. A. T. Weil, N. E. Zinberg, and J. Nelsen, "Clinical and Psychological Effects of Marihuana in Man," *Science* 162 (1969): 1234–42.
48. Zinberg and Robertson, *Drugs and the Public;* J. Kaplan, *Marijuana: The New Prohibition* (New York: World, 1970).

ing the truth, will make everything come out all right. And what makes it considerably harder when thinking about research on powerful intoxicating substances is that general principles about truth and objectivity are not all that is involved; human lives are at stake. It was relatively easy to bear the criticism of marijuana research. The growing popularity of the drug was evident; there were no fatalities reported from its use; the need for more precise information about its effects in order to distinguish myth from fact was pressing. For example, at that time police officers and doctors believed that marijuana dilated the pupils. This misconception, which affected both arrests and medical treatment, needed to be cleared up. But when it became evident that understanding controlled use required looking at drugs whose physical properties, unlike those of marijuana, *demanded* control, the researcher's ethical problem became more serious. Studying heroin meant studying a powerful addicting drug whose potential to kill through a misjudgment on dosage is very great. Disabusing the professional community and the public (by way of the omnipresent media, which seize on anything in the drug area as good copy) of the belief that *any* use is inevitably addicting and destructive ran the risk of reducing the barrier of fear that might have kept someone from using opiates, and this possibility has been and is a tormenting concern. Whatever the devotion to research and the importance of knowledge may be, the work cannot be countenanced if the subjects are not protected from the harm caused by the research, either directly or by withholding information, as, for example, in the unfortunate U.S. Public Health Service research on syphilis that held back a treatment long after it had been proved effective.[49]

Nevertheless, even my preliminary investigations of heroin and other opiate use confirmed what had been found in every investigation of drug use. The reality was far more complex than the simple pharmacological presentation that I had received in medical school. Certainly, heroin is a powerfully addicting drug with great potential for deadly overdose. But there were those who managed to use it in a controlled way, and even those who got into trouble with the drug displayed various patterns of response very different from that of the stereotypical junkie. And, because the truth, although it will not

49. N. Hersey and R. D. Miller, *Human Experimentation and the Law* (Germantown, Md.: Aspen Systems Corp., 1976).

set you free, will usually come out, other investigators such as Leon Hunt and Peter Bourne were beginning to report similar phenomena.[50] Once it became clear that these phenomena were extensive and significant, it was also clear that any attempt to remove from the scientific purview such behavior patterns, because they were morally reprehensible or disapproved of, would reduce the credibility of all scientific enterprise. In addition, in the process of controlling their use, these users might have developed a system of control that could be extremely valuable as a possible method of treatment for addiction.[51]

That research may have a positive application beyond its purely informational value is not a requirement of scientific investigation. Basic research needs no defense here. But as I pointed out earlier, the way the work is received and treated, particularly by the media, can raise extremely serious problems. To what extent researchers who report findings have a responsibility for what is done with them publicly is a moot point. In a basic sense, although these researchers are as accurate and careful in their statements as possible, they cannot control what others say or do with the work. But in the present climate of emotionalism about drug research, they would be naive indeed if they did not realize that certain findings might be picked up by the press. Unfortunately, in order to herald their findings, several researchers have called prepublication press conferences in which they have speculated about far-reaching implications of the work— implications that go beyond the actual published data.[52]

Thus, it is not enough to avoid carelessness in one's actual work and the reporting of it. A researcher must also consider carefully whether the work might cause some people who would not otherwise use drugs to do so. In this context, the potentially positive application of the work as a therapeutic aid may help shift attention away from the overwhelming preoccupation with illicit use. Although dis-

50. Abt Associates, *Drug Use in the State of Ohio: A Study Based upon the Ohio Drug Survey* (Cambridge, Mass.: Abt Associates, 1975); P. G. Bourne, L. G. Hunt, and J. Vogt, *A Study of Heroin Use in the State of Wyoming* (Washington, D.C.: Foundation for International Resources, 1975); L. G. Hunt and C. D. Chambers, *The Heroin Epidemics: A Study of Heroin Use in the United States, 1965-1975* (New York: Spectrum, 1976).

51. N. E. Zinberg et al., *Processes of Control among Different Heroin-using Styles* (Washington, D.C.: NIDA, 1980).

52. *New York Times,* 4 February 1974 and 9 April 1974, interviews with G. G. Nahas and R. C. Kolodny, respectively.

cussing the work from the viewpoint of possible therapeutic applications can lend itself to another brand of sensationalism and overstatement, this danger may be easier to avoid.

The difficulty of knowing what objectivity is and the problem of questioning the ethics of doing certain research and imparting its results are by no means confined to research on illicit drugs. Few people today, in this era of recognition of the overwhelming number of choices faced by each individual, are able to preserve the image of the disinterested scientist burdened by few, if any, values except dedication to the purity of science. A searching article by a prominent jurist in *Science* points out that even when scientists have been able to agree on what is scientific fact—for example, that a certain amount of saccharine can give white mice cancer—they could not, because of the different value-systems influencing their interpretation of those facts, agree on whether this risk was low or moderate for humans.[53]

In his article David L. Bazelon goes on to comment upon matters pertinent to this discussion of illicit drug use, although he did not have that particular subject in mind.

> In reaction to the public's often emotional response to risk, scientists are tempted to disguise controversial value decisions in the cloak of scientific objectivity, obscuring those decisions from political accountability.
>
> At its most extreme, I have heard scientists say that they would consider not disclosing risks which in their view are significant, but which might alarm the public if taken out of context. This problem is not mere speculation. Consider the recently released tapes of the NRC's deliberation over the accident at Three Mile Island. They illustrate dramatically how concern for minimizing public reaction can overwhelm scientific candor.
>
> This attitude is doubly dangerous. First, it arrogates to the scientists the final say over which risks are important enough to merit public discussion. More important, it leads to the suppression of information that may be critical to developing new knowledge about risks or even to developing ways of avoiding those risks.

Who today is willing to assume the risk of deciding to limit our knowledge? The consequences of such limitation are awesome. I do not mean to equate the social issues of opening areas of research on heroin use with the potentially catastrophic consequences of failing

53. D. L. Bazelon, "Risk and Regulation," *Science* 205 (1979): 277–80.

to disclose problems with nuclear reactors, but the principles are similar. It is understandable that government agencies, already overwhelmed by the number of factors that must be considered before reaching a decision and buttressed by a sense of righteousness that what they are trying to do is for the public good, would want to minimize the confusion and uncertainty that might result from presenting the public with more controversial and conflicting information. Such bureaucracies, in principle, want all the information possible; but, once they are settled on a course or a value position that they can unabashedly support, they believe that anything which raises further doubts will raise greater risks. Also, as our cultural belief in the disinterested scientist wanes and as our disillusionment with the efficacy of the judicial system as a means of righting wrongs grows, we are increasingly tempted to surrender to the ostensible benevolence and wisdom of bureaucrats.

Bazelon makes another point that supports my argument and those of John Kaplan and other researchers.[54] Regulations that attempt to limit risks have their own social cost. This does not mean that we should not have regulations. Of course we should, but even at the price of increasing the uncertainty, the choices, and the number of factors to be considered, there must be a keen assessment of the risk cost of the regulations themselves. In few areas is this as true as it is in the drug area. Certainly much of the damage now resulting from marijuana and heroin use occurs because of the illicit status of these drugs and not from their pharmacology. Whether this would continue to be true under a different regulatory situation, no one knows. Reasoning from the basis of historical precedents and from psychological and social attitudes as well as pharmacology, I believe that the use of drugs such as alcohol, marijuana, and heroin might well be regulated in different ways. But in each case we should not assume, as we now assume automatically, that the regulations will not be socially, psychologically, and clinically costly.

The research on controlled use of illicit drugs has one basic policy implication. If, as this work suggests, the problem is not the simple

54. Kaplan, *Marijuana: The New Prohibition;* Robins, Helzer, and Davis, "Narcotic Use in Southeast Asia and Afterwards"; C. P. Herman and L. T. Kozlowski, "Indulgence, Excess, and Restraint: Perspectives on Consummatory Behavior in Everyday Life," in Zinberg and Harding, eds., *Control over Intoxicant Use,* pp. 77–88; D. Waldorf and P. Biernacki, "National Recovery from Heroin Addiction: A Review of the Incidence Literature," in Zinberg and Harding, eds., *Control over Intoxicant Use,* pp. 173–82.

use of these drugs but rather how they are used—when, with whom, under what conditions, and how much—then a formal social policy is needed that separates use from misuse.[55] It is obvious that misuse, like pregnancy, is avoided under conditions of total abstinence, but with both drugs and sex it is doubtful whether total abstinence is possible. As it now stands, in the case of illicit drugs anyone who is not abstinent is considered a criminal and a social deviant. Under these conditions it is extremely difficult to develop viable nonlegal sanctions and rituals that will prevent the dysfunctional consequences of use. Even when such controls are developed by small social groups, it is not easy for knowledge about them to be transmitted through social learning.

The framers of current formal social policy, by attempting to restrict drug supplies and punish any use whatever, hope to reduce the number of users, arguing that if there are fewer users there will automatically be fewer cases of dysfunctional use.[56] This argument implies a straight-line arithmetical relationship between use and misuse. If there are 1,000 users, for example, and 10 percent of them get into trouble, there will be 100 cases of misuse; with 10,000 users there will be 1,000 cases of misuse, and so on. To pursue this type of argument and policy in relation to alcohol use leads to the highly debatable decision to raise prices in order to discourage use.

But what if current social policy is discouraging only those who use drugs moderately? Certainly regular users, to whom the substance is more vital, would be less easily discouraged. Then, inasmuch as the socially derived sanctions and rituals that help maintain control are developed and embodied most definitively by moderate, occasional users, the conditions conducive to controlled use would gradually give way to conditions conducive to dysfunctional use. Thus, the formal social policy whose goal it is to minimize the number of dysfunctional users may actually be making more and more users dysfunctional.

By following the same simplistic mathematical argument, advocates of current social policy claim that preventing any use is crucial

55. President's Commission on Mental Health, "Report of the Liaison Task Panel on Psychoactive Drug Use/Misuse," in *Volume IV, Appendix: Task Panel Reports Submitted to The President's Commission on Mental Health* (Washington, D.C.: Government Printing Office, 1978).

56. Moore, "Limiting Supplies of Drugs to Illicit Markets."

because of the high percentage of users who are indeed misusing. This circular reasoning leads to the view that what is needed is not a reassessment of policy but more of the same policy, that is, better law enforcement and stricter penalties on trafficking and using. My research on controlled use suggests that greater attention should be paid to conditions of use than to the prevention of use. What are the conditions under which dysfunctional use occurs, and how can these be modified? Conversely, what conditions maintain control in the nonmisusers, and how can they be promulgated?

Firm advocates of current policy fear that use will increase if attention is shifted from the fact of use to the conditions of use. That is an understandable fear if one gives credence to the circular argument. But if that argument is challenged, then, on the basis of my research and the theory underlying it, what is needed is a reassessment of current social policy, with a new focus on preventing the dysfunctional problems of use rather than use itself. This new focus does not mean that all substances should be treated alike. Careful studies of the use of different substances and of the varying conditions of use may well result in a call for different policy strategies. Clearly, this question cannot be settled until drug use is separated from misuse. By means of competent psychosocial research, the myths inherent in the emotionally laden subject of illicit drug use must be exposed, the realities of such use brought to light, and a theoretical framework constructed through which the research results may be understood and perhaps even employed to prevent or treat addiction.

SELECTED BIBLIOGRAPHY—
Part II

Aaronson, Bernard, and Humphry Osmond, eds. *Psychedelics: The Uses and Implications of Hallucinogenic Drugs.* Garden City, N.Y.: Anchor Books, 1970.

Abramson, Harold A., ed. *The Use of LSD in Psychotherapy and Alcoholism.* New York: Bobbs-Merrill, 1967.

Abuzzahab, Faid S., Sr., and Bruce J. Anderson. "A Review of LSD Treatment in Alcoholism." *International Pharmacopsychiatry* 6 (1971): 223–35.

Ackerman, Peggy T., et al. "Methylphenidate Effects on Cognitive Style and Reaction Time in Four Groups of Children." *Psychiatry Research* 7 (1982): 199–213.

Albaugh, Bernard J., and Philip O. Anderson. "Peyote in the Treatment of Alcoholism Among American Indians." *American Journal of Psychiatry* 131 (1974): 1247–51.

Bakalar, James B., and Lester Grinspoon. *Drug Control in a Free Society.* New York: Cambridge University Press, 1984.

Barkley, Russell A. "A Review of Stimulant Research With Hyperactive Children." *Journal of Child Psychology and Psychiatry* 18 (1977): 137–65.

Barre, Felix. "Cocaine as an Abortive Agent in Cluster Headache." *Headache* 22 (1982): 69–73.

Becker, Howard S. "Becoming a Marijuana User." *American Journal of Sociology* 59 (1953): 235–43.

Brady, Joseph V., and Scott E. Lukas, eds. *Testing Drugs for Physical Dependence Potential and Abuse Liability,* NIDA Research Monograph 52. Washington, D.C.: Government Printing Office, 1984.

Braude, Monique C., and Stephen Szara, eds. *Pharmacology of Marihuana.* New York: Raven Press, 1976.

Byck, Robert, ed. *Cocaine Papers: Sigmund Freud.* New York: Stonehill, 1974.

Caldwell, William V. *LSD Psychotherapy.* New York: Grove Press, 1967.

Charles, Linda, and Richard Schain. "A Four-Year Follow-Up Study of the Effects of Methylphenidate on the Behavior and Academic Achievement of Hyperactive Children." *Journal of Abnormal Child Psychology* 9 (1981): 495–505.

Cohen, Sidney. "Lysergic Acid Diethylamide: Side Effects and Complications." *Journal of Nervous and Mental Disease* 130 (1960): 30–40.

Cohen, Sidney, and Richard C. Stillman, eds. *The Therapeutic Potential of Marihuana.* New York: Plenum, 1976.

Conners, C. Keith. "Controlled Trial of Methylphenidate in Preschool Children with Minimal Brain Dysfunction." *International Journal of Mental Health* 4 (1975): 61–74.

Conners, C. Keith, and Leon Eisenberg. "The Effects of Methylphenidate on Symptomatology and Learning in Disturbed Children." *American Journal of Psychiatry* 120 (1963): 458–63.

Consroe, Paul F.; Arnold Martin; and Vigrim Singh. "Antiepileptic Potential of Cannabinoid Analogs." *Journal of Clinical Pharmacology* 21 (1981): 428S–36S.

Dishotsky, Norman I., et al. "LSD and Genetic Damage." *Science* 172 (1971): 431–40.

Drug Abuse Council. *The Facts About 'Drug Abuse.'* New York: Free Press, 1980.

Dykman, Roscoe A.; Peggy T. Ackerman; and David S. McCray. "Effects of Methylphenidate on Selective and Sustained Attention in Hyperactive, Reading-Disabled and Presumably Attention-Disordered Boys." *Journal of Nervous and Mental Disease* 168 (1980): 745–52.

Fabrega, Horacio, and Peter K. Manning. "Health Maintenance Among Peruvian Peasants." *Human Organization* 31 (1973): 243–56.

Fish, Barbara. "The 'One Child, One Drug' Myth of Stimulants in Hyperkinesis." *Archives of General Psychiatry* 25 (1971): 193–203.

Gittelman, Rachel. "Indications for the Use of Stimulant Treatment in

Learning Disorders." *Journal of the American Academy of Child Psychiatry* 19 (1980): 623-36.

Grabowski, John, ed. *Cocaine: Pharmacology, Effects, and Treatment of Abuse,* NIDA Research Monograph 50. Washington, D.C.: Government Printing Office, 1984.

Grinspoon, Lester. *Marihuana Reconsidered.* 2d ed. Cambridge: Harvard University Press, 1977.

Grinspoon, Lester, and James B. Bakalar. *Cocaine: A Drug and Its Social Evolution.* Rev. ed. New York: Basic Books, 1985.

————. *Psychedelic Drugs Reconsidered.* New York: Basic Books, 1979.

————. "Coca and Cocaine as Medicines: An Historical Review." *Journal of Ethnopharmacology* 3 (1981): 149-60.

————, eds. *Psychedelic Reflections.* New York: Human Sciences Press, 1983.

Grinspoon, Lester, and Peter Hedblom. *The Speed Culture: Amphetamine Use and Abuse in America.* Cambridge: Harvard University Press, 1975.

Grof, Stanislav. *LSD Psychotherapy.* Pomona, Calif.: Hunter House, 1980.

Grof, Stanislav, et al. "LSD-Assisted Psychotherapy in Patients with Terminal Cancer." *International Pharmacopsychiatry* 8 (1973): 129-41.

Harner, Michael, ed. *Hallucinogens and Shamanism.* London: Oxford University Press, 1973.

Huxley, Aldous. *Moksha: Writings on Psychedelics and the Visionary Experience (1931-1963).* New York: Stonehill, 1977.

Institute of Medicine. *Marijuana and Health.* Washington, D.C.: National Academy Press, 1982.

Jaffe, Jerome H. "Drug Addiction and Drug Abuse." In A. G. Gilman, L. S. Goodman, and A. Gilman, eds., *The Pharmacological Basis of Therapeutics,* 6th ed., pp. 535-84. New York: Macmillan, 1980.

Jones, Reese T. "Human Effects: An Overview." In R. Petersen, ed., *Marijuana Research Findings: 1980,* NIDA Research Monograph 31, pp. 54-80. Washington, D.C.: Government Printing Office, 1980.

Kalant, Oriana J. *The Amphetamines: Toxicity and Addiction.* Toronto: University of Toronto Press, 1966.

Kandel, Denise B. "Convergences in Prospective Longitudinal Surveys of Drug Use in Normal Populations." In D. Kandel, ed., *Longitudinal Research on Drug Use: Empirical Findings and Methodological Issues,* pp. 3-38. Washington, D.C.: Hemisphere, 1978.

Karler, Ralph, and Stuart A. Turkanis. "The Cannabinoids as Potential Antiepileptics." *Journal of Clinical Pharmacology* 21 (1981): 437S-48S.

Katon, Wayne, and Murray Raskind. "Treatment of Depression in the Medically Ill Elderly with Methylphenidate." *American Journal of Psychiatry* 137 (1980): 963-65.

Leake, Chauncey D. *The Amphetamines: Their Actions and Uses.* Springfield, Ill.: Thomas, 1958.

Leuner, Hanscarl. *Hallucinogene: Psychische Grenzzustande in Forschung ung Psychotherapie.* Bern: Hans Huber, 1981.

Lowinson, Joyce, and Pedro Ruiz, eds. *Substance Abuse: Clinical Problems and Perspectives.* Baltimore: Williams and Wilkins, 1981.

Ludwig, Arnold M.; Jerome Levine; and Louis H. Stark. *LSD and Alcoholism: A Clinical Study of Treatment Efficacy.* Springfield, Ill.: Thomas, 1970.

Martin, Richard T. "The Role of Coca in the History, Religion and Medicine of South American Indians." *Economic Botany* 24 (1970): 422–38.

Mattes, Jeffrey A., and Rachel Gittelman. "Growth of Hyperactive Children on Maintenance Regimen of Methylphenidate." *Archives of General Psychiatry* 40 (1983): 317–21.

McCabe, O. Lee, and Thomas E. Hanlon. "The Use of LSD-Type Drugs in Psychotherapy: Progress and Promise." In O. McCabe, ed., *Changing Human Behavior: Current Therapies and Future Directions,* pp. 221–53. New York: Grune & Stratton, 1977.

McGlothlin, William H., and David O. Arnold. "LSD Revisited: A Ten-Year Follow-Up of Medical LSD Use." *Archives of General Psychiatry* 24 (1971): 35–49.

Mikuriya, Tod H., ed. *Marijuana: Medical Papers 1839–1972.* Oakland, Calif.: Medi-Comp Press, 1973.

Mortimer, W. Golden. *History of Coca.* New York: Vail, 1901.

Naranjo, Claudio. *The Healing Journey.* New York: Ballantine, 1975.

Nelson, Jack E., et al., eds. *Research Issues 26: Guide to Drug Abuse Research Terminology.* Rockville, Md.: USPHS (NIDA), 1982.

Rapaport, Judith L., et al. "Dextroamphetamine: Cognitive and Behavioral Effects in Normal Prepubescent Boys." *Science* 199 (1978): 560–63.

Relman, Arnold S., ed. *Marijuana and Health.* Washington, D.C.: National Academy Press, 1982.

Ritchie, J. Murdoch, and Nicholas M. Greene. "Local Anesthetics." In A. G. Gilman, L. S. Goodman, and A. Gilman, eds., *The Pharmacological Basis of Therapeutics,* 6th ed., pp. 300–320. New York: Macmillan, 1980.

Roffman, Roger A. *Marijuana as Medicine.* Seattle: Madrona, 1982.

Rothschild, Gerald, et al. "Dextroamphetamine Sulfate in Children with Learning Disorders. Effects on Perception, Learning and Achievement." *Archives of General Psychiatry* 21 (1969): 182–90.

Rubin, Vera, and Lambros Comitas. *Ganja in Jamaica: The Effects of Marijuana Use.* Garden City, N.Y.: Anchor Books, 1976.

Sallan, Stephen E.; Norman E. Zinberg; and Emil Frei III. "Antiemetic Effect of Delta-9-tetrahydrocannabinol in Patients Receiving Cancer Chemotherapy." *New England Journal of Medicine* 293 (1975): 795–97.

Schenck, Nicholas L. "Local Anesthesia in Otolaryngology: A Reevaluation." *Annals of Otology, Rhinology and Laryngology* 84 (1975): 65–72.

Schultes, Richard Evans. "The Appeal of Peyote (Lophophora williamsii) as a Medicine." *American Anthropologist* 40 (1938): 698–715.

Shaffer, Howard, and Milton E. Burglass, eds. *Classic Contributions in the Addictions.* New York: Brunner/Mazel, 1981.

Sharp, Charles W., ed. *Mechanisms of Tolerance and Dependence,* NIDA Research Monograph 54. Washington, D.C.: Government Printing Office, 1984.

Siegel, Ronald K. "Cocaine Smoking." *Journal of Psychoactive Drugs* 14 (1982): 271–359.

Siegler, Miriam, and Humphrey Osmond. *Models of Madness, Models of Medicine.* New York: Macmillan, 1974.

Smart, Reginald G., and Karen Bateman. "Unfavorable Reactions to LSD: A Review and Analysis of the Available Case Reports." *Canadian Medical Association Journal* 97 (1967): 1214–21.

Tashkin, Donald P., et al. "Effects of Smoked Marijuana in Experimentally Induced Asthma." *American Review of Respiratory Disease* 112 (1975): 377–86.

Temin, Peter. *Taking Your Medicine: Drug Regulation in the United States.* Cambridge: Harvard University Press, 1980.

Thompson, Travis, and Chris E. Johanson, eds. *Behavioral Pharmacology of Human Drug Dependence,* NIDA Research Monograph 37. Washington, D.C.: Government Printing Office, 1981.

Tucker, Gary J.; Donald Quinlan; and Martin Harrow. "Chronic Hallucinogenic Drug Use and Thought Disturbance." *Archives of General Psychiatry* 27 (1972): 443–47.

Weil, Andrew. "The Therapeutic Value of Coca in Contemporary Medicine." *Journal of Ethnopharmacology* 3 (1981): 367–76.

———. *The Marriage of the Sun and Moon: A Quest for Unity in Consciousness.* Boston: Houghton Mifflin, 1980.

Weil, Andrew, and Winifred Rosen. *Chocolate to Morphine: Understanding Mind-Active Drugs.* Boston: Houghton Mifflin, 1983.

Weiss, Bernard, and Victor G. Laties. "Enhancement of Human Performance by Caffeine and the Amphetamines." *Pharmacological Reviews* 14 (1962): 1–36.

Weiss, Gabrielle, and Lilly Hechtman. "The Hyperactive Child Syndrome." *Science* 205 (1979): 1348–54.

Yensen, Richard, et al. "MDA-Assisted Psychotherapy with Neurotic Out-patients: A Pilot Study." *Journal of Nervous and Mental Disease* 163 (1976): 233–45.

Young, James Harvey. *The Toadstool Millionaires.* Princeton, N.J.: Princeton University Press, 1961.

Zinberg, Norman E. "Social Interactions, Drug Use, and Drug Research." In J. Lowinson and P. Ruiz, eds., *Substance Abuse: Clinical Problems and Perspectives,* pp. 91–108. Baltimore: Williams and Wilkins, 1981.

————. *Drug, Set, and Setting: The Basis for Controlled Intoxicant Use.* New Haven and London: Yale University Press, 1984.

Zinberg, Norman E., and John A. Robertson. *Drugs and the Public.* New York: Simon and Schuster, 1972.

POLICY REFORM: EVIDENCE AND ETHICS

8

THE MARKET FOR HEROIN BEFORE AND AFTER LEGALIZATION

Robert J. Michaels

In the space of one hundred and seventy-six years the Lower Mississippi has short-ened itself two hundred and forty-two miles. That is an average of a trifle over one mile and a third per year. Therefore, any calm person who is not blind or idiotic, can see that in the Old Oolitic Silurian Period, just a million years ago next November, the Lower Mississippi River was upward of one million three hundred thousand miles long, and stuck out over the Gulf of Mexico like a fishing-rod. And by the same token any person can see that seven hundred and forty-two years from now the Lower Mississippi will be only a mile and three-quarters long, and Cairo and New Orleans will have joined their streets together, and be plodding comfortably along under a single mayor and a mutual board of aldermen. There is something fascinating about science. One gets such wholesale returns of con-jecture out of such a trifling investment of fact.

Mark Twain

INTRODUCTION

If Mark Twain were alive today, he could probably be found study-ing either drug abuse or economics. Anyone wishing to predict the consequences of legalized opiates must first invest in some facts. The

289

historical, biological, and statistical sources, however, yield little in the way of verifiable facts or properly constructed data. The conclusions typically drawn after a reading of this literature vary about as widely as the alleged facts and are frequently derived without the aid of elementary logic. In this paper I deal with the inferences about legalization that can reasonably be made on the basis of what is known about the market today. My mode of reasoning will be that of an economist.[1]

Economic analysis can help us to predict the qualitative outlines of a world in which heroin is legal or access to it is granted more liberally. If we wish to predict the outcome quantitatively, we clearly need numerical data about the present situation, summarized into relevant conceptual categories. In addition, we would probably like to have data at our disposal from reasonably similar societies or from adjacent historical periods that were characterized by different opiate regimes. Only with such data could we have much confidence in our estimates. For example, economists were able to predict the consequences of nationwide airline deregulation quite accurately from studies of the previously existing unregulated intrastate air travel market in California.[2] In this case, accurate numbers were available, and one could reasonably assume that an unregulated market in Ohio would function much like the one in California.

As we will see below, none of the conditions for plausible inference are met in the case of heroin. Presently available "data" are produced almost exclusively by the federal government, largely for political purposes. Some of the data are attempts to quantify cate-

---

1. I do not discuss the normative literature that centers on the "cost to society" of heroin use. Such costs are said to include lost economic output (because users seldom work 9:00 to 5:00 at legal jobs) and crime. The former "loss" is no more than a judgment that only market output is of value, and the latter (see Sec. V below) generally assumes, erroneously, that in the absence of heroin most of this crime would vanish. For examples of such methodology, see Ralph E. Berry and James P. Boland, *The Economic Cost of Alcohol Abuse* (New York: Free Press, 1977); Brent L. Rufener, J. Valley Rachal, and Alvin M. Cruze, "Costs of Drug Abuse to Society," in Irving Leveson, ed., *Quantitative Explorations in Drug Abuse Policy* (New York: Spectrum, 1980).

I also do not deal with the normative theoretical literature that attempts to establish rationales for legalization or prohibition. See A. J. Culyer, "Should Social Policy Concern Itself with Drug Abuse?" *Public Finance Quarterly* 1 (October 1973): 449–56; J. Patrick Gunning, "Notes on Two Abuses: Drugs and the Pareto Criterion," *Public Finance Quarterly* 4 (January 1976): 43–49.

2. William A. Jordan, *Airline Regulation in America* (Baltimore: Johns Hopkins University Press, 1970).

gories that are impossible to define, such as "addicts." Those data that are attempts to measure objective quantities (e.g., the purity of street heroin) are grossly inaccurate.[3] Heroin is traded in a market whose current characteristics are largely unknown, or known only through the self-serving and unverifiable testimony of captured or disillusioned participants. Patterns of use in other societies and at other times differ so drastically from those around us that even conjecture seems futile. Despite these formidable problems, we can draw some nontrivial conclusions about legalization.

In the remainder of the introduction, I outline the economic ideas a researcher would use in order to analyze legal and illegal heroin regimes. In Part II, I apply them to the supply side of the heroin market. The analysis depends heavily on recent theories of vertical integration, transaction costs, and information search. I will argue that current structural characteristics of the market stem largely from the illegal nature of the good traded, and that taken by themselves they give little guidance as to what a legal market would look like. This analysis of market structure also allows us to evaluate folklore about monopoly control of the market in the present and future.

In the foregoing analysis of the market, I will have assumed that buyers' preferences for heroin are qualitatively the same as for any other good. As will be seen in Part III, the stereotypes of addiction bear scant resemblance to actual use patterns. There I evaluate what is known about the elasticity of demand and the stability of demand for heroin. In reality, the population of users experiences both in- and out-migration, and habits of use are responsive to market forces. Even if we know enough about the response of users to price changes, however, we are also faced with a problem in which economic analysis appears to be of little value: The characteristics of user populations vary greatly over time, geography, and legal regimes, in ways that apparently cannot be predicted by a simple market model.

In Part IV, I explore the statistical literature on the size and scope of the market. Official statistics on "addicts" or "users" are invariably useless and frequently inconsistent with related data. They are typically constructed in an ad hoc and illogical manner, varying strongly in response to political exigencies. Little can be done to im-

---

3. U.S. General Accounting Office (GAO), *Report to the Attorney General: Heroin Statistics Can Be Made More Reliable,* Report GCD-80-84, July 1980.

prove them. As such they are likely to be of no use as benchmarks from which to predict the consequences of legalization.

As shown in Part V, the relationship between heroin and crime is not an easy one to determine. Understanding it requires an exploration of what is known about the sources and uses of user incomes, along with information on the elasticity of demand for heroin. Contrary to official statistics, few users are currently unemployed in any economically meaningful sense. The hope that legalization will significantly reduce urban crime, however, is probably misplaced. In Part VI, I summarize the paper and draw some conclusions.

What We Need to Know

In the competitive market of elementary economics, price and output are determined by the interactions of large numbers of anonymous suppliers and demanders of a homogeneous good. In this market, buyers and sellers exchange information on their personal valuations of the good and strike deals at mutually agreeable prices. Because people on both sides of the market are assumed to be well informed about the behavior of other traders, price quickly converges to its equilibrium value. To what extent can we apply this paradigm to heroin?

In any market, buyers make their decisions about the amounts they will purchase on the basis of their wealth and the price of the good in question relative to the prices of alternatives. At higher prices for our good, alternatives typically come to look more attractive, and fewer units of our good will be purchased. Certain goods, such as heroin, are sometimes alleged to violate this principle, known as the "first law of demand." Because it is "addictive," some claim that the quantity purchased by users will not vary with price and that rises in price will be accompanied by increases in crime as users attempt to acquire sufficient income to support their need for the substance.

The first important piece of information we need is thus some data on the responsiveness of quantity purchased to price, as summarized in the economist's concept of elasticity of demand. A demand that is completely unresponsive to price has an elasticity of zero; as responsiveness to a given price change becomes proportionally greater, elasticity (formally defined below) takes on a larger value. To evaluate legalization, we also need to know both short-run and long-run elasticities of demand. A user may be "addicted" and unresponsive to price over the short run, but in the long run (i.e., after information is acquired and adjustment costs incurred) he may find substitute drugs (methadone), lower his dosage, or learn abstinence. Similarly, a lower price may fail to induce much additional consumption by preexisting users, but new users may be attracted by it as time passes.

We also need to know about other influences on demand. For example, if incomes of purchasers increase, how will they respond as buyers of heroin, other things (e.g., its price) being equal? If the prices of substitute drugs or other enjoyable items fall relative to the price of heroin, how will buyers alter their consumption patterns? The foregoing are, respectively, questions about the income elasticity and cross-elasticities of demand. In addition, we need to know about the ways in which demand varies due to nonmarket factors ("tastes"). Do users "burn out" or drop their habits with increasing age?[4] Does heroin use display massive unpredictable fluctuations that might be called "fads" or "epidemics"?[5]

The analysis of supply in a market is ultimately the analysis of production technology and the availability of resources. Additional units of a good will be produced in a competitive market if the price for which they can be sold exceeds the cost that supplying firms must pay in order to induce resource owners to leave other activities. Higher prices will accompany the expansion of production if there are resources for which supply limitations are of importance. Thus, in order to evaluate legalization, we would like to know about the production technology, limitational resources, and the behavior of costs as output levels change. Think of legalization as reducing the net price that must be paid by buyers and increasing the net price received by sellers, i.e., the analogue of removing a tax. If costs increase rapidly with industry output, there will be little change in quantity produced as we move from the illegal to the legal equilibrium, since few additional units will be producible profitably. Additionally, we are interested in the possibility that technological

4. Charles Winick, "Some Aspects of Careers of Chronic Heroin Users," in Eric Josephson and Eleanor E. Carroll, eds., *Drug Use: Epidemiological and Sociological Approaches* (Washington, D.C.: Hemisphere, 1974).

5. Robert L. DuPont and Mark H. Greene, "The Dynamics of a Heroin Addiction Epidemic," *Science* 181 (August 24, 1973): 716–22.

innovation or learning from experience will reduce production costs as time passes.

Another important question on the supply side concerns economies of scale and scope. Regarding the first, we are asking about the extent to which average costs of a supplier's production decrease with increased output. If economies of scale are quickly exhausted, individual firms will be small relative to the market. If such economies are extensive, competition among sellers might break down because too few of them remain. Alternatively, suppliers may be few because there are "barriers to entry" of newcomers, such as those stemming from monopoly control of an important resource. For example, some have alleged or assumed that control at the highest level of heroin supply is in the hands of a single "organized crime" enterprise.[6] Is this the case because both legal and illegal variants of the business would be characterized by extensive economies of scale, or is the enterprise an inefficient (high-cost) firm that maintains its monopoly through extralegal methods? Whether legalization implies competition or monopoly depends in part on the nature of scale economies.

We are also confronted with the question of evaluating economies of scope. Consider a good whose raw materials require processing and transport before they become useful to ultimate buyers. The activities may either take place within a single vertically integrated enterprise, or a series of transactions in the market may move the good from specialist to specialist. The degree of integration that arises in the market will depend on the relative costs of the two ways of doing business. These costs include the costs of finding trading partners, and negotiating and enforcing agreements. Traders in an unintegrated situation may have an incentive to behave "opportunistically" if the returns from breaking a previously negotiated contract are high enough relative to the cost of enforcing it.[7] In the illegal heroin market, there might be incentives to disintegrate production. A primary supplier who would also do his own retailing in a legal market may find that illegality raises the cost of his own retailing so substantially that he contracts with others to do it. These contracts,

6. Simon Rottenberg, "The Clandestine Distribution of Heroin, Its Discovery and Suppression," *Journal of Political Economy* 76 (January 1968): 78–90.

7. Oliver E. Williamson, "Transaction-Cost Economics: The Governance of Contractual Relations," *Journal of Law and Economics* 22 (October 1979): 233–61.

however, may be more subject to opportunistic breach in an illegal market. Again, the shape of the firm and the market may change greatly under legalization.

In summary, supply and demand provide the central organizing principles for the analysis of the heroin market. The effects of legalization will be on both the size and the organization of the market. Both demand and supply determine price and output, and their characteristics must be jointly evaluated.[8] I turn first to supply.

SUPPLY IN THE HEROIN MARKET

In the heroin market, reliable information about both the internal structure of supplying units and the relationships among these units is hard to come by. The same forces that shape legal firms and their interactions should nevertheless be present here, despite the fact that illegality contrains their actions in certain important ways.

Vertical Relationships, Opportunism, and Transaction Costs

To organize a firm of any kind is not a trivial task. One can think of an entrepreneur laboriously shepherding various specialized productive inputs into a single organization. Alternatively, one can think of the firm as a set of resource owners who are bound together by elaborate sets of implicit and explicit contractual relationships, many of which are costly to negotiate or renegotiate. In an illegal firm, a complex organization will be more costly to achieve than in an equivalent legal enterprise, since the apprehension of a single component

---

8. There is a fair-sized body of economic literature that attempts to model the illegal heroin market. None of it contains more than a peripheral attempt to compare the legal and illegal markets. Many of the conclusions reached by the various authors depend on such doubtful assumptions as monopoly control of supply or highly inelastic demands by addicts. See Godwin Bernard, "An Economic Analysis of the Illicit Drug Market," *International Journal of the Addictions* 18 (October 1983): 681–700; Billy J. Eatherly, "Drug Law Enforcement: Should We Arrest Pushers or Users?" *Journal of Political Economy* 82 (January 1974): 210–14; Daryl Hellman, *The Economics of Crime* (New York: St. Martin's, 1980), chap. 9; John F. Holahan, "The Economics of Heroin," in Patricia Wald et al., eds., *Dealing With Drug Abuse* (New York: Praeger, 1972), pp. 255–99; James V. Koch and Stanley E. Grupp, "The Economics of Drug Control Policies," *International Journal of the Addictions* 5 (December 1971): 571–84; Mark H. Moore, *Buy and Bust* (Cambridge, Mass.: Lexington, 1977), part 1; Rottenberg, "The Clandestine Distribution of Heroin"; Michael D. White and William A. Luksetich, "Heroin: Price Elasticity and Enforcement Strategies," *Economic Inquiry* 31 (October 1983), pp. 557–64.

of such a firm may put an end to the entire operation. Thus the typical criminal "firm" consists of an independent solo practitioner, and "organized crime" consists of organizations with family or ethnic ties that are quite small relative to the size of legal organizations in the same or similar lines of business.[9] Complex, multiperson production processes will be the exception.

Central to the rationale for a firm is the restraint it places on individuals' opportunistic behavior as regards physical resources or specialized information. An individual who supplies labor or other inputs to an illegal enterprise may have particularly strong incentives to act opportunistically, to the detriment of the firm, either by delivering goods or information to a competitor or by cooperating with enforcement authorities.[10] Deterrence of opportunism by illegal means within the firm is itself a risky activity as well.[11] Firms that survive are thus likely to carry on only a limited range of activities because of these risks. They will be inefficiently small, relative to the size they would attain in an equally competitive legal market, and will engage in an inefficiently restricted set of stages of production and distribution. Because of the generally higher costs of illegal operations, the supply of and demand for heroin will be equated at a higher price and lower output than in a legal market.

Little reliable information exists regarding the structure of heroin supply, and what information exists deals only with New York City. There is agreement on the existence of a basic six-tiered system from importers to final dealers in that city,[12] but it is unclear whether such a structure exists elsewhere, i.e., how the division of labor varies with the extent of the market. (Heroin is generally available to the knowl-

9. Annelise Anderson, *The Business of Organized Crime: A Cosa Nostra Family* (Stanford: Hoover Institution Press, 1979); Peter Reuter and Jonathan B. Rubinstein, "Fact, Fancy, and Organized Crime," *The Public Interest* 53 (Fall 1978): 45–67.

10. The problem is complicated by the fact that a long-term career in organized criminal enterprises is generally available only to a person with a reputation for dependability, much as in ordinary business. See Benjamin Klein and Keith Leffler, "The Role of Market Forces in Assuring Contractual Performance," *Journal of Political Economy* 89 (August 1981): 615–41. The youth and short time horizons of many in the heroin market may render reputation a poor enforcer of noncontractual relationships.

11. Information on the paucity of violent activity in organized crime appears in Reuter and Rubinstein, "Fact, Fancy, and Organized Crime."

12. Moore, *Buy and Bust*, pp. 95–115; Edward Preble and John J. Casey, Jr., "Taking Care of Business—The Heroin User's Life on the Street," *International Journal of the Addictions* 4 (March 1969): 1–24, esp. 9–12.

edgeable in almost any part of the country.[13]) The vertically unintegrated structure of the existing market is an efficient method of dealing with the risk of apprehension[14] at any stage of production and distribution, given that the activity is illegal.[15] Any detained participant can supply only limited information about others, thereby lowering overall risk. Under legalization, one expects to see fewer stages, since in general there will be cost savings through the avoidance of additional middlemen. The stages are fewer than six between manufacturer and ultimate retailer for most legal consumable items, and the general trend in household goods has been toward a reduction in the number of stages. The chain grocer and drugstore displaced smaller independent retailers and jobbers in part because of cost advantages they were able to secure by acting as their own middlemen.

The cost of delivered heroin will likely fall for reasons other than a reduction in the number of redundant distribution stages. Illegality is equivalent to a per-transaction tax on a good, since the likelihood of apprehension increases with the number of such transactions one makes. Part of the transaction price thus consists of a premium for risk. As with any tax, some fraction of it will be borne by the buyer and some by the seller. Since the illegal market is frequently characterized by bilateral monopoly, economics offers us little guidance

13. Evidence for this is provided by the existence of nontrivial enrollments in heroin treatment programs in nearly all states. See U.S. National Institute on Drug Abuse (NIDA), *Data from the Client-Oriented Data Acquisition Process, State Statistics 1980,* Statistical Series E, No. 22 (Washington, D.C., Government Printing Office, 1982). Note that the studies covering New York identify the same structure both before and after the market growth of the 1970s.

14. Since statistics on users and law enforcement activity are uniformly poor (see Section IV below), I cannot make a reasonable estimate of the probability of arrest or the probability that an arrestee will be imprisoned. Citing a 1972 news report, Levin et al. found that in New York "the fraction of people arrested for possessing a pound or more of heroin (presumably for sale) who ended up in prison ranged from 32.2% in the Bronx, 15.7% in Manhattan, 14.3% in Queens, to only 4.4% in Brooklyn." See Gilbert Levin, Edward B. Roberts, and Gary B. Hirsch, *The Persistent Poppy: A Computer-Aided Search for Heroin Policy* (Cambridge, Mass.: Ballinger, 1975), p. 59.

15. Personalized and frequently repetitive transactions in heroin also render the corruption of law enforcers more likely than in other areas of illegal activity. See Peter K. Manning and Laurence Redlinger, "Working Bases for Corruption: Organizational Ambiguities and Narcotics Law Enforcement," in Arnold S. Trebach, ed., *Drugs, Crime, and Politics* (New York: Praeger, 1978). In 1975 Baltimore's chief narcotics officer claimed that 800 criminal narcotics informers worked with police there. See Edward Jay Epstein, *Agency of Fear* (New York: Putnam, 1977), p. 101. In the absence of some understandings between these individuals and the police, it is difficult to explain why any users were still on the street.

in identifying the gains to either side from lifting this tax. Even if there is a monopoly seller after legalization, we would expect to see price fall. After legalization, profits—at least in an accounting sense—will be lower at any stage of the distribution chain. To the extent that they are above those obtainable on competitive investments of equal risk, they will be eroded by the investments of newcomers. As will be seen below, there are few likely sources of long-term supernormal profit in a legal heroin market, after adjustment for ordinary business risk.

Information and Reputation as Resources

The barrier to entry of newcomers that is of greatest importance under illegality stems from the ownership of resources for which it is costly to find alternatives in the short run. To the extent that such resources exist, they may generate longer-lived monopoly gains than would otherwise occur. In the heroin market, the most important of these resources is information, especially information about the identity and reliability of trading partners and the quality and predictable availability of goods. Were such institutions of the legal market as advertising, brand names, etc., available, the value of this information and the associated monopoly gains would be less. In a legal market, contracts can be written and enforced against breach. In an illegal market, one must depend on reputation. Such a reputation is not easy to earn, and there is risk in spreading knowledge of that reputation among more than a handful of potential trading partners. The current market is thus characterized by highly personalized trading relationships that are formed only after large amounts of search. Even the seemingly competitive final street markets are characterized by traders dealing predominantly with recognizable partners and by buyer loyalty to those sellers who are known to sell items of dependable quality.[16] The attenuation of informational flows shrinks the trading possibilities, while decreasing the riskiness of transactions actually made.[17]

16. Richard Stephens and R. Smith, "Copping and Caveat Emptor: The Street Addict as Consumer," *Addictive Diseases* 2 (December 1976): 585–600.

17. The market does contain some channels of information. The employment of "touts," who discreetly publicize the availability and quality of certain sellers' heroin on the street, constitutes a highly restricted form of advertising. See Moore, *Buy and Bust,* p. 49. While street-level packages of heroin sometimes carry "brand names," these names are typically short-lived and undependable, since they do not carry any quality-guaranteeing investment

In Nelson's terminology,[18] heroin sold *by a given seller* is an "experience" good as opposed to a "search" good.[19] An experience good is one that a purchaser can deem satisfactory or unsatisfactory only after actual use. (A search good is one for which unsuitable choices can be eliminated prior to actual purchase, e.g., a vehicle that I can determine from advertising to be too small for my needs.) It is in the experience-good situation that consumer uncertainty about quality is most easily resolved through branding and advertising of the brand name. While advertising in experience-good situations raises costs, it also increases the size of the set of choices perceived by an individual buyer and probably lessens the market power of an individual seller. Thus it has the potential to reduce price—and apparently does so in some situations.[20] Heroin at any stage of illegal distribution is of widely varying quality, both in terms of potency and type of adulterant.[21] One expects that legalization with advertising will stabilize quality and lower price relative to a market without advertising. More precisely, it would lead to a spectrum of qualities, priced roughly according to marginal cost. Given the understandable risk aversion of buyers, there is a good likelihood that both the price-lowering and quality-certifying effects of advertising will operate in ways that increase use.

The input mix chosen by those in the distribution chain would change noticeably with legalization in yet another way. It is estimated

---

behind them that would serve as a performance bond for the user of the name. (These names can also, of course, be counterfeited.) See Klein and Leffler, "The Role of Market Forces in Assuring Contractual Performance"; Paul J. Goldstein et al., "The Marketing of Street Heroin in New York City," *Journal of Drug Issues* 14 (Summer 1984): 553–66.

18. Philip Nelson, "Advertising as Information," *Journal of Political Economy* 82 (August 1974): 729–47.

19. In Sec. IIIB below, I discuss the introduction of users to heroin in general, as opposed to the process of sampling a given seller's wares.

20. Lee Benham, "The Effect of Advertising on the Price of Eyeglasses," *Journal of Law and Economics* 15 (October 1972): 337–52.

21. In those situations where heroin is in short supply, personalized trading relationships are more likely to break down as a result of constraints on availability. This increases the risk to buyers associated with each transaction, because of seller incentives to act opportunistically when repeat purchase is less likely. DuPont and Greene ("The Dynamics of a Heroin Addiction Epidemic," p. 719) claim that supply interdiction during the Washington, D.C., "epidemic" of the early 1970s helped increase the actual average price paid per milligram of pure heroin from $1.53 in February 1972 to $5.80 in March 1973. Sellers diluted the amount in the average bag from 16.4 to 5.2 mg over the period, and the coefficient of variation of heroin content per bag rose from 1.11 to 1.43.

that between one-third and one-half of all pure heroin initially imported ends up being consumed in the distribution process rather than being purchased at street prices by final users.[22] With heroin illegal, playing a part in distribution and thereby establishing dependable contact with a supplier is a method by which a user can cut the costs of searching for a source. Given that an addict middleman has few alternative sources of supply in the short run, he is less likely to turn in his supplier for a reward than a nonaddict who might otherwise be more efficient as a lower-stage agent. The observed method by which heroin is distributed thus reflects input choices and inventory wastage that are largely consequences of its illegal status. Distillers and alcoholics have little reason to seek employment relationships with each other. One expects the cost curve to fall after legalization because a given amount of heroin will be produced or transacted with a more competitive payment scheme and more productive personnel.

Under legalization, there will unquestionably be a radical change in the structure of heroin distribution. The nature of the illegal market is such that trading units in it are inefficiently small, restricted as to the scope of their operations, and dependent on personal rather than commercial channels for the acquisition and dissemination of information. Legalization will lower costs of both production and information and will break down informational barriers to entry and rivalry. Thus, one expects that the legal market will be characterized by a lower equilibrium price, higher output, and more dependable quality. There is no reason to believe that its distribution and retailing cannot be taken over by existing firms in, for example, pharmaceutical markets or that they cannot successfully be undertaken by new specialists. Can we be certain that this will be the long-run supply situation?

Competition and Monopoly in the Market

Despite its importance in the folklore of law enforcement, we know little about the role of "organized crime" as a possible monopolizer of the heroin market. In a production and distribution process that has well-defined "stages," a monopolist need only control one of them in order to extract all profit from the market. There is in gen-

22. Moore, *Buy and Bust,* chap. 2.

eral no gain to be made by expansion into other stages.[23] If a monopoly exists anywhere, it is presumably at the upper stages of production and distribution, where capital requirements might pose a barrier to entry and where transactions are highly personalized and infrequent.[24] Note that even if there is a monopoly at some upper level, we need not see a reduced output relative to competition. Lack of contact between different sociological and geographic segments of the market may make resale among them difficult. In such cases, we might observe price discrimination based on differing elasticities of demand in the different submarkets. To the extent discrimination is finer, output will approach competitive levels.

Whether or not a monopoly or cartel controls some stage of the process depends on whose testimony one reads. Thus the assistant secretary-general of Interpol once stated before Congress that a truce among underworld elements had effectively cartelized the business.[25] At about the same time the commissioner of the Federal Bureau of Narcotics reported to Congress that Cosa Nostra had altered its policy and would henceforth not engage in the heroin business.[26] On the bases of a shaky estimate of users and reports of transaction volumes determined from interviews with addicts,[27] Moore estimated four to six major importers at the top of the pyramid in New York in 1973.[28] Without identifying and observing them,

23. Robert H. Bork, *The Antitrust Paradox* (New York: Basic Books, 1978), chap. 11. The statement of the text is subject to a variety of minor qualifications. Prime among them is that there may be gains in allocative efficiency under some circumstances if a monopolist at one stage ventures into other stages of production.

24. Rottenberg, "The Clandestine Distribution of Heroin." One difficulty with a model of monopoly is that it does not explain the observed fluctuation of price or potency with short-term supply availability. If profits are concave in price (as in the case under reasonable assumptions about demand) and inventories are not too costly to store, the monopolist makes more under a steady price-output strategy than under an unstable one.

25. U.S. Senate, Permanent Subcommittee on Investigations, Committee on Governmental Operations, 88th Congress, *Hearings Pursuant to S. Res. 178, Parts 3 and 4. Organized Crime and Illicit Traffic in Narcotics* (Washington, D.C.: Government Printing Office, 1964), pp. 3028-30.

26. U.S. Senate, Subcommittee to Investigate Juvenile Delinquency, 87th Congress, *Hearings Pursuant to S. Res. 265,* May 9, 17, 20 and August 6, 7, 1962 (Washington, D.C.: Government Printing Office, 1963), pp. 645-46. Commissioner Giordano's testimony cites Cosa Nostra informer Joe Valachi as his source of the assertion.

27. The range for the user estimates is 70,000-150,000. The source of the interviews is Preble and Casey, "Taking Care of Business." The authors, however, do not characterize their sample statistically.

28. Moore, *Buy and Bust,* pp. 95-100.

however, we cannot infer whether they act competitively or collusively. Additionally, the factors that limit an importer's size have never been spelled out. Are there diseconomies of scale beyond those associated with the proliferation of illegal contacts?

We can probably infer that there is considerable turnover at the upper levels of the market and that it results from competition rather than law enforcement. Although the subject is partially folkloric, the sources of raw opium, locations of refining facilities, and ethnic identities of personnel, both inside the United States and abroad, have changed rapidly. The ethnic identification of arrested "Higher Echelon Narcotics Traffickers" during the 1950s and 1960s was overwhelmingly Italian.[29] By the mid-1970s, Mexican heroin had largely replaced heroin of Middle Eastern origin in the eastern United States.[30] The trade was apparently organized by Hispanics who had formerly operated only in the Southwest. During the Vietnam period, Southeast Asia came to compete with Mexico as a source.[31] Finally, as the 1980s arrived, production from the "Golden Crescent" of Afghanistan, Pakistan, and Iran became a more important factor in the American market.[32]

It seems clear that these shifts in supply patterns and personnel abroad were accompanied by equally drastic shifts at upper levels of the domestic market. For other drugs, we have little evidence of sustained monopoly. According to anecdotal evidence, cocaine appears to be reasonably competitive at higher levels and is not dominated by any of the ethnic groups that at various times have allegedly controlled heroin. Marijuana and bootleg pharmaceuticals are clearly competitive at the primary sources of supply to the illegal market.

No other important input appears to act as a barrier to entry in the current production of heroin, and such barriers would be even

29. U.S. Senate, *Hearings Pursuant to S. Res. 178, parts 3 and 4. Organized Crime,* pp. 772–89. Using subjective judgment, I identified 60 out of 86 names on the congressional list as Italian, 9 as Jewish, 2 as Hispanic, and 15 as "other" or unidentifiable. I have found no comparable lists for subsequent years.

30. Mark H. Greene, "The Resurgence of Heroin Abuse in the District of Columbia," *American Journal of Alcohol and Drug Abuse* 2, no. 2 (1975): 141–64.

31. Catherine Lamour and Michael Lamberti, *The International Connection* (New York: Pantheon, 1974).

32. U.S. House of Representatives, Appropriations Committee, *Hearings on Department of Justice Appropriations for 1983,* part 7, March 9, 1982 (Washington, D.C.: Government Printing Office, 1983), p. 37; David J. Bellis, *Heroin and Politicians* (Westport, Conn.: Greenwood Press, 1981), pp. 84–88.

less likely under legalization. As the drug trade has increased in volume and remained competitive as an illegal investment, financial capital has appeared, in part through retained earnings. The poppy crop required for America's estimated current annual consumption of heroin could be grown on 25 square miles of land,[33] and the historical record of shifting sources makes it clear that usable land exists in many locations.[34] There appear to be few relevant scale economies in processing opium into heroin, and no unusually skilled labor is required in production, transport, or distribution. Entry of a producer or distributor can probably be effected at only a single level of the chain, i.e., a processor need not also be a grower or distributor.

By the standards of ordinary manufacturing and distribution, a legalized heroin industry would have few of the elements likely to lead to monopoly or monopolistic behavior, and many likely to lead to competitive behavior. It is characterized by no discernible scale economies that would imply natural monopoly. Even when illegal, it has been characterized by few strong barriers to the entry of new producer or distribution units. There are no known inputs that are even in relatively inelastic supply. Costs in the industry are high today because of the risks imposed by illegality. Because there are no resources supplied inelastically to the industry, the costs of illegality are largely borne by users as higher prices. The inefficient distribution chains and input mixes are also thus borne. The price in a competitive legal market would settle at about marginal cost, adjusted for quality.

Currently used information about the characteristics of production and distribution is thus almost useless for predicting the long-run supply and price of legal heroin. According to one recent report,[35] twenty 10-milligram tablets of heroin, legally prescribable for the terminally ill in England, cost "about $1.[36] A liberal estimate of

33. John Kaplan, "A Primer on Heroin," *Stanford Law Review 27* (February 1975): 801–26, esp. 817.
34. Thomas Szasz, *Ceremonial Chemistry* (Garden City, N.Y.: Doubleday Anchor, 1975), p. 52. Quoting President Nixon's special adviser on drugs, the author states that only 5 percent of the world crop would supply America's users. Although this may indicate a high elasticity of supply to Americans, it should be remembered that virtually all estimates of unknown quantities (crop size, number of users) are worthless.
35. CBS, "Sixty Minutes," 2 December 1984.
36. The figure is roughly consistent with the statement by Kaplan ("A Primer on Heroin," p. 813) that "the morphine equivalent of $30 worth of heroin [presumably in 1975 prices] is available through legal medical channels for about $0.20." Figures on "pharmacy cost" quoted by Szasz (*Ceremonial Chemistry,* p. 192) are considerably lower.

a typical addict habit would be 50 milligrams per day.[37] Even if there is monopoly power on the part of drug producers, this comes to little more than 25 cents per day. Additionally, we do not know (but have reason to suspect) that large-scale commercial production will lead to cost-saving innovations. Such a figure gives one pause. The illegal market wastes incredible amounts of economic resources, apparently only because of illegality rather than monopoly. If the illegal price is $5–$15 for 10 milligrams of uncertain quality, it is clear that we need to investigate the responsiveness of demanders to the drastic changes in the market that legality would induce.

ADDICTION AND THE DEMAND FOR HEROIN

The preferences of buyers ultimately determine what will be supplied to them, and in what quantities. The responsiveness of purchases to price and their predictability when external circumstances change must now be examined.

Elasticity of Demand

To the economist, a concept such as addiction is almost impossible to reconcile with a central tenet of economic theory. According to the "first law of demand," an increase in the relative cost of purchasing any good will lead to a decrease in the quantity of it demanded by buyers. The idea is general enough to include costs that take the form of time losses, risks of incarceration, risks of low quality, and social opprobrium. If different goods are substitute sources of well-being for an individual, then a given level of well-being can be more cheaply attained by substituting against those goods which have become costly relative to others. The economist's "second law of demand" is equally at variance with the popular concept of addiction. The law states that one's demand for a good becomes more elastic (price-sensitive) the longer the time that has elapsed since a change in its price. People become more aware of substitutes as time passes, and they minimize their long-term losses by taking their time in adjusting to changed circumstances. For an addictive good, however, an initial adjustment period is said to lead to a pattern of use for which substitution is impossible.[38]

---

37. Moore, *Buy and Bust,* p. 84.
38. Economists have recently begun work on theories of habit formation and self-control.

If addiction is to be consistent with its popular version, we must interpret it as a vertical demand curve, i.e., one in which quantity purchased is held fixed, regardless of the cost the user must bear. Again, the cost includes a dollar price, time spent searching for a seller, a risk of apprehension for both narcotic and criminal violations, and a risk of poor (or lethal) quality. Let us call their total the "full cost."[39] The elasticity of demand with respect to the full cost of the good is a critical number for the evaluation of both short-run and long-run policy. If crime is a concomitant of addiction, effective policies to raise the price of heroin may increase crime if the demand for heroin is sufficiently inelastic. If new users have more elastic demands than do long-term addicts, policies that raise price to the former and lower it to the latter may be in order.[40] If the long-run elasticity of demand is very high, legalization (which lowers the full cost substantially) may turn us into a nation of users.

While the analysis of the market would be much simpler if in fact users had vertical demand curves, the world is not so obliging. Demanders have heterogeneous tastes, ingesting the drug in various manners and with varying frequencies. Although figures here are notoriously unreliable, large-scale daily dependence probably characterizes no more than half of all users.[41] Addiction can be broken by self-imposed detoxification or by imprisonment, and the odds of imprisonment may be greater for those with larger habits. There is considerable evidence that in times when supplies are short, sporadic, or of uncertain quality, other drugs are substituted for heroin.[42] In the process of substitution, "addiction" must vanish. Methadone maintenance substitutes another, equally habit-forming, substance for heroin, and there is some evidence that enrollments in methadone

---

Their application to "addiction" is uncertain. See Thomas C. Schelling, "Self-Command in Practice, in Policy, and in a Theory of Rational Choice," *American Economic Review* 74 (May 1984): 1–11; Richard H. Thaler and Hersh M. Shefrin, "An Economic Theory of Self-Control," *Journal of Political Economy* 89 (April 1981): 392–406; Gordon C. Winston, "Addiction and Backsliding: A Theory of Compulsive Consumption," *Journal of Economic Behavior and Organization* 1, no. 4 (1980): 295–324.

39. Additionally, time that might be spent working may be necessary to consume the good in a satisfying way. I discuss heroin and employment in Sec. V.

40. Mark H. Moore, "Policies to Achieve Discrimination on the Effective Price of Heroin," *American Economic Review* 63 (May 1973): 270–77.

41. Moore, *Buy and Bust*, p. 90.

42. John R. Pekkanen, "Drug Law Enforcement Efforts," in Drug Abuse Council, *The Facts About "Drug Abuse"* (New York: Free Press, 1980), pp. 63–94, esp. p. 92.

and detoxification programs vary inversely with the full cost to the user.[43] Stories about the difficulty of withdrawal appear to be at variance with the facts. The interesting problem is not habitual use, but rather the frequent restarting of a habit by one who has previously gone through withdrawal.[44]

Time patterns of population use and adjustment patterns of individual use give little support to a simple notion of addiction. There is general agreement that heroin use in the United States is predominantly a habit of the young, and that users "mature out" of their habits, in most cases without medical aid.[45] Use of opiates in nineteenth century American was a middle-class phenomenon, with the majority of users being housewives who had acquired a tolerance for patent remedies that contained them. There is little record of withdrawal problems among them (and no record of criminal problems) following the passage of the Harrison Act, although their number may have been in the millions.[46] Estimates of the percentage of American servicemen who used opiates while in Vietnam center around 30 to 40 percent.[47] Yet one study found that those defined by its author as addicted on or after their return constituted less than 3 percent of those sampled.[48] Equally interestingly, they apparently functioned well while on active duty. As will be seen below, such evidence makes an estimation of postlegalization addiction rates either impossible or meaningless.

43. James Q. Wilson, Mark H. Moore, and I. David Wheat, Jr., "The Problem of Heroin," *The Public Interest* 29 (Fall 1972): 3–28; DuPont and Greene, "The Dynamics of a Heroin Addiction Epidemic."

44. Kaplan, "A Primer on Heroin," p. 807. The difficulty of withdrawal is frequently cited as a justification for methadone programs or medical dispensation of heroin. (See, for example, Trebach, ed., *Drugs, Crime, and Politics.*) The argument seems strained. In the short run, many of my demands will be inelastic, i.e., the fact that there are high costs of "withdrawing" from electricity use does not constitute either an economic or an ethical rationale for its collective production or allocation.

45. Dan Waldorf and Patrick Biernacki, "Natural Recovery from Heroin Addiction: A Review of the Incidence Literature," *Journal of Drug Issues* 16 (Spring 1979): 281–89; Winick, "Some Aspects of Careers of Chronic Heroin Users."

46. David F. Musto, *The American Disease* (New Haven: Yale University Press, 1973); Charles E. Terry and Mildred Pellens, *The Opium Problem* (New York: Bureau of Social Hygiene, 1928).

47. Jim Mintz, Charles P. O'Brien, and Beverly Pomerantz, "The Impact of Vietnam Service in Heroin-Addicted Veterans," *American Journal of Drug and Alcohol Abuse* 6, no. 1 (1979): 39–52; Lee N. Robins, "Estimating Addiction Rates and Locating Target Populations," in NIDA Research Monograph 16 (Washington, D.C.: Government Printing Office, 1977), pp. 25–39.

48. Robins, "Estimating Addiction Rates," p. 29.

Algebraically, elasticity of demand is the ratio of the percentage change in quantity (units) of a good purchased to the percentage change in its cost to the buyer, holding other factors constant. Thus a low value of elasticity indicates relative unresponsiveness of quantity to price changes. If elasticity is 0.3, a 10 percent rise in price will result only in a 3 percent fall in quantity purchased. If elasticity of demand is less than one in value, an increase in the price of the good leads to a greater dollar amount spent on it. If it is greater than one, a rise in price leads to a fall in total spending on the good. Elasticity may vary as we move away from a certain range of prices, i.e., the relative responsiveness of users to market changes may depend on whether the initial price is $1 or $100.[49] As noted in the previous section, we can reasonably expect that after legalization the price of heroin will be about 1 percent of today's full cost. Even with usable estimates of elasticity in the neighborhood of today's price, we can have little confidence in inferences about market situations so far removed from today's. As will be seen below, we also cannot make convincing inferences by examining past periods of legalization or the experiences of other countries.

The literature provides little in the way of elasticity estimates for heroin. This is not surprising, since estimation requires a fair amount of reliable data or market conditions at different times or places, as well as observations on other variables that might account for differences in buyer behavior in dissimilar environments. Fujii[50] cites unpublished estimates of 0.007 and 0.09. The only estimates I have discovered that contain any respect for econometric theory or method were produced by the Center for Naval Analyses in the early and mid-1970s.[51] Using samples based on street purchases in various cities, they corrected for the differences in purity among them. On average they found demand elasticities of about 0.25 with respect to dollar price. Full cost, however, varied widely among cities. Assume for the sake of argument that their estimate of elasticity is correct,

49. Consider a linear demand curve. Although the slope of such a curve is constant, elasticity will vary as we move along it, since elasticity is a ratio of percentage rather than absolute changes.

50. Edwin T. Fujii, "Public Investment in the Rehabilitation of Heroin Addicts," *Social Science Quarterly* 55 (June 1974): 39–51.

51. George F. Brown, Jr. and Lester P. Silverman, "The Retail Price of Heroin: Estimation and Applications," *Journal of the American Statistical Association* 69 (September 1974): 595–606; Lester P. Silverman and Nancy L. Spruill, "Urban Crime and the Price of Heroin," *Journal of Urban Economics* 4 (1977): 80–103.

and that the demand curve in question has a constant elasticity. If legalization led to a fall in the full cost of a pure gram to 1.5 percent of its current level, it would lead to a 187 percent increase in the amount purchased and a decrease in spending on heroin to 6.2 percent of its former level.[52]

Such a projection is no more than conjecture. With no experience in the world even remotely close to that of such a price drop, we can say no more. The elasticity estimate of 0.25, additionally, is a short-run figure. While we can learn little about the speed with which the market will adjust to legalization from the studies mentioned above, we can state with some confidence that theirs are low estimates of the long-run effect of reduced price on consumption. Habits of existing users do not expand instantly upon knowledge that price has fallen, and new users likewise require time to become attracted and habituated. Assume the far less likely alternative of a long-run elasticity of 1.5.[53] The same assumed decrease in price now leads to a 560-fold increase in consumption and a twelvefold increase in expenditure on heroin. If we estimate conservatively (see below) that there are currently 200,000 users among American adults, about half of whom have large habits, we would be forced to conclude that under legalization nearly half of all adults in the country would be heavy users.

Both intuition and history tell us that such a conjecture is meaningless. No estimate cited by Musto for the pre-Harrison Act period comes remotely close, and the highest incidence estimate to which any credence can be given is 8–10 percent of physicians in 1899.[54]

---

52. The logic of the calculation is as follows: I use Moore's estimate (*Buy and Bust*, p. 90) of average daily use over all classes of users as 46 milligrams of pure heroin per day. Brown and Silverman ("The Retail Price of Heroin," p. 597) estimate an average price per pure gram of $231 in Manhattan in 1974. Such a purchase, however, would not normally be made in a day by a final user. Assume that the average purchase is made each day, and that the search time and various risks have a cash value of $5 to the purchaser. Then the full cost per pure gram is approximately $340. Consequently, let legalization reduce the price of a pure gram to $5. (In 1974 dollars, this is considerably higher than the prices mentioned in Sec. II.) Such action will also eliminate search time and most of the risk components of consumption. A drop in price of this magnitude (to 1.47 percent of its former level) leads to the results of the text if elasticity is 0.25.

53. The long-run elasticity assumed here is roughly equivalent to that estimated by others for alcohol. See Rodney T. Smith, "The Legal and Illegal Markets for Taxed Goods: Pure Theory and Application to State Government Taxation of Distilled Spirits," *Journal of Law and Economics* 19 (August 1976): 393–430. It is unlikely that the elasticity along the curve would be everywhere that high. See Note 49 above.

54. Musto, *The American Disease*, p. 275.

The highest reported estimate in the contemporary world is 3 percent for adults in Hong Kong.[55] Only 70 percent of America's adult population uses alcohol.[56] Once we abandon a simple idea of addiction and account for the diversity of potential users and the plausible range of price change after legalization, almost any outcome seems possible.

Shifts of the Demand Curve

Our problems in estimating the response to legalization are not completely solved even if we have a reliable estimate of demand elasticity over the relevant range of prices. The entire demand curve for heroin will shift outward or inward as income,[57] prices of other goods, and tastes of users or potential users change. Even with good price data, one cannot estimate the effect of legalization on consumption without also accounting for these other factors that will be changing contemporaneously with price. In addition, changes over time in these other influences on demand may render it impossible to make predictions about today on the basis of experience in the distant past. Rising wages, for example, will ambiguously affect use. Part of the larger income they give a person might be spent on heroin. Since leisure time is needed to consume it,[58] however, rising wages might alternatively lead to decreased use because work is now more financially rewarding.[59] In the current world, it seems clear that the choice of a substance, at least initially, depends on the alternatives avail-

55. James M. N. Chi'en, "Voluntary Treatment for Drug Abuse in Hong Kong," *Addictive Diseases* 3 (1977): 99–104.

56. I. D. McIntosh, "Population Consumption of Alcohol and Proportion Drinking," *British Journal of Addiction* 76 (1981): 267–79.

57. Using BNDD Register data as the dependent variable in a cross-state multiple regression, Leveson estimated an income elasticity of addiction of 1.7. (See Irving Leveson, "Drug Addiction: Some Evidence on Prevention and Deterrence," in Leveson, ed., *Quantitative Explorations in Drug Abuse Policy*, p. 91.) Since the median income of users bears no necessary relation to median income in the state (the measure Leveson used), the results are questionable. Income elasticity is the ratio of the percentage change in addicts to the percentage change in income as we move between two otherwise identical situations.

58. This assumes more hours of work by the individual in response to rising wages, which need not be the case in general.

59. Although we think of heroin today as consumed by the poorly-off, opium importation in the United States between 1870 and 1914 increased significantly with increasing per capita income. (For import figures, see Terry and Pellens, *The Opium Problem*, pp. 50–51.) The positive "income elasticity" of demand might, however, actually be due to other influences. The price of opium, for example, might have been falling at the same time incomes were rising. Were price data available, multiple regression techniques would allow further analysis.

able. Whether a good is a realistic alternative to heroin or nbt depends on both of their prices.

Even more problematic is the question of the noneconomic characteristics of individuals that may predispose them to use. The changing demographics of American users seem to defy economic explanation. Middle-aged housewives and Civil War veterans apparently constituted the majority of American users in the nineteenth century,[60] and most of them lived in small towns or rural areas.[61] By the end of World War II, users had become predominantly male, split between an older group of white rural southerners and a younger group of urban blacks and Puerto Ricans.[62] The southern whites have apparently since vanished. By the 1970s rhetoric about the spread of heroin to well-off suburban youth had become widespread, but hard evidence on its significance was lacking. Hispanics other than Puerto Ricans, however, had clearly become larger users and sellers.[63] Prior to the mid-1960s, the average educational attainment of users was the same as that of the general population, with few users characterized by either extremely high *or low* levels of schooling.[64] Since then, average attainment has dropped somewhat.

Patterns of use elsewhere are equally paradoxical. In England heroin is almost exclusively a drug for middle-class whites. Despite extensive recent immigration of racial minorities from opium-supplying areas, addiction rates among them pose no significant problem.[65] In cultivating countries, use is greater in rural growing areas than in cities, contrary to the Western pattern. In Hong Kong, the habit is considered a prerogative of old age, and there is little use among the young. The latter, however, have turned to alcohol in increasing

---

60. John C. Ball and Carl D. Chambers, "Overview of the Problem," in Ball and Chambers, eds., *The Epidemiology of Opiate Addiction in the United States* (Springfield, Ill.: Thomas, 1970), p. 9; Terry and Pellens, *The Opium Problem,* pp. 428–67.

61. Terry and Pellens, *The Opium Problem,* chap. 1.

62. John C. Ball, "Two Patterns of Opiate Addiction," in Ball and Chambers, eds., *The Epidemiology of Opiate Addiction,* pp. 81–94. The stories of addiction as a peculiar problem for blacks seem inadequate. According to Johnson, "the propensity of blacks to addiction is explained by the fact that larger proportions of blacks than whites experiment with heroin; but very seldom does such use translate into recent use or addiction for either race." See Bruce D. Johnson, "The Race, Class, and Irreversibility Hypotheses: Myths and Research about Heroin," in NIDA Research Monograph 16 (1977), pp. 51–57, esp. p. 52.

63. Greene, "Resurgence of Heroin Abuse."

64. Ball and Chambers, "Overview of the Problem," p. 10.

65. Horace Freeland Judson, *Heroin Addiction in Britain* (New York: Harcourt Brace Jovanovich, 1974), pp. 46–49.

numbers.[66] Massive increases in use by Iranians characterize the Khomeini years, despite extreme attempts at repression.[67] On the other hand, harsh measures taken after the Chinese revolution are said to have been highly effective in ending opium use there.[68]

There is uniformly strong testimony that people are introduced to opiate use by their acquaintances.[69] Famed though he was in folklore, the pusher who turned samplers into addicts probably never existed.[70] To the extent that heroin use carries with it illegal status, one should expect that an ordinary process of market sampling by the general public will not be observed. Such a process might well be seen after legalization, but even this is by no means certain. Decriminalization of small amounts of marijuana possession in Oregon during the 1970s appeared simultaneously with an increase in the fraction of the population who claimed not to use it because they had no interest in doing so.[71] All of this makes it impossible to predict shifts in the demand curve resulting from shifts in the identities of groups likely to contain interested users. Both social convention and historical accident render predictions about future demand shifts effectively impossible.

ESTIMATING USERS AND ADDICTS

In the United States, governmental production of demographic and economic data is typically characterized by a fair degree of reliability and impartiality, given the cost of collection. While the variables measured (e.g., unemployment) may be imperfect realizations of the theoretical constructs of interest, the statistical methods used are

66. K. Singer, "The Choice of Intoxicant Among the Chinese," *British Journal of the Addictions* 69 (September 1974), pp. 257–68.

67. Arnold S. Trebach, *The Heroin Solution* (New Haven: Yale University Press, 1982), pp. 15–16.

68. Ernest Drucker and Victor Sidel, "The Communicable Disease Model of Heroin Addiction: A Critique," *American Journal of Drug and Alcohol Abuse* 1, no. 3 (1974): 301–11, esp. pp. 308–9.

69. Wilson, Moore, and Wheat, "The Problem of Heroin," pp. 10–12; Denise B. Kandel and Deborah R. Maloff, "Commonalities in Drug Use: A Sociological Perspective," in Peter K. Levison, Dean Gerstein, and Deborah Maloff, eds., *Commonalities in Substance Abuse and Habitual Behavior* (Lexington, Mass.: Lexington, 1983), pp. 3–27.

70. The mythology carries with it some interesting inconsistencies. Why, for example, would a profit-making pusher single out the least affluent part of the community for attention?

71. Robert R. Carr and Erik J. Meyers, "Marijuana and Cocaine: The Process of Change in Drug Policy," in Drug Abuse Council, *The Facts about "Drug Abuse"* (New York: Free Press, 1980), pp. 153–89.

generally of high quality. As one enters the realm of figures with a more obvious political purpose, both reliability and methodological quality drop off rapidly. The statistics on heroin are an ideal example. As the Nixon administration attempted to impress the public with its view of the seriousness of the problem, estimates of the addict population by the U.S. Bureau of Narcotics and Dangerous Drugs (BNDD) rose from 69,000 in 1969 to 560,000 in 1971. The effectiveness of newly instituted control programs was clearly in evidence as they fell to 160,000 in the election year of 1972.[72] Describing the same period, another author claims that the government systematically attempted to understate the size of the addict population in its official estimates, in an attempt to minimize political controversy.[73]

Figures on the numbers of addicts are frequently characterized by gross inconsistencies with harder facts. Singer argued that the state government's estimate of 200,000 addicts in New York City at the time was probably an overstatement by a factor of three, since the volume of property crime (assumed to be a major source of addict support) was far lower than that required to support so many addicts, even after allowance for unreported crime.[74] If we take Governor Rockefeller's estimates of addicts and habit sizes seriously, we are forced to conclude that in 1973 "the average resident of New York would be robbed, mugged, or murdered approximately seven times a year."[75] Despite an astoundingly complex estimating formula, estimates by the National Institute on Drug Abuse of about 500,000 addicts nationwide in 1978 are equally inconsistent with what is known about property crime.[76] In part because of internal bureaucratic criticism,[77] and in part because of the decreasing importance of heroin on the national political agenda, official estimates

---

72. Epstein, *Agency of Fear,* pp. 109, 177.

73. Richard Ashley, *Heroin* (New York: St. Martin's, 1972), pp. 40–47.

74. Max Singer, "The Vitality of Mythical Numbers," *The Public Interest* 23 (Spring 1971): 3–9. As will be seen in Sec. V, the link between drug use and crime is also doubtful.

75. Epstein, *Agency of Fear,* p. 44.

76. Peter Reuter, "The (Continued) Vitality of Mythical Numbers," *The Public Interest* 75 (Spring 1984): 135–47. We might try going the other way and attempt to estimate user populations from crime statistics. This seems equally hopeless. A detailed list of the assumptions that must be made in order to do so appears in John A. Newmeyer and Gregory R. Johnson, "The Heroin Epidemic in San Francisco: Estimates of Incidence and Prevalence," *International Journal of the Addictions* 11 (1976): 417–38, esp. 430–32.

77. GAO, *Report to the Attorney General,* chap. 5.

of the addict or user populations seem to vanish after 1980.[78] Despite the possibilities for making the estimates more accurate,[79] there is virtually no constituency to demand such accuracy.[80]

In 1928, Terry and Pellens collated a set of estimates of the American opium "addict" population made by various methods between 1913 and 1920. The highest estimate (782,000) exceeded the lowest (102,000) by a factor of 7.7.[81] More recently, Moore constructed several estimates of heroin "users" in New York City in 1970.[82] The figures vary by a factor of five, from 54,000 to 252,000. The upper estimate for New York City exceeds some low estimates for the entire United States. The results become more interesting at lower levels of aggregation. The Federal Bureau of Narcotics reported a total of one active addict in Utah in 1959, despite 117 narcotics arrests and 101 convictions in the state between 1953 and 1959.[83] Apparently the law enforcement effort failed to deter crime, since by 1963 he had been joined by a federally estimated second addict.[84]

In part, the problem of identifying and enumerating heroin "users" and "addicts" is a definitional one. As noted above, the distribution of consumption varies smoothly rather than moving abruptly from zero to some addiction-maintenance level. Moore estimates that about 60 percent of all active users have habits of over 50 milligrams of pure heroin per day.[85] Below some threshold, which probably varies with the individual user, heroin is an object of occasional consumption rather than daily obsession. Serious symptoms

78. President Carter's 1980 State of the Union message reported an addict population of 380,000. I have been unable to find an official source for the figure. See Trebach, *The Heroin Solution*, p. 243.

79. Estimates of amounts of heroin seized and unseized might provide additional information, but estimates of total traffic are currently provided only for internal federal use. (See U.S. House of Representatives, Appropriations Committee, *Hearings, Part 7. Department of Justice Appropriations for 1983*, pp. 15, 37.) Publicly available seizure estimates for past years are duplicative (some Customs and DEA seizures are double-counted) and inaccurate. (Gross weights rather than potency-adjusted weights are reported.) (See GAO, *Report to the Attorney General*, pp. 36–39.) In any case, estimates of the amounts of drugs not seized, regardless of who makes them, are pure conjecture.

80. Reuter, "The (Continued) Vitality of Mythical Numbers," pp. 145–46.

81. Terry and Pellens, *The Opium Problem*, p. 42.

82. Moore, *Buy and Bust*, p. 72.

83. William Butler Eldridge, *Narcotics and the Law*, 2d ed. rev. (Chicago: University of Chicago Press, 1967), p. 76.

84. U.S. Senate, *Hearings Pursuant to S. Res. 178, part 3. Organized Crime*, p. 769.

85. Moore, *Buy and Bust*, p. 90.

of physical withdrawal are apparently seldom encountered, but those who withdraw for a period often relapse into using it again.[86] There is also reason to believe that users overstate average habit sizes or the frequency of days on which they consume claimed amounts.[87] Researchers have frequently found that the distributions of alcohol and other recreational drugs consumed daily are logarithmically normal in survey data, characterized by low modal amounts and long upper tails.[88] There is some evidence on heroin that leads to similar conclusions.[89]

If the distribution of users is thus characterized, an estimate of their total number tells us little in the absence of information about the circumstances of individuals in it. If all heavy users are wealthy (as they are not), then crime as a correlate of use will be a small problem at worst. Estimates of users and "problem users" are made in a variety of ways, each of which reduces to a simple idea: Find a population of known users, or one whose size is assumed to be highly correlated with that of the user population. Then find an inflation factor and multiply the known population by it in order to estimate the overall user population. As an ideal example, assume that a perfectly random (in all relevant characteristics) subset of the entire population is injected with truth serum and its members told to describe their drug use. If the sample is large enough we will be able to bound our estimate of users in the population with a considerable degree of confidence. The critical inflation factor will simply be the ratio of population size to sample size.

Surveys of drug use in the real world carry with them little guarantee of truthfulness, and the likelihood that the understaters balance out the exaggerators is unknown.[90] If we are dealing with an

86. Kaplan, "A Primer on Heroin," pp. 807–8.

87. Fred Goldman, "Drug Abuse, Crime and Economics: The Dismal Limits of Social Choice," in James A. Inciardi, ed., *The Drugs-Crime Connection* (Beverly Hills, Calif.: Sage, 1981), p. 164.

88. Diane McDermott and James Scheurich, "The Logarithmic Normal Distribution in Relation to the Epidemiology of Drug Abuse," *Bulletin on Narcotics* 29 (January–March 1977): 13–19; Reginald G. Smart, "The Distribution of Illicit Drug Use: Correlations between Extent of Use, Heavy Use, and Problems," *Bulletin on Narcotics* 30 (January–March 1978): 33–41.

89. Erik J. Meyers, "American Heroin Policy: Some Alternatives," in Drug Abuse Council, *The Facts about "Drug Abuse"* (New York: Free Press, 1980), p. 198.

90. The state of the art, such as it is, is adequately summarized in Adele V. Harrell, "Validation of Self-Report: The Research Record," in NIDA Research Monograph 57 (1985), pp. 12–21.

infrequently encountered attribute, the sample required for reliability will be very large. Glenn reports that it would require $500,000 to produce a statistically accurate estimate for North Carolina alone.[91] To drive home the point, he describes a survey of 2,000 randomly selected persons in that state actually taken by the North Carolina Drug Authority in 1974. Only two of the individuals surveyed admitted to regular heroin use (and they may have been lying). On the basis of this survey, the state officially estimated 2,760 regular users. From the characteristics of the respondents, the state concluded that 1,320 were male and 1,440 female, 1,320 were black and 1,440 white, and all 2,760 were moderate smokers.

In the absence of good information from truly random questionnaire samples, inferences are usually made on the basis of samples whose habits are less in doubt. From such samples we can frequently derive interesting facts about the sampled group, but not necessarily about the population. For example, in 1981 74.0 percent of the 93,678 heroin user admissions[92] to federally funded drug clinics were male and 43.6 percent of the total were black,[93] both of which might sound reasonable and consistent with intuition as descriptions of the population. On the other hand, 56.7 percent of heroin admissions claimed they had not been arrested within twenty-four months of admission.[94] Is this "reasonable" or isn't it? According to an unpublished source cited by Moore,[95] 45 percent of total users are arrested in any given year. If the population is stationary, the fraction never arrested in twenty-four months will be $(1 - .45)^2 = 30.2$ percent. The 45 percent figure, of course, was drawn out of thin air by a police official, and arrest histories given at clinics are usually unverified self-reports. One thing is certain: On the basis of figures for admissions to treatment alone, we cannot identify the size of the

91. William Glenn, "Problems Related to Survey Sampling," in NIDA Research Monograph 10 (1977), pp. 154–59, esp. p. 155.

92. There is a potentially important bias in the reporting of heroin admissions. Federal policy makers apparently have made it clear that "drug abuse" clinics are not to concern themselves with marijuana and alcohol users, and that the funding depends in part on reported heroin treatments. See C. James Sample, "Institutional Data—CODAP," in NIDA Research Monograph 10 (1977), pp. 197–205.

93. NIDA, *Data from the Client-Oriented Data Acquisition Process, Annual Data 1980*, Statistical Series E, No. 21 (Washington, D.C.: Government Printing Office, 1982), p. 6.

94. Ibid., p. 9.

95. Moore, *Buy and Bust*, p. 72, note i.

total user population without making probably untenable assumptions about the representativeness of the clinical sample.[96]

Most estimates of the overall population simply apply a multiplier to a known population. Moore's low estimate of 54,000 New York City users in 1970 applies a multiplier of 2 to the number of New York names on the BNDD register of active users, whose activeness is unverifiable.[97] The multiplier is the unpublished opinion of a second expert, as reported by a third.[98] Moore's high figure of 252,000 is an inflation of the 151,000 names on the New York City Register by a factor of 1.67. The adjustment factor reflects the "finding" that 60 percent of dead users were known to the Narcotics Register. How "user" was defined or determined is unknown. The actual practice for determining and reporting heroin-related deaths violates proper sampling and reporting practice in ways that render the estimates valueless.[99] There is no known way of establishing a stable ratio of overdoses[100] or serum hepatitis episodes to users.[101] Attempts to extrapolate population sizes by comparing criminal and

96. John A. O'Donnell, "Comments on Hunt's Estimation Procedures," in NIDA Research Monograph 16 (1977), pp. 96–102; S. B. Sells, "Reflections on the Epidemiology of Heroin and Narcotic Addiction from the Perspective of Treatment Data," also in NIDA Research Monograph 16 (1977), pp. 147–76, esp. p. 148.

97. Moore, *Buy and Bust*, p. 72. The BNDD Register has no criteria for defining a user or verifying one's status as a user. The General Accounting Office declared that reporting by local police to the BNDD was "limited, incomplete, and erratic" (*Report to the Attorney General,* p. 43). In any case, compilation of the Register ceased in December 1977.

A few other estimates, along the same methodological lines, are given by Marc D. Brodsky, "History of Heroin Prevalence Estimation Techniques," in NIDA Research Monograph 57 (1985), pp. 94–103. A more sophisticated multiplier technique is examined by J. Arthur Woodward, Douglas G. Bonnett, and M. L. Brecht, "Estimating the Size of a Heroin-Abusing Population Using Multiple-Recapture Census," in NIDA Research Monograph 57 (1985), pp. 158–71.

98. Moore, *Buy and Bust*, p. 72.

99. GAO, *Report to the Attorney General,* chap. 3.

100. In general, a death associated with heroin use is indiscriminately referred to as an overdose. It may stem from unexpectedly high potency in a street purchase or from reaction to an adulterant. It may also be a consequence of multiple drug use or of the health status of the user. Some are purposive suicides. For a summary of the possibilities, see David P. Desmond, James F. Maddux, and Aureliano Trevino, "Street Heroin Potency and Deaths from Overdose in San Antonio," *American Journal of Drug and Alcohol Abuse* 5 (March 1978): 39–49.

101. Louis A. Gottschalk and Frederick L. McGuire, "Psychosocial and Biomedical Aspects of Deaths Associated with Heroin and Other Narcotics," in NIDA Research Monograph 16 (1977), pp. 122–29; Leon Gibson Hunt, "Prevalence of Active Heroin Use in the United States," also in NIDA Research Monograph 16, pp. 61–86, esp. p. 77.

medical populations have also shown little promise, in large part because we still have no idea of the number of individuals who have not been noticed by either authority.[102]

NIDA had two basic methods of estimating addicts in the late seventies. The first was a discredited inflation of the BNDD Register.[103] The second was an astonishingly sophisticated use of assumptions and unreliable data. According to the GAO,[104] estimates in later years are adjustments of some *assumed* 1974 and 1975 figures[105] by an elaborate simultaneous-equation model that incorporates estimated heroin-related deaths, estimated heroin-related injuries, and the purity of purchased samples of commercial heroin. NIDA does not specify why it believes that these are the only three relevant factors determining addiction, or how it defines an addict. As noted above, heroin-related deaths and injuries are neither reliably reported nor estimated, and the data on purity are characterized by erratic geographic coverage and overly small sample sizes.[106] Most interestingly of all, over a recent period in which all three indicators rose in value, NIDA's estimate of addicts fell.[107]

We cannot reasonably deny a conclusion that published addict and

---

102. The basic idea here is a statistically sound one, frequently used for counting wildlife populations. Assume that we wish to estimate the number of fish in a closed lake. First, we catch an appropriately sized sample of them, tag them, and wait while they swim around randomly. Using the hypergeometric distribution, we can then estimate the entire population after we learn the number of tagged fish that appear in a subsequent catch. A city is not a closed lake, users do not necessarily remain users, and the probability of a first arrest or treatment may differ from the probability of a second. For a good summary of statistical techniques, which have not since been improved, see Alfred Blumstein, Philip C. Sagi, and Marvin E. Wolfgang, "Problems of Estimating the Number of Heroin Addicts," in U.S. National Commission on Marijuana and Drug Abuse, *Technical Papers of the Second Report,* vol. 2 (Washington, D.C.: Government Printing Office, 1973), pp. 201–11. See also Hunt, "Prevalence of Active Heroin Use," pp. 68–71.

103. GAO, *Report to the Attorney General,* pp. 42–43.

104. Ibid., p. 47.

105. To determine the 1974 and 1975 figures, NIDA calculated an "index" of heroin problems for each of twenty-four metropolitan areas. The five variables included in the index were heroin-related injuries and deaths, retail price, retail purity, and admissions of users to federally funded treatment programs. All except the last are measured with great error, and NIDA has not released the index formula or a rationale for it. Once the index is computed, it must still be inflated to an estimate of users in each area, and then that estimated total must be inflated to a national value. In both inflation procedures, the size of the multiplier is arbitrary. While a large amount of computation is needed, it is fair to say that the resultant "estimates" are really assumed figures.

106. GAO, *Report to the Attorney General,* pp. 11–12.

107. Ibid., p. 48.

user estimates are meaningless. I have attempted to correlate certain NIDA estimates with obvious political variables such as budget size requests and changes, but have been unable to obtain significant results owing to sample size limitations.[108] If the problem is the size of the user or addict population, we have no ability to measure it. Neither we nor anyone else can say much that is useful about how it will change under legalization. The "problem," however, is generally characterized as one of dependency and crime, which expand with the user population. It is to these matters that I turn next.

HEROIN, CRIME, AND EMPLOYMENT

While some Americans are certainly offended by the fact that others consume heroin and derive pleasure from doing so, it is likely that very few would claim that their disgust stems from the sight of consumption per se. Rather, the general distaste for heroin users is usually attributed to their criminality and low economic productivity. In this section I examine these two matters.

Crime

As noted above, the distribution chain in the heroin market is characterized by an inefficiently large number of stages and by enterprises whose sizes are too small to exploit what scale economies do exist. Highly personalized exchanges are a method of coping with uncertain quality and availability. One consequence of these facts is that users will frequently attempt with success to participate as agents, i.e., to become their own middlemen, to an extent not seen in legal markets. Those selling at higher levels are likely to find users more acceptable as customers, since a dependable supply and quality of heroin acts as a method of eliciting desirable conduct at lower levels. A significant part of the crime associated with access to heroin is thus committed in the process of making consensual, albeit illegal, business transactions in the material itself.

Moore, citing unpublished surveys of street users, concluded that 51 percent of the income of "addicts" and "drug dependents" (me-

---

108. A summary of recent budgetary data appears in Peter Goldberg, "The Federal Government's Response to Illicit Drugs, 1969–1978," in Drug Abuse Council, *The Facts about "Drug Abuse,"* pp. 56–60.

dian and larger dose users) in New York was earned by work in heroin distribution.[109] Other studies and surveys cited by Goldman[110] concur in stating that a majority of higher-volume users play some role in distribution. Smaller users appear more likely to finance their consumption through employment, welfare, and borrowing.[111] An unknown fraction of remaining income (probably less than 25 percent) is derived through other consensual crimes, including prostitution and sale of other drugs. According to federal treatment statistics, 71 percent of primary heroin users entering drug treatment in 1980 reported themselves as unemployed, and 75 percent of them claimed not to be seeking work.[112] Seventy-three percent of admittees claimed to have daily habits.[113] Most of their income was apparently derived through illegal work,[114] as opposed to the victimization of others.

Statements by users about their habit sizes are typically not given under conditions likely to elicit honest answers. An individuals' self-esteem may increase with the size of the habit he claims he can afford.[115] At methadone clinics the size of dosage allowed may depend on self-reported use. There is likewise a strong incentive on the part of law enforcement or clinical personnel to accept such figures as an inflated justification for their own activities.[116] The problem is that estimates of the volume of addict property crime are typically based on such statements, combined with assumptions (little hard data seem to exist here) about discounts given by buyers of stolen goods.[117] The breakdown of addict crimes with victims between violent crimes

109. Moore, *Buy and Bust,* p. 94.

110. Goldman, "Drug Abuse, Crime and Economics," pp. 174–75.

111. Moore, *Buy and Bust,* p. 92.

112. NIDA, *Data from the Client-Oriented Data Acquisition Process, Annual Data 1980,* p. 6.

113. Ibid., p. 7.

114. Preble and Casey, "Taking Care of Business."

115. Paul J. Goldstein, "Getting Over: Economic Alternatives to Predatory Crime Among Street Drug Users," in Inciardi, ed., *The Drugs-Crime Connection,* p. 82.

116. Epstein, *Agency of Fear,* p. 296.

117. A survey of Oakland pawnbrokers by James Roumasset and John Hadreas ("Addicts, Fences, and the Market for Stolen Goods," *Public Finance Quarterly* 5 [April 1977]: 247–72, esp. p. 257) yielded the conclusion that, on average, the drug buyer receives 15 percent of the value of a newly sold item. Compare U.S. Senate *Hearings Pursuant to S. Res. 265,* p. 2692, which estimates (without data) that a "fence" gives one-third to one-half of "cost." Cost is undefined.

(mugging) and property crimes is also uncertain. Although violent crime carries a higher physical risk for the criminal, if successful it is more likely to produce cash rather than goods.[118] As a Task Force Report on Narcotics for the President's Commission on Law Enforcement noted, "There is no reliable data to assess properly the common assertion that drug users or addicts are responsible for 50 percent of all crime."[119]

Indirect evidence on the weakness of the link between heroin and crime is easy to find. Differences in crime rates among cities are typically too small to be accounted for by differences in addiction rates.[120] While about half of all crime is unreported, differences in reporting rates between cities are too small to account for known differences in heroin use. Street crime has not risen by an amount that could possibly be consistent with reported "epidemics" of heroin use, and the broad trend in the temporal pattern of reported crime is not consistent with that of any estimated shift in the user population.[121] Some have claimed that drops in the quality and availability of heroin in those cities that have experienced epidemics have been accompanied by drops in the crime rate,[122] while others claim to have found the opposite.[123] The former finding implies either that the demand for heroin is highly elastic, i.e., addiction is a fiction, or that the link between heroin and crime is too weak to be of much value for policy planning.

There is some evidence that delinquency often precedes heroin use,

118. Preble and Casey, "Taking Care of Business," pp. 18–19.

119. U.S. President's Commission on Law Enforcement and Administration of Justice, *Task Force Report: Narcotics and Drug Abuse* (Washington, D.C.: Government Printing Office, 1967), p. 11; Epstein, *Agency of Fear,* p. 40.

120. Using BNDD Register data, "addicts" per 1,000 population in 1969 in major cities ranged from 0.43 (St. Louis) to 5.33 (Paterson, N.J.). (See Leveson "Drug Addiction," p. 76.) The Register, however, is sufficiently unreliable and nonrandom as to call these findings into question. See GAO, *Report to the Attorney General,* pp. 42–43, and also note 96.

121. Adding the BNDD-measured addiction rate to Ehrlich's cross-state multiple regression model of property crime rates yields a significant increase (4 percent) in the explanatory power of the equation (R^2). The implied addiction-elasticity of property crime is a relatively low .04 to .09. See Isaac Ehrlich, "Participation in Illegitimate Activities: A Theoretical and Empirical Investigation," *Journal of Political Economy* 81 (May 1973): 521–65; Leveson, "Drug Addiction," p. 93; DuPont and Greene, "The Dynamics of a Heroin Addiction Epidemic"; Newmeyer and Johnson, "The Heroin Epidemic in San Francisco."

122. DuPont and Greene, "The Dynamics of a Heroin Addiction Epidemic," p. 721.

123. Michael Alexander, "The Heroin Market, Crime and Treatment of Heroin Addiction in Atlanta," in *Proceedings of the Fifth National Conference on Narcotic Treatment* (New York: National Association for the Prevention of Addiction to Narcotics, 1973), pp. 733–51.

frequently by several years.[124] What drug use actually does, according to Chein et al.,[125] is to alter the objectives of one who is already predisposed to and possibly involved in criminal behavior. The mix of crimes committed will change to favor those which facilitate the acquisition of heroin. Finestone[126] found higher rates of larceny and robbery for addict offenders, and higher rates of sex crimes, auto theft, and assault for nonaddict offenders, consistent with this theory. According to Coate and Goldman's survey-based simultaneous equation model,[127] criminal earnings, if one can obtain them, precede drug use.

Observing his sample of street users, Goldstein concluded that "the data suggest that, in many cases, subjects who have opportunistically and successfully seized a chance . . . simply use their gains to produce drugs. . . . Drug use is a major form of conspicious consumption among society's outsiders."[128] Although the folkloric literature frequently states that crime only begins after a well-defined onset of addiction,[129] the proposition would have little empirical backing, even if we could construct usable criteria for the onset of addiction.[130] If heroin use is a movable feast, engaged in by individuals who can switch among crimes, employment, and drugs, then we cannot draw any conclusions, favorable or unfavorable, about the impact of legalization on crime rates. According to one study, individuals entering methadone treatment have lower arrest rates for nondrug crimes during treatment, but afterward arrest rates rise to about 70 percent of pretreatment levels.[131] Epstein cites an unpublished study's findings that the only criminal charges (against those younger users admitted into a methadone program) that declined

124. Harold Finestone, "Narcotics and Criminality," *Law and Contemporary Problems* 22 (1957): 69–85, esp. 74, 80–81; Carl D. Chambers, "Narcotic Addiction and Crime: An Empirical Review," in James Inciardi, ed., *Drugs and the Criminal Justice System* (Beverly Hills, Calif.: Sage, 1974), pp. 125–42.

125. Isidor Chein et al., *The Road to H* (New York: Basic Books, 1964), p. 65.

126. Finestone, "Narcotics and Criminality."

127. Douglas Coate and Fred Goldman, "The Impact of Drug Addiction on Criminal Earnings," in Leveson, ed., *Quantitative Explorations in Drug Abuse Policy,* chap. 4.

128. Goldstein, "Getting Over," p. 82.

129. David P. Ausubel, *Drug Addiction* (New York: Random House, 1958), pp. 67–69.

130. Goldman, "Drug Abuse, Crime and Economics," p. 177.

131. Robert M. J. Haglund and Charles Froland, "Relationship between Addict Crime and Drug Treatment: Two Cohorts Examined," *American Journal of Drug and Alcohol Abuse* 5 (1978): 455–62.

were for drugs, forgery, and prostitution.[132] I have been unable to collect reasonable data on the amount of law enforcement resources that would be freed for the apprehension of other criminals after legalization.[133] More important, it is hard to estimate the marginal deterrent effect on predatory crime of an increase in police resources devoted to controlling it.

Employment

The work incentives of opiate users, as reported by hostile parties, have changed radically with the politics of their times. According to a contemporary authority, an addict "characteristically becomes lethargic, slovenly, undependable, and devoid of ambition."[134] By contrast, at the turn of the century opium became illegal in the United States, in large part due to the efforts of Samuel Gompers. He claimed that its use by Chinese immigrants so increased their productivity that whites were at a disadvantage in the labor market. Additionally, it increased their risk-taking proclivity, as virtually all Chinese were alleged to be heavy gamblers.[135] In reality, the period between the Civil War and World War I was the period of America's greatest sustained proportional economic growth. It was characterized by low unemployment rates, legal opium, and a large population of habitual users. The same was true of Victorian England.

People's choices of work and leisure, or of occupations or employers, are fundamentally dependent on the alternatives available. An individual who works legally gives up the possibility of some illegally obtained income. One who can support a $30/day habit and $10/day in living expenses[136] from illegal activity is earning an income of $14,600 per year, which puts him considerably above any reasonably defined poverty level. An obsession with the concept of addiction leads us to forget that in all but the shortest of runs the money is voluntarily spent on this bundle of goods. Relative to le-

132. Edward Jay Epstein, "Methadone: The Forlorn Hope," *The Public Interest* 36 (Summer 1974): 3–24, esp. 11.

133. Fujii estimates the cost of enforcing the heroin laws at $20.8 million in California in 1970. The assumptions he uses to make the estimate are untenable. See his "Public Investment in the Rehabilitation of Heroin Addicts," p. 50.

134. Ausubel, *Drug Addiction*, p. 13.

135. Szasz, *Ceremonial Chemistry*, pp. 69–75.

136. The proportionate breakdown between drug and other expenses is that cited by Moore, *Buy and Bust*, p. 85.

gitimate alternatives, the street may offer a superior financial incentive and work environment, if this is one's preferred consumption bundle. Given the uncertainty associated with the supply and quality of drugs, a more public life-style is probably a method of reducing one's search costs for drugs and becoming more cognizant of earning opportunities.

Unemployment by the federal definition is not synonymous with leisure for the typical heroin user. As Goldstein notes in his detailed study of the daily lives of 51 of them,[137] they are always on the alert for peculiar circumstances of time and place that will enable them to "get over," i.e., succeed economically for the day. The workplace in which this occurs is unquestionably a competitive one. If heroin use produces an all-consuming lethargy, it is difficult to explain how an addict can support his habit.[138] Those with better opportunities away from drug use are more likely to attempt treatment for their habits. In 1980, 56 percent of all enrollees in heroin treatment programs claimed to have twelve or more years of education.[139]

Even today, those with appropriate skills can support their habits by working, although regular employment probably increases the time-cost of a heroin purchase. The relatively high frequency of use in the health professions[140] may reflect their members' lower full cost of obtaining drugs. For users in less renumerative positions, crime supplements work income. Additionally, size of habit appears to be positively correlated with work income.[141] Although the above gives some reason to be hopeful, we cannot even qualitatively predict the effects of legalization on work time and effort. Cheapening heroin implies that an individual will be more disposed to consume it, an activity that requires both heroin and time. Lowering the value of heroin search time relative to the value of work time, taken by itself, will lead to an increase in work. Which of the two effects will dominate cannot be determined *a priori*. The actual consumption pattern

137. Goldstein, "Getting Over."
138. Economic principles of specialization also seem to hold for the generation of user income. Over 50 percent of the income from predatory crime acquired by the users Goldstein studied ("Getting Over," p. 70) was earned by less than 20 percent of the group. For those active in the distribution chain, there are a variety of specialized roles (ibid., pp. 71–74).
139. NIDA, *Data from the Client-Oriented Data Acquisition Process, Annual Data 1980*, p. 6.
140. Eldridge, *Narcotics and the Law*, p. 27.
141. Goldman, "Drug Abuse, Crime and Economics," pp. 170–72.

of Chinese opium smokers was typically one of moderate use after the day's work was finished.[142] Their world, however, was characterized by minimal uncertainty about quality or availability.

SUMMARY AND CONCLUSIONS

In several important respects, the prohibition on heroin has clearly been effective. It has imposed a structure of supply and distribution whose complexity and costs are very high relative to those that would be seen in an unregulated market. What we know about the technology and history of supply indicates that after legalization the market would be workably competitive. With no patented production processes or monopolized inputs, the market would be open to any newcomer willing to make an investment in it. With no discernibly great economies of scale or scope in the unregulated market, it is unlikely that monopoly would result. In the existing market, illegality makes the economically optimal distribution chain a peculiarly high-cost one, i.e., one dependent on the use of addicts as agents. This too would end with legalization.

Illegality may have imposed high costs on the supply side of the market, but without knowledge of demand conditions we cannot say anything about how effectively it has curbed the use of heroin. If users truly are addicts and must support their habits regardless of price, the illegality will have done no more than raise the expense of obtaining the same quantity that would have been sold to them under a regime of legality. It is clear that such a simplistic characterization of users is incorrect, and that demand in the market is not perfectly inelastic. Existing estimates of demand elasticity, however, are unable to give us usable predictions about the consequences of a price drop of the magnitude that would follow legalization. Additionally, demographic patterns of use change rapidly and vary widely among cultures. Such instability of demand is difficult to capture in the economist's market model and adds an even greater hazard to predicting the consequences of legalization.

To predict those consequences numerically requires that we have a reasonably accurate statistical picture of the existing market at our disposal. While they are frequently circulated and quoted with alarm,

142. John C. Kramer, "Speculations on the Nature and Pattern of Opium Smoking," *Journal of Drug Issues* 12 (Spring 1979): 247–55.

figures on the numbers of users and the volume of crime for which they are responsible are meaningless political constructs. They are highly sensitive to the use of arbitrary assumptions and are dependent on surveys or registers whose methodology is questionable and whose coverage is poor. Judicial and legislative testimony about the market invariably comes either from self-interested former participants or self-styled experts whom only a television reporter could take seriously. Some of the literature alleges that the statistics overstate the problem, while the remainder claims that they conceal a much larger one. No one outside of elective office assumes they are correct.

If we know little about the extent of heroin use, we know even less about the careers of users, in particular about their criminal habits and other sources of income. The case for almost any type of public policy toward heroin depends in large part on the strength of the correlation between crime and heroin use. Such a correlation is both hard to find in the literature and inconsistent with the actual experience of crime during "epidemics" of heroin use. Because we know so little about the user population, we cannot say much about that fraction of users known to support their habits through legal employment, or how that fraction would change after legalization. It is hard to think of an unskilled individual as unindustrious if he is attempting to support his habit at today's prices.

All statistics are imperfect, but those related to drug use are egregiously bad. There is some room for improving the latter at reasonable cost,[143] but little reason to expect that this will be done.[144] The suppliers and demanders of meaningless statistics are both heavily concentrated in government, and what numbers appear in newsprint do so as the consequence of a carefully orchestrated process. As a typical voter, I have so little influence on electoral outcomes that it is not worth my while to ascertain the actual magnitude of the heroin problem, if one exists. As a comparison, consider the activity of the U.S. Census Bureau. A large number of individuals outside of government (e.g., marketing experts) have an interest in accurate demographic statistics, and ultimately a biased or incomplete federal census imposes on them costs that will lead to pressure for accuracy. There is no such well-defined set of losers from poor heroin statistics.

---

143. GAO, *Report to the Attorney General.*
144. Reuter, "The (Continued) Vitality of Mythical Numbers."

The pattern has been seen time and again. If the specious figures on oil reserves announced at the start of the "energy crisis" were correct, America would have by now been immobilized and frozen. The "crisis," of course, was no more than an attempt to politicize and bureaucratize the allocation of a good for which market conditions had changed. As an issue loses political saliency, the crisis fades away. We thus move from one statistical crisis to another— from vanishing farmland to environmental cancer to heroin epidemics to illegal aliens. Some of these matters may actually be problems on which accurate statistics could shed considerable light. The policy-making process, however, is unlikely to produce either good statistics or good policy.

9

THE MORALITY
OF DRUG CONTROLS

Thomas Szasz

In wise hands, poison is medicine; in foolish hands, medicine is poison.

—Casanova

DRUG CONTROL AS A MORAL ISSUE

Traditionally, in Judeo-Christian cultures, sexual behavior has constituted the core concern of morality, with other aspects of personal conduct occupying distinctly peripheral positions. This reigning role of sex in the moral calculus of our forebears is exemplified by the parable of the Fall. Although that act has always been interpreted, no doubt correctly, as referring to sexual intercourse between man and woman, it is important to remember that the Bible writers did not name that "crime" directly but only alluded to it through the metaphor of partaking of the Forbidden Fruit.

Inasmuch as that primal act of defiance of God's authority has always been couched in metaphorical terms, it has not proved overly difficult to replace sex with drugs in the grand morality play of human existence. No longer are men, women, and children tempted, corrupted, and ruined by the irresistibly sweet pleasures of sex; instead, they are tempted, corrupted, and ruined by the irresistibly sweet pleasures of drugs. Thus, youth's defiance of adult authority and, more generally, man's defiance of societal conventions, is now enacted through ceremonies of drug use, called "drug abuse"; at the same time the collective celebration of the legitimacy and power of parental, societal, and scientific authority is now enacted through the counterceremonies of drug controls, called the "war on drugs."

THE WAR ON DRUGS

Ostensibly, the war on drugs is a struggle against "dangerous" drugs. But the substances we now call "drugs" are simply the products of nature (for example, coca leaves) or of human inventiveness (for example, LSD). They are material objects—leaves and liquids, powders and pills—like trees or trucks. How, then, can human beings wage war against drugs? One would have to be blind not to recognize that the war on drugs must be a metaphorical war. But that cannot be all there is to it. Another part of the story has to do with our stubborn determination not to come to grips with what a drug is: in other words, with our refusal to recognize that the term "drug" is not only a medical but also a political concept.

In order to appreciate this, all we need to do is ask, for example, what is the difference between lithium as the third element in the Periodic Table of Elements and lithium as a now-fashionable "antipsychotic" medication? The difference between them is, of course, the same as between description and prescription, fact and value, science and politics. In short, while seemingly the word "drug" is a part of the vocabulary of science, it is even more importantly a part of the vocabulary of politics. This explains why there is no such thing—why, indeed, there can be no such thing—as a "neutral" drug: A drug is either good or bad, effective or ineffective, therapeutic or noxious, licit or illicit. Precisely herein lie the vast powers of drugs in modern societies: We deploy them simultaneously as technical tools in our fight against medical diseases and as scapegoats in our struggle for personal security and political stability.

If history teaches us anything at all, it teaches us that human beings have a powerful need to form groups and that the sacrificial victimization of scapegoats is often an indispensable ingredient for maintaining social cohesion among the members of such groups. Perceived as the very embodiment of evil, the scapegoat's actual characteristics or behavior are thus impervious to rational analysis. Since the scapegoat is evil, the good citizen's task is not to understand him (or her, or it), but to hate him and to rid the community of him. Attempts to analyze and grasp such a ritual purgation of society of its scapegoats is perceived as disloyalty to, or even an attack on, the "compact majority" and its best interests.

In my opinion, the American "war on drugs" represents merely a new variation in humanity's age-old passion to "purge" itself of its "impurities" by staging vast dramas of scapegoat persecutions.[1] In the past, we have witnessed religious or "holy" wars waged against people who professed the wrong faith; more recently, we have witnessed racial or "eugenic" wars, waged against people who possessed the wrong genetic makeup; now we are witnessing a medical or "therapeutic" war, waged against people who use the wrong drugs.

Let us not forget that the modern state is a political apparatus with a monopoly on waging war: It selects its enemies, declares war on them, and thrives on the enterprise. In saying this I am, of course, merely repeating Randolph Bourne's now classic observation that "war is the health of the State. It automatically sets in motion throughout society those irresistible forces for uniformity, for passionate cooperation with the Government in coercing into obedience the minority groups and individuals which lack the larger herd sense."[2]

Let us not forget, too, that only fifty years have passed since Hitler incited the German people against the Jews—by "explaining" the various ways in which the Jews were "dangerous" to the Germans individually and to Germany as a nation. Millions of Germans—among them leaders in science, in medicine, in law, in the media—came to believe in the reality of the "dangerous Jew." Indeed, they more than believed in it; they loved the imagery of that racial myth, felt exhilarated by the increased self-esteem and solidarity it gave them, and were thrilled by the prospect of "cleansing" the nation of its "racial impurities." Today, hardly anyone in Germany believes

1. T. S. Szasz, *The Manufacture of Madness: A Comparative Study of the Inquisition and the Mental Health Movement* (New York: Harper & Row, 1970), esp. pp. 242–75.
2. R. Bourne, *The Radical Will: Selected Writings, 1911–1918* (New York: Urizen Books, 1977), p. 360.

the myth of the "dangerous Jew"—a change in point of view that surely had nothing to do with more research on, or fresh scientific discoveries about, the problem of "dangerous Jews."

Mutatis mutandis, every American president since John F. Kennedy, and countless other American politicians, have incited the American people against "dangerous drugs"—by "explaining" the various ways in which such drugs threaten Americans individually and the United States as a nation. Millions of Americans—among them leaders in science, in medicine, in law, in the media—believe in the reality of "dangerous drugs." Indeed, they more than believe in it: They love the imagery of this pharmacological myth and are inspired by the prospect of cleansing the nation of illicit drugs. In short, we are now in the midst of a medical or "therapeutic" war waged against "drugs" and the people who sell and buy them.

THE "DRUG" AS SCAPEGOAT

In 1980, crime and violence, long endemic to New York City, erupted in a new epidemic. Singly and in packs, hoodlums rampaged through the subways and the commuter trains, ripping gold chains off the necks of women. One such public mass robbery was described as follows: "Seconds after a packed Amtrak passenger train collided with a freight train last night, a wave of chain-snatching broke out at the scene. Gold chains and purses were ripped from commuters in a second passenger train, which screeched to a halt behind the Amtrak wreck near Dobbs Ferry."[3]

The public was horrified. The police were helpless. Although (New York State) Governor Hugh Carey could offer neither protection for the public nor compensation for the victims, he could—and did—offer an explanation for this mayhem. "The epidemic of gold-snatching in the city," he declared, "is the result of a Russian design to wreck America by flooding the nation with deadly heroin. In the streets, you know what's going on. Women are afraid to walk with a chain around their neck. Why? Somebody's grabbing that chain to get enough money for a fix. . . . [If the Russians] were using nerve gas on us, we'd certainly call out the troops. This is more insidious than nerve gas. Nerve gas passes off. This doesn't. It kills. I'm not overstating the case."[4]

3. *New York Post,* 8 November 1980, p. 5.
4. *New York Post,* 26 September 1980, p. 10.

When Governor Carey spoke these words (at a press conference in New York City on September 25, 1980), the American war against "dangerous drugs," especially heroin, had been going on for more than a quarter of a century. The political rhetoric about "drug abuse," the medical mendacity about "drug rehabilitation," the legislative prohibition of "illicit drugs," and the judicial persecution of drug users ("addicts") and drug sellers ("pushers"), aided and abetted by the popular media intoxicated with a blind faith in a holy war against unholy drugs—all this has been going on for much longer than the First and Second World Wars combined; much longer than Prohibition, or Nazism, or the war in Vietnam. Still, America's war against "dangerous drugs"—which has spread to Europe, to Australia, to Japan, and to any Third World nation the U.S. government is able to intimidate—shows no signs of letting up. Alas, Governor Carey's comments are simply the most immoderate example of the views commonly voiced by government officials when discussing the drug "problem."

The result is that the public is regularly faced with self-intoxicated politicians, posing as protectors of the people. Moreover, although the public is indeed endangered, it is endangered not by the threat from which the politician promises protection, but by the threat from which the politician is quite unable to protect it because he himself (together with his fellow politicians) has helped to create and unleash it. For the people from whom we need protection—those who are robbing, maiming, and killing us—are not foreign "drug pushers," as our protectors claim, but American thugs. Obviously, for anyone not in the grip of the scapegoater's ideology, the now fashionable antidrug exhortations are nothing but propaganda of the cheapest sort.

A SYNOPTIC HISTORY OF THE WAR ON DRUGS, 1974–1984

To appreciate better the nature and scope of current American drug controls, the context in which politicians continually seek to escalate the war on drugs while people continue to support it, and the cancerous growth of unenforceable and unenforced drug prohibitions that have resulted from this mad scramble for protection from "dangerous drugs"—I shall next present, in synoptic form, a series of illustrative excerpts from newspapers, magazines, and books.[5] (For the sake of brevity I am limiting the following summary to the last decade, that is, the period from 1974 until 1984.)

1974   An article in the *American Journal of Psychiatry* advocates treating alcoholism in American Indians with peyote (an illicit drug), because it "offers the alcoholic Indian both occupational and cultural therapy including participation in the services of the Native American Church (peyote meetings)."[6]

1975   Jerome H. Jaffe, former top White House drug abuse official, "urge[s] that people who smoke a pack [of cigarettes] a day or more be described as suffering from a 'compulsive smoking disorder.'" To a Third World Conference on Smoking and Health, Jaffe explains that "a new term—'compulsive smoking syndrome'—has been proposed as a disorder to be listed in the Diagnostic and Statistical Manual of the American Psychiatric Association."[7]

The family of Frank Olson, a civilian biochemist who died in 1953 after being drugged, without his knowledge or consent, in a secret CIA project involving psychoactive substances, settles its claim against the U.S. government "in return for a payment of $1.25 million and the release of all CIA files concerning the case."[8]

1976   An article in the *New York Times Magazine* entitled "Valiumania" warns that "Americans are spending almost half a billion dollars a year on a drug [Valium] to relieve their anxiety—a fact that is in itself a considerable cause for anxiety."[9]

It is revealed that between 1972 and 1975, the United States government "has helped to pay for the shipment overseas of hundreds of tons of pesticides so poisonous that they are not permitted to be used in the United States. . . . Leptophos, DDT, aldrin, heptachlor, and chlordane were all included on the list of commodities for which U.S. government financing

5. For more details, see T. S. Szasz, *Ceremonial Chemistry: The Ritual Persecution of Drugs, Addicts, and Pushers* (Garden City, N.Y.: Doubleday, 1974), pp. 183–212.

6. B. J. Albaugh and P. O. Anderson, "Peyote in the Treatment of Alcoholism Among American Indians," *American Journal of Psychiatry* 131 (1974): 1247.

7. *New York Times*, 5 June 1975, p. 38.

8. *International Herald-Tribune*, 20–21 December 1975, p. 3.

9. *New York Times Magazine*, 1 February 1976, p. 34.

was available to foreign buyers. The use of these chemicals either has never been authorized or has been sharply circumscribed."[10]

1977   A British story on the war against laetrile reports that "U.S. Federal Marshals last month seized 50 tons of apricot stones . . . probably the largest seizure of an illegal drug base in the history of U.S. law enforcement."[11]

The Labor Department directs employers with federal contracts "to take 'affirmative action' to hire alcoholics and drug abusers. . . . Alcoholics and drug abusers are covered by the 1973 Rehabilitation Act, which protects 'handicapped people' against job discrimination. 'Employers who fail to consider qualified alcoholics and drug abusers for employment because of their handicap are clearly violating the law,' Mr. Elisburg [Donald Elisburg, assistant secretary of labor for employment standards] said."[12]

1978   Peter Bourne, special assistant to the president [Carter] and director of the White House Office of Drug Abuse Policy, writes an illegal prescription for Quaaludes for one of his aides and is forced to resign. On leaving the White House, he tells the press that there is a "high incidence of marijuana use . . . [and] occasional use of cocaine" by members of the White House staff.[13]

1979   In Jacksonville, Florida, actress Linda Blair is "ordered to become a crusader against drug abuse as part of her probation after pleading guilty to a federal misdemeanor charge of conspiracy to possess cocaine."[14]

1980   Dr. Lee Macht, a Harvard professor of psychiatry who treated David Kennedy, admits that "he prescribed drugs illegally to the 24-year-old nephew of Senator Edward Kennedy. . . . [He is] fined $1,000 and . . . his license to prescribe Class 2 drugs [is] suspended for at least one year. The Middlesex County assistant district attorney said that at least 50 prescrip-

10. *International Herald-Tribune,* 9 December 1976, p. 1.

11. J. T. M. Murphy-Ferris and L. Torrey, "The Apricot Connection," *New Scientist* (London), 30 June 1977, p. 766.

12. *International Herald-Tribune,* 7 June 1977, p. 4.

13. T. S. Szasz, *The Therapeutic State: Psychiatry in the Mirror of Current Events* (Buffalo, N.Y.: Prometheus Books, 1984), pp. 284–96.

14. *International Herald-Tribune,* 7 September 1979, p. 16.

tions over a 2½-year period were written for the young Kennedy, involving the drugs Percodan, Dilaudid . . . and Quaaludes.''[15]

Japan agrees to provide concessions to the U.S. tobacco industry "that could increase sales there from $35 million to about $350 million [annually].'' In a new trade agreement announced by Steve Lande, assistant U.S. trade representative for bilateral affairs, Japan would "reduce tariffs on cigarettes . . . increase the number of retailers selling imported tobacco products . . . [and] permit U.S. companies to advertise in Japan.''[16]

Christopher Lawford, son of Peter Lawford and Patricia Kennedy Lawford and nephew of Senator Edward Kennedy, is arraigned in Boston on a charge of possessing heroin.[17]

1981   Responding to questions concerning the problems created by the PCB contamination of a state office building in Binghamton, New York, Governor Hugh Carey volunteers "to drink a glass of PCB's . . . to demonstrate that the building was safe. 'I offer here and now [said Carey] to walk into Binghamton or any part of that building and swallow an entire glass of PCB's.'"[18]

Janet Cooke, a *Washington Post* reporter, wins a Pulitzer Prize for her story entitled "8-Year-Old Heroin Addict Lives for a Fix,'' which turns out to be a complete fabrication. The *Post*'s executive editor, Benjamin Bradlee, attributes the fraud to mental illness, explaining to an interviewer: "We're going to take care of her. We're going to see that she has professional help.''[19]

The U.S. Supreme Court upholds the constitutionality of "a 40-year prison sentence imposed on a Virginia man for possession and distribution of nine ounces of marijuana worth about $200. The unsigned decision, which the Court reached by a vote of 6 to 3 . . . reverses ruling by two lower Federal courts that the sentence was so harsh in proportion to the

15. *International Herald-Tribune,* 21 January 1980, p. 16.
16. *Washington Post,* 22 November 1980, p. C-1.
17. *International Herald-Tribune,* 17 December 1980, p. 16.
18. *New York Times,* 5 March 1981, p. B2.
19. T. S. Szasz, "The Protocols of the Learned Experts on Heroin,'' *Libertarian Review,* July 1981, p. 297; reprinted in Szasz, *The Therapeutic State,* p. 297.

crime as to violate the Eighth Amendment's prohibition against cruel and unusual punishment.''[20]

In Tucson, Arizona, a 21-year-old man is sentenced to two years in prison for sniffing paint, under an Arizona law that reads: "A person shall not knowingly breathe, inhale, or drink a vapor-releasing substance containing a toxic substance." Police and prosecutors are said to favor the law because "intoxicated sniffers can grow violent."[21]

An editorial in the *New York Post* declares: "Drugs are now the scourge of our society. . . . [Parents] should ask their children this question: What did John Belushi have in common with Elvis Presley, Freddie Prinze, Janis Joplin, Jimi Hendrix, Billie Holiday, Lenny Bruce, Frankie Lymon, Miguel Berrios, and Charlie Parker? Answer: They all took drugs and they all killed themselves doing so."[22]

1983   The Drug Enforcement Agency acknowledges using entrapment in fighting the war on drugs. "Federal drug agents seeking to draw out potential producers of hallucinogens and other illicit drugs have been operating bogus chemical companies that sell materials and instructions for the manufacture of such dangerous drugs. Then they arrest their customers. . . . The tactic . . . has already led to convictions."[23]

John V. Lindsay, Jr., son of former New York City Mayor John V. Lindsay, is sentenced to six months in prison for selling three grams of cocaine to an undercover agent.[24]

1984   In Rapid City, South Dakota, Robert F. Kennedy, Jr., a former assistant district attorney in New York City, pleads guilty to a felony charge of possessing heroin.[25]

Responding to David Kennedy's suicide (with an overdose of cocaine, Demerol, and Mellaril), New York City Mayor Edward Koch demands the death penalty for "drug dealers." Kennedy, Koch declares, " 'was killed by a drug pusher. I believe the person who sold him those drugs is guilty of murder.'

20. *New York Times,* 13 January 1982, p. B-15.
21. *Ithaca Journal,* 11 February 1982, p. 29.
22. *New York Post,* 10 March 1982, p. 24.
23. *New York Times,* 11 August 1983, p. A-1.
24. *Syracuse Herald-Journal,* 1 October 1983, p. A-9.
25. *New York Times,* 18 February 1984, p. A-8.

. . . Koch said he wanted to see capital punishment for such crimes on a national level."[26]

School officials order the suspension of any Wilmington, Massachusetts, high school student "caught with drugs—including aspirin and over-the-counter medications." The rule, "written with the help of the U.S. Drug Enforcement Administration . . . requires students to store drugs and pills in the school clinic." Robert Stutmant, head of the Boston office of the DEA, explained that the ruling was required because "a drop of LSD can be concealed in an aspirin tablet."[27]

Speaking in the House Rayburn Office Building, Democratic presidential candidate Walter F. Mondale "accuses President Reagan of failing 'to match tough talk with tough action' in fighting illicit drug traffic." Mondale promises that, if elected, "he would direct the armed forces to join in the war on drugs. . . . 'I will get tough on foreign countries that continue to produce the drugs that kill American kids,' he said. 'In my Administration, no country will receive foreign aid or military assistance unless it follows a plan to stop producing or peddling narcotics.'"[28]

According to a survey conducted by the New York State Division of Substance Abuse Services, 31 percent of seventh grade students "reported using a drug before reaching that grade. About 60 percent of all students responding to the survey said they had at least one experience with illicit drugs." At the same time, it was reported that New York City police and school officials agreed "to send undercover police officers into city high schools in search of drug dealers. . . . [The officers would] impersonate teachers, custodians, or students."[29]

DRUG CONTROLS

As the evidence cited so far illustrates, and as I shall now try to demonstrate, it is a serious error to view currently fashionable drug controls as most people now view them and as their proponents want

26. *Syracuse Herald-Journal,* 1 May 1984, p. A-2.
27. *Washington Post,* 8 September 1984, p. A-16.
28. *New York Times,* 4 October 1984, p. B-17.
29. Ibid., 18 October 1984, pp. A-1, B-3, B-7.

us to view them, namely, as if they were similar to measures aimed against the spread of, say, typhoid fever by contaminated water or food. Instead of resembling controls based on objective (technical, scientific) considerations, contemporary drug controls resemble the prohibition of countless substances whose control rests on religious (ritual, social) considerations. In this connection, we must not forget that there is hardly any object or behavior that has not been prohibited somewhere, some time, and whose prohibition was not viewed by those who believed in it and enforced it as rational, that is, as theologically or scientifically "valid." The following is but a brief and quite incomplete list of such prohibitions, with a few comments about them.

Taboo and Avoidance: Some Examples of Ritual Prohibitions

The dietary laws set forth in the Old Testament, which form one of the pillars of Judaism, prohibit the ingestion of numerous edible things. Although conformity to these rules is now often rationalized on historical-hygienic grounds, they have nothing whatever to do with health; instead, they have to do with holiness, that is, with being dutiful toward God, in an effort to gain His favor. By glorifying what one may or may not eat as a matter of the gravest concern to an all-caring deity, true believers elevate ordinary events—say, eating a shrimp cocktail—to acts that are, spiritually speaking, matters of life and death. Similar proscriptions of food characterize other religions—for example, Muslims are forbidden to eat pork, Hindus to eat beef.

Most religious codes also proscribe, as well as prescribe, certain drinks. Jewish and Christian religious ceremonies require the use of alcohol, which, in turn, is forbidden in the Koran. When secular alcohol-prohibition is superimposed on Judeo-Christian customs, the result is the banning of a substance that, at the same time, is recognized to be indispensable for religious (and, usually, medical) purposes.

Like eating and drinking, sexual activity is a basic human urge whose free exercise, with some exceptions, has also been closely controlled by custom, religion, and law. Among the forms of sexual activity that have been, or are still, forbidden, the following spring quickly to mind: masturbation; homosexuality; heterosexual intercourse outside of marriage; heterosexual intercourse with the sole purpose of sexual enjoyment; heterosexual intercourse with the use of condoms, diaphragms, or other "artificial" birth control devices; nongenital heterosexual intercourse; incest; and prostitution. For about two hundred years—well into the twentieth century— self-abuse (as masturbation was then called) was thought to be the greatest threat to the medical and moral well-being of mankind. Preoccupation with self-abuse, both popular and professional, has since been displaced by a similar preoccupation with drug abuse.

Verbal and pictorial representation of certain ideas or images are perhaps the prime products of human inventiveness prohibited by human inventiveness. This behavior, too, has its roots in religious ritual, exemplified by the Jewish prohibition against graven images, that is, making pictures of God and hence of man, created in His image. This is why, prior to the modern era, there were no Jewish painters or sculptors. With the development of literacy among the laity, the Catholic church quickly "criminalized" translating the Bible into the "vulgar" tongues. Thus, in the fifteenth century, possessing an English Bible was an offense much like possessing heroin is today, except that the penalty for it was death by burning at the stake. Since then, there followed an almost limitless variety of prohibitions against the printed word and the painted picture, such as prohibitions of blasphemy, heresy, subversion, sedition, obscenity, pornography, and so forth; these prohibitions have been implemented by such institutionalized interventions as the Roman Catholic Index of Prohibited Books, the Comstock laws (in the United States), the Nazi book burnings, and the censorship policies of the various communist countries.

Money, as precious metal or paper, is another product of human inventiveness widely prohibited throughout history. Although the United States is regarded as the very pillar of the Western capitalist world, owning gold was, until recently, prohibited in this country. Private ownership of this metal (in forms other than personal ornaments) is, of course, prohibited in all communist countries; and so, too, is the free movement, across national boundaries, of paper money. Prohibitions against lending money at interest are deeply ingrained in the Christian and Mohammedan religions. Charging any interest was sometimes viewed as an evil that must be proscribed; at other times, only charging "excessive" interest, called "usury," was prohibited. Interest rates charged or paid by American banks today would, of course, have been considered usurious in the Middle Ages.

Although gambling was prevalent and permitted in antiquity, in the Christian world-view it, too, came to be seen as a sin and was generally prohibited. Conducted as a private enterprise, gambling is still treated as a criminal offense in most parts of the United States; however, if it is conducted by the state—offering much poorer odds for the gambler than do private gaming establishments—it is regarded as a positively virtuous undertaking, aggressively promoted by the government.

Since the modern state has a monopoly on coercion, it is not surprising that individuals are prohibited from possessing powerful weapons, such as tanks, warships, or bombs. However, even in the politically most tightly controlled countries, individuals can own knives, sticks, ropes, automobiles, poisons, and other means useful for inflicting harm on others or oneself. Yet, it is illegal to own an empty hypodermic syringe.

In short, there is virtually no material object or human behavior that has not been found to be "dangerous" or "harmful"—to God, king, the public interest, national security, bodily health, or mental health—and thus prohibited by religious, legal, medical, or psychiatric authorities. In every case of such prohibition, we are confronted with certain ceremonial-ritual rules rationalized and justified on pragmatic-scientific grounds: Typically, we are told that such prohibitions protect the health or well-being of particularly vulnerable individuals or groups; actually, the rules protect the well-being—that is, the integrity—of the community as a whole (which is what is meant by saying that certain behavioral rules have a ceremonial function).

The Danger in "Dangerous Drugs"

In what way are drugs a danger to Americans individually or to the United States as a nation? What do the officially persecuted drugs—especially heroin, cocaine, and marijuana—do that is so different from what other drugs do? And if these drugs are such a grave danger to Americans, why were they not a danger to them in, say, 1940 or 1900? Anyone who reflects on these matters must realize that our culturally accepted drugs—in particular, alcohol, tobacco, and "mind-altering" drugs legitimated as "psychotherapeutic"—pose a much graver threat, and cause much more demonstrable harm, to people than do the prohibited or so-called dangerous drugs.

There are, of course, complex religious, historical, and economic reasons, which we cannot consider here, that play a part in determining which drugs people use and which they avoid. But regardless of such cultural-historical determinants, and regardless of the pharmacological properties of the "dangerous drugs" in question, one simple fact remains—namely, that no one has to ingest, inject, or smoke any of these substances unless he or she wants to do so. This simple fact compels one to see the "drug problem" in a light totally different from that in which it is now officially portrayed. The official line is that "dangerous drugs" pose an "external" threat to people—that is, a threat like a natural disaster, such as an erupting volcano or a hurricane. The inference drawn from this image is that it is the duty of a modern, scientifically enlightened state to protect its citizens from such dangers, and it is the duty of the citizens to submit to the protections so imposed on them for the benefit of the community as a whole.

But "dangerous drugs" pose no such threat. Obviously the danger posed by so-called dangerous drugs is quite unlike that posed by hurricanes or plagues, but is rather like the danger posed (to some people) by, say, eating pork or masturbating. The point is that certain threats—so-called natural disasters, in particular—strike us down as "passive victims," whereas certain other threats—for example, "forbidden" foods or sexual acts—strike us down as "active victims," that is, only if we succumb to their temptation. Thus, an Orthodox Jew may be tempted to eat a ham sandwich and a Catholic may be tempted to use artificial contraception, but that does not make most of us view pork products or birth-control devices as "dangers" from which the state should protect us. On the contrary, we believe that free access to such foods and devices is our right (or "constitutional right," as Americans put it).

In actuality—that is, at the present time, and especially in the United States—the so-called "drug problem" has several distinct dimensions. First, there is the problem posed by the pharmacological properties of the drugs in question. This problem is technical: All new scientific or practical inventions not only offer us certain solutions for old problems, but also create new problems for us. Drugs are no exception. Secondly, there is the problem posed to the individual by the temptation certain drugs present, especially those believed to possess the power to "give" pleasure. This problem is moral and psychological: Some drugs offer us certain new temptations that we must learn to resist or enjoy in moderation. They, too, are no exception. Thirdly, there is the problem posed by the prohibition of certain drugs. This problem is partly political and economic, and partly moral and psychological. Drug prohibition and persecution constitute a type of scapegoating, as discussed earlier.

Moreover, the drug prohibition itself generates a wide range of otherwise unavailable economic and existential options and opportunities. Thus, for members of the upper and middle classes, the war on drugs provides opportunities for gaining self-esteem, public recognition for benevolence, life meaning, jobs, and money. For example, it enables First Ladies (of both major parties) to play a combination of Santa Claus and Doctor Schweitzer vis-à-vis their involuntary beneficiaries, who, without the compassion and largesse of these ladies, are ostensibly unable to abstain from illegal drugs. Similarly, it enables physicians, especially psychiatrists, to claim special skills in treating the mythical disease of drug abuse, a claim politicians and others are only too eager to authenticate. These examples are, of course, only the tip of the proverbial iceberg: There is no need to list the numerous jobs in the "drug rehabilitation" racket, and their ripple effects on the economy, with which everyone is only too familiar. For members of lowest and lower classes, the war on drugs is perhaps only slightly less useful. For example, for unemployed and perhaps unemployable youngsters, the war provides an opportunity for making a living as drug dealers and, after they have recovered from "drug abuse," as drug abuse counselors; for unskilled but employable persons, it provides countless opportunities for staffing and running the infrastructure of the drug abuse empire. Last but not least, for persons at all levels of society, the war on drugs offers a ready-made opportunity for dramatizing their lives and aggrandizing their individuality by defying certain modern "medical" taboos.

The role of defiance in so-called drug abuse is, indeed, quite obvious. It is clearly displayed in the various contemporary subcultures' righteous rejection of conventional or legal drugs and its passionate embrace of the use of unconventional or illegal drugs. The perennial confrontation between authority and autonomy, the permanent tension between behavior based on submission to coercion and the free choice of one's own course in life—these basic themes of human morality and psychology are now enacted on a stage on which the principal props are drugs and laws against drugs. In this connection, the following tragedy, typical of countless similar stories reported in the press, is especially revealing.

> A young couple about to be sentenced on drug charges [possessing marijuana and cocaine] horrified a packed courtroom when they swallowed cyanide and fell dying to the floor. After the probation judge refused to grant probation, William Melton, 27, put a white powder in his mouth and collapsed seconds later. His wife, Tracey Lee, 21, walked over to her husband and patted him softly on the head and then put some cyanide powder in her own mouth. . . . They died in a local hospital. "It was crazy. It was as if they were going to the gas chamber," said court clerk Howard Smith. "They weren't even going to get a long sentence."[30]

THE POLITICS OF DRUG CONTROL

We Americans regard freedom of speech and religion as fundamental rights. Until 1914, we also regarded the freedom of choosing our diets and drugs as fundamental rights. Obviously, this is no longer true today. What is behind this fateful moral and political transformation, which has resulted in the rejection, by the overwhelming majority of Americans, of their right to self-control over their diets and drugs? How could it have come about in view of the obvious parallels between the freedom to put things into one's mind and its restriction by the state by means of censorship of the press, and the freedom to put things into one's body and its restriction by the state by means of drug controls?

The answer to these questions lies basically in the fact that our society is therapeutic in much the same sense in which medieval Spanish society was theocratic. Just as the men and women living in a theocratic society did not believe in the separation of church and state but, on the contrary, fervently embraced their union, so we, living in a therapeutic society, do not believe in the separation of medicine and the state but fervently embrace their union. The censorship of drugs follows from the latter ideology as inexorably as the censorship of books followed from the former. That explains why liberals and conservatives—and people in that imaginary center as well—all favor drug controls. In fact, persons of all political and religious convictions (save libertarians) now favor drug controls.

---

30. *New York Post,* 8 November 1980, p. 4.

Viewed as a political issue, drugs, books, and religious practices all present the same problem to a people and its rulers. The state, as the representative of a particular class or dominant ethic, may choose to embrace some drugs, some books, and some religious practices and reject the others as dangerous, depraved, demented, or devilish. Throughout history, such an arrangement has characterized most societies. Or the state, as the representative of a constitution ceremonializing the supremacy of individual choice over collective comfort, may ensure a free trade in drugs, books, and religious practices. Such an arrangement has traditionally characterized the United States. Its Constitution explicitly guarantees the right to freedom of religion and the press and it can with some justification be argued that it also implicitly guarantees the right to freedom of self-determination with respect to what we put into our bodies.

The Right to Drugs

The framers of the Constitution did not explicitly guarantee the right to take drugs for a variety of reasons, but for our purposes, two are particularly worthy of note. First, two hundred years ago medical science was not even in its infancy; medical practice was socially unorganized and therapeutically worthless. Second, there was then no conceivable danger of an alliance between medicine and the state. The very idea that the government should lend its police power to physicians to deprive people of their free choice to ingest certain substances would have seemed absurd to the drafters of the Bill of Rights.

This conjecture is strongly supported by a casual remark by Thomas Jefferson, clearly indicating that he regarded our freedom to put into our bodies whatever we want as essentially similar to our freedom to put into our minds whatever we want. "Was the government to prescribe to us our medicine and diet," wrote Jefferson in 1782, "our bodies would be in such keeping as our souls are now. Thus in France the emetic was once forbidden as a medicine, the potato as an article of food."[31]

Jefferson poked fun at the French for their pioneering efforts to

31. T. Jefferson, "Notes on the State of Virginia" (1781), in A. Koch and W. Peden, eds., *The Life and Selected Writings of Thomas Jefferson* (New York: Modern Library, 1944), p. 275.

prohibit drugs and diets. What, then, would he think of the state that now forbids the use of harmless sweeteners while encouraging the use of dangerous contraceptives? That labels marijuana a narcotic and prohibits it while calling tobacco an agricultural product and promoting it? That defines the voluntary use of heroin as a disease and the legally coerced use of methadone as a treatment for it?

Freedom of religion is indeed a political idea of transcendent importance. As that idea has been understood in the United States, it does not mean that members of the traditional churches—that is, Christians, Jews, and Muslims—may practice their faith unmolested by the government but that others—for example, Jehovah's Witnesses—may not. American religious freedom is effectively unconditional; it is not contingent on any particular church proving, to the satisfaction of the state, that its principles or practices possess "religious efficacy." The requirement that the supporters of a religion establish its theological credentials in order to be tolerated is the hallmark of a theological state. The fact that we accept the requirement that the supporters of a drug establish its therapeutic credentials before we tolerate its sale or use shows that we live in a therapeutic state.

The argument that people need the protection of the state from dangerous drugs but not from dangerous ideas is unpersuasive. No one has to ingest any drug he does not want, just as no one has to read a book he does not want. Insofar as the state assumes control over such matters, it can only be in order to subjugate its citizens—by protecting them from temptation, as befits children, and by preventing them from assuming self-determination over their lives, as befits an enslaved population.

The Fear of Drugs

Conventional wisdom now approves—indeed, assumes as obvious—that it is the legitimate business of the state to control certain substances we take into our bodies, especially so-called psychoactive drugs. According to this view, as the state must, for the benefit of society, control dangerous persons, so it must also control dangerous drugs. The obvious fallacy in this analogy is obscured by the riveting together of the notions of dangerous drugs and dangerous acts: As a result, people now "know" that dangerous drugs cause people to behave dangerously and that it is just as much the duty of the state to protect its citizens from dope as it is to protect them from murder and theft. The trouble is that all these supposed facts are false.

Today, the average person does not want to keep an open mind about drug controls. Instead of thinking about the problem, he tends to dismiss it with some cliché such as, "Don't tell me that heroin is not a dangerous drug!" He thus implies or indeed asserts, "Don't tell me that it doesn't make good sense to prohibit its production, sale, and possession!"

What is wrong with this argument? Quite simply, everything. In the first place, the proposition that heroin is dangerous must be qualified and placed in relation to the dangerousness of other drugs and other artifacts that are not drugs. Second, the social policy that heroin should be prohibited does not follow, as a matter of logic, from the proposition that it is dangerous (even if it is "dangerous").

Admittedly, heroin is more dangerous than aspirin, in the sense that it gives more pleasure to its users than does aspirin; heroin is therefore more likely than aspirin to be taken for the self-induction of euphoria. Heroin is also more dangerous than aspirin in the sense that it is easier to kill oneself with it; heroin is therefore more likely to be used for committing suicide.

The fact that people take heroin to make themselves feel happy or high—and use other psychoactive drugs for their mind-altering effects—raises a simple but basic issue that the drug-prohibitionists like to avoid, namely: What is wrong with people using drugs for that purpose? Why shouldn't people make themselves happy by means of self-medication? Let me say at once that I believe these are questions to which honest and reasonable men may offer different answers. For example, some people say that individuals should not take heroin because it diverts them from doing productive work, making those who use the drugs, as well as those economically dependent on them, burdens on society. Others say that whether individuals use, abuse, or avoid heroin is, unless they harm others, their private business. And still others opt for a compromise between the total prohibition of heroin and a free trade in it.

There is, however, more to the prohibitionist's position than his concern that hedonic drugs seduce people from hard labor to happy leisure. Actually, the objects we now call "dangerous drugs" are metaphors for all that we consider sinful and wicked; that is why they are prohibited, rather than because they are demonstrably more harmful than countless other objects in the environment that do not now symbolize sin for us. In this connection, it is instructive to consider the cultural metamorphosis we have undergone during the past half-century, shifting our symbols of sin from sexuality to chemistry.

Indeed, our present views on drugs, especially psychoactive drugs, are strikingly similar to our former views on sex, especially masturbation. Until relatively recently, masturbation—or self-abuse, as it used to be called—was professionally declared, and popularly accepted, as both the cause and the symptom of a variety of illnesses, especially insanity. Today no medical authority accepts, much less supports, this concept of self-abuse. However, no medical authority now questions, much less rejects, the concept of drug abuse. On the contrary, expert medical opinion now holds that drug abuse is a major medical, psychiatric, and public-health problem. Conventional wisdom maintains that (1) drug addiction is a disease similar to diabetes, requiring prolonged (or lifelong) and medically carefully supervised treatment; (2) taking or not taking drugs is primarily a matter of medical concern and responsibility; and (3) doctors cannot discharge their responsibility for controlling and "curing" drug abuse unless the state empowers them to use fraud and force to combat this worldwide "plague."

A CRITIQUE OF DRUG CONTROLS

Like any social policy, drug controls, or antidrug laws, may be examined from two entirely different points of view: technical and moral. Our present inclination is either to ignore the moral perspective or to mistake the technical for the moral.

Illustrative of our misplaced overreliance on a technical approach to the so-called drug problem is the professionalized mendacity about the dangerousness of certain types of drugs. Since most propagandists against drug abuse seek to justify their repressive policies by appeals to the alleged dangerousness of various drugs, they falsify the facts about the pharmacological properties of the drugs they seek to prohibit. They do so for two reasons: first, because many substances in daily use are just as harmful as the substances they want to prohibit; second, because they realize that dangerousness alone is never a sufficiently persuasive argument to justify the prohibition of any drug, substance, or artifact. Accordingly, the more they ignore the moral dimensions of the problem, the more they must escalate their fraudulent claims about the dangers of drugs.

To be sure, some drugs are more dangerous than others. It is easier to kill oneself with heroin than with aspirin, just as it is easier to kill oneself by jumping off a high building than a low one. In the case of drugs, we regard their potentiality for self-injury as a justification for their prohibition; in the case of buildings, we do not. Furthermore, we systematically blur and confuse the two quite different ways in which narcotics can cause death: by a deliberate act of suicide and by accidental overdose.

Suicide is an act, not a disease. In other words, suicide resembles other acts of killing persons, such as murder and execution, and differs from diseases, such as cancer or diabetes. The now fashionable argument that suicide, say self-poisoning with a barbiturate, is a medical matter because it results in the subject's ("patient's") death is no more and no less valid than would be the argument that executing a convicted murderer, say by poisoning him with cyanide, is a medical matter because it results in the subject's ("patient's") death. Neither the suicidal person nor the person condemned to death are patients (in the conventional sense of that word), though either or both may be so treated by medical or political authorities. This is why I maintain that it is morally absurd—and, in a free society, it is also politically illegitimate—to deprive a *particular* adult of certain drugs because he might use them to kill himself; and it is even more absurd and illegitimate to deprive *all* adults of certain drugs because *some* adults might use them to kill themselves. Indeed, to do so is tantamount to treating people as if they were suicidal patients, and politicians as if they were psychiatrists whose job was to prevent suicide.

Death by accidental overdose is an altogether different matter. But can anyone doubt that this danger now looms so large precisely because the sale of narcotics and many other drugs is illegal? Persons buying illicit drugs cannot be sure what they are getting or how much of it. Free trade in drugs, with governmental action at most limited to safeguarding the purity of the product and the veracity of labeling, would reduce the risk of accidental overdose with so-called dangerous drugs to the same levels that prevail, and that we find acceptable, with respect to other chemical agents and physical artifacts that abound in our complex technological society.

In my view, regardless of their dangerousness, all drugs should be "legalized" (a misleading term that I employ reluctantly as a concession to common usage). Although I realize that the use of some drugs—notably heroin, among those now in vogue—may have dangerous consequences, I favor free trade in drugs for the same reason the Founding Fathers favored free trade in ideas: In a free society it is none of the government's business what ideas a man puts into his mind; likewise, it should be none of its business what drugs he puts into his body.

Clearly, the argument that heroin or cocaine is prohibited because it is addictive or dangerous cannot be supported by facts. For one thing, there are many drugs, from insulin to penicillin, that are neither addictive nor dangerous but are nevertheless also prohibited: They can be obtained only through a physician's prescription. For another, there are many things, from poisons to guns, that are much more dangerous than narcotics (especially to others) but are not prohibited. As everyone knows, it is still possible in the United States to walk into a store and walk out with a shotgun. We enjoy that right, not because we do not believe that guns are dangerous, but because we believe even more strongly that civil liberties are precious. At the same time, it is not possible in the United States to walk into a store and walk out with a bottle of barbiturates or codeine or, indeed, even with an empty hypodermic syringe. We are now deprived of that right because we have come to value medical paternalism more highly than the right to obtain and use drugs without recourse to medical intermediaries.

I submit, therefore, that our so-called drug-abuse problem is an integral part of our present social ethic that accepts "protections" and repressions justified by appeals to health similar to those which medieval societies accepted when they were justified by appeals to faith. Drug abuse (as we now know it) is one of the inevitable consequences of the medical monopoly over drugs—a monopoly whose value is daily acclaimed by science and law, state and church, the professions and the laity. As formerly the church regulated man's relations to God, so medicine now regulates his relations to his body. Deviation from the rules set forth by the church was then considered heresy and was punished by appropriate theological sanctions; deviation from the rules set forth by medicine is now considered drug abuse (or some sort of "mental illness") and is punished by appropriate medical sanctions, called treatment.

The problem of drug abuse will thus be with us as long as we live under medical tutelage. That is not to say that if all access to drugs were free, some people would not medicate themselves in ways that might upset us or harm them. That, of course, is precisely what happened when religious practices became free. People proceeded to engage in all sorts of religious behaviors that true believers in traditional faiths found harmful and upsetting. Nevertheless, in the conflict between freedom and coerced religion, the American political system has come down squarely for the former and against the latter.

THE ETHICS OF DRUG CONTROLS

I believe that just as we regard freedom of speech and religion as fundamental rights, so should we also regard freedom of self-medication as a fundamental right; and that, instead of mendaciously opposing or mindlessly promoting illicit drugs, we should, paraphrasing Voltaire, make this maxim our rule: "I disapprove of what you take, but I will defend to the death your right to take it!"

Sooner or later we shall have to confront the basic moral dilemma underlying the so-called drug problem: Does a person have the right to take a drug, any drug, not because he needs it to cure an illness but because he wants to take it?

It is a fact that we Americans have a right to read a book—any book—not because we are uninformed and want to learn from it, nor because a government-supported educational authority claims that it will be good for us, but simply because we want to read it and because the government—as our servant rather than our master—does not have the right to meddle in our private reading affairs. I believe that we also have a right to eat, drink, or inject a substance—any substance—not because we are sick and want it to cure us, nor because a government-supported medical authority claims that it will be good for us, but simply because we want to take it and because the government—as our servant rather than our master—does not have the right to meddle in our private dietary and drug affairs.

Of course, this belief is not universally shared. On the contrary, it is a minority view, held only by persons who support the moral and political principles of a free society, by which I here mean principally a society in which individuals are expected to control their own self-regarding behavior. The First Amendment's protection of religious freedom exemplifies this posture: Americans are not expected to look to the government to provide them with those religious beliefs and organizations that are good for them, while protecting them against those that are bad for them. Our system of drug controls exemplifies the opposite principle: Americans are expected to look to the government to provide them with those drugs and drug-dispensing organizations that are good for them, while protecting them from those that are bad for them. The results speak for themselves.

Sad to say, we Americans have collectively chosen to cast away our freedom to determine what we should eat, drink, or smoke. In this large and ever expanding area of our lives, we have rejected the principle that the state is our servant rather than our master. This proposition is painfully obvious when people plaintively insist that we need the government to protect us from the hazards of "dangerous" drugs. The demand for, and expectation of, governmental protection from what is, in effect, the temptation to take drugs is, in my opinion, emblematic of our collective belittling of ourselves as children unable to control themselves, and of our collective glorification of the state as our benevolent parent whose duty is to control its childlike subjects.

To be sure, drugs are potentially potent influences, for good or ill, on our bodies and our health. Hence, we need private voluntary associations—or also, some might argue, the government—to warn us of the dangers of heroin, salt, or a high-fat diet. But it is one thing for our would-be protectors to inform us of what they regard as dangerous substances, and it is quite another thing for them to punish us if we disagree with them or defy their wishes.

DRUGS AND SELF-DETERMINATION

According to the formula made famous by the Caesars, the masses of mankind need only two things: *panem et circenses,* bread and circuses. This is still true. Today, farms and factories supply us with an abundance of "bread," while drugs and drug controls give us our "circuses." In other words, the contemporary preoccupation with the use and abuse of drugs, together with the persecution of (illicit) drugs, "addicts," and "pushers," is best understood as a secular ritual that now amuses, fascinates, terrorizes, and satisfies Americans, much as gladiatoral contests and Christian wonder-workings fascinated and satisfied the Romans.

As I noted earlier, this is, of course, not the way people see their own important rituals. Hence, it should not surprise us that the ritual nature of the war on drugs does not make people doubt the validity of their premises concerning our so-called drug problem or the legitimacy of the social policies ostensibly aimed at combating it. Indeed, why should it? If people want to deny that the danger in "dangerous drugs" lies not in the substances themselves but in the human propensity to take them and in the personal decisions of those who use them, then they will deny it. And, having denied it, they will proceed to lose sight of such old-fashioned but eternally valid ideas as temptation and self-control, and will end up denying the reality of personal freedom and responsibility as well. Finally, people will convince themselves, as most Americans have, that the "drug problem" is something historically novel, a new disease requiring new treatment. This is a costly illusion.

SELECTED BIBLIOGRAPHY—
Part III

Alexander, Michael. "The Heroin Market, Crime and Treatment of Heroin Addiction in Atlanta." In *Proceedings of the Fifth National Conference on Narcotic Treatment,* pp. 733–51. New York: National Association for the Prevention of Addiction to Narcotics, 1973.

Anderson, Annelise. *The Business of Organized Crime: A Cosa Nostra Family.* Stanford: Hoover Institution Press, 1979.

Ashley, Richard. *Heroin.* New York: St. Martin's, 1972.

Ausubel, David P. *Drug Addiction.* New York: Random House, 1958.

Ball, John C. "Two Patterns of Opiate Addiction." In J. Ball and C. Chambers, eds., *The Epidemiology of Opiate Addiction in the United States,* chap. 5, pp. 81–94. Springfield, Ill.: Thomas, 1970.

Ball, John C., and Carl D. Chambers, eds. *The Epidemiology of Opiate Addiction in the United States.* Springfield, Ill.: Thomas, 1970.

———. "Overview of the Problem." In J. Ball and C. Chambers, eds., *The Epidemiology of Opiate Addiction in the United States,* pp. 5–21. Springfield, Ill.: Thomas, 1970.

Bellis, David J. *Heroin and Politicians.* Westport, Conn.: Greenwood Press, 1981.

Benham, Lee. "The Effect of Advertising on the Price of Eyeglasses." *Journal of Law and Economics* 15 (October 1972): 337–52.

Bernard, Godwin. "An Economic Analysis of the Illicit Drug Market." *International Journal of the Addictions* 18 (October 1983): 681–700.

Berry, Ralph E., and James P. Boland. *The Economic Cost of Alcohol Abuse.* New York: Free Press, 1977.

Blumstein, Alfred; Philip C. Sagi; and Marvin E. Wolfgang. "Problems of Estimating the Number of Heroin Addicts." In U.S. National Commission on Marijuana and Drug Abuse, *Technical Papers of the Second Report,* vol. 2, pp. 201–11. Washington, D.C.: Government Printing Office, 1973.

Bork, Robert H. *The Antitrust Paradox.* New York: Basic Books, 1978.

Brecher, Edward M., and Consumer Reports Editors. *Licit and Illicit Drugs: The Consumers Union Report on Narcotics, Stimulants, Depressants, Inhalants, Hallucinogens & Marijuana—Including Caffeine, Nicotine and Alcohol.* Boston: Little, Brown, 1972.

Brodsky, Marc D. "History of Heroin Prevalence Estimation Techniques." In National Institute on Drug Abuse (NIDA), *Self-Report Methods of Estimating Drug Use: Meeting Current Challenges to Validity,* NIDA Research Monograph 57, pp. 94–103. Washington, D.C.: Government Printing Office, 1985.

Brown, Clinton C., and Charles Savage, eds. *The Drug Abuse Controversy.* Baltimore: Friends Medical Science Research Center, 1971.

Brown, George F., Jr., and Lester P. Silverman. "The Retail Price of Heroin: Estimation and Applications." *Journal of the American Statistical Association* 69 (September 1974): 595–606.

Bruun, Kettil; L. Pan; and I. Rexed. *The Gentlemen's Club: International Control of Drugs and Alcohol.* Chicago: University of Chicago Press, 1975.

Carr, Robert R., and Erik J. Meyers. "Marijuana and Cocaine: The Process of Change in Drug Policy." In Drug Abuse Council, *The Facts About 'Drug Abuse,'* pp. 153–89. New York: Free Press, 1980.

Chambers, Carl D. "Narcotic Addiction and Crime: An Empirical Review." In J. Inciardi, ed., *Drugs and the Criminal Justice System,* pp. 125–42. Beverly Hills, Calif.: Sage, 1974.

Chein, Isidor, et al. *The Road to H.* New York: Basic Books, 1964.

Chi'en, James M. N. "Voluntary Treatment for Drug Abuse in Hong Kong." *Addictive Diseases* 3 (1977): 99–104.

Coate, Douglas, and Fred Goldman. "The Impact of Drug Addiction on Criminal Earnings." In I. Leveson, ed., *Quantitative Explorations in Drug Abuse Policy,* chap. 4. New York: Spectrum, 1980.

Culyer, Anthony J. "Should Social Policy Concern Itself with Drug Abuse?" *Public Finance Quarterly* 1 (October 1973): 449–56.

Desmond, David P.; James F. Maddux; and Aureliano Trevino. "Street Heroin Potency and Deaths from Overdose in San Antonio." *American Journal of Drug and Alcohol Abuse* 5 (March 1978): 39–49.

Douglas, Mary. *Purity and Danger: An Analysis of the Concepts of Pollution and Taboo.* Middlesex, England: Routledge & Kegan Paul, 1978.

Drucker, Ernest, and Victor Sidel. "The Communicable Disease Model of Heroin Addiction: A Critique." *American Journal of Drug and Alcohol Abuse* 1, no. 3 (1974): 301–11.

Drug Abuse Council. *The Facts About 'Drug Abuse.'* New York: Free Press, 1980.

DuPont, Robert L., and Mark H. Greene. "The Dynamics of a Heroin Addiction Epidemic." *Science* 181 (August 24, 1973): 716–22.

Duster, Troy. *The Legislation of Morality: Law, Drugs, and Moral Judgment.* New York: Free Press, 1970.

Eatherly, Billy J. "Drug Law Enforcement: Should We Arrest Pushers or Users?" *Journal of Political Economy* 82 (January 1974): 210–14.

Ehrlich, Isaac. "Participation in Illegitimate Activities: A Theoretical and Empirical Investigation." *Journal of Political Economy* 81 (May 1973): 521–65.

Eldridge, William Butler. *Narcotics and the Law.* 2d ed. rev. Chicago: University of Chicago Press, 1967.

Epstein, Edward Jay. "Methadone: The Forlorn Hope." *The Public Interest* 36 (Summer 1974): 3–24.

———. *Agency of Fear.* New York: Putnam, 1977.

Finestone, Harold. "Narcotics and Criminality." *Law and Contemporary Problems* 22 (1957): 69–85.

Fujii, Edwin T. "Public Investment in the Rehabilitation of Heroin Addicts." *Social Science Quarterly* 55 (June 1974): 39–51.

Glenn, William. "Problems Related to Survey Sampling." In National Institute on Drug Abuse (NIDA), *The Epidemiology of Drug Abuse: Current Issues,* NIDA Research Monograph 10, pp. 154–59. Washington, D.C.: Government Printing Office, 1977.

Goldberg, Peter. "The Federal Government's Response to Illicit Drugs, 1969–1978." In Drug Abuse Council, *The Facts About 'Drug Abuse,'* pp. 20–62. New York: Free Press, 1980.

Goldman, Fred. "Drug Abuse, Crime and Economics: The Dismal Limits of Social Choice." In J. Inciardi, ed., *The Drugs-Crime Connection,* chap. 7. Beverly Hills, Calif.: Sage, 1981.

Goldstein, Paul J. "Getting Over: Economic Alternatives to Predatory Crime Among Street Drug Users." In J. Inciardi, ed., *The Drugs-Crime Connection,* chap. 3. Beverly Hills, Calif.: Sage, 1981.

Goldstein, Paul, et al. "The Marketing of Street Heroin in New York City." *Journal of Drug Issues* 14 (Summer 1984): 553–66.

Goode, Erich. *Drugs in American Society.* New York: Knopf, 1972.

Gottschalk, Louis A., and Frederick L. McGuire. "Psychosocial and Biomedical Aspects of Deaths Associated with Heroin and Other Narcotics." In National Institute on Drug Abuse (NIDA), *The Epidemiology of Heroin and Other Narcotics,* NIDA Research Monograph 16, pp. 122–24. Washington, D.C.: Government Printing Office, 1977.

Greene, Mark H. "The Resurgence of Heroin Abuse in the District of Columbia." *American Journal of Alcohol and Drug Abuse* 2, no. 2 (1975): 141–64.

Gunning, J. Patrick. "Notes on Two Abuses: Drugs and the Pareto Criterion." *Public Finance Quarterly* 4 (January 1976): 43–49.

Haglund, Robert M. J., and Charles Froland. "Relationship between Addict Crime and Drug Treatment: Two Cohorts Examined." *American Journal of Drug and Alcohol Abuse* 5 (1978): 455–62.

Harrell, Adele V. "Validation of Self-Report: The Research Record." In National Institute on Drug Abuse (NIDA), *Self-Report Methods of Estimating Drug Use: Meeting Current Challenges to Validity,* NIDA Research Monograph 57, pp. 12–21. Washington, D.C.: Government Printing Office, 1985.

Hellman, Daryl. *The Economics of Crime.* New York: St. Martin's, 1980.

Holahan, John F. *"The Economics of Heroin."* In P. Wald et al., eds., *Dealing With Drug Abuse,* pp. 255–99. New York: Praeger, 1972.

Hunt, Leon Gibson. "Prevalence of Active Heroin Use in the United States." In National Institute on Drug Abuse (NIDA), *The Epidemiology of Heroin and Other Narcotics,* NIDA Research Monograph 16, pp. 61–86. Washington, D.C.: Government Printing Office, 1977.

Inciardi, James A., ed. *The Drugs-Crime Connection.* Beverly Hills, Calif.: Sage, 1981.

Inglis, Brian. *The Forbidden Game: A Social History of Drugs.* London: Hodder and Stoughton, 1975.

Johnson, Bruce D. "The Race, Class, and Irreversibility Hypotheses: Myths and Research About Heroin." In U.S. National Institute on Drug Abuse (NIDA), *The Epidemiology of Heroin and Other Narcotics,* NIDA Research Monograph 16, pp. 51–60. Washington, D.C.: Government Printing Office, 1977.

Jordan, William A. *Airline Regulation in America.* Baltimore: Johns Hopkins University Press, 1970.

Judson, Horace Freeland. *Heroin Addiction in Britain: What Americans Can Learn from the English Experience.* New York: Harcourt Brace Jovanovich, 1974.

Kandel, Denise B., and Deborah R. Maloff. "Commonalities in Drug Use: A Sociological Perspective." In P. Levison, D. Gerstein, and D. Maloff, eds., *Commonalities in Substance Abuse and Habitual Behavior,* pp. 3–27. Lexington, Mass.: Lexington, 1983.

Kaplan, John. *Marijuana: The New Prohibition.* New York: Pocket Books, 1972.

Kaplan, John. "A Primer on Heroin." *Stanford Law Review* 27 (February 1975): 801–26.

King, Rufus. *The Drug Hang-Up: America's Fifty-Year Folly.* New York: Viking, 1972.

Klein, Benjamin, and Keith Leffler. "The Role of Market Forces in Assuring Contractual Performance." *Journal of Political Economy* 89 (August 1981): 615–41.

Koch, James V., and Stanley E. Grupp. "The Economics of Drug Control Policies." *International Journal of the Addictions* 5 (December 1971): 571–84.

Kramer, John C. "Speculations on the Nature and Pattern of Opium Smoking." *Journal of Drug Issues* 12 (Spring 1979): 247–55.

Lamour, Catherine, and Michael Lamberti. *The International Connection.* New York: Pantheon, 1974.

Leveson, Irving. "Drug Addiction: Some Evidence on Prevention and Deterrence." In I. Leveson, ed., *Quantitative Explorations in Drug Abuse Policy,* pp. 73–97. New York: Spectrum, 1980.

———, ed. *Quantitative Explorations in Drug Abuse Policy.* New York: Spectrum, 1980.

Levin, Gilbert; Edward B. Roberts; and Gary B. Hirsch. *The Persistent Poppy: A Computer-Aided Search for Heroin Policy.* Cambridge, Mass.: Ballinger, 1975.

Manning, Peter K., and Laurence Redlinger. "Working Bases for Corruption: Organizational Ambiguities and Narcotics Law Enforcement." In A. Trebach, ed., *Drugs, Crime, and Politics,* pp. 60–89. New York: Praeger, 1978.

McDermott, Diane, and James Scheurich. "The Logarithmic Normal Distribution in Relation to the Epidemiology of Drug Abuse." *Bulletin on Narcotics* 29 (January–March 1977): 13–19.

McIntosh, I. D. "Population Consumption of Alcohol and Proportion Drinking." *British Journal of Addiction* 76 (1981): 267–79.

Meyers, Erik J. "American Heroin Policy: Some Alternatives." In Drug Abuse Council, *The Facts About 'Drug Abuse,'* pp. 190–247. New York: Free Press, 1980.

Mintz, Jim; Charles P. O'Brien; and Beverly Pomerantz. "The Impact of Vietnam Service on Heroin-Addicted Veterans." *American Journal of Drug and Alcohol Abuse* 6, no. 1 (1979): 39–52.

Moore, Mark H. "Policies to Achieve Discrimination on the Effective Price of Heroin." *American Economic Review* 63 (May 1973): 270–77.

———. *Buy and Bust.* Cambridge, Mass.: Lexington, 1977.

Musto, David F. *The American Disease: Origins of Narcotic Control.* New Haven: Yale University Press, 1973.

Nelson, Philip. "Advertising as Information." *Journal of Political Economy* 82 (August 1974): 729–47.

Newmeyer, John A., and Gregory R. Johnson. "The Heroin Epidemic in San Francisco: Estimates of Incidence and Prevalence." *International Journal of the Addictions* 11 (1976): 417–38.

O'Donnell, John A. "Comments on Hunt's Estimation Procedures." In National Institute on Drug Abuse (NIDA), *The Epidemiology of Heroin and Other Narcotics*, NIDA Research Monograph 16, pp. 96–102. Washington, D.C.: Government Printing Office, 1977.

Pekkanen, John R. "Drug Law Enforcement Efforts." In Drug Abuse Council, *The Facts About 'Drug Abuse,'* pp. 63–94. New York: Free Press, 1980.

Preble, Edward, and John J. Casey, Jr. "Taking Care of Business—The Heroin User's Life on the Street." *International Journal of the Addictions* 4 (March 1969): 1–24.

Regush, Nicholas M. *The Drug Addiction Business*. New York: Dial Press, 1971.

Reuter, Peter. "The (Continued) Vitality of Mythical Numbers." *The Public Interest* 75 (Spring 1984): 135–47.

Reuter, Peter, and Jonathan B. Rubinstein. "Fact, Fancy, and Organized Crime." *The Public Interest* 53 (Fall 1978): 45–67.

Robins, Lee N. "Estimating Addiction Rates and Locating Target Populations." In National Institute on Drug Abuse (NIDA), *The Epidemiology of Heroin and Other Narcotics*, NIDA Research Monograph 16, pp. 25–39. Washington, D.C.: Government Printing Office, 1977.

Rottenberg, Simon. "The Clandestine Distribution of Heroin, Its Discovery and Suppression." *Journal of Political Economy* 76 (January 1968): 78–90.

Roumasset, James, and John Hadreas. "Addicts, Fences, and the Market for Stolen Goods." *Public Finance Quarterly* 5 (April 1977): 247–72.

Rufener, Brent L.; J. Valley Rachal; and Alvin M. Cruze. "Costs of Drug Abuse to Society." In I. Leveson, ed., *Quantitative Explorations in Drug Abuse Policy*, pp. 1–12. New York: Spectrum, 1980.

Sample, C. James. "Institutional Data—CODAP." In National Institute on Drug Abuse (NIDA), *The Epidemiology of Drug Abuse: Current Issues*, NIDA Research Monograph 10, pp. 197–205. Washington, D.C.: Government Printing Office, 1977.

Schelling, Thomas C. "Self-Command in Practice, in Policy, and in a Theory of Rational Choice." *American Economic Review* 74 (May 1984): 1–11.

Sells, S. B. "Reflections on the Epidemiology of Heroin and Narcotic Addiction from the Perspective of Treatment Data." In National Institute on Drug Abuse (NIDA), *The Epidemiology of Heroin and Other Nar-*

cotics, NIDA Research Monograph 16, pp. 147–76. Washington, D.C.: Government Printing Office, 1977.

Silverman, Lester P., and Nancy L. Spruill. "Urban Crime and the Price of Heroin." *Journal of Urban Economics* 4 (1977): 80–103.

Sinclair, Andrew. *Era of Excess: A Social History of the Prohibition Movement.* New York: Harper-Colophon, 1964.

Singer, K. "The Choice of Intoxicant Among the Chinese." *British Journal of the Addictions* 69 (September 1974): 257–68.

Singer, Max. "The Vitality of Mythical Numbers." *The Public Interest* 23 (Spring 1971): 3–9.

Smart, Reginald G. "The Distribution of Illicit Drug Use: Correlations between Extent of Use, Heavy Use, and Problems." *Bulletin on Narcotics* 30 (January–March 1978): 33–41.

Smith, Rodney, T. "The Legal and Illegal Markets for Taxed Goods: Pure Theory and Application to State Government Taxation of Distilled Spirits." *Journal of Law and Economics* 19 (August 1976): 393–430.

Solomon, David, ed. *The Marihuana Papers.* New York: Signet, 1968.

Stephens, Richard, and R. Smith. "Copping and Caveat Emptor: The Street Addict as Consumer." *Addictive Diseases* 2 (December 1976): 585–600.

Szasz, Thomas S. *Ceremonial Chemistry: The Ritual Persecutions of Drugs, Addicts, and Pushers.* Garden City, N.Y.: Doubleday, 1974. Reprint, 1985.

———. *The Therapeutic State: Psychiatry in the Mirror of Current Events.* Buffalo, N.Y.: Prometheus Books, 1984.

Terry, Charles E., and Mildred Pellens. *The Opium Problem.* New York: Bureau of Social Hygiene, 1928.

Thaler, Richard H., and Hersh M. Shefrin. "An Economic Theory of Self-Control." *Journal of Political Economy* 89 (April 1981): 392–406.

Trebach, Arnold S., ed. *Drugs, Crime, and Politics.* New York: Praeger, 1978.

———. *The Heroin Solution.* New Haven: Yale University Press, 1982.

———. "The Potential Impact of 'Legal' Heroin in America." In A. Trebach, ed., *Drugs, Crime, and Politics,* pp. 154–75. New York: Praeger, 1978.

U.S. Congress. House of Representatives. Appropriations Committee. *Hearings on Department of Justice Appropriations for 1983.* Part 7, March 9, 1982. Washington, D.C.: Government Printing Office, 1983.

U.S. Congress. Senate. Subcommittee to Investigate Juvenile Delinquency, *Hearings Pursuant to S. Res. 265.* 87th Congress. May 9, 17, and 20, and Aug. 6, and 7, 1962. Washington, D.C.: Government Printing Office, 1963.

U.S. Congress. Senate. Permanent Subcommittee on Investigations, Committee on Governmental Operations. *Hearings Pursuant to S. Res. 178,*

Parts 3 & 4. Organized Crime and Illicit Traffic in Narcotics. 88th Congress. Washington, D.C.: Government Printing Office, 1964.

U.S. General Accounting Office. Report to the Attorney General: Heroin Statistics Can Be Made More Reliable. Report GCD-80-84. Washington, D.C.: Government Printing Office, July 1980.

U.S. National Institute on Drug Abuse (NIDA). The Epidemiology of Drug Abuse: Current Issues, NIDA Research Monograph 10. Washington, D.C.: Government Printing Office, 1977.

——. The Epidemiology of Heroin and Other Narcotics, NIDA Research Monograph 16. Washington, D.C.: Government Printing Office, 1977.

——. Data from the Client-Oriented Data Acquisition Process, Annual Data 1980. Statistical Series E, No. 21. Washington, D.C.: Government Printing Office, 1982.

——. Data from the Client-Oriented Data Acquisition Process, State Statistics 1980. Statistical Series E, No. 22. Washington, D.C.: Government Printing Office, 1982.

U.S. President's Commission on Law Enforcement and Administration of Justice. Task Force Report: Narcotics and Drug Abuse. Washington, D.C.: Government Printing Office, 1967.

Waldorf, Dan, and Patrick Biernacki. "Natural Recovery from Heroin Addiction: A Review of the Incidence Literature." Journal of Drug Issues 16 (Spring 1979): 281–89.

White, Michael D., and William A. Luksetich. "Heroin: Price Elasticity and Enforcement Strategies." Economic Inquiry 31 (October 1983): 557–64.

Williamson, Oliver E. "Transaction-Cost Economics: The Governance of Contractual Relations." Journal of Law and Economics 22 (October 1979): 233–61.

Wilson, James Q.; Mark H. Moore; and I. David Wheat, Jr. "The Problem of Heroin." The Public Interest 29 (Fall 1972): 3–28.

Winick, Charles. "Some Aspects of Careers of Chronic Heroin Users." In E. Josephson and E. Carroll, eds., Drug Use: Epidemiological and Sociological Approaches. Washington, D.C.: Hemisphere, 1974.

Winston, Gordon C. "Addiction and Backsliding: A Theory of Compulsive Consumption." Journal of Economic Behavior and Organization 1, no. 4 (1980): 295–324.

Woodward, J. Arthur; Douglas G. Bonnett; and M. L. Brecht. "Estimating the Size of a Heroin-Abusing Population Using Multiple-Recapture Census." In National Institute on Drug Abuse (NIDA), Self-Report Methods of Estimating Drug Abuse; Meeting the Current Challenges to Validity, NIDA Research Monograph 57, pp. 158–71. Washington, D.C.: Government Printing Office, 1985.

Young, Jock. The Drugtakers: The Social Meaning of Drug Use. London: Paladin, 1962.

ABOUT THE EDITOR

Ronald Hamowy is Professor of History at the University of Alberta (Canada). He received his B.A. from the City College of New York and his Ph.D. from the University of Chicago. He has held teaching positions at the City University of New York (Brooklyn College), Stanford University, and Simon Fraser University in British Columbia.

Professor Hamowy has written a number of articles on the history of medical legislation in the United States and Canada. He is the author of *Canadian Medicine: A Study in Restricted Entry.*

ABOUT THE AUTHORS

James B. Bakalar is Lecturer in Law in the Department of Psychiatry at Harvard Medical School and Assistant Editor of the Harvard Medical School Mental Health Letter. He received his A.B. from Harvard College and his J.D. from Harvard Law School. Dr. Bakalar has also acted as consultant for the Project on Drug Regulation at the Hastings Center for the Study of Society, Ethics, and Life Sciences.

Dr. Bakalar is the coauthor of *Drug Control in a Free Society* (with L. Grinspoon), *Psychedelic Drugs Reconsidered* (with L. Grinspoon), and *Cocaine: A Drug and Its Social Evolution* (with L. Grinspoon). He has coauthored chapters (with L. Grinspoon) in *Research Developments in Drug and Alcohol Use* (R. B. Millman, P. Cushman, and J. Lowinson, eds.); *Marihuana Reconsidered* (L. Grinspoon, ed.); *Ampnetamine Use, Misuse, and Abuse* (D. Smith et al., eds.); and *Substance Abuse in the United States: Clinical Problems and Perspectives* (J. Lowinson and P. Ruiz, eds.). Dr. Bakalar's articles have appeared in *American Journal of Psychotherapy,*

Journal of Ethnopharmacology, Journal of Psychoactive Drugs, Psychiatric Annals, and *Social Science and Medicine.*

Randy E. Barnett is Associate Professor of Law at the Illinois Institute of Technology, Chicago-Kent College of Law. He is also the Director of the Law and Philosophy Program of the Institute for Humane Studies at George Mason University. Professor Barnett received his B.A. from Northwestern University and his J.D. from Harvard Law School. From 1977–1981, he served as an Assistant State's Attorney in the Criminal Prosecutions Bureau of the State's Attorney's Office of Cook County, Illinois.

Professor Barnett is the coeditor of *Assessing the Criminal: Restitution, Retribution and the Legal Process.* He has written articles and reviews that have appeared in the *Columbia Law Review, Criminal Justice Ethics, Emory Law Journal, Ethics, Harvard Journal of Law and Public Policy, Harvard Law Review,* and *Social Philosophy and Policy.*

Robert Byck is Professor of Psychiatry and Pharmacology at the Yale University School of Medicine and Associate Physician at the Yale-New Haven Hospital. He received his A.B. from the University of Pennsylvania and his M.D. from the University of Pennsylvania School of Medicine. Dr. Byck is a member of the advisory board of *The Medical Letter on Drugs and Therapeutics.*

Dr. Byck has published a number of articles, some of which have appeared in *American Journal of Psychiatry, Clinical Pharmacology and Therapeutics, The Encyclopedia Americana, Journal of the American Medical Association,* and *Journal of Physiology.* He has also contributed to the *New York Times, Science,* and *Scientific American.*

Lester Grinspoon is Associate Professor of Psychiatry at the Harvard Medical School. He received his B.S. from Tufts College and his M.D. from Harvard Medical School. Dr. Grinspoon is the editor of The Harvard Medical School Mental Health Letter.

Dr. Grinspoon is the author of *Marihuana Reconsidered, The Speed Culture: Amphetamine Use and Abuse in America* (with P. Hedblom), *Cocaine: A Drug and Its Social Evolution* (with J. Bakalar), *Drug Control in a Free Society* (with J. Bakalar), and *Psychedelic Drugs Reconsidered* (with J. Bakalar). His articles and reviews have been published in the *American Journal of Psychiatry, Archives of General Psychiatry, Drug Therapy, International Journal of Psychiatry, New England Journal of Medicine,* and *New York Law Journal.*

Jonathan Marshall is Editorial Page Editor for the *Oakland Tribune.* He received his B.A. in economics and history from Stanford University and his M.A. in American history from Cornell University. He has been an editorial writer for the *San Jose Mercury News* and Associate Editor for *Inquiry* magazine.

Mr. Marshall's articles and reviews have appeared in the *Wall Street Journal* and many other newspapers.

Robert J. Michaels is Professor of Economics at California State University, Fullerton. He received his A.B. in economics from the University of Chicago and his Ph.D. in economics from the University of California, Los Angeles. He serves as coeditor of *Contemporary Policy Issues.*

Dr. Michaels has written articles for *Journal of Economics and Business, Journal of Legal Studies, Policy Analysis, Public Choice* and other publications.

David F. Musto is Professor of Psychiatry (Child Study Center) and of the History of Medicine at the Yale School of Medicine. He received his B.A. from the University of Washington, his M.A. from Yale, and his M.D. from the University of Washington. He has served as Special Assistant to the Director of the National Institute of Mental Health and has been Program Director of the National Humanities Institute at Yale.

Dr. Musto is the author of *The American Disease: Origins of Narcotic Control* and numerous chapters and articles on the history of drugs and drug policy.

Thomas Szasz is Professor of Psychiatry at the State University of New York, Syracuse (Health Science Center). He received his A.B. and M.D. from the University of Cincinnati. Dr. Szasz serves on the editorial boards of several scholarly journals including the *Journal of Law and Human Behavior.*

Among Dr. Szasz's many books are *Ceremonial Chemistry: The Ritual Persecution of Drugs, Addicts, and Pushers; Insanity: The*

Idea and Its Consequences; Law, Liberty, and Psychiatry: An Inquiry into the Social Uses of Mental Health Practices and *The Myth of Mental Illness*. He has written over 400 articles, reviews, newspaper columns, and letters to the editor.

Arnold S. Trebach is Professor in the School of Justice at the American University and Director of its Institute on Drugs, Crime, and Justice. He holds an M.A. and Ph.D. in politics from Princeton University and a J.D. from the New England School of Law. He has been Chief, Administration of Justice Section, for the U.S. Commission on Civil Rights and has served as a consultant to the U.S. Department of Justice, Congress, and other policymaking agencies.

Dr. Trebach is the author of *The Rationing of Justice* and *The Heroin Solution*. His most recent book is *The Great Drug War,* published in 1987. He was the lead author of the *1961 Justice Report,* U.S. Commission on Civil Rights. Dr. Trebach's articles have appeared in the *Journal of Drug Issues, Journal of Psychoactive Drugs, Justice Quarterly, Rutgers Law Review,* and in newspapers such as *Chicago Tribune, Newsday, Philadelphia Inquirer, San Francisco Chronicle, Toronto Star, USA Today,* and *Wall Street Journal.*

Norman E. Zinberg is Clinical Professor of Psychiatry at Harvard Medical School and Staff Psychiatrist and Director of Psychiatric Training at The Cambridge Hospital. He received his A.B. from the University of Maryland and his M.D. from the University of Maryland School of Medicine. He also serves on the editorial boards of *Contemporary Drug Problems—A Law Quarterly* and *Advances in Alcohol and Substance Abuse.*

Dr. Zinberg is the author of *Drug, Set, and Setting: The Basis for Controlled Intoxicant Use* and coauthor of *Drugs and the Public* (with J. A. Robertson). His journal articles have appeared in professional publications such as *American Journal of Drug and Alcohol Abuse, Contemporary Drug Problems, Harvard Review, International Journal of Addictions, Journal of Drug Issues, New Society,* and *New York Law Journal.*

INDEX

Acute tolerance, 238
Adaptive tolerance, 238
Addiction: and cocaine use, 229–230, 233–235, 242–243; and controlled use, 251–252; correlation of, with drug use, 78; cure for, 65; of drug-law advocates, 73–75; and elasticity of demand, 304–309; legal v. scientific definitions of, 15–16, 28–29; maintenance of, 47, 48, 58, 62–65; and marijuana use, 232–235, 242; manipulation of statistics concerning, 312–318, 324–325; multi-variable causation, 257–258; pharmacologic factors in, 255; physiological v. psychological, 74n, 239; semantics of, 221, 233–243; shifting patterns of, 309–311; as slavery, 33n.80; and social setting, 252, 264–265, 266; treatment of—deregulation of choices in,

128–129. *See also* "addiction" and "consumption" subentries under names of specific drugs
Advertising: of legal heroin, 299; of patent medicines, 44–45
Afghanistan: covert operations in, 165; as heroin source, 302
Agency for International Development, 155
Agency of Fear (Epstein), 106
Ahmad, Encik Mohamed Noorbin Haji, 110
Alcohol: medical use of, 184, 185; pharmacologic effects of, 244 (table); pharmacologic properties affecting choice of, 253, 254; pharmacologic variables governing effects of, 225–226; prohibition of, as precedent for "narcotic" controls, 46–47, 55–56; recreational use of, 185; reform of controls on, 277; ritual prescription/proscription

367

PACIFIC RESEARCH INSTITUTE
FOR PUBLIC POLICY

The Pacific Research Institute for Public Policy is an independent, tax-exempt research and educational organization. The Institute's program is designed to broaden public understanding of the nature and effects of market processes and government policy.

With the bureaucratization and politicization of modern society, scholars, business and civic leaders, the media, policymakers, and the general public have too often been isolated from meaningful solutions to critical public issues. To facilitate a more active and enlightened discussion of such issues, the Pacific Research Institute sponsors in-depth studies into the nature of and possible solutions to major social, economic, and environmental problems. Undertaken regardless of the sanctity of any particular government program, or the customs, prejudices, or temper of the times, the Institute's studies aim to ensure that alternative approaches to currently problematic policy areas are fully evaluated, the best remedies discovered, and these findings made widely available. The results of this work are published as books and monographs, and form the basis for numerous conference and media programs.

Through this program of research and commentary, the Institute seeks to evaluate the premises and consequences of government policy, and provide the foundations necessary for constructive policy reform.

PACIFIC STUDIES IN PUBLIC POLICY

FORESTLANDS
Public and Private
Edited by Robert T. Deacon and M. Bruce Johnson
Foreword by B. Delworth Gardner

URBAN TRANSIT
The Private Challenge to Public Transportation
Edited by Charles A. Lave
Foreword by John Meyer

POLITICS, PRICES, AND PETROLEUM
The Political Economy of Energy
By David Glasner
Foreword by Paul W. MacAvoy

RIGHTS AND REGULATION
Ethical, Political, and Economic Issues
Edited by Tibor M. Machan and M. Bruce Johnson
Foreword by Aaron Wildavsky

FUGITIVE INDUSTRY
The Economics and Politics of Deindustrialization
By Richard B. McKenzie
Foreword by Finis Welch

MONEY IN CRISIS
The Federal Reserve, the Economy, and Monetary Reform
Edited by Barry N. Siegel
Foreword by Leland B. Yeager

NATURAL RESOURCES
Bureaucratic Myths and Environmental Management
By Richard Stroup and John Baden
Foreword by William Niskanen

FIREARMS AND VIOLENCE
Issues of Public Policy
Edited by Don B. Kates, Jr.
Foreword by John Kaplan

WATER RIGHTS
Scarce Resource Allocation, Bureaucracy, and the Environment
Edited by Terry L. Anderson
Foreword by Jack Hirshleifer

LOCKING UP THE RANGE
Federal Land Controls and Grazing
By Gary D. Libecap
Foreword by Jonathan R. T. Hughes

THE PUBLIC SCHOOL MONOPOLY
A Critical Analysis of Education and the State in American Society
Edited by Robert B. Everhart
Foreword by Clarence J. Karier